Honda NTV600 & 650 V-Twins

Service and Repair Manual

by Matthew Coombs

(3243-216-7W1)

Models covered

NTV600 Revere. 583 cc. February 1988 to January 1993
NTV650. 647 cc. December 1992-on

© **Haynes Publishing 1997**

ABCDE
FGHIJ
KLMNO
PQRS

A book in the **Haynes Service and Repair Manual Series**

ISBN **1 85960 243 6**

British Library Cataloguing in Publication Data
A catalogue record for this book is available from the British Library.

Printed by **J H Haynes & Co. Ltd, Sparkford, Nr Yeovil, Somerset BA22 7JJ**

Haynes Publishing
Sparkford, Nr Yeovil, Somerset BA22 7JJ, England

Haynes North America, Inc
861 Lawrence Drive, Newbury Park, California 91320, USA

Editions Haynes S.A.
147/149, rue Saint Honoré, 75001 PARIS, France

Haynes Publishing Nordiska AB
Box 1504, 751 45 UPPSALA, Sweden

Contents

LIVING WITH YOUR HONDA NTV

Introduction

Daily (pre-ride) checks

MAINTENANCE

Routine maintenance and servicing

Contents

REPAIRS AND OVERHAUL

Engine, transmission and associated systems

Chassis components

Bodywork components

Electrical system

Wiring diagrams

REFERENCE

Index

The Birth of a Dream

by Julian Ryder

There is no better example of the Japanese post-War industrial miracle than Honda. Like other companies which have become household names, it started with one man's vision. In this case the man was the 40-year old Soichiro Honda who had sold his piston-ring manufacturing business to Toyota in 1945 and was happily spending the proceeds on prolonged parties for his friends. However, the difficulties of getting around in the chaos of post-War Japan irked Honda, so when he came across a job lot of generator engines he realised that here was a way of getting people mobile again at low cost.

A 12 by 18-foot shack in Hamamatsu became his first bike factory, fitting the

1970 Honda C90 OHV-engined model

generator motors into pushbikes. Before long he'd used up all 500 generator motors and started manufacturing his own engine, known as the 'chimney', either because of the elongated cylinder head or the smoky exhaust or perhaps both. The chimney made all of half a horsepower from its 50 cc engine but it was a major success and became the Honda A-type. Less than two years after he'd set up in Hamamatsu, Soichiro Honda founded the Honda Motor Company in September 1948. By then, the A-type had been developed into the 90 cc B-type engine, which Mr Honda decided deserved its own chassis not a bicycle frame. Honda was about to become Japan's first post-War manufacturer of complete motorcycles. In August 1949 the first prototype was ready. With an output of three horsepower, the 98 cc D-type was still a

simple two-stroke but it had a two-speed transmission and most importantly a pressed steel frame with telescopic forks and hard tail rear end. The frame was almost triangular in profile with the top rail going in a straight line from the massively braced steering head to the rear axle. Legend has it that after the D-type's first tests the entire workforce went for a drink to celebrate and try and think of a name for the bike. One man broke one of those silences you get when people are thinking, exclaiming 'This is like a dream!' 'That's it!' shouted Honda, and so the Honda Dream was christened.

'This is like a dream!' 'That's it' shouted Honda

Mr Honda was a brilliant, intuitive engineer and designer but he did not bother himself with the marketing side of his business. With hindsight, it is possible to see that employing Takeo Fujisawa who would both sort out the home market and plan the eventual expansion into overseas markets was a masterstroke. He arrived in October 1949 and in 1950 was made Sales Director. Another vital new name was Kiyoshi Kawashima, who along with Honda himself, designed the company's first four-stroke after Kawashima had told them that the four-stroke opposition to Honda's two-strokes sounded nicer and therefore sold better. The result of that statement was the overhead-valve 148 cc E-type which first ran in July 1951 just two months after the first drawings were made. Kawashima was made a director of the Honda Company at 34 years old.

The E-type was a massive success, over 32,000 were made in 1953 alone, but Honda's lifelong pursuit of technical innovation sometimes distracted him from commercial reality. Fujisawa pointed out that they were in danger of ignoring their core business, the motorised bicycles that still formed Japan's main means of transport. In May 1952 the F-type Cub appeared, another two-stroke despite the top men's reservations. You could buy a complete machine or just the motor to attach to your own bicycle. The result was certainly distinctive, a white fuel tank with a circular profile went just below and behind the saddle on the left of the bike, and the motor with its horizontal cylinder and bright red cover just below the rear axle on the same side of the bike. This was the machine that turned Honda into the biggest bike maker in Japan

The CB250N Super Dream became a favorite with UK learner riders of the late seventies and early eighties

with 70% of the market for bolt-on bicycle motors, the F-type was also the first Honda to be exported. Next came the machine that would turn Honda into the biggest motorcycle manufacturer in the world.

The C100 Super Cub was a typically audacious piece of Honda engineering and marketing. For the first time, but not the last, Honda invented a completely new type of motorcycle, although the term 'scooterette' was coined to describe the new bike which had many of the characteristics of a scooter but the large wheels, and therefore stability, of a motorcycle. The first one was sold in August 1958, fifteen years later over nine-million of them were on the roads of the world. If ever a machine can be said to have brought mobility to the masses it is the Super Cub. If you add in the electric starter that was added for the C102 model of 1961, the design of the Super Cub has remained substantially unchanged ever since, testament to how right Honda got it first time. The Super Cub made Honda the world's biggest manufacturer after just two years of production.

Honda's export drive started in earnest in 1957 when Britain and Holland got their first bikes, America got just two bikes the next year. By 1962 Honda had half the American market with 65,000 sales. But Soichiro Honda had already travelled abroad to Europe and the USA, making a special point of going to the Isle of Man TT, then the most important race in the GP calendar. He realised that no matter how advanced his products were, only racing success would convince overseas markets

for whom 'Made in Japan' still meant cheap and nasty. It took five years from Soichiro Honda's first visit to the Island before his bikes were ready for the TT. In 1959 the factory entered five riders in the 125. They did not have a massive impact on the event being benevolently regarded as a curiosity, but sixth, seventh and eighth were good enough for the team prize.

The bikes were off the pace but they were well engineered and very reliable. The TT was the only time the West saw the Hondas in '59, but they came back for more the following year with the first of a generation of bikes which shaped the future of motorcycling - the double-overhead-cam four-cylinder 250. It was fast and reliable - it revved to 14,000 rpm -

The GL1000 introduced in 1975, was the first in Honda's line of Goldwings

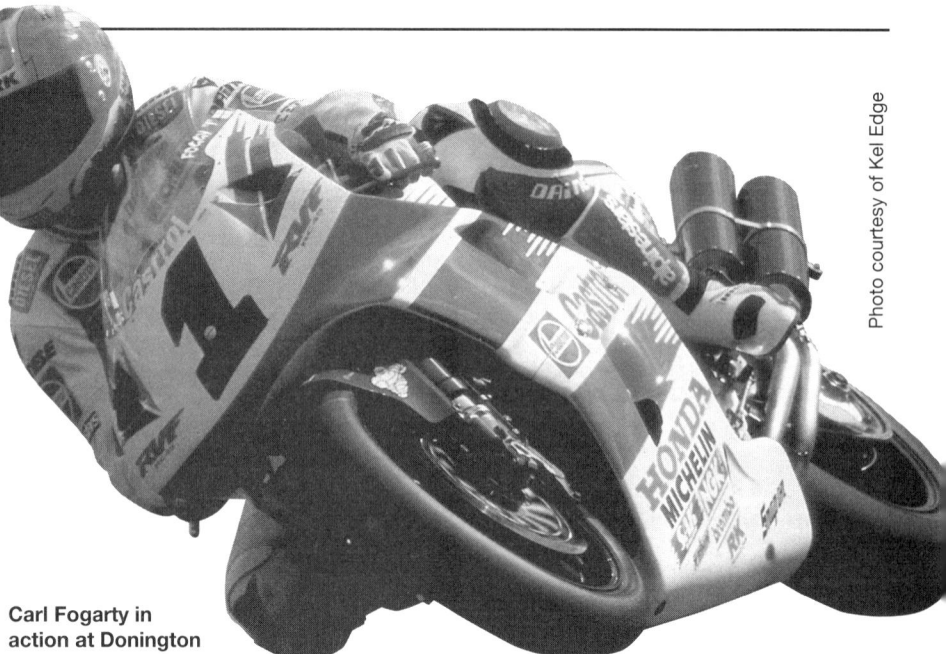

Photo courtesy of Kel Edge

but didn't handle anywhere near as well as the opposition. However, Honda had now signed up non-Japanese riders to lead their challenge. The first win didn't come until 1962 (Aussie Tom Phillis in the Spanish 125 GP) and was followed up with a world-shaking performance at the TT. Twenty-one year old Mike Hailwood won both 125 and 250 cc TTs and Hondas filled the top five positions in both races. Soichiro Honda's master plan was starting to come to fruition, Hailwood and Honda won the 1961 250 cc World Championship. Next year Honda won three titles. The other Japanese factories fought back and inspired Honda to produce some of the most fascinating racers ever seen: the awesome six-cylinder 250, the five-cylinder 125, and the 500 four with which the immortal Hailwood battled Agostini and the MV Agusta. When Honda pulled out of racing in '67 they had won sixteen rider's titles, eighteen manufacturer's titles, and 137 GPs, including 18 TTs, and introduced the concept of the modern works team to motorcycle racing. Sales success followed racing victory as Soichiro Honda had predicted, but only because the products advanced as rapidly as the racing machinery. The Hondas that came to Britain in the early '60s were incredibly sophisticated. They had overhead cams where

Carl Fogarty in action at Donington on the RC45

An early CB750 Four

the British bikes had pushrods, they had electric starters when the Brits relied on the kickstart, they had 12V electrics when even the biggest British bike used a 6V system. There seemed no end to the technical wizardry and when in 1968 the first four-cylinder CB750

road bike arrived the world changed for ever. They even had to invent a new word for it: superbike. Honda raced again with the CB750 at Daytona and won the World Endurance title with a prototype DOHC version that became the CB900 roadster. There was the six-cylinder CBX, the first turbocharged production bike, they invented the full-dress tourer with the Goldwing and came back to GPs with the revolutionary oval-pistoned NR500 four-stroke, a much-misunderstood bike that was more rolling experiment than racer. It was true, though, that Mr Honda was not keen on two-strokes - early motocross engines had to be explained away to him as lawnmower motors! However, in 1982 Honda raced the NS500, an agile three-cylinder lightweight against the big four-cylinder opposition in 500 GPs. The bike won in the first year and in '83 took the world title for Freddie Spencer. In four-stroke racing the V4 layout took over from the straight four, dominating TT, F1 and Endurance championships and when Superbike arrived Honda were ready with the RC30. On the roads the VFR V4 became an instant classic while the CBR600 invented another new class of bike on its way to becoming a best-seller.

And then there was the NR750. This limited-edition technological tour-de-force embodied many of Soichiro Honda's ideals. It used the latest techniques and materials in every component, from the oval-piston, 32-valve V4 motor to the titanium coating on the windscreen, it was - as Mr Honda would have wanted - the best it could possibly be. A fitting memorial to the man who has shaped the motorcycle industry and motorcycles as we know them today.

The Honda NTVs

When it was unveiled at a luxury hotel near Windsor, Honda's management described the Revere as 'motorcycling's best-kept secret' and 'the motorcycle for the new breed of rider'. Behind the hyperbole was a brave attempt to perform a trick that only Honda has ever managed to do - invent a new market sector. The marketing men perceived that the industry's emphasis on race replicas through most of the 1980s had polarised the market leaving a large gap which could be filled by a modern motorcycle for a rapidly emerging new breed of customer, the so-called born-again bikers returning to two wheels in their 30s and 40s.

The result was the Revere, based around a slightly tuned version of the 600 cc V-twin motor first seen in the XL600 Transalp. All the rest was new though, and was determinedly non-racy - there was no fairing not even a headlight cowl - but it tried very hard to exude a high-tech image. The steel chassis, painted to look like aluminium, was a major styling point, running almost straight from the steering head to the swinging arm pivot. Honda was keen to point out that the tubing used had a complex hexagonal cross-section for maximum strength, a typical piece of attention to technical detail from the world's biggest manufacturer.

The ohc motor used the three-valves-per-cylinder layout first seen on the Dream and an offset crankpin arrangement to reduce vibration from the 90° V-twin. However, the designers took great pains not to totally eliminate all vibration in an attempt to engineer in that indefinable thing 'character'.

User-friendliness was seen as important, so the Revere got shaft drive and - surprisingly - the Pro-Arm single-sided swingarm, a feature so far only seen on bikes like the RC30 race-replica which got into the shops just three months before the 600. The three-spoke wheels were similarly racy but the overall

NTV 650 model

effect was of a rugged, solid machine rather than a racer.

The UK market seemed a trifle confused by the worthy Revere. At £3299 in 1988 rising to £3499 in '89 it was seen as too expensive to be a natural successor to the CX and VT water-cooled V-twins that had carried a generation of big-city despatch riders. The Revere concept was a bigger success in the USA and on the Japanese home market where the bikes got much sportier, 650 cc chain-drive treatment. One American magazine described the 650 Hawk (A revival of the CB77's model name from the '60s) as 'proof the Japanese can build a Ducati'.

In Japan the bike was called the Bros and was sold in 400 and 650 cc versions known as Product 1 and Product 2. In its five years as a UK model from February 1988 to late 1992, the Revere sold around 2000 units under the model designations NTV600J, K and M. While this was not seen as underachievement, it

was perceived that the bike's image was a little staid and the price was too high. The UK didn't get the sporty Hawk/Bros 650, but for the 1993 model year the Revere name was dropped and the cylinder bore upped from 75 to 79 mm to produce the NTV650. Most significantly, the price was slashed from £4399 to £3635 which helped increase sales.

The second-generation NTV seemed much happier without the handicap of being labelled as a bike specifically for the born-agains. As with the CX500 before it, the extra cc's gave the motor that extra muscle it always needed and sales show that the market is happier, too. The Revere may not have changed the face of motorcycling but after a faltering start it has become an established part of the Honda range with the reputation of being a solid all-rounder, equally at home commuting into the city or touring two-up with luggage - and you can't say that about many bikes!

Acknowledgements

Our thanks are due to Bridge Motorcycle World of Exeter for supplying the NTV650 featured in the photographs throughout this manual, and to Mel Rawlings A. I. R. T. E. of MHR Engineering who carried out the mechanical work. NGK Spark Plugs (UK) Ltd supplied the colour spark plug condition photographs and the Avon Rubber Company provided information on tyre fitting.

Thanks are also due to Honda (UK) Ltd and Kel Edge for supplying colour transparencies, and to Andrew Dee who carried out the front cover photography. The Honda introduction, "The Birth of a Dream" was written by Julian Ryder.

About this Manual

The aim of this manual is to help you get the best value from your motorcycle. It can do so in several ways. It can help you decide what work must be done, even if you choose to have it done by a dealer; it provides information and procedures for routine maintenance and servicing; and it offers diagnostic and repair procedures to follow when trouble occurs.

We hope you use the manual to tackle the work yourself. For many simpler jobs, doing it yourself may be quicker than arranging an appointment to get the motorcycle into a dealer and making the trips to leave it and pick it up. More importantly, a lot of money

can be saved by avoiding the expense the shop must pass on to you to cover its labour and overhead costs. An added benefit is the sense of satisfaction and accomplishment that you feel after doing the job yourself.

References to the left or right side of the motorcycle assume you are sitting on the seat, facing forward.

We take great pride in the accuracy of information given in this manual, but motorcycle manufacturers make alterations and design changes during the production run of a particular motorcycle of which they do not inform us. No liability can be accepted by the authors or publishers for loss, damage or injury caused by any errors in, or omissions from, the information given.

Professional mechanics are trained in safe working procedures. However enthusiastic you may be about getting on with the job at hand, take the time to ensure that your safety is not put at risk. A moment's lack of attention can result in an accident, as can failure to observe simple precautions.

There will always be new ways of having accidents, and the following is not a comprehensive list of all dangers; it is intended rather to make you aware of the risks and to encourage a safe approach to all work you carry out on your bike.

Asbestos

● Certain friction, insulating, sealing and other products - such as brake pads, clutch linings, gaskets, etc. - contain asbestos. Extreme care must be taken to avoid inhalation of dust from such products since it is hazardous to health. If in doubt, assume that they do contain asbestos.

Fire

● Remember at all times that petrol is highly flammable. Never smoke or have any kind of naked flame around, when working on the vehicle. But the risk does not end there - a spark caused by an electrical short-circuit, by two metal surfaces contacting each other, by careless use of tools, or even by static electricity built up in your body under certain conditions, can ignite petrol vapour, which in a confined space is highly explosive. Never use petrol as a cleaning solvent. Use an approved safety solvent.

● Always disconnect the battery earth terminal before working on any part of the fuel or electrical system, and never risk spilling fuel on to a hot engine or exhaust.

● It is recommended that a fire extinguisher of a type suitable for fuel and electrical fires is kept handy in the garage or workplace at all times. Never try to extinguish a fuel or electrical fire with water.

Fumes

● Certain fumes are highly toxic and can quickly cause unconsciousness and even death if inhaled to any extent. Petrol vapour comes into this category, as do the vapours from certain solvents such as trichloroethylene. Any draining or pouring of such volatile fluids should be done in a well ventilated area.

● When using cleaning fluids and solvents, read the instructions carefully. Never use materials from unmarked containers - they may give off poisonous vapours.

● Never run the engine of a motor vehicle in an enclosed space such as a garage. Exhaust fumes contain carbon monoxide which is extremely poisonous; if you need to run the engine, always do so in the open air or at least have the rear of the vehicle outside the workplace.

The battery

● Never cause a spark, or allow a naked light near the vehicle's battery. It will normally be giving off a certain amount of hydrogen gas, which is highly explosive.

● Always disconnect the battery ground (earth) terminal before working on the fuel or electrical systems (except where noted).

● If possible, loosen the filler plugs or cover when charging the battery from an external source. Do not charge at an excessive rate or the battery may burst.

● Take care when topping up, cleaning or carrying the battery. The acid electrolyte, evenwhen diluted, is very corrosive and should not be allowed to contact the eyes or skin. Always wear rubber gloves and goggles or a face shield. If you ever need to prepare electrolyte yourself, always add the acid slowly to the water; never add the water to the acid.

Electricity

● When using an electric power tool, inspection light etc., always ensure that the appliance is correctly connected to its plug and that, where necessary, it is properly grounded (earthed). Do not use such appliances in damp conditions and, again, beware of creating a spark or applying excessive heat in the vicinity of fuel or fuel vapour. Also ensure that the appliances meet national safety standards.

● A severe electric shock can result from touching certain parts of the electrical system, such as the spark plug wires (HT leads), when the engine is running or being cranked, particularly if components are damp or the insulation is defective. Where an electronic ignition system is used, the secondary (HT) voltage is much higher and could prove fatal.

Remember...

✗ **Don't** start the engine without first ascertaining that the transmission is in neutral.

✗ **Don't** suddenly remove the pressure cap from a hot cooling system - cover it with a cloth and release the pressure gradually first, or you may get scalded by escaping coolant.

✗ **Don't** attempt to drain oil until you are sure it has cooled sufficiently to avoid scalding you.

✗ **Don't** grasp any part of the engine or exhaust system without first ascertaining that it is cool enough not to burn you.

✗ **Don't** allow brake fluid or antifreeze to contact the machine's paintwork or plastic components.

✗ **Don't** siphon toxic liquids such as fuel, hydraulic fluid or antifreeze by mouth, or allow them to remain on your skin.

✗ **Don't** inhale dust - it may be injurious to health (see Asbestos heading).

✗ **Don't** allow any spilled oil or grease to remain on the floor - wipe it up right away, before someone slips on it.

✗ **Don't** use ill-fitting spanners or other tools which may slip and cause injury.

✗ **Don't** lift a heavy component which may be beyond your capability - get assistance.

✗ **Don't** rush to finish a job or take unverified short cuts.

✗ **Don't** allow children or animals in or around an unattended vehicle.

✗ **Don't** inflate a tyre above the recommended pressure. Apart from overstressing the carcass, in extreme cases the tyre may blow off forcibly.

✔ **Do** ensure that the machine is supported securely at all times. This is especially important when the machine is blocked up to aid wheel or fork removal.

✔ **Do** take care when attempting to loosen a stubborn nut or bolt. It is generally better to pull on a spanner, rather than push, so that if you slip, you fall away from the machine rather than onto it.

✔ **Do** wear eye protection when using power tools such as drill, sander, bench grinder etc.

✔ **Do** use a barrier cream on your hands prior to undertaking dirty jobs - it will protect your skin from infection as well as making the dirt easier to remove afterwards; but make sure your hands aren't left slippery. Note that long-term contact with used engine oil can be a health hazard.

✔ **Do** keep loose clothing (cuffs, ties etc. and long hair) well out of the way of moving mechanical parts.

✔ **Do** remove rings, wristwatch etc., before working on the vehicle - especially the electrical system.

✔ **Do** keep your work area tidy - it is only too easy to fall over articles left lying around.

✔ **Do** exercise caution when compressing springs for removal or installation. Ensure that the tension is applied and released in a controlled manner, using suitable tools which preclude the possibility of the spring escaping violently.

✔ **Do** ensure that any lifting tackle used has a safe working load rating adequate for the job.

✔ **Do** get someone to check periodically that all is well, when working alone on the vehicle.

✔ **Do** carry out work in a logical sequence and check that everything is correctly assembled and tightened afterwards.

✔ **Do** remember that your vehicle's safety affects that of yourself and others. If in doubt on any point, get professional advice.

● **If** in spite of following these precautions, you are unfortunate enough to injure yourself, seek medical attention as soon as possible.

Frame and engine numbers

The frame serial number is stamped into the right side of the steering head. The engine number is stamped into the right side of the crankcase at the base of the rear cylinder. Both of these numbers should be recorded and kept in a safe place so they can be furnished to law enforcement officials in the event of a theft. There is also a carburettor identification number on the intake side of each carburettor body, and a model colour identification label under the seat on the right-hand frame rail.

The frame serial number, engine serial number, carburettor identification number and colour code should also be kept in a handy place (such as with your driver's licence) so they are always available when purchasing or ordering parts for your machine.

The procedures in this manual identify the bikes by their model code letter. To determine which model code applies to your machine, refer to the frame and engine number in the table below. Note that the date of registration can be used as a guide, but note that this ofter differs from the production year.

Dates of availability	Model code	Frame No.	Engine No.
Feb '88 to Oct '88	600 J	PC22-2000002 to 2000519	PC22E-2000002 to 2000520
Oct '88 to Apr '91	600 K	PC22-2100001 to 2101405	PC22E-2100001 to 2101408
Apr '91 to Jan '93	600 M	PC22-2300002 to 2300271	PC22E-2300002 to 2300271
Dec '92 to Jan '95	650 P	RC33-2400924 onward	RC33E-2400956 onward
Jan '95 to Nov '95	650 S	RC33-2500200 onward	RC33E-2500203 onward
Nov '95 on	650 T	RC33A*-TM000001 onward	RC33E-2600001 onward

Note:The asterisk (*) in the frame number of the 650 T represents a number indicating the machine's power output.

Buying spare parts

Once you have found all the identification numbers, record them for reference when buying parts. Since the manufacturers change specifications, parts and vendors (companies that manufacture various components on the machine), providing the ID numbers is the only way to be reasonably sure that you are buying the correct parts.

Whenever possible, take the worn part to the dealer so direct comparison with the new component can be made. Along the trail from the manufacturer to the parts shelf, there are numerous places that the part can end up with the wrong number or be listed incorrectly.

The two places to purchase new parts for your motorcycle - the accessory store and the franchised dealer - differ in the type of parts they carry. While dealers can obtain virtually every part for your motorcycle, the accessory dealer is usually limited to normal high wear items such as shock absorbers, tune-up parts, various engine gaskets, cables, chains, brake parts, etc. Rarely will an accessory outlet have major suspension components, cylinders, transmission gears, or cases.

Used parts can be obtained for roughly half the price of new ones, but you can't always be sure of what you're getting. Once again, take your worn part to the breaker for direct comparison.

Whether buying new, used or rebuilt parts, the best course is to deal directly with someone who specialises in parts for your particular make.

The engine number is on the right-hand side crankcase above the clutch cover

The model identification plate is mounted on the right-hand side frame spar

The frame number is stamped into the steering head

1 Engine/transmission oil level

1 Unscrew the oil filler cap from the right-hand side crankcase cover. The dipstick is integral with the oil filler cap, and is used to check the engine oil level.

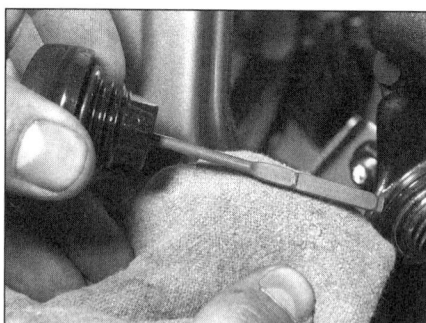

2 Using a clean rag or paper towel, wipe off all the oil from the dipstick, then insert the clean dipstick back into the engine, but do not screw it in.

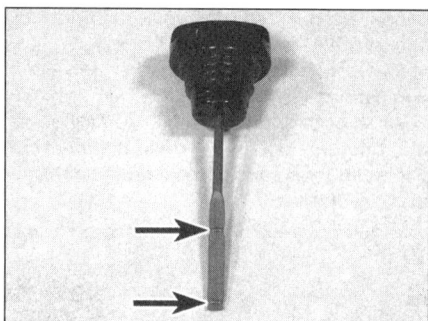

3 Remove the dipstick and observe the level of the oil, which should lie between the upper and lower level marks (arrows).

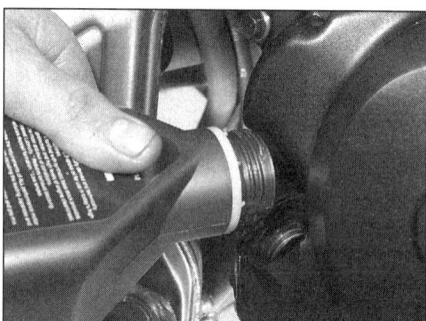

4 If the level is below the lower mark, top the engine up with the recommended oil, to bring the level up to the upper mark on the dipstick.

Before you start:

✔ Take the motorcycle on a short run to allow it to reach operating temperature. *Caution: Do not run the engine in an enclosed space such as a garage or workshop.*

✔ Stop the engine and place the motorcycle on its centre stand, or support it in an upright position using an auxiliary stand. Allow it to stand undisturbed for a few minutes to allow the oil level to stabilise. Make sure the motorcycle is on level ground.

Bike care:

● If you have to add oil frequently, you should check whether you have any oil leaks. If there is no sign of oil leakage from the joints and gaskets the engine could be burning oil (see Fault Finding).

The correct oil

● Modern, high-revving engines place great demands on their oil. It is very important that the correct oil for your bike is used.
● Always top up with a good quality oil of the specified type and viscosity and do not overfill the engine.

Oil type	API grade SE, SF or SG
Oil viscosity	SAE 10W40

2 Coolant level

⚠ *Warning: DO NOT remove the radiator pressure cap to add coolant. Topping up is done via the coolant reservoir tank filler. DO NOT leave open containers of coolant about, as it is poisonous.*

Before you start:

✔ Make sure you have a supply of coolant available (a mixture of 50% distilled water and 50% corrosion inhibited ethylene glycol antifreeze is needed).
✔ Always check the coolant level when the engine is at normal working temperature. Take the motorcycle on a short run to allow it to reach normal temperature. *Caution: Do not run the engine in an enclosed space such as a garage or workshop.*
✔ Place the motorcycle on its centre stand, or support it in an upright position using an auxiliary stand. Make sure the motorcycle is on level ground.

Bike care:

● Use only the specified coolant mixture (see above). It is important that antifreeze is used in the system all year round, and not just in the winter. Do not top up using only water, as the system will become too diluted.
● Do not overfill the reservoir tank. If the coolant is well above the UPPER level line at any time, the surplus should be siphoned or drained off to prevent the possibility of it being expelled out of the overflow hose.
● If the coolant level falls steadily, check the system for leaks (see Chapter 1). If no leaks are found and the level continues to fall, it is recommended that the machine is taken to a Honda dealer for a pressure test.

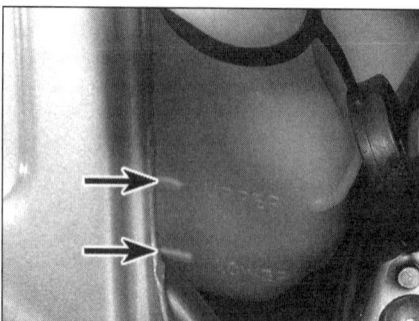

1 The coolant reservoir is located behind the left-hand side panel (see Chapter 8 for removal of the panel). The coolant UPPER and LOWER level markings are visible on the front of the reservoir (arrows).

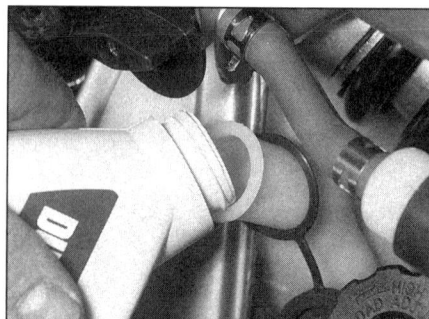

2 If the coolant level is not between the UPPER and LOWER markings, remove the filler cap and top the level up with recommended coolant mixture.

3 Brake fluid levels

⚠️ *Warning: Brake hydraulic fluid can harm your eyes and damage painted surfaces, so use extreme caution when handling and pouring it and cover surrounding surfaces with rag. Do not use fluid that has been standing open for some time, as it absorbs moisture from the air which can cause a dangerous loss of braking effectiveness.*

Before you start:

✔ Make sure you have the correct hydraulic fluid. DOT 4 is recommended.

✔ Position the motorcycle on its centre stand, or support it in an upright position using an auxiliary stand, and turn the handlebars until the top of the master cylinder is as level as possible. If necessary, tilt the motorcycle to make it level. Remove the right-hand side cover for access to the rear brake fluid reservoir.

Bike care:
● The fluid in the front and rear brake master cylinder reservoirs will drop slightly as the brake pads wear down.
● If either fluid reservoir requires repeated topping-up this is an indication of a leak somewhere in the system, which should be investigated immediately.

1 The front brake fluid level is checked via the sightglass in the reservoir - it must lie above the LOWER level mark (arrow).

● Check for signs of fluid leakage from the hydraulic hoses and components - if found, rectify immediately.
● Check the operation of both brakes before taking the machine on the road; if there is evidence of air in the system (spongy feel to lever or pedal), it must be bled as described in Chapter 7.

2 If the level is below the LOWER level mark (arrows), remove the two screws (arrows) to free the front brake fluid reservoir cover, and remove the cover, the diaphragm plate and the diaphragm.

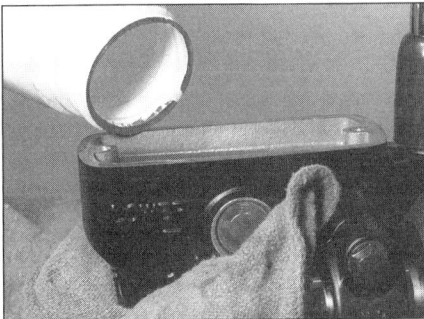

3 Top up with new clean hydraulic fluid of the recommended type, until the level is above the lower mark. Take care to avoid spills (see **Warning** above).

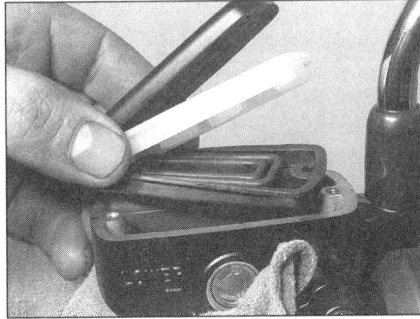

4 Ensure that the diaphragm is correctly seated before installing the plate and cover.

5 The rear brake fluid level can be seen through the translucent body of the reservoir behind the right-hand side panel (see Chapter 8 for removal of the panel). The fluid must lie between the UPPER and LOWER level marks (arrows). If necessary, top up the fluid level using the same procedure for the front brake reservoir.

4 Suspension, steering and final drive

Suspension and steering:
● Check that the front and rear suspension operate smoothly without binding.
● Check that the suspension is adjusted as required.

● Check that the steering moves smoothly from lock-to-lock.

Final drive:
● Check for signs of oil leakage around the final drive housing. If any is evident, check the final drive oil level (Chapter 1).

5 Tyres

The correct pressures:
● The tyre pressures must be checked when **cold**, not immediately after riding. If the motorcycle has just been ridden the tyres will be warm and their pressures will have increased. Note that extremely low tyre pressures may cause the tyre to slip on the rim or come off. High tyre pressures will cause abnormal tread wear and unsafe handling.

● Use an accurate pressure gauge.

● Proper air pressure will increase tyre life and provide maximum stability and ride comfort.

Tyre care:
● Check the tyres carefully for cuts, tears, embedded nails or other sharp objects and excessive wear. Operation of the motorcycle with excessively worn tyres is extremely hazardous, as traction and handling are directly affected.
● Check the condition of the tyre valve and ensure the dust cap is in place.
● Pick out any stones or nails which may have become embedded in the tyre tread.
● If tyre damage is apparent, or unexplained loss of pressure is experienced, seek the advice of a tyre fitting specialist without delay.

Tyre tread depth:
● At the time of writing UK law requires that tread depth must be at least 1 mm over 3/4 of the tread breadth all the way around the tyre, with no bald patches. Many riders, however, consider 2 mm tread depth minimum to be a safer limit. Honda recommend a minimum tread depth of 1.5 mm for the front tyre, and 2.0 mm for the rear.
● Many tyres now incorporate wear indicators in the tread. Identify the triangular pointer or TWI mark on the tyre sidewall to locate the indicator bars and replace the tyre if the tread has worn down to the bar.

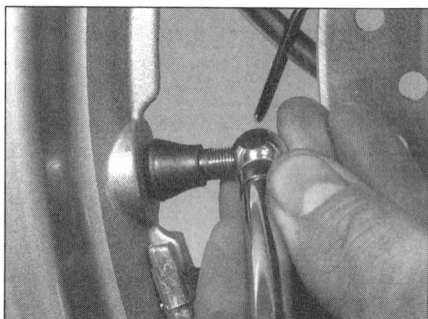

1 Check the tyre pressures when the tyres are **cold** and keep them properly inflated.

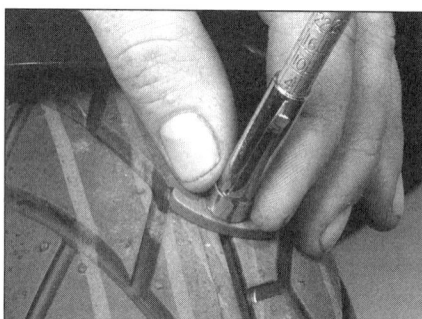

2 Measure tread depth at the centre of the tyre using a tread depth gauge.

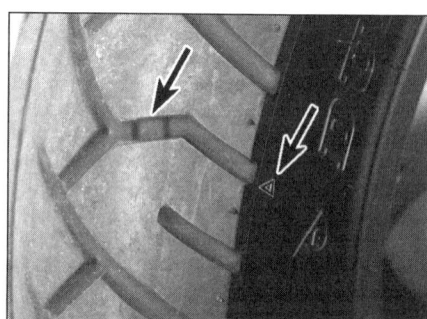

3 Tyre tread wear indicator bar and its location marking on the sidewall (arrows).

Loading/speed	Front	Rear
Rider only	33 psi (2.3 Bar)	33 psi (2.3 Bar)
Rider and passenger	33 psi (2.3 Bar)	41 psi (2.8 Bar)

6 Legal and safety checks

Lighting and signalling:
● Take a minute to check that the headlight, taillight, brake light and turn signals all work correctly.
● Check that the horn sounds when the switch is operated.
● A working speedometer is a statutory requirement in the UK.

Safety:
● Check that the throttle grip rotates smoothly and snaps shut when released, in all steering positions.
● Check that the engine shuts off when the kill switch is operated.
● Check that side stand return spring holds the stand securely up when retracted. The same applies to the centre stand.
● Following the procedure in your owner's manual, check that the engine cuts out if the sidestand is lowered when the engine is running and in gear.

Fuel:
● This may seem obvious, but check that you have enough fuel to complete your journey. If you notice signs of fuel leakage - rectify the cause immediately.
● Ensure you use the correct grade unleaded fuel - see Chapter 4 Specifications.

Chapter 1
Routine maintenance and servicing

Contents

Degrees of difficulty

Easy, suitable for novice with little experience | **Fairly easy,** suitable for beginner with some experience | **Fairly difficult,** suitable for competent DIY mechanic | **Difficult,** suitable for experienced DIY mechanic | **Very difficult,** suitable for expert DIY or professional

Specifications

Engine

Spark plugs
  Type
    Standard . . . . NGK DPR8EA-9 or Nippondenso X24EPR-U9
    For cold climate (below 5°C) . . . . NGK DPR7EA-9 or Nippondenso X22EPR-U9
    For extended high speed riding . . . . NGK DPR9EA-9 or Nippondenso X27EPR-U9
  Electrode gap . . . . 0.8 to 0.9 mm
Valve clearances (COLD engine)
  Intake valves . . . . 0.13 to 0.17 mm
  Exhaust valves . . . . 0.18 to 0.22 mm
Engine idle speed
  600 engine . . . . 1200 ± 100 rpm
  650 engine . . . . 1100 ± 100 rpm
Carburettor synchronisation
  Maximum difference between cylinder readings . . . . 40 mm Hg
Cylinder compression . . . . 192 ± 28 psi (13.25 ± 1.9 Bar)

Miscellaneous

Freeplay adjustments
    Throttle grip . . . . 2 to 6 mm
    Clutch lever . . . . 10 to 20 mm

Tyre pressures (cold)	**Front**	**Rear**
Solo rider	33 psi (2.3 Bar)	33 psi (2.3 Bar)
Rider and pillion	33 psi (2.3 Bar)	41 psi (2.8 Bar)

Torque settings

Spark plugs . . . . 14 Nm
Crankshaft end cap . . . . 15 Nm
Timing mark inspection cap . . . . 10 Nm
Valve clearance adjuster locknuts . . . . 23 Nm
Valve cover bolts . . . . 10 Nm
Oil drain plug . . . . 35 Nm
Oil filter cartridge . . . . 10 Nm
Final drive oil filler cap . . . . 12 Nm
Final drive oil drain bolt . . . . 20 Nm
Side stand pivot bolt . . . . 38 Nm
Swingarm right pivot bolt . . . . 10 Nm
Swingarm right pivot bolt locknut (using special tool) . . . . 90 Nm
Swingarm left pivot bolt . . . . 100 Nm
Steering stem nut . . . . 105 Nm
Steering head bearing adjuster nut . . . . 22 Nm
Top yoke fork clamp bolts . . . . 23 Nm

Recommended lubricants and fluids

Engine/transmission oil type . . . . SE, SF or SG motor oil
Engine/transmission oil viscosity . . . . SAE 10W40
Engine/transmission oil capacity
    Oil and filter change . . . . 2.6 litres
    Following engine overhaul - dry engine, new filter . . . . 3.0 litres
Final drive oil type . . . . SAE 80 Hypoid gear oil
Final drive oil capacity . . . . Approx. 110 cc
Brake fluid . . . . DOT 4
Coolant type . . . . 50% distilled water, 50% corrosion inhibited ethylene glycol antifreeze
Coolant capacity
    After draining . . . . 1.6 litres
    Total capacity . . . . 2.2 litres
Fork oil level*
    J model . . . . 182 mm
    K, M and P models . . . . 123 mm
    S and T models . . . . 106 mm
Fork oil capacity
    J model . . . . 405 cc
    K, M and P models . . . . 466 cc
    S and T models . . . . 482 cc
Fork oil type . . . . ATF
*Fork oil level is measured from the top of the tube, with the fork tube compressed and the spring removed.

Miscellaneous

Wheel bearings . . . . Multi-purpose grease
Rear suspension bearings . . . . Multi-purpose grease
Steering head bearings . . . . Multi-purpose grease
Cables, lever and stand pivot points . . . . Motor oil
Throttle grip . . . . Multi-purpose grease or dry film lubricant

Note: *Always perform the daily (pre-ride) checks at every maintenance interval (in addition to the procedures listed). The intervals listed below are the intervals recommended by the manufacturer for each particular operation during the model years covered in this manual. Your owner's manual may have different intervals for your model.*

Daily (pre-ride) checks

- ☐ See *'Daily (pre-ride) checks'* at the beginning of this manual.

After the initial 600 miles (1000 km)

Note: *This check is usually performed by a Honda dealer after the first 600 miles (1000 km) from new. Thereafter, maintenance is carried out according to the following intervals of the schedule.*

Every 4000 miles (6000 km) or 6 months

Carry out all the items under the Daily (pre-ride) checks
- ☐ Clean the crankcase breather (Section 1)
- ☐ Check the spark plug gaps (Section 2).
- ☐ Check and adjust the idle speed (Section 3).
- ☐ Check the brake pads for wear (Section 4).
- ☐ Check the operation of the clutch (Section 5).
- ☐ Check the tyre and wheel condition, and the tyre tread depth (Section 6).

Every 8000 miles (12 000 km) or 12 months

Carry out all the items under the 4000 mile (6000 km) check, plus the following:
- ☐ Check the fuel hoses and system components (Section 7).
- ☐ Check throttle/choke cable operation and freeplay (Section 8).
- ☐ Replace the spark plugs (Section 9).
- ☐ Check the valve clearances (Section 10).
- ☐ Change the engine oil and replace the oil filter (Section 11).
- ☐ Check carburettor synchronisation (Section 12).
- ☐ Check the cooling system (Section 13).
- ☐ Check the final drive oil level (Section 14).
- ☐ Check the operation of the brakes, and for fluid leakage (Section 15).
- ☐ Check the headlight aim (Section 16).
- ☐ Check the side stand (Section 17).
- ☐ Check the front and rear suspension (Section 18).

Every 8000 miles (12 000 km) or 12 months (continued)

- ☐ Check the swingarm bearings (Section 19).
- ☐ Check the steering head bearing freeplay (Section 20).
- ☐ Check the wheel bearings (Section 21).
- ☐ Lubricate the stand(s), lever pivots and cables (Section 22).
- ☐ Check the tightness of all nuts and bolts (Section 23).

Every 12 000 miles (18 000 km) or 18 months

Carry out all the items under the 4000 mile (6000 km) check, plus the following:
- ☐ Replace the air filter (Section 24).
- ☐ Change the brake fluid (Section 25).

Every 24 000 miles (36 000 km) or 2 years

Carry out all the items under the 8000 (12 000 km) and the 12 000 mile (18 000 km) check, plus the following:
- ☐ Change the coolant (Section 26).

Every 24 000 miles (36 000 km) or 3 years

Carry out all the items under the 8000 (12 000 km) and the 12 000 mile (18 000 km) check, plus the following:
- ☐ Change the final drive oil (Section 27).

1

Non-scheduled maintenance

- ☐ Change the front fork oil (Section 28).
- ☐ Check the cylinder compression (Section 29).
- ☐ Re-grease the steering head bearings (Section 30).
- ☐ Re-grease the swingarm bearings (Section 31).
- ☐ Replace the brake master cylinder and caliper seals (Section 32).
- ☐ Replace the brake hoses (Section 33).

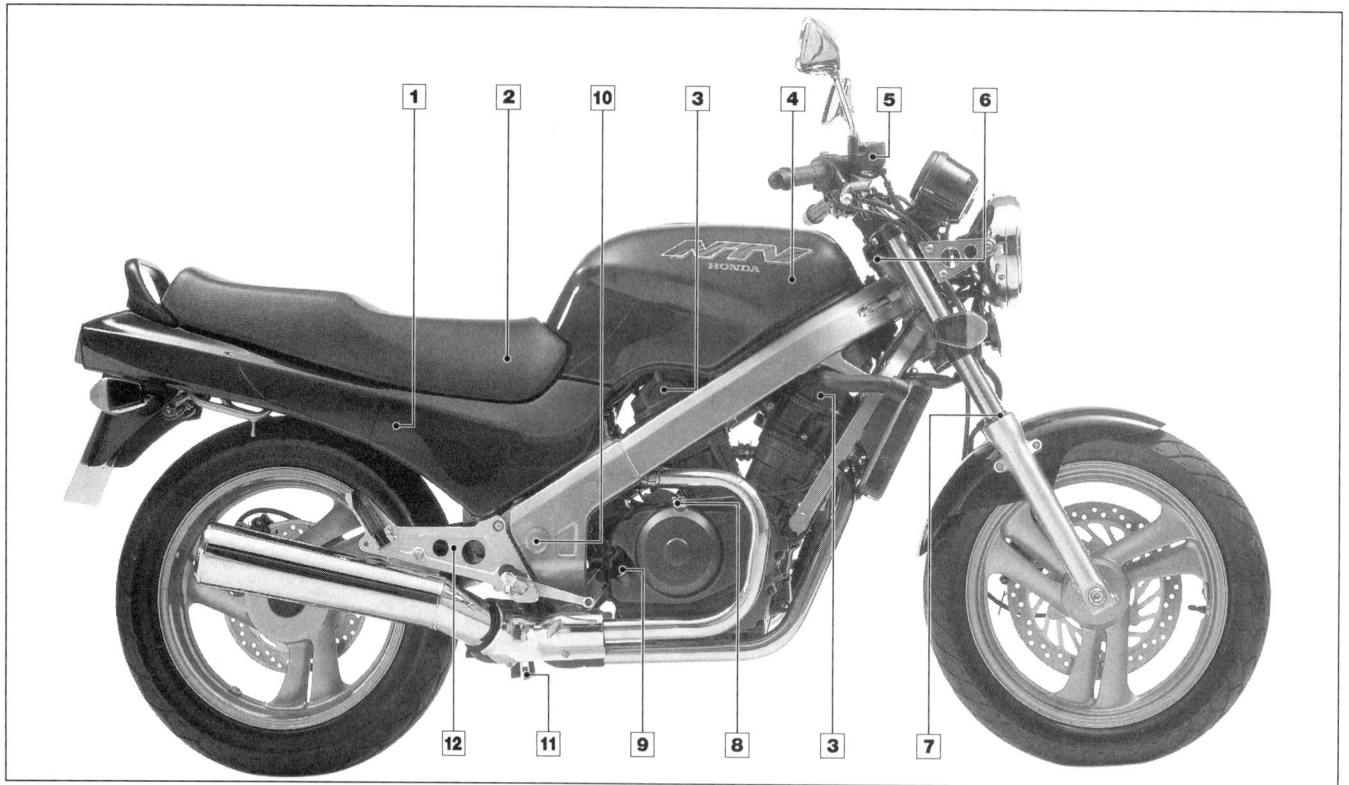

1 Rear brake fluid reservoir
2 Battery
3 Valves and spark plugs
4 Air filter
5 Front brake fluid reservoir
6 Steering head bearings
7 Fork seals
8 Clutch cable lower adjuster
9 Engine oil filler/dipstick
10 Swingarm pivot
11 Crankcase breather tube
12 Rear brake light switch

1 Radiator pressure cap
2 Engine idle speed adjuster
3 Carburettors
4 Coolant reservoir
5 Fuel filter
6 Brake calipers
7 Final drive oil filler/level plug
8 Final drive oil drain plug
9 Engine oil filter
10 Coolant drain plug
11 Engine oil drain plug
12 Rotor inspection cap

1 This Chapter is designed to help the home mechanic maintain his/her motorcycle for safety, economy, long life and peak performance.

2 Deciding where to start or plug into the routine maintenance schedule depends on several factors. If the warranty period on your motorcycle has just expired, and if it has been maintained according to the warranty standards, you may want to pick up routine maintenance as it coincides with the next mileage or calendar interval. If you have owned the machine for some time but have never performed any maintenance on it, then you may want to start at the nearest interval and include some additional procedures to ensure that nothing important is overlooked. If you have just had a major engine overhaul, then you may want to start the maintenance routine from the beginning. If you have a used machine and have no knowledge of its history or maintenance record, you may desire to combine all the checks into one large service initially and then settle into the maintenance schedule prescribed.

3 Before beginning any maintenance or repair, the machine should be cleaned thoroughly, especially around the oil filter, spark plugs, valve cover, side panels, carburettors, etc. Cleaning will help ensure that dirt does not contaminate the engine and will allow you to detect wear and damage that could otherwise easily go unnoticed.

4 Certain maintenance information is sometimes printed on decals attached to the motorcycle. If the information on the decals differs from that included here, use the information on the decal.

Every 4000 miles (6000 km) or 6 months

1 Crankcase breather - draining

1 Remove the plug from the bottom of the crankcase breather tube located behind the side stand (see illustration). Allow the deposits to drain into a suitable container, then fit the plug back into the bottom of the tube. Note: The crankcase breather should be drained more often if the bike is ridden frequently in the rain or at full throttle, or if the bike is washed or has been dropped. Drain the tube at any time when deposits are seen in the clear part of the tubing.

2 Spark plug gaps - check and adjustment

1 This motorcycle is equipped with two spark plugs per cylinder. One plug is located on the side of the engine, the other is located within the valve cover (there is no need to remove the valve cover to access the plug for removal) (see illustrations). Make sure your spark plug socket is the correct size before attempting to remove the plugs - a suitable one is supplied in the motorcycle's tool kit.

2 Remove the seat and disconnect the battery negative (-ve) lead.

3 Remove the fuel tank (see Chapter 4).

4 Clean the area around the valve cover and plug caps to prevent any dirt falling into the spark plug channels.

5 Check that the cylinder location number is marked on each plug lead, then pull the spark plug caps off the spark plugs. Using a socket type wrench, unscrew the plugs from the cylinder head (see illustration). Lay the plugs out in relation to their cylinder; if either plug shows up a problem it will then be easy to identify the troublesome cylinder.

6 Inspect the electrodes for wear. Both the centre and side electrodes should have square edges and the side electrode should be of uniform thickness. Look for excessive deposits and evidence of a cracked or chipped insulator around the centre electrode. Compare your spark plugs to the colour spark plug reading chart at the end of this manual. Check the threads, the washer and the ceramic insulator body for cracks and other damage.

7 If the electrodes are not excessively worn, and if the deposits can be easily removed with a wire brush, the plugs can be regapped and re-used (if no cracks or chips are visible in the insulator). If in doubt concerning the condition of the plugs, replace them with new ones, as the expense is minimal.

8 Cleaning spark plugs by sandblasting is permitted (though not recommended), provided you clean the plugs with a high flash-point solvent afterwards.

9 Before installing the plugs, make sure they are the correct type and heat range and check the gap between the electrodes (they are not pre-set on new plugs). For best results, use a

1.1 Remove the plug and allow any deposits to drain from the crankcase breather

2.1a Each cylinder has a spark plug on the side of the engine . . .

2.1b . . . and one within the valve cover

2.5 Remove the spark plugs using the tool provided in the tool kit or a deep plug socket

1

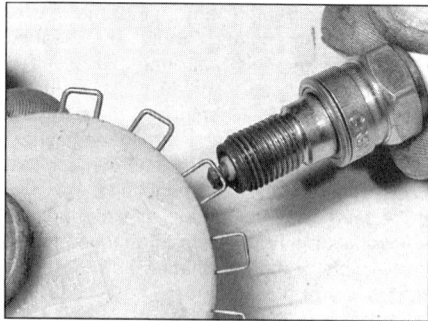

2.9a A wire type gauge is recommended to measure the spark plug electrode gap

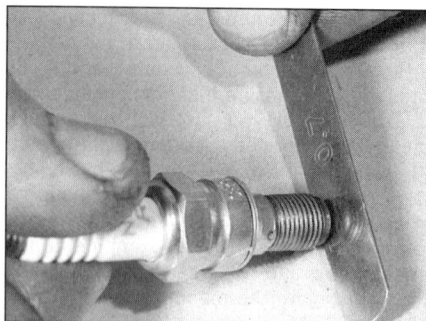

2.9b A blade type feeler gauge can also be used

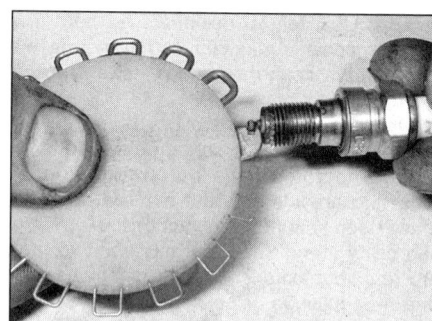

2.9c Adjust the electrode gap by bending the side electrode

2.10 Thread the plug in as far as possible by hand

3.3 Idle speed adjusting screw (throttle stop screw) (arrow)

wire-type gauge rather than a flat (feeler) gauge to check the gap. Compare the gap to that specified and adjust as necessary. If the gap must be adjusted, bend the side electrode only and be very careful not to chip or crack the insulator nose **(see illustrations)**. Make sure the washer is in place before installing each plug.

10 Since the cylinder head is made of aluminium, which is soft and easily damaged, thread the plugs into the heads by hand **(see illustration)**. Once the plugs are finger-tight, the job can be finished with a socket. Tighten the spark plugs to the specified torque listed in this Chapter's Specifications; do not over-tighten them.

11 Reconnect the spark plug caps, making sure they are securely connected to the correct cylinder.

12 Install the fuel tank (see Chapter 4).

3 Idle speed - check and adjustment

1 The idle speed should be checked and adjusted before and after the carburettors are synchronised and when it is obviously too high or too low. Before adjusting the idle speed, make sure the valve clearances and spark plug gaps are correct. Also, turn the handlebars back-and-forth and see if the idle speed changes as this is done. If it does, the throttle cable may not be adjusted correctly, or may be worn out. This is a dangerous condition that can cause loss of control of the bike. Be sure to correct this problem before proceeding.

2 The engine should be at normal operating temperature, which is usually reached after 10 to 15 minutes of stop and go riding. Place the

motorcycle on its centre stand, or hold it upright, and make sure the transmission is in neutral.

3 With the engine idling, adjust the idle speed by turning the throttle stop screw in or out until the idle speed listed in this Chapter's Specifications is obtained. The throttle stop screw is located under the carburettors behind the left-hand side frame spar **(see illustration)**.

4 Snap the throttle open and shut a few times, then recheck the idle speed. If necessary, repeat the adjustment procedure.

5 If a smooth, steady idle can't be achieved, the fuel/air mixture may be incorrect. Refer to Chapter 4 for additional carburettor information.

4 Brake pads - wear check

1 The OE (original equipment) brake pads have three wear indicator grooves (single groove on the rear brake) that can be viewed without removing the pads from the caliper. The pad wear indicator grooves are visible by looking up at the bottom of the pad **(see illustrations)**. If the pads are worn to or beyond the base of the groove(s), they must be replaced. If you are in any doubt about the amount on pad material remaining, remove the pads for thorough inspection (see Chapter 7).

2 Refer to Chapter 7 for details of pad replacement.

HAYNES HINT *Since the plugs are recessed, slip a short length of hose over the end of the plug to use as a tool to thread it into place. The hose will grip the plug well enough to turn it, but will start to slip if the plug begins to cross-thread in the hole - this will prevent damaged threads and the resultant repair costs.*

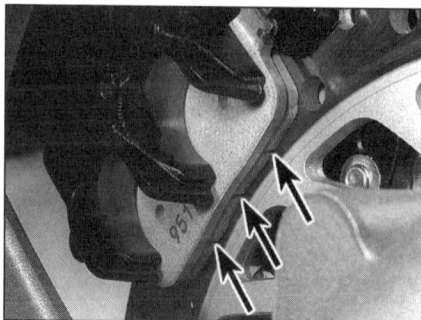

4.1a Front brake pad wear indicator grooves (arrows)

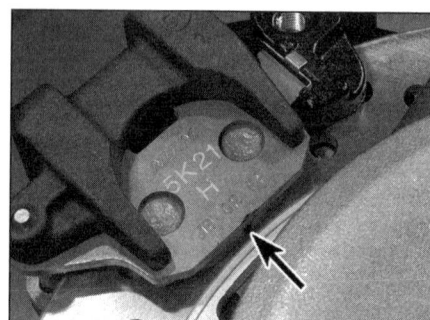

4.1b Rear brake pad wear indicator groove (arrow)

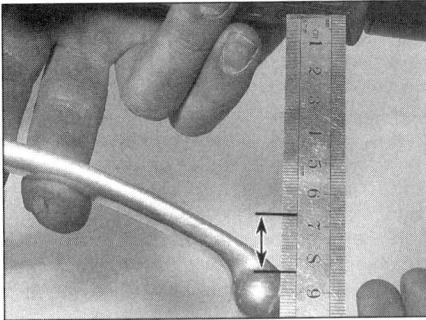

5.1 Measuring clutch lever freeplay

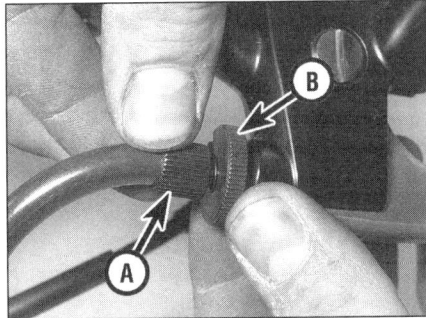

5.2 Clutch cable (lever end) adjuster (A) and lockring (B)

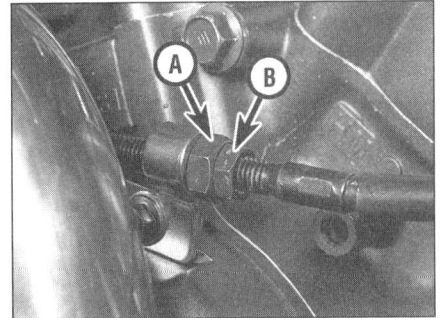

5.3 Clutch cable (clutch end) adjuster (A) and locknut (B)

5 Clutch - check

1 Periodic adjustment of the clutch cable is necessary to compensate for wear of the clutch plates and stretch in the cable. Check that the amount of freeplay at the clutch lever end is within the specifications listed at the beginning of the Chapter (see illustration). If adjustment is required, it can be made at either the lever end of the cable or at the clutch end.

2 To adjust cable freeplay at the lever, pull back the rubber cover, then loosen the locking ring and turn the adjuster in or out until the required amount of freeplay is obtained (see illustration). To increase freeplay, turn the adjuster clockwise. To reduce freeplay, turn the adjuster anticlockwise. Tighten the locking ring securely.

3 To adjust cable freeplay at the clutch, loosen the locknut and turn the adjuster nut until the required amount of freeplay is obtained (see illustration). To increase freeplay, turn the adjuster nut anti-clockwise. To reduce freeplay, turn the adjuster nut clockwise. Tighten the locknuts securely.

4 If all the adjustment has been taken up at the lever, reset the adjuster to give the maximum amount of freeplay, then set the correct amount of freeplay using the adjuster at the clutch end of the cable. Subsequent adjustments can now be made using the lever adjuster only.

6 Wheels and tyres - general check

Wheels

1 Cast wheels are virtually maintenance free, but they should be kept clean and checked periodically for cracks and other damage. Also check the wheel runout and alignment (see Chapter 7). Never attempt to repair damaged cast wheels; they must be replaced with new ones. Check the tyre valve rubber for signs of damage or deterioration and have it replaced if necessary. Also, make sure the valve stem dust cap is in place and tight.

Tyres

2 Check the tyre condition and tread depth thoroughly - see Daily (pre-ride) checks.

Every 8000 miles (12 000 km) or 12 months

1

7 Fuel system - check

⚠️ Warning: Petrol is extremely flammable, so take extra precautions when you work on any part of the fuel system. Don't smoke or allow open flames or bare light bulbs near the work area, and don't work in a garage where a natural gas-type appliance is present. If you spill any fuel on your skin, rinse it off immediately with soap and water. When you perform any kind of work on the fuel system, wear safety glasses and have a fire extinguisher suitable for a Class B type fire (flammable liquids) on hand.

Check

1 Remove the fuel tank (see Chapter 4) and check the tank, the tap, and the fuel hose for signs of leakage, deterioration or damage; in particular check that there is no leakage from the fuel hose. Replace any hoses which are cracked or deteriorated.

2 If the fuel tap is leaking, tightening its nut and screws may help. If leakage persists, remove the tap from the tank as described in Chapter 4. Unscrew the screws and disassemble the tap, noting how the components fit. Inspect all components for wear or damage, and replace the O-ring at the tap and tank joint. If any of the components are worn or damaged beyond repair a new tap must be fitted as components are not available individually.

3 If the carburettor gaskets are leaking, the carburettors should be disassembled and rebuilt using new gaskets and seals (see Chapter 4).

Filter cleaning

4 Cleaning or replacement of the fuel filters is advised after a particularly high mileage has been covered. It is also necessary if fuel starvation is suspected.

5 The fuel tap incorporates a gauze type filter inside the fuel tank. Remove the fuel tap (see Chapter 4) and clean the filter, being careful not to tear the gauze. If the gauze is damaged, replace it with a new one.

6 The fuel hose incorporates an in-line filter between the tank and the fuel pump; remove the left-hand side panel for access (see illustration). This is a sealed unit and cannot be cleaned or serviced. If it is suspected of being blocked, replace it with a new one. To replace the filter, turn the fuel tap OFF, and with a rag held under the filter to catch any fuel spills, disconnect both pipes from the filter. Work the filter out of its housing. Install the new filter, noting that the arrow on its

7.6 In-line fuel filter is located in hose from tap to fuel pump

8.3 Throttle cable freeplay is measured in terms of free twistgrip rotation (arrow)

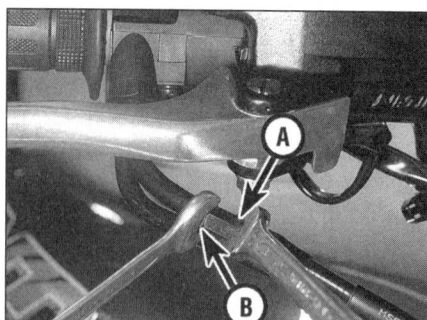

8.4 Throttle cable adjuster (A) and locknut (B)

body must point in the direction of fuel flow (ie towards the fuel pump). Install the fuel pipes and secure them with their clips. Turn the fuel tap ON and check that there is no sign of fuel leakage from the filter connections. Install the side panel.

8 Throttle and choke cables - check

Throttle cables

1 Make sure the throttle grip rotates easily from fully closed to fully open with the front wheel turned at various angles. The grip should snap shut automatically when released.

2 If the throttle sticks, this is probably due to a cable fault. Remove the cables (see Chapter 4) and lubricate them. Install the cables, making sure that they are correctly routed. If this fails to improve the operation of the throttle, the cables must be replaced. Note that in very rare cases the fault could lie in the carburettors rather than the cables, necessitating the removal of the carburettors and inspection of the throttle linkage (see Chapter 4).

3 With the throttle operating smoothly, check for a small amount of freeplay at the grip **(see illustration)**. The amount of freeplay in the throttle cable, measured in terms of twistgrip rotation, should be as given in this Chapter's Specifications. If adjustment is necessary, adjust the idle speed first (see Section 3).

4 The accelerator (opening) cable is adjustable at either the throttle end or the carburettor end. Minor adjustments should be made at the throttle end. To adjust the cable freeplay, slacken the locknut on the cable adjuster and rotate the adjuster until the correct amount of freeplay is obtained, then tighten the locknut against the adjuster **(see illustration)**. If all the adjustment has been taken up at the throttle, re-set the adjuster to give maximum freeplay and then set the correct amount of freeplay by adjusting the accelerator (opening) cable at the carburettor. Subsequent adjustments can now be made at the throttle.

5 After adjustment check that the throttle twistgrip operates smoothly and snaps shut quickly when released.

6 With the engine idling, turn the handlebars through the full extent of their travel. The idle speed should not change. If it does, the cable may be incorrectly routed.

Caution: Correct this condition before riding the bike (see Chapter 4).

Choke cable

7 If the choke does not operate smoothly this is probably due to a cable fault. Remove the cable as described in Chapter 4 and lubricate it. Install the cable, routing it so it takes the smoothest route possible. If this fails to improve the operation of the choke, the cable must be replaced. Note that in very rare cases the fault could lie in the carburettors rather than the cable, necessitating the removal of the carburettors and inspection of the choke valves (see Chapter 4).

8 There should be a very small amount of freeplay at the choke lever when the choke is in the OFF position; this ensures that the choke is not in operation when the engine is running normally. An adjuster elbow immediately underneath the handlebar switch enables adjustment of the cable.

9 To check the choke cable setting, remove the fuel tank (see Chapter 4) and trace the choke cables (single cable from the handlebar splits into two) to the carburettors. Peel back the rubber cover and unscrew the retaining nut to allow the plunger to be withdrawn from each carburettor body. With the choke lever in

the OFF (fully forwards) position, measure the distance from the choke plunger to the retaining nut on both carburettors. It should be between 10 to 11 mm. If not, back off the locknut at the cable elbow under the handlebar switch and rotate the elbow to make cable adjustment - tighten the locknut on completion.

10 Install the choke plungers in the carburettors and secure them with their retaining nuts. Slip the rubber covers back into place. Install the fuel tank as described in Chapter 4.

9 Spark plugs - replacement

See Section 2 'Spark plug gap check' under the 4000 mile (6000 km) or 6 months heading for details.

10 Valve clearances - check and adjustment

1 The engine must be completely cool for this maintenance procedure, so let the machine sit overnight before beginning.

2 Remove the fuel tank and the air filter housing (see Chapter 4).

3 Pull out the three trim clips securing the heat guard to the frame and remove the guard **(see illustration)**.

4 Remove the radiator and the thermostat housing (not necessary if working the on rear cylinder only).

5 Unscrew the crankshaft end cap and the timing mark inspection cap from the left-hand side crankcase cover **(see illustration)**.

6 Remove the valve cover from each cylinder (see Chapter 2). Unscrew the spark plugs to allow the engine to be turned over easier.

7 The engine can be turned over by rotating the crankshaft anti-clockwise using a suitable socket on the flywheel bolt **(see illustration)**. Starting with the front cylinder, rotate the engine until it is at TDC (Top Dead Centre) on the compression stroke. At this point the "FT" mark on the flywheel aligns with the notch in

10.3 The heat guard is secured by three trim clips (arrows)

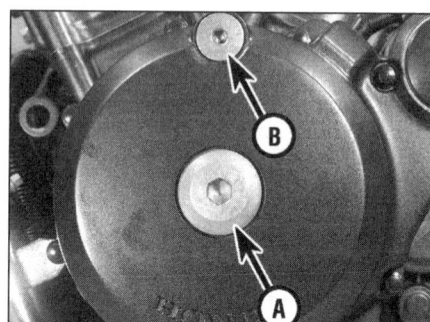

10.5 Crankshaft end cap (A) and timing mark inspection cap (B)

10.7a Use a socket on the flywheel bolt behind the crankshaft end cap to rotate the engine

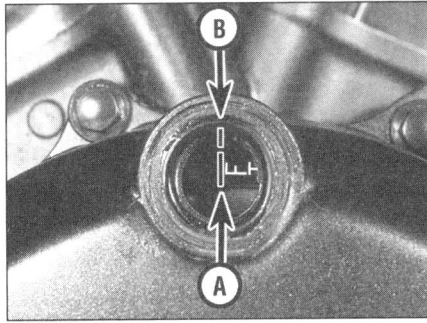

10.7b Align the "FT" mark (A) with the notch (B) in the inspection hole

11 Engine oil and oil filter - change

Warning: Be careful when draining the oil, as the exhaust pipes, the engine, and the oil itself can cause severe burns.

1 Consistent routine oil and filter changes are the single most important maintenance procedure you can perform on a motorcycle. The oil not only lubricates the internal parts of the engine, transmission and clutch, but it also acts as a coolant, a cleaner, a sealant, and a protectant. Because of these demands, the oil takes a terrific amount of abuse and should be replaced often with new oil of the recommended type and viscosity. Saving a little money on the difference in cost between a good oil and a cheap oil won't pay off if the engine is damaged.

2 Before changing the oil, warm up the engine so the oil will drain easily.

3 Put the bike on its side stand and place a clean drain tray below the engine. Unscrew the oil filler cap on the right-hand side crankcase cover to vent the crankcase and to act as a reminder that there is no oil in the engine.

4 Next, unscrew the oil drain plug from the left-hand side of the engine and let the oil flow into the drain tray (see illustration). Discard the drain plug sealing washer as it should be replaced whenever the plug is removed.

10.7c Check the valve clearance using a feeler gauge

10.8 Adjust the valve clearance by turning the adjuster (arrow) whilst counter-holding the locknut

the timing mark inspection hole (see illustration), and both camshaft lobes will be pointing almost downwards (see illustration 8.25b in Chapter 2). Insert a feeler gauge of the correct thickness (see Specifications) between each rocker arm adjuster screw and valve and check that it is a firm sliding fit (see illustration).

8 If it is not, unscrew the locknut and rotate the adjuster until a firm sliding fit is obtained, then tighten the locknut to the torque setting specified at the beginning of the Chapter, making sure the adjuster does not rotate as you do so (see illustration). Re-check the clearances, not forgetting that there is a difference between the inlet valve clearance and the exhaust valve clearance.

9 Moving to the rear cylinder, rotate the engine until it is at TDC (Top Dead Centre) on the compression stroke. At this point the "RT" mark on the flywheel aligns with the notch in the inspection hole, and both camshaft lobes will be pointing almost downwards. Check and adjust the valve clearance as described in Steps 7 and 8 above.

10 Install all disturbed components in a reverse of the removal sequence, referring to the relevant Chapters where necessary. Apply engine oil to the valve assemblies and camshafts before installing the valve covers. Apply a smear of molybdenum disulphide grease to the threads of the crankshaft end cap and the timing mark inspection cap and tighten them to their specified torque settings.

5 Position the oil drain tray so that it is below the oil filter (see illustration). Using an oil filter removing tool (there are several types commercially available at little cost), unscrew the filter from the rear of the engine. Clean the filter thread and housing on the crankcase using clean rag. Wipe off any remaining oil from the filter sealing area

6 When the oil has completely drained, fit a new sealing washer over the drain plug. Fit the plug to the crankcase and tighten it to the torque setting specified at the beginning of the Chapter. Avoid overtightening, as damage to the threads will result.

7 Apply a smear of clean engine oil to the rubber sealing ring on the new filter, then install the filter onto the engine (see illustration). Using an oil filter wrench (if

1

11.4 Engine oil drain plug location (arrow)

11.5 Engine oil filter location

11.7 Apply a smear of motor oil to the sealing ring of the filter on installation

available), tighten the filter to the specified torque setting. If the wrench is not available, tighten the filter firmly by hand. Do not overtighten the filter as the seal will be damaged and the filter will leak.

8 Refill the crankcase with oil to the proper level (see *Daily (pre-ride) checks*) and install the filler cap. Start the engine and let it run for two or three minutes (make sure that the oil pressure light extinguishes after a few seconds). Shut it off, wait a few minutes, then check the oil level. If necessary, add more oil to bring the level up to the upper mark on the dipstick. Check around the drain plug and filter for leaks.

9 The old oil drained from the engine cannot be re-used and should be disposed of properly. Check with your local refuse disposal company, disposal facility or environmental agency to see whether they will accept the used oil for recycling. Don't pour used oil into drains or onto the ground.

HAYNES HiNT *Check the old oil carefully - if it is very metallic coloured, then the engine is experiencing wear from running-in (new engine) or from insufficient lubrication. If there are flakes or chips of metal in the oil, then something is drastically wrong internally and the engine will have to be disassembled for inspection and repair. If there are pieces of fibre-like material in the oil, the clutch is experiencing excessive wear and should be checked.*

OIL CARE
OIL BANK LINE
0800 66 33 66

Note: It is antisocial and illegal to dump oil down the drain. To find the location of your local oil recycling bank, call this number free.

12 Carburettors - synchronisation

⚠️ **Warning: Petrol is extremely flammable, so take extra precautions when you work on any part of the fuel system. Don't smoke or allow open flames or bare light bulbs near the work area, and don't work in a garage where a natural gas-type appliance is present. If you spill any fuel on your skin, rinse it off immediately with soap and water. When you perform any kind of work on the fuel system, wear safety glasses and have a fire extinguisher suitable for a Class B type fire (flammable liquids) on hand.**

⚠️ **Warning: Take great care not to burn your hand on the hot engine unit when accessing the gauge take-off points on the intake manifolds. Do not allow exhaust gases to build up in the work area; either perform the check outside or use an exhaust gas extraction system.**

1 Carburettor synchronisation is simply the process of adjusting the carburettors so they pass the same amount of fuel/air mixture to each cylinder. This is done by measuring the vacuum produced in each cylinder. Carburettors that are out of synchronisation will result in decreased fuel mileage, increased engine temperature, less than ideal throttle response and higher vibration levels. Before synchronising the carburettors, make sure the valve clearances are properly set.

2 To properly synchronise the carburettors, you will need some sort of vacuum gauge set-up, preferably with a gauge for each cylinder, or a manometer, which is a calibrated tube arrangement that utilises columns of mercury or steel rods to indicate engine vacuum.

3 A manometer can be purchased from a motorcycle dealer or accessory shop and should have the necessary rubber hoses supplied with it for hooking into the vacuum take-off stubs.

4 A vacuum gauge set-up can also be purchased from a dealer or mail-order specialist or fabricated from commonly available hardware and automotive vacuum gauges.

5 The manometer is the more reliable and accurate instrument, and for that reason is preferred over the vacuum gauge set-up; however, if using a mercury manometer, extra precautions must be taken during use and storage of the instrument as mercury is a liquid, and extremely toxic.

6 Because of the nature of the synchronisation procedure and the need for special instruments, most owners leave the task to a Honda dealer.

7 Start the engine and let it run until it reaches normal operating temperature, then shut it off.

8 Remove the fuel tank (see Chapter 4).

9 Unscrew the vacuum take-off plug from the intake port on each cylinder and install the

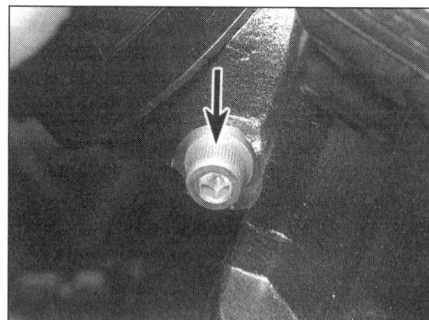

12.9 The vacuum take-off plug (arrow) is located in the intake port of each cylinder

vacuum take-off adapter in its place **(see illustration)**. If your vacuum gauge set or manometer does not contain the correct size adapters, they are available from a Honda dealer (Pt. No. 16124-MBO-000).

10 Connect the gauge hoses to the take-off adapters. Make sure there are no air leaks as false readings will result.

11 Arrange a temporary fuel supply, either by using a small temporary tank or by using extra long fuel pipes to the now remote fuel tank. Alternatively, position the tank on a suitable base on the motorcycle, taking care not to scratch any paintwork, and making sure that the tank is safely and securely supported.

12 Start the engine and make sure the idle speed is as specified at the beginning of the Chapter. If it isn't, adjust it (see Section 3). If the gauges are fitted with damping adjustment, set this so that the needle flutter is just eliminated but so that they can still respond to small changes in pressure.

13 The vacuum readings for both of the cylinders should be the same, or at least within the tolerance listed in this Chapter's Specifications. If the vacuum readings vary, proceed as follows.

14 The carburettors are adjusted by turning the synchronising screw situated in-between the carburettors, in the throttle linkage **(see illustration)**. The screw is accessed using a long screwdriver inserted through the hole in the air cleaner housing **(see illustration)**. Turn the screw until the reading on each gauge is the same. **Note:** *Do not press down on the screw whilst adjusting it, otherwise a false*

12.14a Carburettor synchronisation screw (arrow) (with air filter housing removed)

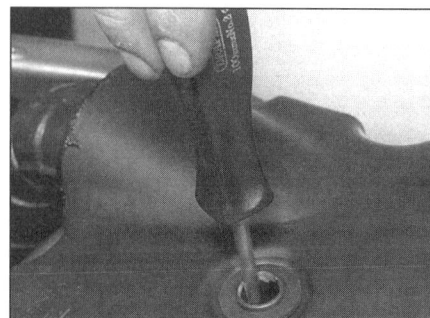

12.14b Adjust the synchronisation screw through the hole in the air filter housing

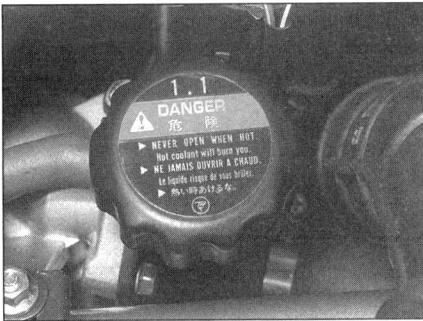

13.6 Observe caution when releasing the radiator pressure cap

14.2a Unscrew the oil filler cap from the final drive housing . . .

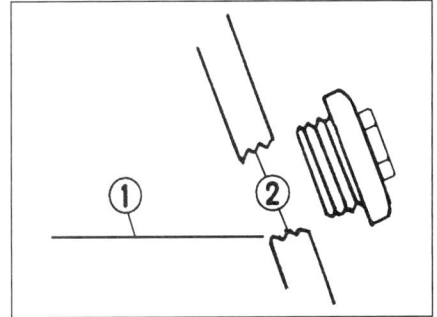

14.2b . . . and check that the oil (1) is up to the edge of the filler hole (2)

reading will be obtained. When the carburettors are synchronised, open and close the throttle quickly to settle the linkage, and recheck the gauge readings, readjusting if necessary.

15 When the adjustment is complete, recheck the vacuum readings, then stop the engine. Remove the vacuum gauge or manometer and install the blanking plugs, complete with their sealing washers.

16 Detach the temporary fuel supply and install the fuel tank (see Chapter 4).

13 Cooling system - check

Warning: The engine must be cool before beginning this procedure.

1 Check the coolant level (see *Daily (pre-ride) checks*).

2 The entire cooling system should be checked for evidence of leakage. Examine each rubber coolant hose along its entire length. Look for cracks, abrasions and other damage. Squeeze each hose at various points. They should feel firm, yet pliable, and return to their original shape when released. If they are dried out or hard, replace them with new ones.

3 Check for evidence of leaks at each cooling system joint. Tighten the hose clips carefully to prevent future leaks.

4 Check the radiator for leaks and other damage. Leaks in the radiator leave telltale scale deposits or coolant stains on the outside of the core below the leak. If leaks are noted, remove the radiator (see Chapter 3) and have it repaired professionally or replace it with a new one.

Caution: Do not use a liquid leak stopping compound to try to repair leaks.

5 Check the radiator fins for mud, dirt and insects, which may impede the flow of air through the radiator. If the fins are dirty, clean them using water or low pressure compressed air directed through the fins from the rear side. If the fins are bent or distorted, straighten them carefully with a screwdriver. If the air flow is restricted by bent or damaged

fins over more than 30% of the radiator's surface area, replace the radiator.

6 Remove the fuel tank to access the radiator pressure cap (see Chapter 4). Remove the pressure cap from the filler neck by turning it anti-clockwise until it reaches a stop **(see illustration)**. If you hear a hissing sound (indicating there is still pressure in the system), wait until it stops. Now press down on the cap and continue turning the cap until it can be removed. Check the condition of the coolant in the system. If it is rust-coloured or if accumulations of scale are visible, drain, flush and refill the system with new coolant (See Section 26). Check the cap seal for cracks and other damage. If in doubt about the pressure cap's condition, have it tested by a Honda dealer or replace it with a new one. Install the cap by turning it clockwise until it reaches the first stop, then push down on the cap and continue turning until it can turn no further. Install the fuel tank.

7 Check the antifreeze content of the coolant with an antifreeze hydrometer. Sometimes coolant looks like it's in good condition, but might be too weak to offer adequate protection. If the hydrometer indicates a weak mixture, drain, flush and refill the system (see Section 26).

8 Start the engine and let it reach normal operating temperature, then check for leaks again. As the coolant temperature increases, the fan should come on automatically and the temperature should begin to drop. If it does not, refer to Chapter 3 and check the fan and fan circuit carefully.

9 If the coolant level is consistently low, and no evidence of leaks can be found, have the entire system pressure checked by a Honda dealer.

10 Periodically, check the drainage hole on the underside of the water pump cover (see Chapter 3). Leakage from this hole indicates failure of the pump's mechanical seal.

14 Final drive oil level - check

1 Place the motorcycle on its centre stand, or support it in an upright position using an

auxiliary stand, making sure it is on level ground.

2 The check should be made after the machine has been standing for a few hours. Unscrew the oil filler cap and check that the oil is up to the edge of the filler hole **(see illustrations)**. If the level is below this, look for signs of leakage, such as oil staining on the underside of the casing. If leakage is evident, the problem must be rectified to avoid the possibility of damage to the final drive and oil contaminating the rear tyre (see Chapter 6).

3 Replenish the oil if necessary to the correct level using the type specified at the beginning of the Chapter, then install the filler cap, using a new O-ring smeared with clean oil, and tighten it to the torque setting specified at the beginning of the Chapter.

15 Brake system - check

1 A routine general check of the brake system will ensure that any problems are discovered and remedied before the rider's safety is jeopardised.

2 Check the brake lever and pedal for loose connections, excessive play, bends, and other damage. Replace any damaged parts with new ones (see Chapter 7).

3 Make sure all brake fasteners are tight. Check the brake pads for wear and make sure the fluid level in the reservoirs is correct (see *Daily (pre-ride) checks*). Look for leaks at the hose connections and check for cracks in the hoses. If the lever or pedal is spongy, bleed the brakes (see Chapter 7).

4 Make sure the brake light operates when the front brake lever is depressed. The front brake light switch is not adjustable. If it fails to operate properly, check it (see Chapter 9).

5 Make sure the brake light is activated just before the rear brake pedal takes effect. If adjustment is necessary, hold the switch and turn the adjusting nut on the switch body until the brake light is activated when required **(see illustration)**. If the switch doesn't operate the brake lights, check it (see Chapter 9).

6 Check the position of the brake pedal tip in relation to the top of the footrest. Honda do

1

15.5 Rear brake light adjusting nut (arrow) - viewed from inside

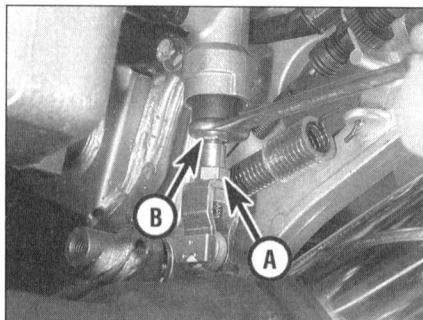

15.6 Slacken the locknut (A) and adjust the pedal height using the nut (B) on the pushrod

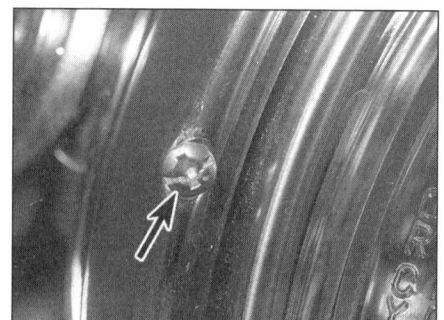

16.2 Headlight horizontal adjustment screw (arrow)

16.3 Slacken the headlight mounting bolts (arrow) for vertical adjustment

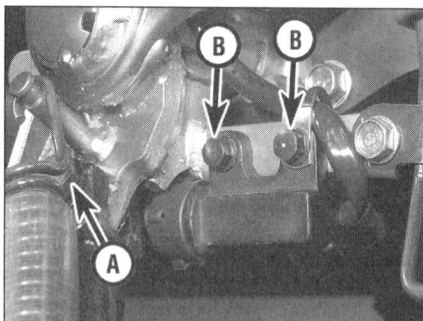

17.4a Side stand pivot bolt (A) and side stand switch bolts (B)

17.4b Side stand switch plunger (arrow)

not supply an actual setting for the brake pedal height, but it can be adjusted to suit rider preference. Adjustment is made by slackening the locknut on the master cylinder pushrod, then turning the pushrod until the pedal is at the correct height **(see illustration)**. Tighten the locknut securely. Always check and if necessary adjust the rear brake light switch after adjusting the pedal height (see Step 5). **Note:** *A setting is given for master cylinder pushrod length in Chapter 7 and it is advised that you do not deviate too far from this setting when making adjustments.*

16 Headlight aim - check and adjustment

Note: *An improperly adjusted headlight may cause problems for oncoming traffic or provide poor, unsafe illumination of the road ahead. Before adjusting the headlight aim, be sure to consult with local traffic laws and regulations and refer to MOT Test Checks in the Reference section of this Manual.*

1 The headlight beam can adjusted both horizontally and vertically. Before making any adjustment, check that the tyre pressures are correct and the suspension is adjusted as required. Make any adjustments to the headlight aim with the machine on level ground, with the fuel tank half full and with an assistant sitting on the seat. If the bike is

usually ridden with a passenger on the back, have a second assistant to do this.

2 Horizontal adjustment is made by turning the adjuster screw in the headlight rim **(see illustration)**. Turn it clockwise to move the beam to the left, and anti-clockwise to move it to the right.

3 Vertical adjustment is made by slackening the headlight mounting bolts and tilting the unit up or down as required **(see illustration)**. Tighten the bolts securely after the adjustment has been made.

17 Side stand - check

1 The side stand return spring must be capable of retracting the stand fully and holding the stand retracted when the motorcycle is in use. If the spring is sagged or broken it must be replaced.

2 Lubricate the side stand pivot regularly (see Section 22). Make sure the pivot bolt is tightened to the torque setting specified at the beginning of the Chapter **(see illustration 17.4a)**.

3 The side stand switch prevents the engine being started if the stand is extended and the motorcycle is in gear. Check its operation by shifting the transmission into neutral, retracting the stand and starting the engine. Pull in the clutch lever and select a gear. Extend the side stand. The engine should stop

as the side stand is extended. If the side stand switch does not operate as described, check its circuit (see Chapter 9).

4 Check that the switch mounting bolts are secure and that the switch plunger moves freely in and out of the switch **(see illustrations)**.

18 Suspension - check

1 The suspension components must be maintained in top operating condition to ensure rider safety. Loose, worn or damaged suspension parts decrease the motorcycle's stability and control.

Front suspension

2 While standing alongside the motorcycle, apply the front brake and push on the handlebars to compress the forks several times. See if they move up-and-down smoothly without binding. If binding is felt, the forks should be disassembled and inspected (see Chapter 6).

3 Inspect the area above the dust seal for signs of oil leakage, then carefully lever off the dust seal using a flat-bladed screwdriver and inspect the area around the fork seal **(see illustrations)**. If leakage is evident, the seals must be replaced (see Chapter 6).

4 Check the tightness of all suspension nuts and bolts to be sure none have worked loose.

18.3a Lever off the dust seal . . .

18.3b . . . and inspect the area above the oil seal for signs of oil leakage

Rear suspension

5 Inspect the rear shock for fluid leakage and tightness of its mountings. If leakage is found, the shock should be replaced.

6 With the aid of an assistant to support the bike, compress the rear suspension several times. It should move up and down freely without binding. If binding is felt, the shock absorber should be removed and examined further. Also check the swingarm bearings (see Section 19).

7 Position the motorcycle on its centre stand or on an auxiliary stand so that the rear wheel is off the ground. Grab the swingarm and rock it from side to side - there should be no discernible movement at the rear. If there's a little movement or a slight clicking can be heard, make a further check of the swingarm bearings (see Section 19).

8 Inspect the tightness of the rear suspension mounting bolts and nuts.

19 Swingarm bearings - check

1 To make an accurate assessment of the swingarm bearings, remove the rear wheel (see Chapter 7) and the shock absorber lower mounting bolt (see Chapter 6). Swing the shock absorber backwards to provide clearance for the swingarm to be moved.

2 Grasp the rear of the swingarm with one hand and place your other hand at the junction of the swingarm and the frame. Try to move the rear of the swingarm from side-to-side. Any wear (play) in the bearings should be felt as movement between the swingarm and the frame at the front. If there is any play the swingarm will be felt to move forward and backward at the front (not from side-to-side). Next, move the swingarm up and down through its full travel. It should move freely, without any binding or rough spots.

3 If any play in the swingarm is noted, check that the bearings are loaded to the correct torque setting. Prise off the dust cover from the right-hand side of the swingarm pivot, then counter-hold the pivot bolt on the right-hand side and slacken the locknut **(see illustration)**. This requires the use of a Honda

service tool (Pt. No. 07908-ME90000) which is a special wrench that fits the locknut slots **(see illustration)**. There is no alternative to the use of this tool; if you do not have access to it, the swingarm pivot locknut must be unscrewed and later tightened by a Honda dealer. Check that the pivot bolt is tightened to the torque setting specified at the beginning of the Chapter, and adjust if necessary. Install the locknut and tighten it to the specified torque setting using a torque wrench applied to the socket in the arm of the special tool **(see illustration)**. **Note:** *The specified torque setting takes into account the extra leverage provided by the service tool and cannot be duplicated without it.* Counter-hold the pivot bolt to stop it from turning whilst tightening the locknut.

4 Also check that the left-hand side pivot bolt is tightened to the correct torque setting. Install the dust caps in the frame.

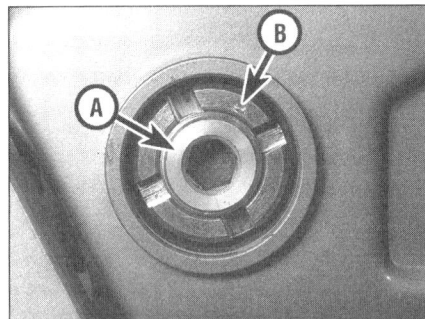

19.3a Swingarm pivot bolt (A) and locknut (B) on right-hand side

19.3c Tighten the locknut using the special tool whilst counter-holding the pivot bolt

5 If any freeplay still exists or if the swingarm does not move freely, the bearings must be removed for inspection or replacement (see Chapter 6).

20 Steering head bearings - freeplay check and adjustment

1 This motorcycle is equipped with caged-ball type steering head bearings. Head bearings can become dented, rough or loose during normal use of the machine, and in extreme cases, worn or loose steering head bearings can cause steering wobble - a condition that is potentially dangerous.

Check

2 Place the motorcycle on its centre stand, or support it using an auxiliary stand. Raise the front wheel off the ground either by having an assistant push down on the rear or by placing a support under the engine.

3 Point the front wheel straight-ahead and slowly move the handlebars from side-to-side. Any dents or roughness in the bearing races will be felt and the bars will not move smoothly and freely.

4 Next, grasp the fork sliders and try to move them forward and backward **(see illustration)**. Any looseness in the steering head bearings will be felt as front-to-rear movement of the forks. If play is felt in the bearings, adjust the steering head as follows **(see Haynes Hint)**.

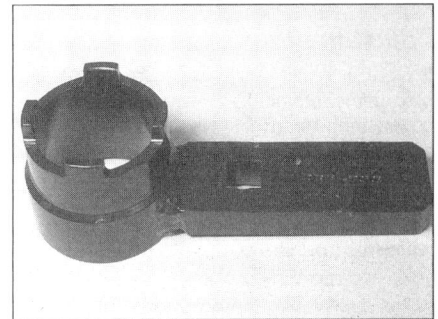

19.3b This Honda special tool is essential for adjusting the swingarm bearings

20.4 Checking for looseness in the steering head bearings

1

20.7a Remove the steering stem nut and washer

20.7b Slacken the fork clamp bolts (arrows), then lift off the top yoke

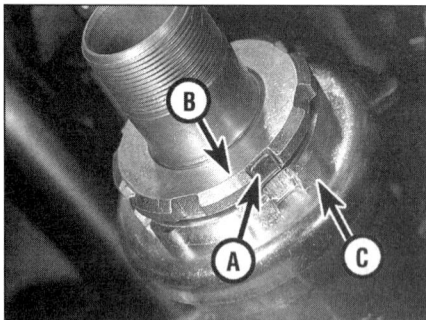

the steering is able to move freely **(see illustration)**. Note that Honda specify a torque setting for the adjuster nut - if this is applied, check afterwards that the steering is still able to move freely from side to side. The object is to set the adjuster nut so that the bearings are under a very light loading, just enough to remove any freeplay.

Caution: Take great care not to apply excessive pressure because this will cause premature failure of the bearings.

10 If the bearings cannot be set up properly, or if there is any binding, roughness or notchiness, they will have to be removed for inspection or replacement (see Chapter 5).

11 With the bearings correctly adjusted, install the lockwasher, and bend down two of its opposite tabs to secure the adjuster nut. Install the locknut, and tighten it finger-tight as far as possible, then tighten it further (to a maximum of 90°) until its slots align with the remaining tabs on the lock washer. Counterhold the adjuster nut whilst doing this to prevent it from moving. Bend up the two remaining tabs to secure the locknut.

12 Fit the top yoke to the steering stem, making sure the rubbers are in place on the top prongs of the headlight frame and that they fit into the holes in the underside of the top yoke **(see illustration)**. Install the steering stem washer and nut, tightening it and both fork clamp bolts to their specified torques **(see illustrations)**. On P, S and T models install the handlebars (Chapter 5) and instrument cluster (Chapter 9) onto the top yoke

13 Check the bearing adjustment as described above and re-adjust if necessary.

20.8 Steering head bearing lockwasher tab (A), locknut (B) and adjuster nut (C)

20.9 Adjust the head bearing adjuster nut using a C-spanner

HAYNES HiNT *Freeplay in the fork due to worn fork bushes can be misinterpreted for steering head bearing play - do not confuse the two.*

Adjustment

5 On J, K and M models, unscrew the fuse box cover retaining screws and remove the cover, then remove the screws securing the fuse box to the top yoke and move the fuse box aside, leaving its wiring connected and noting its routing.

6 On P, S and T models, unscrew the bolts securing the instrument cluster to the top yoke and move the cluster aside to allow the top yoke to be moved (see Chapter 9 if necessary) - there is no need to disconnect the instrument cluster wiring or speedometer cable. Also displace the handlebars (see

Chapter 5) to gain access to the steering stem nut.

7 Unscrew and remove the steering stem nut and washer, then slacken the fork clamp bolts in the top yoke and lift the top yoke off the steering stem **(see illustrations)**. Support the headlight as the top yoke is removed, and note how the prongs and their rubbers on the top of the headlight bracket frame fit into the holes in the underside of the yoke. Support the assembly carefully whilst adjusting the head bearings.

8 Bend back the tabs of the steering stem lockwasher to release it from the locknut, then unscrew and remove the locknut using a suitable C-spanner **(see illustration)**. Remove the lockwasher and discard it as a new one must be used.

9 Slacken the adjuster nut slightly (using the C-spanner) until pressure is just released, then tighten it until all freeplay is removed, yet

21 Wheel bearings - check

1 Place the motorcycle on its centre stand, or support it using an auxiliary stand, and check for any play in the bearings by pushing and pulling the wheel against the hub. Also rotate the wheel and check that it rotates smoothly.

2 If any play is found in the hub, or the wheel does not rotate smoothly (and this is not due to brake drag), the wheel bearings must be inspected for wear or damage (see Chapter 7).

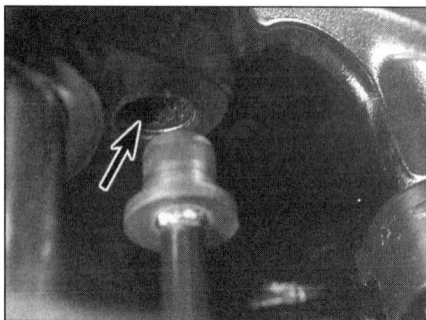

20.12a Headlight frame prongs fit in holes in the underside of the top yoke (arrow)

20.12b Install the steering stem washer . . .

20.12c . . . and tighten the nut to the specified torque setting

22 Stand(s), lever pivots and cables - lubrication

1 Since the controls, cables and various other components of a motorcycle are exposed to the elements, they should be lubricated periodically to ensure safe and trouble-free operation.

2 The footrests, clutch and brake levers, brake pedal, gearshift lever linkage and stand pivot(s) should be lubricated frequently. In order for the lubricant to be applied where it will do the most good, the component should be disassembled. However, if chain and cable lubricant is being used, it can be applied to the pivot joint gaps and will usually work its way into the areas where friction occurs. If motor oil or light grease is being used, apply it sparingly as it may attract dirt (which could cause the controls to bind or wear at an accelerated rate). **Note:** *One of the best lubricants for the control lever pivots is a dry-film lubricant (available from many sources by different names).*

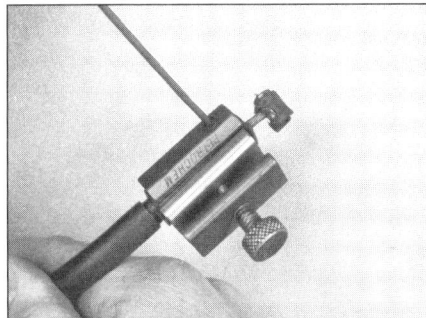

22.3 Lubricating a cable with a pressure lubricator. Make sure the tool seals around the inner cable

3 To lubricate the cables, disconnect the relevant cable at its upper end, then lubricate the cable with a pressure adapter **(see illustration)**. See Chapter 4 for the choke and throttle cable removal procedures and Chapter 2 for the clutch cable removal procedure.

4 The speedometer cable should be removed (see Chapter 9) and the inner cable withdrawn from the outer cable and lubricated with motor oil or cable lubricant. Do not lubricate the upper few inches of the cable as the lubricant may travel up into the speedometer head.

23 Nuts and bolts - tightness check

1 Since vibration of the machine tends to loosen fasteners, all nuts, bolts, screws, etc. should be periodically checked for proper tightness.

2 Pay particular attention to the following:
Spark plugs
Engine oil drain plug
Gearshift pedal bolt
Footrest and stand bolts
Engine mounting bolts
Shock absorber mounting bolts
Handlebar and yoke bolts
Front axle and clamp bolts
Rear axle bolt
Exhaust system bolts/nuts

3 If a torque wrench is available, use it along with the torque specifications at the beginning of this, or other, Chapters.

Every 12 000 miles (18 000 km) or 18 months

24 Air filter - replacement

1 Remove the fuel tank (see Chapter 4).

2 Remove the screws securing the air filter housing cover and remove the cover **(see illustration)**.

3 Remove the old air filter element and install a new one, making sure it is correctly seated **(see illustration)**.

4 Install the air filter housing cover and tighten its screws securely **(see illustration)**.

5 Although it is not a scheduled service item, when replacing the air filter element it is advisable to also clean the sub-air filter element, as follows. The sub-air filter connects via hoses to the carburettor breather passages.

6 Remove the air filter housing (see Chapter 4).

7 Remove the two screws securing the sub-air filter element cover to the base of the air filter housing and remove the cover and the element **(see illustrations)**.

8 Wash the element in non-flammable solvent, then squeeze it out and leave it to dry. Soak the element in SAE 80 or 90 gear oil, then squeeze out the excess.

9 Install the element into its housing, then

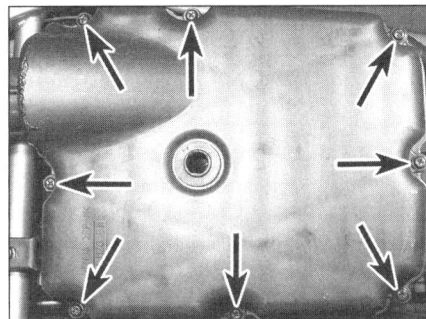

24.2 The air filter housing cover is secured by eight screws (arrows)

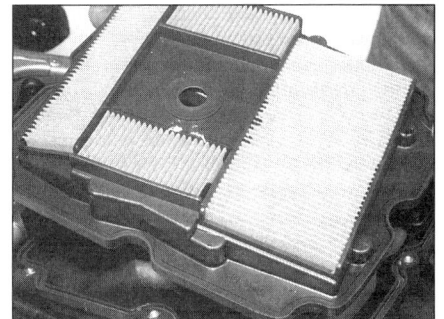

24.3 Installing the new air filter element

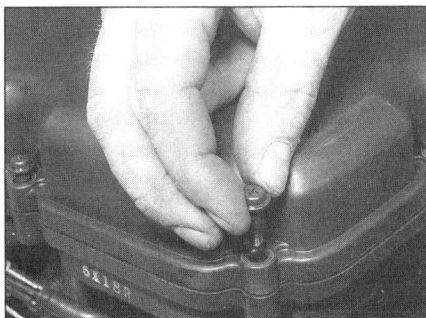

24.4 Secure the air filter housing cover with the eight screws

24.7a Unscrew the two sub-air filter element housing screws (arrows) . . .

24.7b . . . and remove the element

1

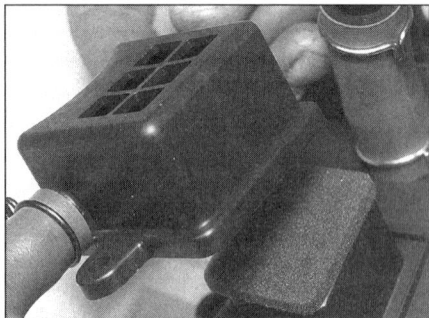

24.9 Install the cover over the element

install the cover and tighten its screws securely **(see illustration)**.
10 Install the air filter housing (refer to Chapter 4).
11 Install the fuel tank (see Chapter 4).

25 Brake fluid - change

1 The brake fluid should be replaced at the prescribed interval or whenever a master cylinder or caliper overhaul is carried out. Refer to the brake bleeding section in Chapter 7, noting that all old fluid must be pumped from the fluid reservoir before filling with new fluid.

> **HAYNES HiNT** *Old brake fluid is invariably much darker in colour than new fluid, making it easy to see when all old fluid has been expelled from the system.*

Every 24 000 miles (36 000 km) or 2 years

26 Cooling system - draining, flushing and refilling

⚠ **Warning: Allow the engine to cool completely before performing this maintenance operation. Also, don't allow antifreeze to come into contact with your skin or the painted surfaces of the motorcycle. Rinse off spills immediately with plenty of water. Antifreeze is highly toxic if ingested. Never leave antifreeze lying around in an open container or in puddles on the floor; children and pets are attracted by its sweet smell and may drink it. Check with local authorities (councils) about disposing of antifreeze. Many communities have collection centres which will see that antifreeze is disposed of safely. Antifreeze is also combustible, so don't store it near open flames.**

Draining

1 Remove the fuel tank to access the pressure cap (see Chapter 4). Remove the pressure cap by turning it anti-clockwise until it reaches a stop **(see illustration 13.6)**. If you hear a hissing sound (indicating there is still pressure in the system), wait until it stops. Now press down on the cap and continue turning the cap until it can be removed.
2 Position a suitable container beneath the water pump, then remove the drain bolt and its sealing washer from the pump cover **(see illustration)**. Discard the washer as a new one must be used.
3 Drain the coolant reservoir. Refer to Chapter 3 for the reservoir removal procedure. Wash out the reservoir with fresh water.

Flushing

4 Flush the system with clean tap water by inserting a garden hose in the radiator filler neck. Allow the water to run through the system until it is clear and flows cleanly out of the drain hole. If the radiator is extremely corroded, remove it by referring to Chapter 3 and have it cleaned by a professional.
5 Clean the drain hole then install the drain bolt with its sealing washer.
6 Fill the cooling system with clean water mixed with a flushing compound. Make sure the flushing compound is compatible with aluminium components, and follow the manufacturer's instructions carefully.
7 Start the engine and allow it reach normal operating temperature. Let it run for about ten minutes.
8 Stop the engine. Let it cool for a while, then cover the pressure cap with a heavy rag and turn it anti-clockwise to the first stop, releasing any pressure that may be present in the system. Once the hissing stops, push down on the cap and remove it completely.
9 Drain the system once again, taking care to avoid scalding your hands.
10 Fill the system with clean water and repeat the procedure in Steps 7 through 9.

Refilling

11 Fit a new sealing washer to the drain bolt and tighten it securely.
12 Fill the system with the proper coolant mixture (refer to this Chapter's Specifications) (see illustration). **Note:** *Pour the coolant in slowly to minimise the amount of air entering the system.*
13 When the system is full (all the way up to the top of the radiator filler neck), install the pressure cap. Also top up the coolant reservoir to the UPPER level mark (see *Daily (pre-ride) checks*).
14 Start the engine and allow it to idle for 2 to 3 minutes. Flick the throttle twistgrip part open 3 or 4 times, so that the engine speed rises to approximately 4000 - 5000 rpm, then stop the engine. This process will bleed any air from the system.
15 Let the engine cool then remove the pressure cap as described in Step 1. Check that the coolant level is still up to the radiator filler neck. If it's low, add the specified mixture until it reaches the top of the filler neck. Reinstall the cap. Install the fuel tank (see Chapter 4).
16 Check the coolant level in the reservoir and top up if necessary.
17 Check the system for leaks.
18 Do not dispose of the old coolant by pouring it down the drain. Instead pour it into a heavy plastic container, cap it tightly and take it to an authorised disposal site or service station - see **Warning** at the beginning of this Section.

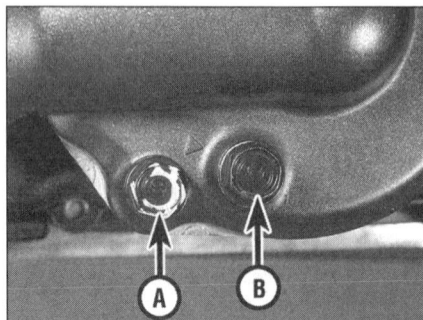

26.2 Coolant drain bolt - J, K and M models (A), P, S and T models (B)

26.12 Fill the cooling system via the filler neck

Every 24 000 miles (36 000 km) or 3 years

27 Final drive oil - change

1 Place the motorcycle on its centre stand, or support it using an auxiliary stand, making sure it is on level ground.
2 Place an oil drain pan under the drain bolt in the final drive housing. Unscrew the filler cap (see illustration 14.2a) and the drain bolt, and allow the oil to drain into the pan (see illustration).
Caution: Make sure that no oil contacts the rear tyre - raise the drain tray or make up a cardboard chute to prevent this.
3 Check the condition of the drain bolt sealing washer and replace it if necessary (it is advisable to replace it as a matter of course). Install the drain bolt and tighten it to the torque setting specified at the beginning of the Chapter. Fill the housing using the amount and type of oil specified at the beginning of the Chapter (also marked on the housing itself) (see illustration). The oil should come up to the edge of the filler hole (see illustration 14.2b).
4 Install the filler cap, using a new O-ring smeared with clean oil, and tighten it to the specified torque setting (see illustration).

27.2 Final drive oil drain bolt

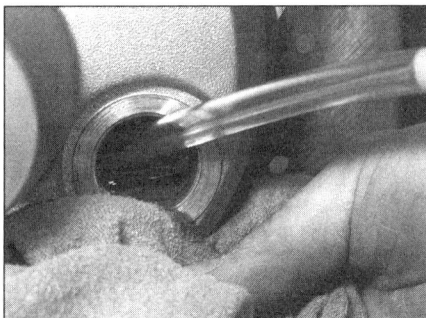

27.3 Fill the final drive housing with the correct quantity and grade of oil

27.4 Install the filler cap using a new O-ring

Non-scheduled maintenance

28 Front fork oil - change

1 Although not specified as part of the maintenance schedule, fork oil will degrade over a period of time and lose its damping qualities. It can be changed without removing the forks from the yokes.
2 Remove the handlebars from the top yoke, but leave the levers and switch housings intact (see Chapter 6). Although movement of the handlebars is restricted by the wiring, cables and brake hose, they can be displaced sufficiently to gain access to the fork top bolts. On J, K and M models support the right handlebar, and on P, S and T models the whole handlebar assembly, so the brake master cylinder is upright and no strain is placed on the hose
3 Slacken the fork clamp bolts in the top yokes (see illustration 20.7b), then remove the fork top bolt cover and unscrew the top bolt.

⚠️ Warning: The fork spring is pressing on the fork top bolt with considerable pressure. Unscrew the bolt very carefully, keeping a downward pressure on it and release it slowly as it is likely to spring clear. It is advisable to wear some form of eye and face protection when carrying out this operation.

4 Remove the spacer and spring seat from the top of the spring, then remove the spring from the fork tube, noting which way up it fits.

HAYNES HiNT *Slackening the fork pinch bolts in the top yoke releases pressure on the fork top bolt. This makes it much easier to remove and helps to preserve the threads.*

5 Place a drain pan under the fork leg, then unscrew the drain screw on the back of the leg and drain the oil into the pan.
6 Pump the forks up and down several times to expel all the old oil, then install the drain screw, using a new sealing washer if the old one shows any signs of damage or deterioration. Tighten the screw securely.
7 Fully compress the fork, and pour in the oil using the amount and type specified at the beginning of the Chapter. Slowly pump the forks up and down a few times to fully distribute the oil. The oil level should also be measured and adjustment made by adding or subtracting oil. Fully compress the fork tubes into the sliders and measure the fork oil level from the top of each tube. Add or subtract fork oil until the oil is at the level specified in the Specifications Section of this Chapter.
Note: It is important that the level in each fork tube is identical.
8 Install the spring, with its closer-wound coils at the bottom, followed by the spring seat, with its shoulder inserted into the spring, and the spacer.
9 Inspect the O-ring on the fork top bolt and replace it if it shows any signs of damage or deterioration. Install the top bolt carefully into the fork tube, making sure it is not cross-threaded, and tighten it to the torque setting specified at the beginning of the Chapter.

⚠️ Warning: It will be necessary to compress the spring by pressing it down using the top bolt to engage the threads of the top bolt with the fork tube. This is a potentially dangerous operation and should be performed with care, using an assistant if necessary. Wipe off any excess oil before starting to prevent the possibility of slipping.

TOOL TiP *Use a ratchet-type tool when installing the fork top bolt. This makes it unnecessary to remove the tool from the bolt whilst threading it in making it easier to maintain a downward pressure on the spring.*

10 Install the top bolt cap, and tighten the fork clamp bolts to the torque setting specified at the beginning of the Chapter.
11 Install the handlebars onto the top yoke (see Chapter 6).

1

29 Cylinder compression - check

1 A compression test will provide useful information about an engine's condition and if performed regularly, can give warning of trouble before any other symptoms become apparent.
2 Refer to the procedure under the *Fault Finding Equipment* heading in the Reference section of this Manual. The cylinder compression figure is given in the Specifications at the beginning of this Chapter.

30 Steering head bearings - re-greasing

1 Over a period of time the grease will harden or may be washed out of the bearings by incorrect use of jet washes.

2 Disassemble the steering head for re-greasing of the bearings. Refer to Chapter 6 for details.

31 Swingarm bearings - re-greasing

1 Over a period of time the grease will harden or dirt will penetrate the bearing due to failed dust seals.
2 The swingarm is not equipped with grease nipples. Remove the swingarm as described in Chapter 6 for greasing of the bearings.

32 Brake caliper and master cylinder - seal replacement

1 Brake piston fluid and dust seals will deteriorate with age and must be replaced with new ones.

2 Refer to Chapter 7 and dismantle the components for seal replacement.

33 Brake hoses - replacement

1 The flexible brake hoses will in time deteriorate with age and must be replaced with new ones.
2 Refer to Chapter 7 and disconnect the brake hoses from the master cylinders and calipers. The hoses should be replaced regardless of their condition. Always replace the banjo union sealing washers with new ones.

Chapter 2
Engine, clutch and transmission

Contents

2

Degrees of difficulty

Easy, suitable for novice with little experience	**Fairly easy,** suitable for beginner with some experience	**Fairly difficult,** suitable for competent DIY mechanic	**Difficult,** suitable for experienced DIY mechanic	**Very difficult,** suitable for expert DIY or professional

Specifications

General

Capacity	
600 cc engine (J, K, M models)	583 cc
650 cc engine (P, S, T models)	647 cc
Bore	
600 cc engine (J, K, M models)	75.0 mm
650 cc engine (P, S, T models)	79.0 mm
Stroke	66.0 mm
Compression ratio	9.2 to 1
Cylinder compression	192 ± 28 psi (13.25 ± 1.9 Bar)

Camshafts, rockers and cam chain

Cam chain tensioner projection (max) .... 6 mm
Camshaft
   Intake lobe height
      Standard .... 38.189 mm
      Service limit .... 38.17 mm
   Exhaust lobe height
      Standard .... 38.123 mm
      Service limit .... 38.19 mm
   Journal diameter
      Standard .... 21.959 to 21.980 mm
      Service limit .... 21.95 mm
   Camshaft bearing oil clearance
      Standard .... 0.040 to 0.093 mm
      Service limit .... 0.11 mm
   Camshaft runout
      Standard .... 0.03 mm
      Service limit .... 0.05 mm
   Rocker shaft diameter
      Standard .... 11.966 to 11.984 mm
      Service limit .... 11.96 mm
   Rocker arm internal diameter
      Standard .... 12.000 to 12.018 mm
      Service limit .... 12.03 mm

Cylinder head

Warpage (max) .... 0.10 mm

Valves, guides and springs

Intake valve
   Stem diameter
      Standard .... 5.475 to 5.490 mm
      Service limit .... 5.47 mm
   Guide bore diameter
      Standard .... 5.500 to 5.512 mm
      Service limit .... 5.53 mm
   Stem-to-guide clearance
      Standard .... 0.010 to 0.037 mm
      Service limit .... 0.07 mm
   Seat width
      Standard .... 0.9 to 1.1 mm
      Service limit .... 1.5 mm
   Spring free lengths
      Inner spring .... 36.47 mm
      Outer spring .... 40.58 mm
   Guide projection height .... 19.4 to 19.6 mm
Exhaust valve
   Stem diameter
      Standard .... 6.555 to 6.570 mm
      Service limit .... 6.55 mm
   Guide bore diameter
      Standard .... 6.600 to 6.615 mm
      Service limit .... 6.66 mm
   Stem-to-guide clearance
      Standard .... 0.030 to 0.060 mm
      Service limit .... 0.11 mm
   Seat width
      Standard .... 0.9 to 1.1 mm
      Service limit .... 1.5 mm
   Spring free lengths
      Inner spring .... 37.51 mm
      Outer spring .... 41.25 mm
   Guide projection height .... 17.9 to 18.1 mm
Valve clearances .... see Chapter 1

Cylinder block

Bore diameter
  600 cc engine
    Standard . . . . 75.00 to 75.015 mm
    Wear limit . . . . 75.10 mm
  650 cc engine
    Standard . . . . 79.00 to 79.015 mm
    Wear limit . . . . 79.05 mm
Taper (max) . . . . 0.06 mm
Ovality (max) . . . . 0.06 mm
Warpage (max) . . . . 0.10 mm

Pistons

Piston diameter (measured 10.0 mm up from skirt, at 90° to piston pin axis)
  600 cc engine
    Standard . . . . 74.965 to 74.990 mm
    Service limit . . . . 74.90 mm
  650 cc engine
    Standard . . . . 78.970 to 78.990 mm
    Service limit . . . . 78.92 mm
1st oversize . . . . +0.25 mm
2nd oversize . . . . +0.50 mm
Piston-to-bore clearance
  Standard . . . . 0.010 to 0.035 mm
  Service limit . . . . 0.13 mm
Piston pin diameter
  600 cc engine
    Standard . . . . 17.994 to 18.000 mm
    Service limit . . . . 17.98 mm
  650 cc engine
    Standard . . . . 19.994 to 20.000 mm
    Service limit . . . . 19.98 mm
Piston pin bore
  600 cc engine
    Standard . . . . 18.002 to 18.008 mm
    Service limit . . . . 18.05 mm
  650 cc engine
    Standard . . . . 20.002 to 20.008 mm
    service limit . . . . 20.02 mm
Piston pin-to-bore clearance
  Standard . . . . 0.002 to 0.014 mm
  Service limit . . . . 0.034 mm
Connecting rod small-end internal diameter
  600 cc engine
    Standard . . . . 18.016 to 18.034 mm
    Service limit . . . . 18.07 mm
  650 cc engine
    Standard . . . . 20.016 to 20.034 mm
    Service limit . . . . 20.04 mm
Piston pin-to-connecting rod small-end clearance
  Standard . . . . 0.016 to 0.040 mm
  Service limit . . . . 0.060 mm

Piston rings

Ring-to-groove clearance
  Top ring
    Standard . . . . 0.025 to 0.055 mm
    Service limit . . . . 0.11 mm
  2nd ring
    Standard . . . . 0.015 to 0.045 mm
    Service limit . . . . 0.10 mm

2

Piston rings (continued)

End gap (installed)
  Top ring
    Standard . . . . 0.20 to 0.35 mm
    Service limit . . . . 0.65 mm
  2nd ring
    Standard . . . . 0.35 to 0.50 mm
    Service limit . . . . 0.65 mm
  Oil ring
    Standard . . . . 0.2 to 0.8 mm
    Service limit . . . . 0.95 mm

Connecting rods

Side clearance
  Standard . . . . 0.05 to 0.20 mm
  Service limit . . . . 0.3 mm
Bearing oil clearance
  Standard . . . . 0.028 to 0.052 mm
  Service limit . . . . 0.08 mm
Big-end internal diameter
  Size code 1 . . . . 39.000 to 39.006 mm
  Size code 2 . . . . 39.006 to 39.012 mm
Crankpin diameter
  Size code A . . . . 35.994 to 36.000 mm
  Size code B . . . . 35.988 to 35.994 mm
For connecting rod small-end specifications see under "Pistons".

Crankshaft and bearings

Main bearing oil clearance
  Standard . . . . 0.025 to 0.041 mm
  Service limit . . . . 0.06 mm
Runout (max) . . . . 0.05 mm

Clutch

Friction plate (see Section 17 for identification)
  Type A
    Quantity 1
    Thickness . . . . 2.92 to 3.08 mm
    Service limit . . . . 2.6 mm
  Type B
    Quantity 6
    Thickness . . . . 2.62 to 2.78 mm
    Service limit . . . . 2.3 mm
  Type C
    Quantity 1
    Thickness . . . . 2.62 to 2.78 mm
    Service limit . . . . 2.3 mm
Plain plate
  Quantity 7
  Warpage (max) . . . . 0.3 mm
Springs
  Free length . . . . 44.4 mm
  Service limit . . . . 42.8 mm
Mainshaft diameter at clutch housing guide
  Standard . . . . 21.967 to 21.980 mm
  Service limit . . . . 21.92 mm
Clutch housing guide
  Internal diameter
    Standard . . . . 21.991 to 22.016 mm
    Service limit . . . . 22.09 mm
  External diameter
    Standard . . . . 31.959 to 31.975 mm
    Service limit . . . . 31.92 mm
Clutch housing internal diameter
  Standard . . . . 32.000 to 32.025 mm
  Service limit . . . . 32.10 mm
Oil pump drive sprocket internal diameter
  Standard . . . . 32.000 to 32.025 mm
  Service limit . . . . 32.10 mm

Starter clutch

Starter driven gear hub external diameter
    Standard . . . .   57.749 to 57.768 mm
    Service limit . . . .   57.60 mm

Transmission

Type
    Gearbox . . . .   5 speed, constant mesh
    Final drive . . . .   Shaft
Gear ratios (No. of teeth)
    Primary reduction
        600 cc engine . . . .   1.888 to 1 (68/36T)
        650 cc engine . . . .   1.763 to 1 (67/38T)
    Secondary reduction . . . .   0.882 to 1 (30/34T)
    Tertiary reduction . . . .   1.058 to 1 (18/17T)
    Final drive . . . .   2.909 to 1 (32/11T)
    1st gear . . . .   2.571 to 1 (36/14T)
    2nd gear . . . .   1.882 to 1 (32/17T)
    3rd gear . . . .   1.500 to 1 (30/20T)
    4th gear . . . .   1.240 to 1 (31/25T)
    5th gear . . . .   1.074 to 1 (29/27T)
Gear ID
    Mainshaft 4th and 5th gears
        Standard . . . .   28.000 to 28.021 mm
        Service limit . . . .   28.03 mm
    Countershaft 1st gear
        Standard . . . .   24.000 to 24.021 mm
        Service limit . . . .   24.03 mm
    Countershaft 2nd and 3rd gears
        Standard . . . .   28.000 to 28.021 mm
        Service limit . . . .   28.03 mm
    Output drive shaft driven gear
        Standard . . . .   24.000 to 24.021 mm
        Service limit . . . .   24.10 mm
Gear bushing OD
    Mainshaft 4th and 5th gears
        Standard . . . .   27.959 to 27.980 mm
        Service limit . . . .   27.95 mm
    Countershaft 1st gear
        Standard . . . .   23.959 to 23.980 mm
        Service limit . . . .   23.95 mm
    Countershaft 2nd and 3rd gears
        Standard . . . .   27.959 to 27.980 mm
        Service limit . . . .   27.95 mm
    Output drive shaft driven gear
        Standard . . . .   23.959 to 23.980 mm
        Service limit . . . .   23.70 mm
Gear bushing ID
    Mainshaft 4th gear
        Standard . . . .   25.000 to 25.021 mm
        Service limit . . . .   25.03 mm
    Countershaft 1st gear
        Standard . . . .   20.016 to 20.037 mm
        Service limit . . . .   20.05 mm
    Countershaft 2nd and 3rd gears
        Standard . . . .   25.000 to 25.021 mm
        Service limit . . . .   25.03 mm
    Output drive shaft driven gear
        Standard . . . .   20.020 to 20.041 mm
        Service limit . . . .   20.10 mm
Gear-to-bushing clearance
    Mainshaft 4th and 5th gear
        Standard . . . .   0.020 to 0.062 mm
        Service limit . . . .   0.08 mm
    Countershaft 1st, 2nd and 3rd gear
        Standard . . . .   0.020 to 0.062 mm
        Service limit . . . .   0.08 mm

2

Transmission (continued)

Mainshaft OD at 4th gear bushing point
    Standard . . . . 24.959 to 24.980 mm
    Service limit . . . . 24.95 mm
Countershaft OD
    1st gear bushing point
        Standard . . . . 19.980 to 19.993 mm
        Service limit . . . . 19.97 mm
    2nd gear bushing point
        Standard . . . . 24.972 to 24.990 mm
        Service limit . . . . 24.96 mm
    3rd gear bushing point
        Standard . . . . 24.959 to 24.980 mm
        Service limit . . . . 24.95 mm
Shaft-to-bushing clearance
    Mainshaft 4th gear
        Standard . . . . 0.020 to 0.062 mm
        Service limit . . . . 0.08 mm
    Countershaft 2nd gear
        Standard . . . . 0.010 to 0.049 mm
        Service limit . . . . 0.07 mm
    Countershaft 3rd gear
        Standard . . . . 0.020 to 0.062 mm
        Service limit . . . . 0.08 mm
Output drive shaft OD
    Standard . . . . 19.979 to 20.000 mm
    Service limit . . . . 19.97 mm
Damper spring free length
    J model
        Standard . . . . 58.40 mm
        Service limit . . . . 56.00 mm
    All other models
        Standard . . . . 62.30 mm
        Service limit . . . . 59.70 mm
Output shaft backlash
    Standard . . . . 0.40 mm
    Maximum difference between measurements . . . . 0.10 mm

Selector drum and forks

Selector fork end thickness
    Standard . . . . 5.93 to 6.00 mm
    Service limit . . . . 5.83 mm
Selector fork bore ID
    Standard . . . . 13.000 to 13.018 mm
    Service limit . . . . 13.03 mm
Selector fork shaft OD
    Standard . . . . 12.966 to 12.984 mm
    Service limit . . . . 12.96 mm
Selector drum OD at the left-hand journal
    Standard . . . . 11.966 to 11.984 mm
    Service limit . . . . 11.96 mm

Lubrication system

Oil pressure . . . . 64 psi @ 6000 rpm
Oil pump rotor tip-to-outer rotor clearance
    Standard . . . . 0.15 mm
    Service limit . . . . 0.20 mm
Oil pump outer rotor-to-body clearance
    Standard . . . . 0.15 to 0.22 mm
    Service limit . . . . 0.35 mm
Oil pump rotor end float
    Standard . . . . 0.02 to 0.07 mm
    Service limit . . . . 0.10 mm

Torque settings

Engine mounting bolts	
Front	40 Nm
Frame cross-member to engine bolts	25 Nm
Rear upper	40 Nm
Rear lower	40 Nm
Rear mounting bracket bolts	22 Nm
Gearchange linkage arm pinch bolt	12 Nm
Valve cover bolts	10 Nm
Crankshaft end cap	15 Nm
Timing mark inspection cap	10 Nm
Camshaft main holder bolts and nut	23 Nm
Camshaft end holder bolts	10 Nm
Camshaft sprocket bolts	23 Nm
Cam chain tensioner mounting bolts	10 Nm
Ignition timing rotor/primary drive gear bolt	90 Nm
Cylinder head nuts	
Domed nuts	43 Nm
Plain nut	23 Nm
Long bolts	23 Nm
Short bolt	10 Nm
External oil pipe (J and K models only)	
Upper bolts	10 Nm
Lower bolt	23 Nm
Clutch nut	130 Nm
Gear selector drum stopper plate bolt	26 Nm
Starter clutch bolts	30 Nm
Output driveshaft bolt	50 Nm
Crankcase bolts	
8 mm bolts	23 Nm
6 mm bolts	12 Nm
Cylinder studs	
8 mm stud	20 to 30 Nm
10 mm studs	30 to 50 Nm
Oil pump driven sprocket bolt	18 Nm
Output shaft housing assembly bolts	32 Nm
Output drive shaft bearing housing bolts	32 Nm
Output driven shaft bearing housing bolts	32 Nm
Crankcase cover bolts (left-hand side)	10 Nm
Crankcase cover bolts (right-hand side)	10 Nm
Connecting rod nuts	34 Nm

2

1 General information

The engine/transmission unit is a water-cooled 52° V-twin, fitted parallel with the frame. The engine has three valves per cylinder, two for the intake and one for the exhaust, operated by a single overhead camshaft via rocker arms. The camshafts are chain driven off the crankshaft.

The engine/transmission unit is constructed in aluminium alloy with the crankcase being divided vertically. The crankcase incorporates a wet sump, pressure fed lubrication system, and houses a chain driven oil pump. The one-piece forged crankshaft runs in two main bearings. The left-hand end of the crankshaft carries the alternator rotor, whilst the right-hand end carries the ignition rotor and pulse generator coils.

The clutch is of the wet multi-plate type and is gear driven off the crankshaft. The transmission is of the five-speed constant mesh type. Drive is then turned through 90° by the output drive and driven shafts, then transmitted to the rear wheel by shaft.

2 Operations possible with the engine in the frame

The components and assemblies listed below can be removed without having to remove the engine/transmission assembly from the frame. If however, a number of areas require attention at the same time, removal of the engine is recommended.

Valve covers
Cam chain tensioners
Camshafts and rockers
Cylinder heads
Cylinder blocks, pistons and piston rings
Water pump
Ignition rotor and pulse generator coils
Clutch
*Gearchange mechanism
  (external components)*
Starter motor
Alternator
Starter clutch and idle gear

3 Operations requiring engine removal

It is necessary to remove the engine/transmission assembly from the frame and separate the crankcase halves to gain access to the following components.

Transmission shafts
Crankshaft and bearings
Connecting rod big-ends and bearings
*Selector drum and forks (gearchange
  mechanism internal components)*
Oil pump

4 Major engine repair - general note

1 It is not always easy to determine when or if an engine should be completely overhauled, as a number of factors must be considered.

2 High mileage is not necessarily an indication that an overhaul is needed, while low mileage, on the other hand, does not preclude the need for an overhaul. Frequency of servicing is probably the single most important consideration. An engine that has regular and frequent oil and filter changes, as well as other required maintenance, will most likely give many miles of reliable service. Conversely, a neglected engine, or one which has not been run in properly, may require an overhaul very early in its life.

3 Exhaust smoke and excessive oil consumption are both indications that piston rings and/or valve guides are in need of attention, although make sure that the fault is not due to oil leakage.

4 If the engine is making obvious knocking or rumbling noises, the connecting rod and/or main bearings are probably at fault.

5 Loss of power, rough running, excessive valve train noise and high fuel consumption rates may also point to the need for an overhaul, especially if they are all present at the same time. If a complete tune-up does not remedy the situation, major mechanical work is the only solution.

6 An engine overhaul generally involves restoring the internal parts to the specifications of a new engine. The piston rings and main and connecting rod bearings are usually replaced and the cylinder walls honed or, if necessary, re-bored during a major overhaul. Generally the valve seats are reground, since they are usually in less than perfect condition at this point. The end result should be a like new engine that will give as many trouble-free miles as the original.

7 Before beginning the engine overhaul, read through the related procedures to familiarise yourself with the scope and requirements of the job. Overhauling an engine is not all that difficult, but it is time consuming. Plan on the motorcycle being tied up for a minimum of two weeks. Check on the availability of parts and make sure that any necessary special tools, equipment and supplies are obtained in advance.

8 Most work can be done with typical workshop hand tools, although a number of precision measuring tools are required for inspecting parts to determine if they must be replaced. Often a dealer will handle the inspection of parts and offer advice concerning reconditioning and replacement. As a general rule, time is the primary cost of an overhaul so it does not pay to install worn or substandard parts.

9 As a final note, to ensure maximum life and minimum trouble from a rebuilt engine, everything must be assembled with care in a spotlessly clean environment.

5 Engine - removal and installation

Note: *The engine is very heavy. Engine removal and installation should be carried out with the aid of at least one assistant; personal injury or damage could occur if the engine falls or is dropped. A hydraulic or mechanical floor jack should be used to support and lower or raise the engine if possible.*

Removal

1 Position the bike on its centre stand or support it securely in an upright position using an auxiliary stand. Work can be made easier by raising the machine to a suitable working height on a hydraulic ramp or a suitable platform.

2 If the engine is dirty, particularly around its mountings, wash it thoroughly before starting any major dismantling work. This will make work much easier and rule out the possibility of caked on lumps of dirt falling into some vital component.

3 Drain the engine oil and remove the oil filter (see Chapter 1).

4 Drain the coolant (see Chapter 1).

5 Remove the seat and the side panels (see Chapter 8) and disconnect the battery negative (-ve) lead (see Chapter 9).

6 Remove the fuel tank (see Chapter 4).

7 Remove the air filter housing (see Chapter 4).

8 Remove the carburettors (see Chapter 4). Plug the engine intake manifolds with clean rag.

9 Remove the radiator (see Chapter 3).

10 Unscrew the clamps securing the coolant hoses to the cylinder head pipes and detach the hoses **(see illustration)**. Release the clamp securing the overflow hose to the filler neck and secure the hose clear of the engine **(see illustration)**.

11 Pull out the clips securing the heat guard and remove the guard **(see illustration)**.

12 Remove the exhaust system (Chapter 4).

13 Pull back the rubber boot on the starter motor, then unscrew the nut securing the lead to the motor **(see illustration)**. Also unscrew the front starter motor mounting bolt to release the earth cable **(see illustration)**.

14 Detach the clutch cable from the clutch housing (see Section 18). Release the cable

5.10a Release the clamps (arrows) and detach the coolant hoses from the cylinder heads

5.10b Release the overflow hose clamp (arrow) and detach the hose from the filler neck

5.11 The heat guard is secured by three trim clips

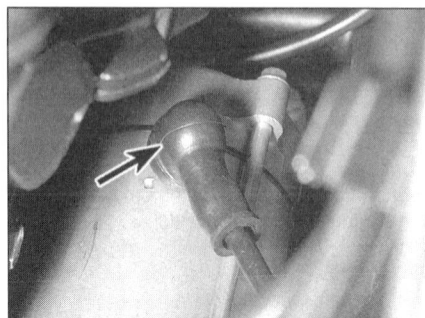

5.13a Pull back the rubber boot (arrow) to expose the starter motor lead securing nut

5.13b Unscrew the starter motor front bolt to release the earth lead (arrow)

5.15a Unscrew the wiring guide bolt (arrow) . . .

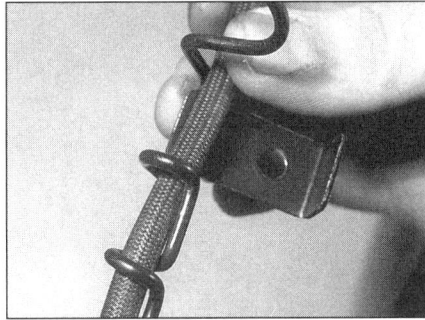

5.15b . . . and release the wiring from the guide

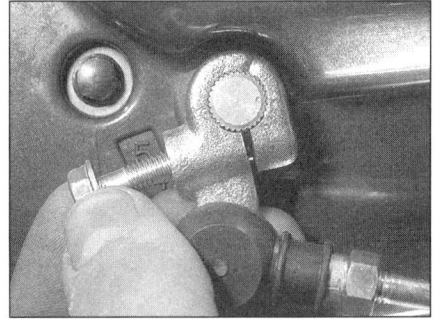

5.16 Remove the pinch bolt and slide the gearchange linkage off the shaft

5.17a Left-hand side crankcase rear cover bolts (arrows)

5.17b Pull off the neutral switch wiring connector

5.17c Unscrew the oil pressure switch wiring connector (arrow)

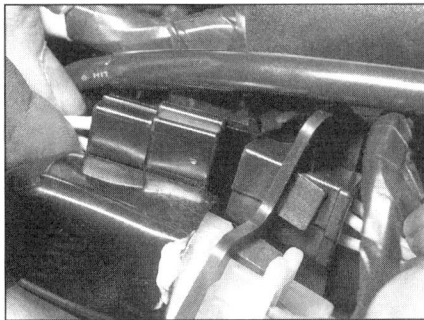

5.18 The alternator wiring connector is behind the right-hand side panel

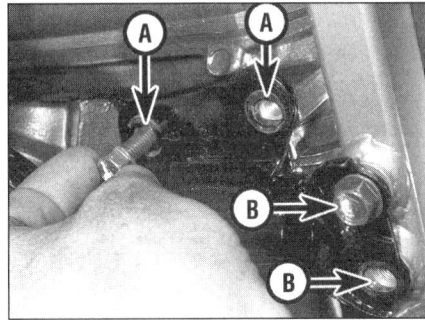

5.23 The cross-member is secured to the engine by two bolts (A) and to each frame downtube by two bolts (B)

from the guide on the right-hand side frame downtube and secure it clear of the engine.
15 Trace the ignition pulse generator wiring and disconnect it at the connector. Unscrew the wiring guide bolt from the frame and release the wiring from the guide, noting how it fits **(see illustrations)**. Coil the wiring between the cylinders so it does not impede engine removal.
16 Unscrew the gearchange linkage arm pinch bolt and remove the linkage arm from the shaft **(see illustration)**. Note the punch marks on the arm and the shaft which must be aligned on installation.
17 Unscrew the bolts securing the left-hand side crankcase rear cover and remove the cover **(see illustration)**. Pull off the neutral switch wiring connector **(see illustration)**. Pull back the rubber boot on the oil pressure switch, then unscrew the screw securing the wiring connector to the switch **(see illustration)**. Secure the wiring clear of the engine.

18 Trace the alternator wiring and disconnect it at the connector behind the right-hand side panel, then coil the wiring in between the cylinders so that it does not impede engine removal **(see illustration)**.

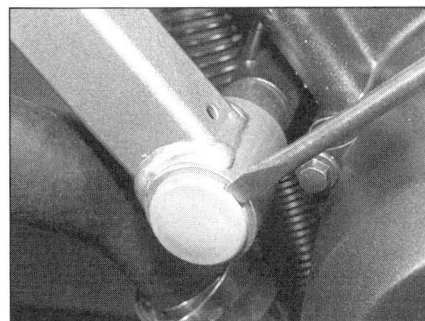

5.24a Prise off the front engine mounting bolt caps using a flat-bladed screwdriver

19 Disconnect the spark plug leads from the plugs and secure them clear of the engine.
20 Remove the rear wheel (see Chapter 7).
21 Remove the final drive housing along with the driveshaft and universal joint as an assembly (see Chapter 6).
22 At this point, position an hydraulic or mechanical jack under the engine with a block of wood between the jack head and sump. Make sure the jack is centrally positioned so the engine will not topple in any direction when the last mounting bolt is removed. Take the weight of the engine on the jack.
23 Unscrew the bolts securing the frame cross-member to the engine, then unscrew the bolts securing the frame cross-member to the frame downtubes and remove the cross-member **(see illustration)**.
24 Remove the cap from each end of the front engine mounting bolt, then unscrew the nut and withdraw the bolt **(see illustrations)**. Note

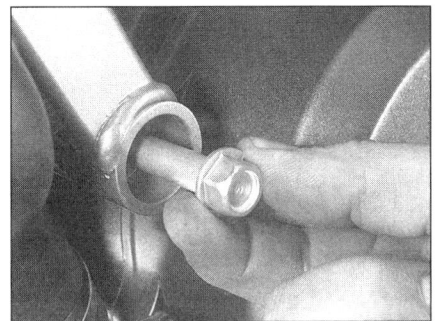

5.24b Unscrew the nut and withdraw the bolt

2

5.25a Prise off the rear upper engine mounting bolt caps

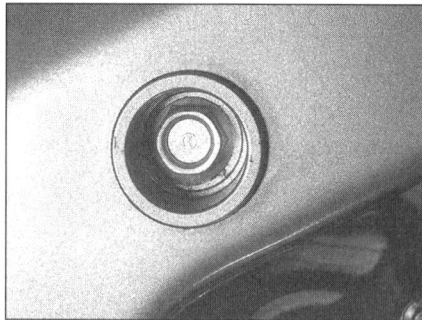

5.25b Rear upper engine mounting bolt

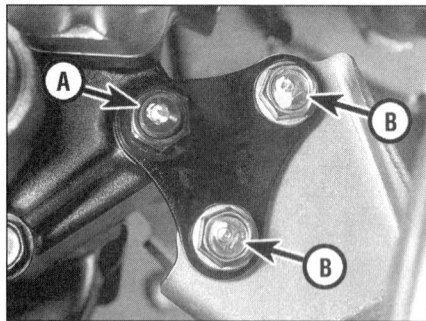

5.26 Rear lower engine mounting bolt nut (A) and bracket bolts (B)

5.27 Removing the engine from the frame

how the spacers fit in between the frame downtubes and the engine, and that the longer spacer fits on the left-hand side.

25 Remove the cap from each end of the rear upper engine mounting bolt, then unscrew the nut and withdraw the bolt **(see illustrations)**. Note how the spacer fits in between the frame and the engine.

26 Make sure the engine is properly supported on the jack, then unscrew the rear lower engine mounting bolt nut and withdraw the bolt **(see illustration)**. Unscrew the bolts securing the mounting bolt bracket to the frame and remove the bracket.

27 The engine can now be removed from the frame. Check that all wiring, cables and hoses are well clear, then lower the jack and manoeuvre the engine out **(see illustration)**.

Installation

28 Installation is the reverse of removal, noting the following points:

a) Make sure no wires, cables or hoses become trapped between the engine and the frame when installing the engine.

b) Make sure the driveshaft rubber boot is in position on the front of the swingarm and with its "UP" mark facing up.

c) When installing the front engine mounting bolt, make sure the short spacer is on the right-hand side of the engine and the long spacer is on the left **(see illustration)**.

d) When installing the rear upper engine mounting bolt, make sure the spacer is fitted on the left-hand side of the engine and with its protrusion pointing down and curving inwards **(see illustration)**.

e) Do not tighten any of the engine mounting bolts until they have all been installed. Make sure the spacers are correctly positioned.

f) Tighten the engine mounting bolts and any other bolts to the torque settings specified at the beginning of the Chapter.

g) Use new gaskets at all exhaust pipe connections.

h) Align the punch marks on the gearchange linkage arm and shaft when installing the arm on the shaft, and tighten the pinch bolt to the specified torque setting **(see illustration)**.

i) Make sure all wires, cables and hoses are correctly routed and connected, and secured by any clips or ties.

j) Refill the engine with oil (see Chapter 1).

k) Refill the cooling system with coolant (see Chapter 1).

l) Adjust the throttle and clutch freeplay (see Chapter 1).

6 Engine disassembly and reassembly - general information

Note: Refer to "Maintenance techniques, tools and working facilities" in the Reference section of this manual for further information.

Disassembly

1 Before disassembling the engine, the external surfaces of the unit should be thoroughly cleaned and degreased. This will prevent contamination of the engine internals, and will also make working a lot easier and cleaner. A high flash-point solvent, such as paraffin can be used, or better still, a proprietary engine degreaser. Use old paintbrushes and toothbrushes to work the solvent into the various recesses of the engine casings. Take care to exclude solvent or water from the electrical components and intake and exhaust ports.

⚠ **Warning: The use of petrol as a cleaning agent should be avoided because of the risk of fire.**

5.28a The longer spacer for the front engine mounting bolt fits on the left-hand side

5.28b Rear upper engine mounting bolt spacer (arrow)

5.28c Align the punch mark on the gearchange linkage arm with that on the shaft (arrows)

6.4 An engine support made from pieces of 2 x 4 inch wood

2 When clean and dry, arrange the unit on the workbench, leaving suitable clear area for working. Gather a selection of small containers and plastic bags so that parts can be grouped together in an easily identifiable manner. Some paper and a pen should be on hand to permit notes to be made and labels attached where necessary. A supply of clean rag is also required.

3 Before commencing work, read through the appropriate section so that some idea of the necessary procedure can be gained. When removing various engine components it should be noted that great force is seldom required, unless specified. In many cases, a component's reluctance to be removed is indicative of an incorrect approach or removal method. If in any doubt, re-check with the text.

4 An engine support stand made from short lengths of 2 x 4 inch wood bolted together into a rectangle will help support the engine **(see illustration)**. The perimeter of the mount should be just big enough to accommodate the sump within it so that the engine rests on its crankcase.

5 When disassembling the engine, keep "mated" parts together (including gears, cylinders, pistons, connecting rods, valves, etc. that have been in contact with each other during engine operation). These "mated" parts must be re-used or replaced as an assembly.

6 Engine/transmission disassembly should be done in the following general order with reference to the appropriate Sections.

Remove the valve covers
Remove the camshafts and cam chain tensioners
Remove the cylinder heads
Remove the cylinder blocks
Remove the pistons
Remove the water pump (see Chapter 3)
Remove the ignition rotor and pulse generator coils (see Chapter 5)
Remove the clutch
Remove the gearchange mechanism external components
Remove the starter motor (see Chapter 9)
Remove the alternator (see Chapter 9)
Remove the starter clutch and idle gear
Separate the crankcase halves

Remove the oil pump
Remove the transmission shafts/gears
Remove the selector drum and forks
Remove the crankshaft and the connecting rods

Reassembly

7 Reassembly is accomplished by reversing the general disassembly sequence.

7   Valve covers - removal and installation

Note: *The valve covers can be removed with the engine in the frame. If the engine has been removed, ignore the steps which do not apply.*

Removal

1 Remove the seat and the side panels (see Chapter 8) and disconnect the battery negative (-ve) lead.

2 Remove the fuel tank and the air filter housing (see Chapter 4).

3 Remove the radiator and the thermostat housing (not necessary if only removing the rear valve cover) (see Chapter 3). Unscrew the clamps securing the coolant hoses to the cylinder head pipes and detach the hoses (not necessary if only removing the rear valve cover) **(see illustration 5.10a)**.

4 Remove the three clips securing the heat guard and remove the guard (not necessary if only removing the rear valve cover) **(see illustration 5.11)**.

5 Disconnect the spark plug leads from the plugs and secure them clear of the engine.

6 Unscrew the valve cover bolts, then remove them with their rubber washers and seals **(see illustration)**.

7 Lift the valve cover off the cylinder head. If it is stuck, do not try to lever it off with a screwdriver. Tap it gently around the sides with a rubber hammer to dislodge it. Remove the front cylinder valve cover through the front of the frame.

Installation

8 Examine the valve cover gasket for signs of damage or deterioration and replace it if necessary **(see illustration)**. Also check the cover bolt washers and seals and replace them if necessary.

9 Clean the mating surfaces of the cylinder head and the valve cover with lacquer thinner, acetone or brake system cleaner.

10 Install the rubber gasket into the valve cover, making sure it fits correctly into the groove.

11 Position the cover on the cylinder head, making sure the gasket stays in place **(see illustration)**. Install the cover bolts with their seals and washers and tighten them to the torque setting specified at the beginning of the Chapter **(see illustration)**.

12 Install the remaining components in the reverse order of removal.

7.6 Each valve cover is secured by two bolts (arrows)

7.8 Make sure the gasket is in good condition before re-using it

7.11a Install the valve cover . . .

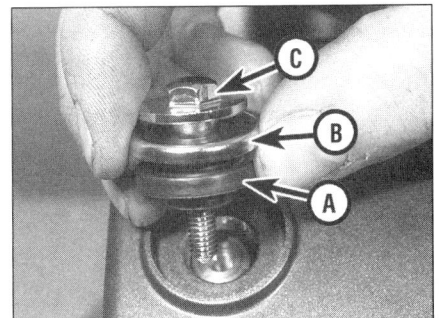

7.11b . . . and secure it with its bolts, making sure the seal (A) and washer (B) are installed with the bolt (C)

2

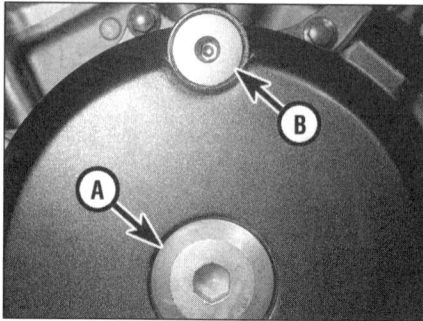

8.2a Crankshaft end cap (A) and timing mark inspection cap (B)

8.2b Use a socket on the flywheel bolt behind the crankshaft end cap to rotate the engine

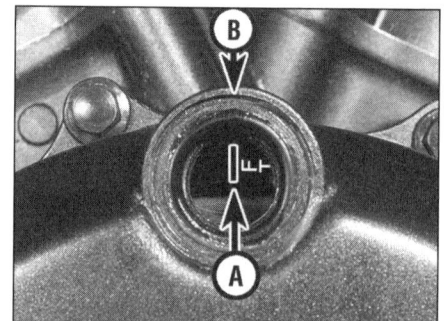

8.2c Align the "FT" or "RT" mark (A) with the notch (B) in the inspection hole

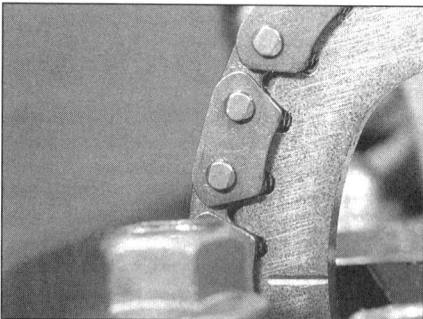

8.2d The index lines on the sprocket (arrow) should align with the surface of the cylinder head

8.3a Measure the amount of projection of the front wedge on top of the cam chain tensioner

8.3b Pull up the rear wedge and insert a suitable pin or nail through its hole to secure it in the raised position

8 Camshafts and rockers - removal, inspection and installation

Note: *The camshafts and rockers can be removed with the engine in the frame.*

Removal

1 Remove the valve cover (see Section 7).
2 Unscrew the crankshaft end cap and the timing mark inspection cap from the left-hand side crankcase cover **(see illustration)**. Using a suitable socket on the alternator rotor bolt **(see illustration)**, rotate the engine anti-clockwise so that it is at TDC (Top Dead Centre) on the compression stroke of the cylinder being worked on. At this point the "FT" mark (if removing the front camshaft) or

the "RT" mark (if removing the rear camshaft) should align with the notch in the inspection hole **(see illustration)**, the index lines on the camshaft sprocket should align with the top of the cylinder head mating surface **(see illustration)**, and both camshaft lobes should face down. If necessary to ease reassembly, make your own alignment marks on the sprockets, chain and camshafts with a felt pen.
3 At this point, measure the amount of projection of the front wedge on the top of the cam chain tensioner **(see illustration)**. If the amount of projection exceeds the limit specified at the beginning of the Chapter, the cam chain must be replaced (see Section 9). Having taken the measurement, pull the rear wedge straight up using a pair of pliers and secure it in position using a 2 mm pin inserted

through the whole in the wedge **(see illustration)**. Slacken, but do not remove, the lower cam chain tensioner bolt **(see illustration 10.4a)**.
4 Unscrew the two bolts securing the end camshaft holder adjacent to the cam chain sprocket and remove the holder, noting which way round it fits **(see illustration)**. Remove the two dowels if they are loose **(see illustration)**.
5 Rotate the engine to reveal the lower sprocket bolt and remove it, then return the engine to TDC on the compression stroke and remove the other sprocket bolt **(see illustration)**. Use the socket on the alternator rotor bolt to stop the engine rotating while unscrewing the bolts. Slip the sprocket from its boss on the camshaft. **Caution:** Do *not rotate the camshaft after the cam chain has*

8.4a Camshaft end holder bolts (arrows)

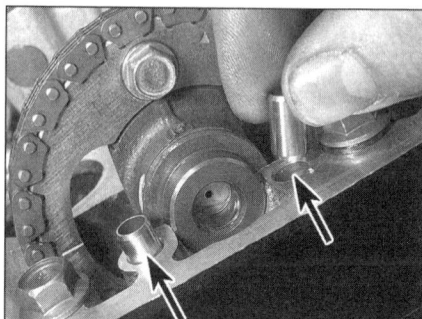

8.4b Remove the dowels (arrows) if they are loose

8.5 Remove the two sprocket bolts

8.6a Main camshaft holder has 3 bolts (A) and a nut (B) on J & K models, or 3 bolts (A) and 2 nuts (B) and (C) on M, P, S & T models. Note how oil guide plate (D) fits

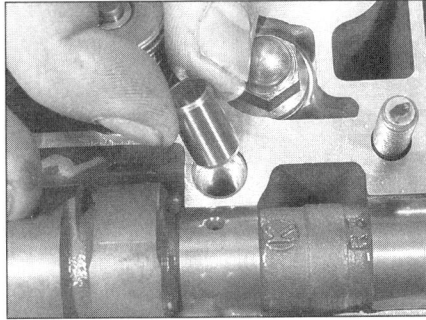

8.6b Remove the dowels if they are loose

8.8a Withdraw the rocker arm shafts . . .

8.8b . . . then remove each rocker arm . . .

8.8c along with its wave washer

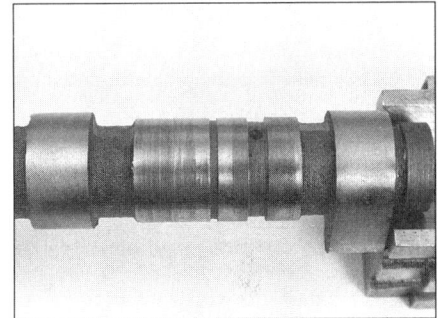

8.9a Check the journal surfaces of the camshaft for scratches or wear

8.9b Check the lobes of the camshaft for wear - damage like this will require replacement (or repair) of the camshaft

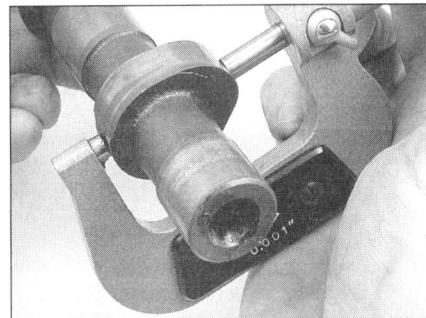

8.9c Measure the height of the camshaft lobes with a micrometer

Inspection

Note: *Before replacing the camshafts or the cylinder head and camshaft holders because of damage, check with local machine shops specialising in motorcycle engineering work. In the case of the camshafts, it may be possible for cam lobes to be welded, reground and hardened, at a cost far lower than that of a new camshaft. If the bearing surfaces in the cylinder head are damaged, it may be possible for them to be bored out to accept bearing inserts. Due to the cost of a new cylinder head, it is recommended that all options be explored.*

9 Inspect the cam bearing surfaces of the head and the holder. Look for score marks, deep scratches and evidence of spalling (a pitted appearance). Check the camshaft lobes for heat discoloration (blue appearance), score marks, chipped areas, flat spots and spalling **(see illustrations)**. Measure the height of each lobe with a micrometer and compare the reading with the specifications at the beginning of the Chapter **(see illustration)**. If wear is excessive the amount of valve lift is reduced which results in poor engine performance. The camshaft must be replaced, but first refer to the **Note** preceding this Step.

10 Camshaft runout can be checked by supporting each end of the camshaft on V-blocks, and measuring any runout using a dial gauge. If the runout exceeds the specified limit the camshaft must be replaced.

11 The camshaft bearing oil clearance should then be checked using a product known as Plastigauge.

been disengaged as damage may occur if a valve contacts a piston. The crankshaft can be rotated as long as the valves are closed or if the camshaft has been removed.

6 Unscrew the three bolts and the two nuts (one nut only on J and K models) securing the main camshaft holder **(see illustration)**. Slacken them evenly in a criss-cross pattern, then remove the holder along with the oil guide plate, noting how the assembly fits. Retrieve the two dowels if they are loose **(see illustration)**. Mark each holder according to its cylinder (ie front or rear).

7 Slip the cam chain off the sprocket and withdraw the camshaft and sprocket. Tie the cam chain up to prevent it from dropping down into the crankcase, and do not allow it to go slack as it could bind between the crankshaft sprocket and the crankcase. Cover

the top of the cylinder head with a rag to prevent anything falling into the engine. Mark each camshaft and sprocket according to its cylinder (ie front or rear. The camshafts come with their cylinder identity already marked on their end ("F" or "R"). Check that it is visible and make your own mark if necessary). Note the "IN" mark on the sprocket which must face inwards on installation.

8 Remove the rocker arm shafts from the camshaft holder, using a soft-faced mallet if necessary to drift them out **(see illustration)**. If the shafts are difficult to remove, carefully drift them out. Remove the rocker arms and their wave washers, noting how they fit. Mark each shaft and rocker arm according to its position (ie front or rear cylinder, intake or exhaust valve), and/or install each rocker arm back onto its shaft in its original position.

2

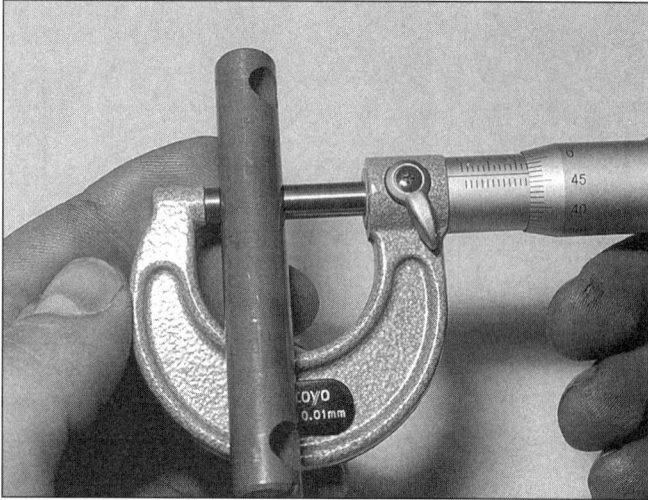

8.21a Measure the diameter of the rocker arm shaft . . .

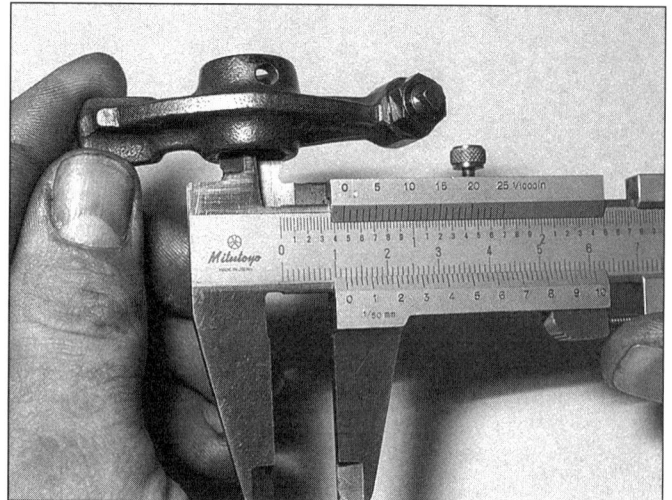

8.21b . . . and the internal diameter of the rocker arm bore

12 Clean the camshaft, the bearing surfaces in the cylinder head and the holders with a clean, lint-free cloth, then lay the camshaft in place in the cylinder head.

13 Cut strips of Plastigauge and lay one piece on each bearing journal parallel with the camshaft centreline, making sure none is placed over the oil hole. Make sure the camshaft holder dowels are installed and fit the holders. Ensuring the camshafts are not rotated at all, tighten the holder bolts and nut(s) evenly, a little at a time, in a criss-cross sequence, until the specified torque setting is reached.

14 Now unscrew the bolts and nut(s) evenly, a little at a time, in a criss-cross sequence and carefully lift off the holders, again making sure the camshaft is not rotated.

15 To determine the oil clearance, compare the crushed Plastigauge (at its widest point) on each journal to the scale printed on the Plastigauge container.

16 Compare the results to this Chapter's Specifications. If the oil clearance is greater than specified, measure the diameter of the camshaft bearing journal with a micrometer. If it is within specifications, replace the cylinder head and cam holders with new components. If the journal diameter is less than the specified limit, replace the camshaft with a new one and recheck the clearance. If the clearance is still too great, also replace the cylinder head and cam holders. Before replacing any worn parts with new ones, bear in mind the information in the Note preceding Step 9.

17 Except in cases of oil starvation, the cam chain wears very little. If the chain has stretched excessively, which makes it difficult to maintain proper tension, it must be replaced (see Section 9).

18 Check the sprocket for cracks and other damage, replacing it if necessary. Note that if a new sprocket is installed, a new cam chain must also be installed. If the sprockets are worn, the cam chain is also worn, and also the sprocket on the crankshaft (which can only be remedied by replacing the crankshaft). If wear this severe is apparent, the entire engine should be disassembled for inspection.

19 If available, blow through the oil passages in the rocker arms and camshaft holder with compressed air. Inspect the rocker arm contact points for pitting, spalling, score marks, cracks and rough spots. If the rocker arms are damaged they must be replaced along with the shafts as a set.

20 Check the condition of the wave washers and replace them if they are damaged or deteriorated.

21 Measure the diameter of the rocker arm shafts in the area of contact with the rocker arms **(see illustration)**. Also measure the internal diameter of the rocker arm bores **(see illustration)**. Compare the measurements to the specifications listed at the beginning of the Chapter. If any components are worn beyond their limits, replace all the shafts and arms as a set.

Installation

22 Apply a smear of molybdenum disulphide grease to the contact faces of each rocker arm, then install the arms and their wave washers into the camshaft holder, making sure they are returned to their original positions **(see illustrations 8.8c and 8.8b)**. The wave washers fit on the inside of the intake rocker arms, on the left-hand side of the front cylinder exhaust rocker arm, and on the right-hand side of the rear cylinder exhaust arm.

23 Apply a smear of molybdenum disulphide grease to the rocker arm shafts, then slide the shafts into the camshaft holder, making sure they are installed in their original positions, and that they pass through the rocker arms and wave washers **(see illustration 8.8a)**. Position the shafts so that the grooves in the ends of the shafts are vertical and the holes in the shafts align with the bolt holes in the camshaft holder **(see illustration)**. Check that the arms move freely on the shafts.

24 If only the front camshaft has been removed, position the crankshaft at TDC on the compression stroke for the rear cylinder (see Step 2), then rotate the crankshaft anticlockwise 488° (at which point the "FT" mark on the rotor will align with the notch in the inspection hole). This positions the front cylinder at TDC on the compression stroke, and the front camshaft can be installed. If only the rear camshaft has been removed, position the crankshaft at TDC for the front cylinder (see Step 2), then rotate the crankshaft anti-clockwise 232° (at which point the "RT" mark on the rotor will align with the notch in the inspection hole). This positions the rear cylinder at TDC on the compression stroke, and the rear camshaft can be installed. If both camshafts have been removed, install the front one first, with the crankshaft positioned so that the "FT" mark on the rotor aligns with the notch in the inspection hole, then rotate the crankshaft anti-clockwise 232° (at which point the "RT" mark on the rotor will align with the notch in the inspection hole). This positions the rear cylinder at TDC on the compression stroke, and the rear camshaft can be installed.

8.23 Position the shafts so that the grooves in the shaft ends are as shown

8.25a The "IN" mark (arrow) must face inwards

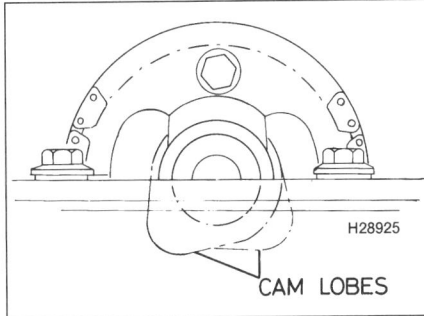

8.25b Position the camshaft so that the lobes face down as shown

8.25c Fit the camchain onto the sprocket

8.27a Make sure the dowels are in place (arrows) before installing the main holder

8.27b Install the oil guide plate

8.27c Tighten the bolts and nut(s) to the specified torque setting

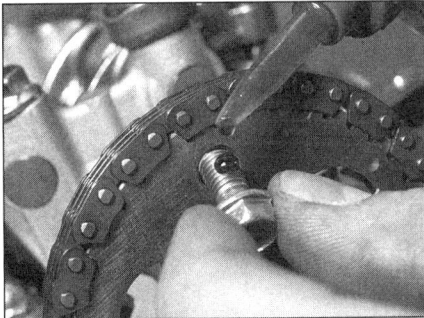

8.28a Apply thread locking compound to the sprocket bolt threads . . .

8.28b . . . and tighten them to the specified torque setting

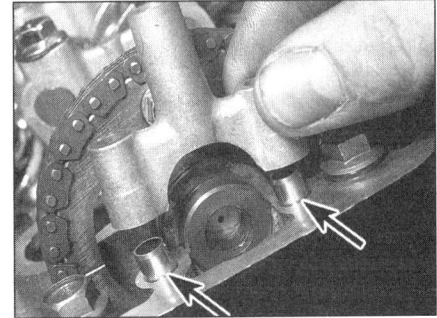

8.29a Install the end holder onto its two dowels (arrows) . . .

2

25 Check that the cam chain is engaged around the lower sprocket teeth on the crankshaft and that the crankshaft is positioned as described in Step 24. Apply a smear of molybdenum disulphide grease to the camshaft journals and install the correct camshaft for the cylinder being worked on (the one marked "F" for the front cylinder, the one marked "R" for the rear), with its sprocket loose on the shaft and with the sprocket's "IN" mark facing inwards, through the cam chain and position it so that the cam lobes are facing down (see illustrations). Keeping the front run of the chain taut engage the chain on the sprocket teeth with the sprocket positioned loose on the camshaft but so that the index lines on the sprocket align with the cylinder head mating surface and its mounting holes align with those on the camshaft (see illustration). With the chain engaged on the sprocket, mount the sprocket onto its boss on

the camshaft, and install the top sprocket bolt finger-tight only. Check that the chain is tight at the front of the engine so that there is no slack between the crankshaft sprocket and the camshaft sprocket. If any slack is evident, move the chain around the sprocket so that the slack is taken up. Any slack in the chain must lie in the portion of the chain in the back of the cylinder so that it is then taken up by the tensioner.
26 Before proceeding further, check that everything aligns as described in Step 2. If it doesn't, the valve timing will be inaccurate and the valves will contact the piston when the engine is turned over.
27 If removed, install the main camshaft holder dowels into the cylinder head, then install the holder, making sure it is the right way round and seats correctly onto the dowels (see illustration). Install the oil guide plate onto the holder with its guide facing the intake

valves (see illustration), then install the holder bolts and nuts (one only on J and K models) and tighten them evenly in a criss-cross pattern to the torque setting specified at the beginning of the Chapter (see illustration).
28 Apply a suitable non-permanent thread locking compound to the camshaft sprocket bolt threads, then tighten the top bolt to the specified torque setting, using a socket on the alternator rotor bolt to stop the engine from rotating if necessary (see illustrations). Rotate the crankshaft anti-clockwise to reveal the lower sprocket bolt and tighten that to the specified torque setting, then return the engine to TDC on the compression stroke for the cylinder being worked on.
29 If removed, install the end camshaft holder dowels into the cylinder head, then install the holder, making sure its flat surface faces inwards and it seats correctly onto the dowels (see illustration). Install the holder

8.29b ... and secure it with its bolts

bolts and tighten them evenly to the specified torque setting **(see illustration)**.

30 With both holders tightened down, check that the valve timing marks still align (see Step 2). Check that each camshaft is not pinched by turning it a few degrees in each direction using a suitable socket on the alternator rotor bolt. Lubricate the camshaft lobes with a mixture of engine oil and molybdenum disulphide grease.

31 Tighten the lower cam chain tensioner bolt to the specified torque setting **(see illustration 10.4a)**. Remove the 2 mm pin securing the bottom wedge on the cam chain tensioner.

32 Rotate the engine anti-clockwise through 720° degrees and re-check that the valve timing for both cylinders is correct (see Step 2).

33 Check the valve clearances (Chapter 1) and adjust if necessary.

34 Apply a smear of molybdenum disulphide grease to the threads of the crankshaft end cap and the timing mark inspection cap, and install them into the left-hand side crankcase cover and tighten them to the specified torque setting.

35 Install the valve cover (see Section 7).

36 Check the engine oil level and top up if necessary (see Chapter 1).

9 Cam chains - removal and installation

Note: *The cam chains can be removed with the engine in the frame.*

Front cylinder cam chain

Removal

1 Drain the engine oil (see Chapter 1).

2 Remove the camshaft (see Section 8).

3 Remove the alternator rotor/starter clutch and starter driven gear (see Section 20).

4 Unscrew the bolt securing the cam chain tensioner set plate to the crankcase and remove the plate, noting how it fits **(see illustration)**.

5 Hook a piece of wire to the top of the cam chain, then drop the chain down through its tunnel. Detach the wire and remove the cam chain from the end of the crankshaft.

Installation

6 Hook the new cam chain to the piece of wire and draw the chain up through its tunnel, making sure its bottom end engages around the sprocket on the crankshaft **(see illustration)**. Secure the chain at the top to prevent it falling back down the tunnel.

7 Install the cam chain tensioner set plate and tighten its bolt securely **(see illustration)**.

8 Install the starter driven gear and alternator/starter clutch (see Section 20).

9 Install the camshaft (see Section 8). Replenish the engine oil (see Chapter 1).

Rear cylinder cam chain

Removal

10 Drain the engine oil (see Chapter 1).

11 Remove the camshaft (see Section 8).

12 Remove the ignition pulse generator coil assembly (see Chapter 5).

13 The crankshaft must be locked so that the timing rotor bolt can be slackened. Honda provide a special tool (Pt. No. 07724-0010100) which locks the primary drive gear and the clutch. Alternatively, if the engine is in the frame, select a gear and have an assistant apply the rear brake. If the engine has been removed, install the universal joint onto the output driven shaft and engage 5th gear, then fit a suitable spanner onto the flats of the universal joint and secure it against the work surface **(see illustration 17.8a)**. With the crankshaft locked, unscrew the timing rotor bolt and remove the rotor **(see illustration)**.

14 Remove the clutch (see Section 17).

15 Remove the primary drive gear from the end of the crankshaft. Note the "OUT" mark on the gear which must face outwards.

16 Hook a piece of wire to the top of the cam chain, then drop the chain down through its tunnel. Detach the wire and remove the cam chain from the end of the crankshaft. Slide the cam chain sprocket off the end of the crankshaft and check it for wear or damage to both the outer teeth and the inner splines **(see illustration)**.

Installation

17 Align the extra wide spline on the crankshaft with that on the sprocket, then slide the sprocket onto the crankshaft. Hook the new cam chain to the piece of wire and

9.4 The cam chain tensioner set plate is secured by a single bolt (shown with tensioner removed)

9.6 Make sure the cam chain engages properly on the crankshaft sprocket

9.7 Install the cam chain tensioner set plate (shown with tensioner removed)

9.13 Ignition timing rotor (A) and its bolt (B)

9.16 Check the cam chain sprocket for wear or damage

9.17 Make sure the cam chain engages properly on the sprocket

9.18 Align the wide splines (arrows) and make sure the "OUT" mark faces outwards

9.20a Install the timing rotor onto the crankshaft

9.20b Install the rotor bolt with its washer . . .

9.20c . . . and tighten it to the specified torque setting

draw the chain up through its tunnel, making sure its bottom end engages around the sprocket (see illustration). Secure the chain at the top to prevent it falling back down the tunnel.

18 Align the extra wide spline on the crankshaft with that on the primary drive gear and install the gear onto the crankshaft with its "OUT" mark facing out (see illustration).
19 Install the clutch (see Section 17).
20 Align the extra wide spline on the crankshaft with that on the timing rotor, and install the rotor onto the end of the crankshaft (see illustration). Install the rotor bolt with its washer, then, using the method employed in Step 13 to lock the crankshaft, tighten the bolt to the torque setting specified at the beginning of the Chapter (see illustrations).
21 Install the camshaft (see Section 8). Replenish the engine oil (see Chapter 1).

10 Cam chain tensioners and guide blades - removal, inspection and installation

Note: The cam chain tensioners and guide blades can be removed with the engine in the frame.

Cam chain tensioner

Removal

1 Remove the valve cover (see Section 7). The cam chain tensioner is located in the back of the cam chain tunnel. Note the position of the rubber cushion behind the top of the tensioner (see illustration).
2 At this point, measure the projection of the front wedge on the top of the cam chain tensioner (see illustration 8.3a). If the amount

of projection exceeds the limit specified at the beginning of the Chapter, the cam chain must be replaced (see Section 9). Having taken the measurement, pull the rear wedge straight up using a pair of pliers and secure it in position using a 2 mm pin inserted through the whole in the wedge (see illustration 8.3b). Slacken, but do not yet remove, the lower cam chain tensioner bolt (see illustration 10.4a).
3 Unscrew the crankshaft end cap and the timing mark inspection cap from the left-hand side crankcase cover (see illustration 8.2a). Using a suitable socket on the alternator rotor bolt (see illustration 8.2b), rotate the engine anti-clockwise as required to access the two cam chain sprocket mounting bolts. Unscrew each bolt as it is exposed and displace the sprocket off the camshaft. Note: Do not disengage the cam chain from the sprocket or the valve timing will have to be reset (see Section 8). Caution: Do not rotate either the camshaft or the crankshaft whilst the cam chain sprocket is displaced as damage could occur if a valve contacts a piston.
4 Unscrew the two bolts securing the cam chain tensioner and withdraw the tensioner from the cylinder head along with its rubber cushion, noting which way up the cushion fits (see illustrations).

Inspection

5 Examine the sliding surface of the tensioner for wear or damage, and replace it if necessary.
6 Check the tensioner spring for damage or a loss of tension, and replace it if necessary.

10.1 The cam chain tensioner is located behind the sprocket. Note the position of the rubber cushion (arrow)

10.4a Unscrew the two cam chain tensioner mounting bolts (arrows) . . .

10.4b . . . and withdraw the tensioner

10.7 Make sure the rubber cushion is correctly installed

10.9 Use new sealing washers on the tensioner mounting bolts if necessary

10.15 Make sure the lugs on the guide blade fit in the slots in the head (arrows)

Installation

7 Install the tensioner into the back of the cam chain tunnel in the cylinder head, making sure the base of the tensioner is correctly seated in its slot. Install the rubber cushion with its widest end uppermost behind the top of the tensioner **(see illustration)**. The top of the cushion sits flush with the top of the cylinder head **(see illustration 10.1)**. Loosely install the lower cam chain tensioner bolt.

8 Mount the cam chain and sprocket onto its boss on the camshaft. Apply a suitable non-permanent thread locking compound to the camshaft sprocket bolt threads, then tighten the exposed bolt to the specified torque setting, using a socket on the alternator bolt to stop the engine from rotating if necessary **(see illustrations 8.28a and 8.28b)**. Rotate the crankshaft anti-clockwise to reveal the other sprocket bolt and tighten that to the specified torque setting. Before proceeding further, check that everything aligns as described in Section 8, Step 2. If it doesn't, the valve timing will be inaccurate and the valves will contact the piston when the engine is turned over.

9 Make sure the sealing washers on the tensioner mounting bolts are in good condition, and replace them with new ones if necessary. Install the bolts and tighten them to the torque setting specified at the beginning of the Chapter **(see illustration)**.

10 Remove the 2 mm pin from the wedge. The tensioner will automatically set itself to the correct tension against the cam chain.

11 Install the valve cover (see Section 7).

Cam chain guide blade

Removal

12 Remove the cylinder head (Section 11).

13 Lift the cam chain guide blade out of the front of the cam chain tunnel in the cylinder block, noting how it fits.

Inspection

14 Examine the sliding surface of the guide blade for wear or damage, and replace it if necessary.

Installation

15 Install the guide blade into the front of the cam chain tunnel, making sure its lugs seat correctly in their slots **(see illustration)**.

16 Install the cylinder head (see Section 11).

11 Cylinder heads - removal and installation

Caution: The engine must be completely cool before beginning this procedure or the cylinder head may become warped.
Note: *The heads can be removed with the engine in the frame. If the engine has been removed, ignore the steps which don't apply.*

Removal

Front cylinder

1 Drain the coolant (see Chapter 1).

2 Remove the valve cover (see Section 7).

3 Unscrew the bolts securing the frame

cross-member to the engine, then unscrew the bolts securing the frame cross-member to the frame downtubes and remove the cross-member **(see illustration 5.23)**.

4 Remove the front cylinder exhaust pipe (see Chapter 4).

5 Remove the carburettors (see Chapter 4).

6 Remove the spark plugs (see Chapter 1).

7 Remove the camshaft (see Section 9).

8 On J and K models unscrew the four bolts securing the external oil pipe and remove the pipe; do not bend it. Discard the pipe's sealing washers as new ones must be used.

9 Unscrew the bolt securing the coolant pipe to the back of the cylinder head **(see illustration)**. Withdraw the pipe from its socket and remove the O-ring, noting that it fits with its thicker section uppermost **(see illustration)**. Discard the O-ring as a new one must be used.

10 Detach the clutch cable from the clutch housing (see Section 18). Release the cable from the guide on the right-hand side frame downtube and secure it clear of the engine. Trace the ignition pulse generator wiring and disconnect it at the connector. Unscrew the bolt securing the wiring guide to the frame and release the wiring from the guide, noting how it fits **(see illustrations 5.15a and 5.15b)**. Secure the wiring out of the way.

11 Remove the cam chain tensioner (see Section 10).

12 The cylinder head is secured by four domed nuts, one plain nut (which on all except J and K models also secures the main camshaft holder and has already been removed), two long bolts and one short bolt **(see illustration)**. Slacken these evenly a little

11.9a Unscrew the water pipe bolt (arrow) . . .

11.9b . . . and withdraw the pipe and its O-ring (arrow)

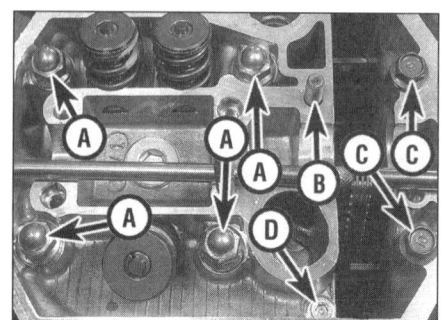
11.12 The cylinder head has four domed nuts (A), one plain nut (B) (see text), two long bolts (C) and one short bolt (D)

11.15 Remove the two dowels
if they are loose (arrows)

11.25a Detach the coolant hose
from the pipe

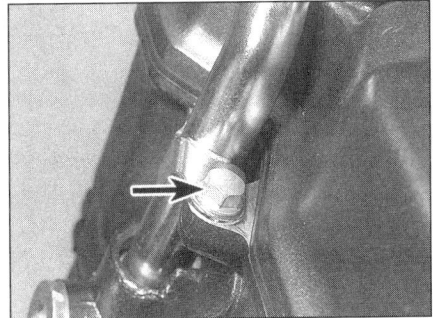

11.25b Unscrew the coolant pipe bolt
(arrow) . . .

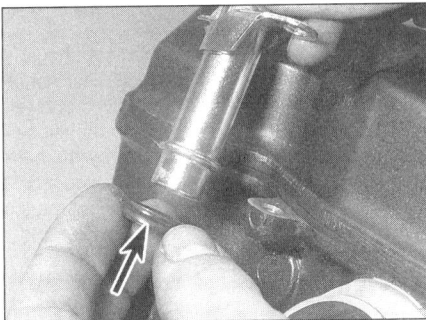

11.25c . . . and withdraw the pipe
and its O-ring (arrow)

11.34 Install the two dowels over the studs
and onto the cylinder block

at a time and in a criss-cross pattern until they are all loose. Remove all the nuts and their washers, and remove the short bolt and the front long bolt. Take great care not to drop any of the nuts or washers into the crankcase. The rear long bolt can only be fully removed once the cylinder head has been lifted off the block and brought forward to provide clearance from the frame.

13 Pull the cylinder head up off the studs. If it is stuck, tap around the joint faces of the cylinder head with a soft-faced mallet to free the head. Do not try to free the head by inserting a screwdriver between the head and cylinder block - you'll damage the sealing surfaces.

14 Lift the head off the block, and remove it from the engine via the front frame downtubes. The rear long bolt can be removed when the head is half way out of the frame. Remove the old gasket and stuff a clean rag into the cam chain tunnel to prevent any debris falling into the engine.

15 If they are loose, remove the two dowels from the cylinder block studs **(see illustration)**. If either appears to be missing it is probably stuck in the underside of the cylinder head. Also remove the cam chain guide blade from the front of the cam chain tunnel (see Section 10).

16 Check the cylinder head gasket and the mating surfaces on the cylinder head and block for signs of leakage, which could indicate warpage. Refer to Section 13 and check the flatness of the cylinder head.

17 Clean all traces of old gasket material from the cylinder head and block. If a scraper is used, take care not to scratch or gouge the

soft aluminium. Be careful not to let any of the gasket material fall into the crankcase, the cylinder bores or the oil passages.

Rear cylinder

18 Drain the coolant (see Chapter 1).

19 Remove the valve cover (see Section 7).

20 Remove the rear cylinder exhaust pipe (see Chapter 4).

21 Remove the carburettors (see Chapter 4).

22 Remove the spark plugs (see Chapter 1).

23 Remove the camshaft (see Section 9).

24 On J and K models unscrew the four bolts securing the external oil pipe and remove the pipe; take care not to bend it. Discard the pipe's sealing washers as new ones must be used.

25 Slacken the coolant hose clamp and detach the coolant hose from the pipe on the front of the cylinder head (if not already done) **(see illustration)**. Unscrew the bolt securing the coolant pipe to the cylinder head **(see illustration)**. Withdraw the pipe from its socket and remove the O-ring, noting that it fits with its thicker section uppermost **(see illustration)**. Discard the O-ring as a new one must be used.

26 Remove the cam chain tensioner (see Section 10).

27 The cylinder head is secured by four domed nuts, one plain nut (which on all except J and K models also secures the main camshaft holder and has already been removed), two long bolts and one short bolt **(see illustration 11.12)**. Slacken these evenly a little at a time and in a criss-cross pattern until they are all loose, then remove them with their washers. Take great care not to drop any of the nuts or washers into the crankcase.

28 Pull the cylinder head off the studs. If it is stuck, tap around the joint faces of the cylinder head with a soft-faced mallet to free the head. Do not attempt to free the head by inserting a screwdriver between the head and cylinder block - you'll damage the sealing surfaces.

29 Lift the head off the block, and remove it from the engine. Remove the old gasket and stuff a clean rag into the cam chain tunnel to prevent any debris falling into the engine.

30 If they are loose, remove the two dowels from the cylinder block studs **(see illustration 11.15)**. If either appears to be missing it is probably stuck in the underside of the cylinder head. Also remove the cam chain guide blade from the front of the cam chain tunnel (see Section 10).

31 Check the cylinder head gasket and the mating surfaces on the cylinder head and block for signs of leakage, which could indicate warpage. Refer to Section 13 and check the flatness of the cylinder head.

32 Clean all traces of old gasket material from the cylinder head and block. If a scraper is used, take care not to scratch or gouge the soft aluminium. Be careful not to let any of the gasket material fall into the crankcase, the cylinder bores or the oil passages.

Installation

33 Install the cam chain guide blade into the front of the cam chain tunnel (see Section 10) **(see illustration 10.15)**.

34 If removed, install the two dowels onto the cylinder block studs **(see illustration)**. Lubricate the cylinder bores with engine oil.

2

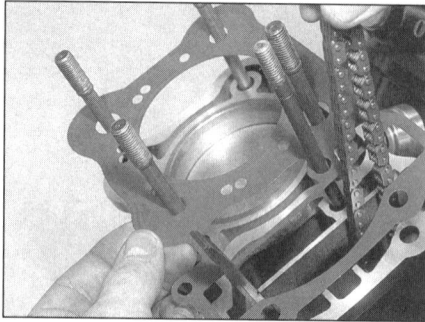

11.35 Always use a new cylinder head gasket

11.36 Carefully lower the cylinder head onto the block

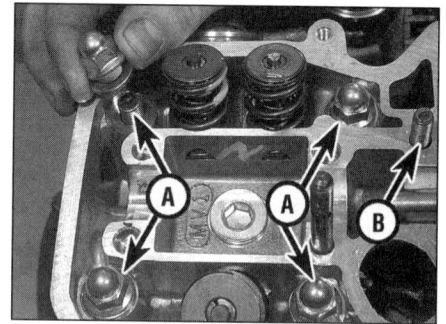

11.37a Install the four domed nuts and washers (A), the plain nut and washer (B) (J and K models only) . . .

11.37b . . . the long bolts and washers . . .

11.37c . . . and the short bolt

35 Ensure both cylinder head and block mating surfaces are clean, then lay the new head gasket in place on the cylinder block (see illustration). The gasket can only fit one way, so if the holes do not line up properly the gasket is upside down. Never re-use the old gasket.

36 When installing the front cylinder head, install the rear long bolt into the head as the head is being manoeuvred through the front frame downtubes (unless the engine has been removed from the frame). Carefully lower the cylinder head over the studs and onto the block (see illustration). It is helpful to have an assistant to pass the cam chain up through the tunnel and slip a piece of wire through it to prevent it falling back into the engine. Keep the chain taut to prevent it becoming disengaged from the crankshaft sprocket).

37 Install the domed nuts with washers, the plain nut with washer (J and K models only), the long bolts with washers and the short bolt; tighten them finger-tight at this stage (see illustrations).

38 Tighten the cylinder head nuts and bolts evenly a little at a time and in a criss-cross pattern to the torque setting specified at the beginning of the Chapter.

39 Install all other components that have been removed in a reverse of the removal procedure, referring to the relevant sections where necessary. On J and K models (front cylinder only) blow through the external oil pipe and its bolts using compressed air if available, then install the pipe using new

sealing washers and tighten its bolts to the specified torque setting. Also tighten the frame cross-member bolts to the specified torque setting (front cylinder only).

12 Valves/valve seats/valve guides - servicing

1 Because of the complex nature of this job and the special tools and equipment required, most owners leave servicing of the valves, valve seats and valve guides to a professional.

2 The home mechanic can, however, remove the valves from the cylinder head, clean and check the components for wear and grind in the valves (see Section 13).

3 After the valve service has been performed, the head will be in like-new condition. When the head is returned, be sure to clean it again very thoroughly before installation on the engine to remove any metal particles or abrasive grit that may still be present from the valve service operations. Use compressed air, if available, to blow out all the holes and passages.

13 Cylinder head and valves - disassembly, inspection and reassembly

1 As mentioned in the previous section, valve servicing, valve seat recutting and valve guide

replacement should be left to a Honda dealer. However, disassembly, cleaning and inspection of the valves and related components can be done (if the necessary special tools are available) by the home mechanic. This way no expense is incurred if the inspection reveals that overhaul is not required at this time.

2 To disassemble the valve components without the risk of damaging them, a valve spring compressor is absolutely necessary.

Disassembly

3 Before proceeding, arrange to label and store the valves along with their related components in such a way that they can be returned to their original locations without getting mixed up. A good way to do this is to obtain a container which is divided into six compartments, and to label each compartment with the identity of the valve which will be stored in it (ie front or rear cylinder, intake or exhaust valve, left or right intake valve).

4 If not already done, clean all traces of old gasket material from the cylinder head. If a scraper is used, take care not to scratch or gouge the soft aluminium. Carefully scrape all carbon deposits out of the combustion chamber area. A hand-held wire brush or a piece of fine emery cloth can be used once the majority of deposits have been scraped away. Do not use a wire brush mounted in a drill motor, or one with extremely stiff bristles, as the head material is soft and may be eroded away or scratched by the wire brush.

5 Compress the valve spring on the first valve with a spring compressor, then remove the collets and the retainer from the valve assembly (see illustration). Do not compress the springs any more than is absolutely necessary. Carefully release the valve spring compressor and remove the springs and the valve from the head. If the valve binds in the guide (won't pull through), push it back into the head and deburr the area around the collet groove with a very fine file or whetstone (see illustration).

6 Repeat the procedure for the remaining valves. Remember to keep the parts for each valve together so they can be reinstalled in the same location.

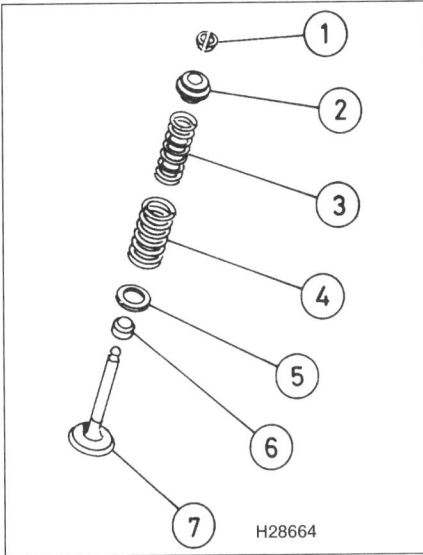

13.5a Valve components

1 Collets   5 Spring seat
2 Spring retainer 6 Stem seal
3 Inner spring   7 Valve
4 Outer spring

7 Once the valves have been removed and labelled, pull the valve stem seals off the top of the valve guides with pliers and discard them (the old seals should never be re-used), then remove the spring seats.

8 Next, clean the cylinder head with solvent and dry it thoroughly. Compressed air will speed the drying process and ensure that all holes and recessed areas are clean.

9 Clean all of the valve springs, collets, retainers and spring seats with solvent and dry them thoroughly. Do the parts from one valve at a time so that no mixing of parts between valves occurs.

10 Scrape off any deposits that may have formed on the valve, then use a motorised wire brush to remove deposits from the valve heads and stems. Again, make sure the valves do not get mixed up.

Inspection

11 Inspect the head very carefully for cracks and other damage. If cracks are found, a new head will be required. Check the cam bearing surfaces for wear and evidence of seizure. Check the camshafts and rockers for wear as well (see Section 8).

12 Using a precision straightedge and a feeler gauge of the same thickness as the warpage limit listed in the specifications at the beginning of the Chapter, check the head gasket mating surface for warpage. Lay the straightedge lengthways, across the head and diagonally, intersecting the stud holes, and try to slip the feeler gauge under it on either side of the combustion chamber **(see illustration)**. If the feeler gauge can be inserted between the straight edge and the cylinder head, the head is warped and must be either machined or, if warpage is excessive, replaced with a new one.

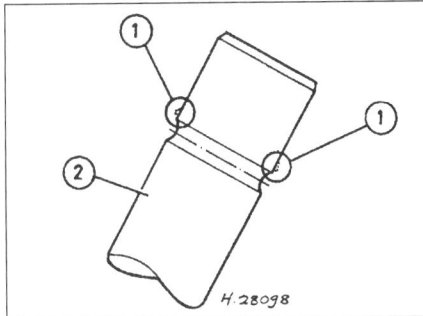

13.5b Remove any burrs (1) if the valve stem (2) won't pull through the guide

13 Examine the valve seats in the combustion chamber. If they are pitted, cracked or burned, the head will require work beyond the scope of the home mechanic. Measure the valve seat width and compare it to this Chapter's Specifications **(see illustration)**. If it exceeds the service limit, or if it varies around its circumference, valve overhaul is required.

14 Clean the valve guides to remove any carbon build-up, then measure the inside diameters of the guides (at both ends and the centre of the guide) with a small hole gauge and micrometer **(see illustrations)**. Record the measurements for future reference. These measurements, along with the valve stem diameter measurements, will enable you to compute the valve stem-to-

13.13 Measure the valve seat width with a ruler (or for greater precision use a vernier caliper)

13.14b Measure the small hole gauge with a micrometer

13.12 Lay a precision straightedge across the cylinder head and try to slide a feeler gauge of the specified thickness (equal to the maximum allowable warpage) under it

guide clearance. This clearance, when compared to the Specifications, will be one factor that will determine the extent of the valve service work required. The guides are measured at the ends and at the centre to determine if they are worn in a bell-mouth pattern (more wear at the ends). If the guides are worn they must be replaced.

15 Carefully inspect each valve face for cracks, pits and burned spots. Check the valve stem and the collet groove area for cracks **(see illustration)**. Rotate the valve and check for any obvious indication that it is bent. Check the end of the stem for pitting and excessive wear. The presence of any of the above conditions indicates the need for valve servicing.

2

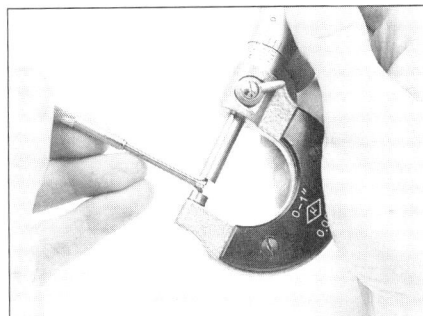

13.14a Insert a small hole gauge into the valve guide and expand it so there's a slight drag when it's pulled out

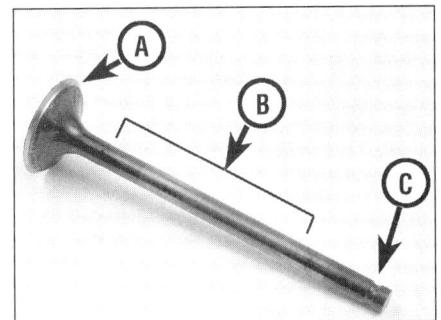

13.15 Check the valve face (A), stem (B) and collet groove (C) for wear and damage

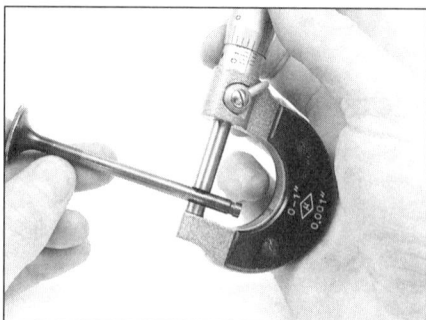

13.16 Measure the valve stem diameter with a micrometer

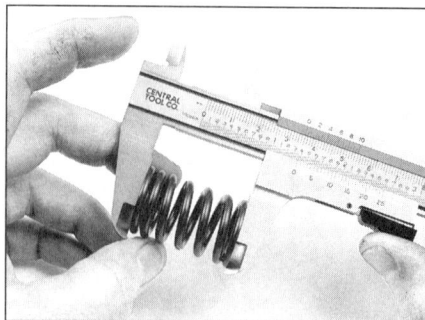

13.17a Measure the free length of the valve springs

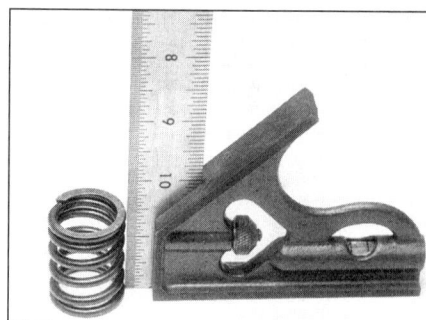

13.17b Check the valve springs for squareness

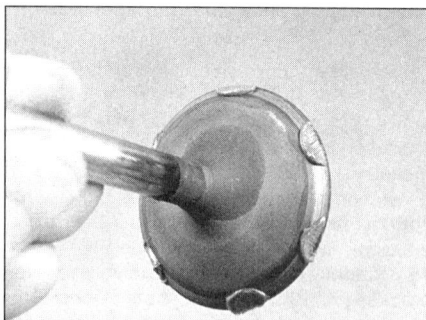

13.21 Apply the lapping compound very sparingly, in small dabs, to the valve face only

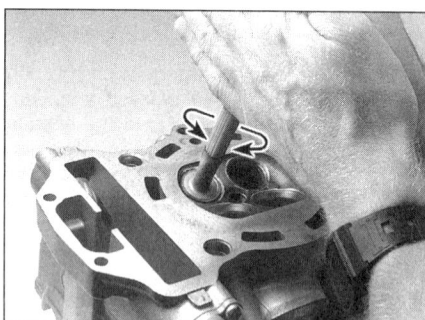

13.22a Rotate the valve grinding tool between the palms of your hands

13.22b The face should be the specified width (arrow) with a smooth, unbroken appearance

16 Measure the valve stem diameter **(see illustration)**. By subtracting the stem diameter from the valve guide bore diameter, the valve stem-to-guide clearance is obtained. If the stem-to-guide clearance is greater than that listed in the specifications, the valves and guides must be replaced.

17 Check the end of each valve spring for wear and pitting. Measure the spring free length and compare it to that listed in the specifications **(see illustration)**. If any spring is shorter than specified it has sagged and must be replaced. Also place the spring upright on a flat surface and check it for bend by placing a ruler against it **(see illustration)**. If the bend in any spring is excessive, it must be replaced.

18 Check the spring retainers and collets for obvious wear and cracks. Any questionable parts should not be re-used, as extensive damage will occur in the event of failure during engine operation.

19 If the inspection indicates that no overhaul work is required, the valve components can be reinstalled in the head.

Reassembly

20 Before installing the valves in the head, they should be ground in (lapped) to ensure a positive seal between the valves and seats. This procedure requires coarse and fine valve grinding compound and a valve grinding tool. If a grinding tool is not available, a piece of rubber or plastic hose can be slipped over the

valve stem (after the valve has been installed in the guide) and used to turn the valve.

21 Apply a small amount of coarse grinding compound to the valve face, then slip the valve into the guide **(see illustration)**. **Note:** *Make sure each valve is installed in its correct guide and be careful not to get any grinding compound on the valve stem.*

22 Attach the grinding tool (or hose) to the valve and rotate the tool between the palms of your hands. Use a back-and-forth motion (as though rubbing your hands together) rather than a circular motion (ie so that the valve rotates alternately clockwise and anti-clockwise rather than in one direction only) **(see illustration)**. Lift the valve off the seat and turn it at regular intervals to distribute the grinding compound properly. Continue the grinding procedure until the valve face and seat contact area is of uniform width and unbroken around the entire circumference of the valve face and seat **(see illustration)**.

23 Carefully remove the valve from the guide and wipe off all traces of grinding compound. Use solvent to clean the valve and wipe the seat area thoroughly with a solvent soaked cloth.

24 Repeat the procedure with fine valve grinding compound, then repeat the entire procedure for the remaining valves.

25 Lay the spring seats in place in the cylinder head, then install new valve stem seals on each of the guides. Use an appropriate size deep socket to push the

seals over the end of the valve guide until they are felt to clip into place. Don't twist or cock them, or they will not seal properly against the valve stems. Also, don't remove them again or they will be damaged.

26 Coat the valve stems with molybdenum disulphide grease, then install one of them into its guide, rotating it slowly to avoid damaging the seal. Check that the valve moves up and down freely in the guide. Next, install the springs and retainer, compress the springs and install the collets. **Note:** *Install the springs with the closely-wound coils at the bottom, towards the valve head* **(see illustration)**. When compressing the springs with the valve spring compressor, depress them only as far as is absolutely necessary to slip the collets into place. Apply a small

13.26a Install the springs with their closely-wound coils down (against the cylinder head)

13.26b A small dab of grease will help to keep the collets in place on the valve while the spring is released

14.2a Remove one of the clips . . .

14.2b . . . and slide the coolant joint collar off the opposite stub

amount of grease to the collets to help hold them in place as the pressure is released from the springs (see illustration). Make certain that the collets are securely locked in their retaining grooves.

27 Support the cylinder head on blocks so the valves can't contact the workbench top, then very gently tap each of the valve stems with a soft-faced hammer. This will help seat the collets in their grooves.

> **HAYNES HiNT** Check for proper sealing of the valves by pouring a little solvent into the valve ports. If the solvent leaks past any valve into the combustion chamber area the valve grinding operation on that valve should be repeated.

14 Cylinder blocks - removal, inspection and installation

Note: The cylinder blocks can be removed with the engine in the frame. The procedure is the same for both front and rear cylinders.

Removal

1 Remove the cylinder head (see Section 11).
2 Release one of the clips securing the coolant joint collar that connects between the two cylinder blocks (see illustration). Slide the collar either forwards or backwards (depending on which clip was removed) so that it is detached from the stub on one or other of the blocks (see illustration). Also release the clamp securing the coolant inlet hose to the union on the front of the front cylinder block and remove the hose (see illustrations). If necessary, unscrew the two bolts securing the hose union and remove the union. Discard the O-ring as a new one must be used.
3 Lift the cylinder block up to remove it from the studs. If it is stuck, tap around the joint faces of the block with a soft-faced mallet to free it from the crankcase. Don't attempt to free the block by inserting a screwdriver between it and the crankcase - you'll damage the sealing surfaces. When the block is removed, stuff clean rags around the piston to prevent anything falling into the crankcase.

14.2c Slacken the hose clamp . . .

14.2d . . . and detach the coolant hose from the union

14.4 Remove the dowels if they are loose (arrows)

14.5 Remove the coolant joint collar and both O-rings

4 Note the location of the two dowels which will be either on the bottom of the block or in the crankcase (see illustration). Remove them if they are loose.
5 Remove the coolant joint collar from whichever block it is attached to, then remove the collar O-ring from the stub on each block (see illustration). Discard them as new ones must be used.
6 Remove the gasket and clean all traces of old gasket material from the cylinder block and crankcase mating surfaces. If a scraper is used, take care not to scratch or gouge the soft aluminium. Don't let any gasket material fall into the crankcase or the oil passages.

Inspection

Note: Do not attempt to separate the cylinder liners from the cylinder block.
7 Check the cylinder walls carefully for scratches and score marks. A rebore will be necessary to remove any deep scores.

8 Using telescoping gauges (see Tools and Working facilities), check the dimensions of each cylinder to assess the amount of wear, taper and ovality. Measure near the top (but below the level of the top piston ring at TDC), centre and bottom (but above the level of the oil ring at BDC) of the bore both parallel to and across the crankshaft axis (see illustration). Calculate any differences between the measurements taken to

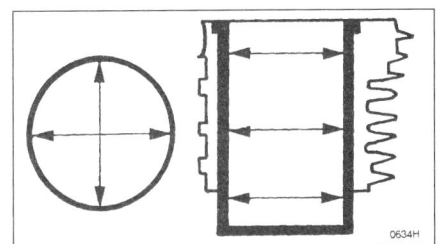

14.8 Cylinder bore wear measurement points

2

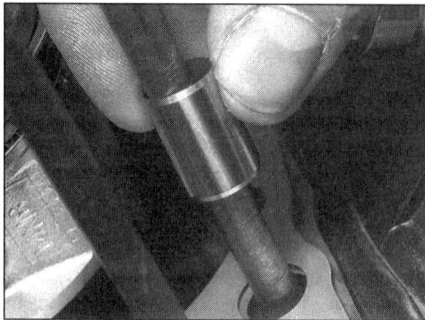

14.16 Install the two dowels over the studs and into their crankcase recesses

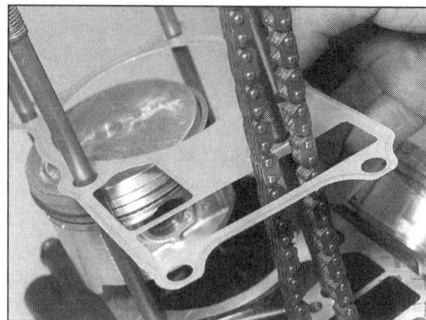

14.17 Always use a new base gasket

14.20 Feed the piston rings into the bore as the block is lowered

determine any taper and ovality in the bore. Compare the results to the specifications at the beginning of the Chapter. If the cylinders are tapered, oval, or worn beyond the service limits, or badly scratched, scuffed or scored, have them rebored and honed by a Honda dealer or specialist motorcycle repair shop. If the cylinders are rebored, they will require oversize pistons and rings.

9 If the precision measuring tools are not available, take the block to a Honda dealer or specialist motorcycle repair shop for assessment and advice.

10 If the cylinders are in good condition and the piston-to-bore clearance is within specifications (see Section 15), the cylinders should be honed (de-glazed). To perform this operation you will need the proper size flexible hone with fine stones (see *Tools and Working facilities*), or a bottle-brush type hone, plenty of light oil or honing oil, some clean rags and an electric drill motor.

11 Hold the block sideways (so that the bore is horizontal rather than vertical) in a vice with soft jaws or cushioned with wooden blocks. Mount the hone in the drill motor, compress the stones and insert the hone into the cylinder. Thoroughly lubricate the cylinder, then turn on the drill and move the hone up and down in the cylinder at a pace which produces a fine cross-hatch pattern on the cylinder wall with the lines intersecting at an angle of approximately 60 degrees. Be sure to use plenty of lubricant and do not take off any more material than is necessary to produce the desired effect. Do not withdraw the hone from the cylinder while it is still turning. Switch off the drill and continue to move it up and down in the cylinder until it has stopped turning, then compress the stones and withdraw the hone. Wipe the oil from the cylinder and repeat the procedure on the other cylinder. Remember, do not take too much material from the cylinder wall.

12 Wash the cylinders thoroughly with warm soapy water to remove all traces of the abrasive grit produced during the honing operation. Be sure to run a brush through the bolt holes and flush them with running water. After rinsing, dry the cylinders thoroughly and apply a thin coat of light, rust-preventative oil to all machined surfaces.

13 If you do not have the equipment or desire to perform the honing operation, take the block to a Honda dealer or specialist motorcycle repair shop.

Installation

14 Install a new O-ring onto the coolant joint collar stub on each cylinder block, then slide the collar as far as possible onto the stub of one of the blocks (see illustration 14.5).

15 Check that the mating surfaces of the cylinder block and crankcase are free from oil or pieces of old gasket.

16 If removed, install the dowels into their correct locations in the crankcase, and push them firmly home (see illustration).

17 Remove the rags from around the piston, and lay the new base gasket in place on the crankcase (see illustration). The gasket can only fit one way, so if the holes do not line up properly the gasket is upside down. Never re-use the old gasket.

18 If required, install a piston ring clamp onto the piston to ease its entry into the bore as the block is lowered. This is not essential as the cylinder has a good lead-in, enabling the piston rings to be hand-fed into the bore. If possible, have an assistant support the block while this is done.

19 Lubricate the cylinder bore, piston and piston rings with clean engine oil, then install the block down over the studs until the piston crown fits into the bore. At this stage feed the cam chain up through the block and secure it in place with a piece of wire to prevent it from falling back down.

20 Gently push down on the cylinder block, making sure the piston enters the bore squarely and does not get cocked sideways. If you are doing this without a piston ring clamp, carefully compress and feed each ring into the bore as the block is lowered (see illustration). If necessary, use a soft mallet to gently tap the block down, but do not use force if the block appears to be stuck as the piston and/or rings will be damaged. If clamps are used, remove them once the piston is in the bore.

21 When the piston is correctly installed in the cylinder, press the block down onto the base gasket.

22 If removed, fit a new O-ring to the coolant inlet hose union and install the union onto the front of the front cylinder block, tightening its bolts securely. Fit the coolant inlet hose onto the union and secure it with its clamp (see illustration 14.2c and 14.2d).

23 Slide the coolant joint collar across and over the O-ring so that it is central on the stubs between the cylinder blocks, then secure it in place with its clips (see illustration 14.2a).

24 Install the cylinder head (see Section 11).

15 Pistons - removal, inspection and installation

Note: *The pistons can be removed with the engine in the frame.*

Removal

1 Remove the cylinder block (see Section 14).

2 Before removing the piston from the connecting rod, stuff a clean rag into the hole around the rod to prevent the circlips or anything else from falling into the crankcase. Use a felt marker pen to write the cylinder identity on the crown of each piston (or on the skirt if the piston is dirty and going to be cleaned). Each piston should also have "IN" marked on its crown which should face the intake side (see illustration). If this is not visible, mark the piston accordingly so that it can be installed the correct way round.

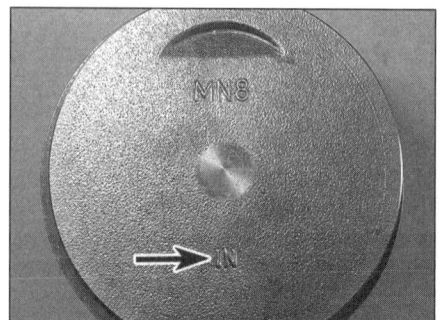

15.2 Note the "IN" mark (arrow) on the piston which faces the intake side

15.3a Prise the piston pin circlip out from one side of the piston . . .

15.3b . . . then push the piston pin out from the other side until you can grasp it and pull it out the rest of the way

15.5 Remove the piston rings with a ring removal and installation tool

3 Prise out the circlip on one side of the piston using needle-nose pliers or a small flat-bladed screwdriver inserted into the notch **(see illustration)**. Push the piston pin out from the other side to free the piston from the connecting rod **(see illustration)**. Rotate the crankshaft so that the best access is obtained for each piston. Remove the other circlip and discard them as new ones must be used.

> **HAYNES HiNT** *if a piston pin is a tight fit in the piston bosses, soak a rag in boiling water then wring it out and wrap it around the piston - this will expand the alloy piston sufficiently to release its grip on the pin.*

Inspection

4 Before the inspection process can be carried out, the piston must be cleaned and the old piston rings removed. Note that if the cylinders are being rebored, piston inspection can be overlooked as new ones will be fitted.
5 Using your thumbs or a piston ring removal and installation tool, carefully remove the rings from the piston **(see illustration)**. Do not nick or gouge the piston in the process. Carefully note which way up each ring fits in its groove as they must be installed in their original positions if being re-used.

6 Scrape all traces of carbon from the tops of the piston. A hand-held wire brush or a piece of fine emery cloth can be used once most of the deposits have been scraped away. Do not, under any circumstances, use a wire brush mounted in a drill motor to remove deposits from the piston; the piston material is soft and will be eroded away by the wire brush.
7 Use a piston ring groove cleaning tool to remove any carbon deposits from the ring grooves. If a tool is not available, a piece broken off an old ring will do the job. Be very careful to remove only the carbon deposits. Do not remove any metal and do not nick or gouge the sides of the ring grooves.
8 Once the deposits have been removed, clean the piston with solvent and dry it thoroughly. If the identification previously marked on the piston is cleaned off, be sure to re-mark it with the correct identity. Make sure the oil return holes below the oil ring groove are clear.
9 Carefully inspect each piston for cracks around the skirt, at the pin bosses and at the ring lands. Normal piston wear appears as even, vertical wear on the thrust surfaces of the piston and slight looseness of the top ring in its groove. If the skirt is scored or scuffed, the engine may have been suffering from overheating and/or abnormal combustion,

which caused excessively high operating temperatures. The oil pump should be checked thoroughly. Also check that the circlip grooves are not damaged.
10 A hole in the piston crown, an extreme to be sure, is an indication that abnormal combustion (pre-ignition) was occurring. Burned areas at the edge of the piston crown are usually evidence of spark knock (detonation). If any of the above problems exist, the causes must be corrected or the damage will occur again.
11 Measure the piston ring-to-groove clearance by laying a new piston ring in the ring groove and slipping a feeler gauge in beside it **(see illustration)**. Check the clearance at three or four locations around the groove. If the clearance is greater than specified, the piston is worn and must be replaced. **Note:** *Make sure you have the correct ring for the groove - the two compression rings can be identified by their profile (see illustration 16.13).*
12 Check the piston-to-bore clearance by measuring the bore (see Section 14) and the piston diameter. Make sure each piston is matched to its correct cylinder. Measure the piston 10.0 mm up from the bottom of the skirt and at 90° to the piston pin axis **(see illustration)**. Subtract the piston diameter from the bore diameter to obtain the clearance. If it

2

15.11 Measure the piston ring-to-groove clearance with a feeler gauge

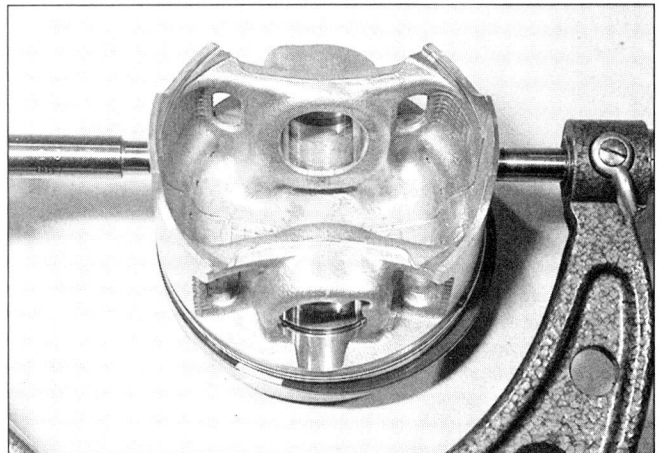

15.12 Measure piston diameter with a micrometer at the specified distance from the bottom of the skirt

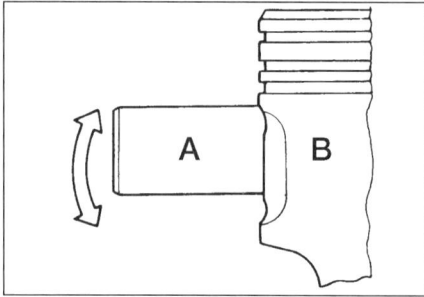

15.13a Slip the pin (A) into the piston (B) and try to rock it back and forth. If it's loose, replace the piston and pin

15.13b Measure the external diameter of the pin . . .

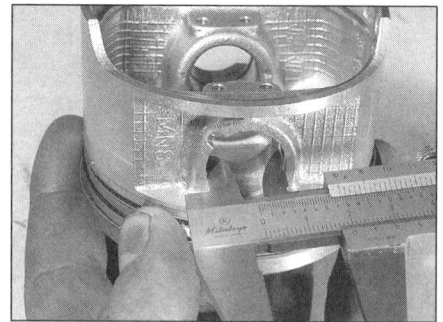

15.13c . . . the internal diameter of the bore in the piston . . .

15.13d . . . and the internal diameter of the connecting rod small-end

15.17a Secure the piston pin with new circlips

15.17b Make sure open end of the circlip (A) is away from the notch in the piston (B)

is greater than the specified figure, the piston must be replaced (assuming the bore itself is within limits, otherwise a rebore is necessary).
13 Apply clean engine oil to the piston pin, insert it into the piston and check for any freeplay between the two **(see illustration)**. Measure the pin external diameter and the pin bore in the piston and compare the measurements to the specifications at the beginning of the Chapter **(see illustrations)**. Calculate the difference between the measurements taken to obtain the piston pin-to-bore clearance and compare the result to the specifications. Repeat the measurements between the pin and the connecting rod small-end **(see illustration)**. Replace components that are worn beyond the specified limits.
14 If the pistons are to be replaced, ensure the correct size of piston is ordered. Honda produce two oversize pistons as well as the standard piston. The oversize pistons available are: +0.25 mm and +0.50 mm. **Note:** *Oversize pistons have their relevant size stamped on top of the piston crown, eg a 0.50 mm oversize piston will be marked 0.50.*

Installation

15 Inspect and install the piston rings (see Section 16).
16 Lubricate the piston pin and the connecting rod small-end bore with molybdenum disulphide grease.
17 Install a new circlip in one side of the piston (do not re-use old circlips) **(see illustration)**. Line up the piston on its correct connecting rod, making sure the "IN" mark faces the intake side, and insert the piston pin

from the other side **(see illustration 15.3b)**. Secure the pin with the other new circlip. When installing the circlips, compress them only just enough to fit them in the piston, and make sure they are properly seated in their grooves with the open end away from the removal notch **(see illustration)**.

16 Piston rings - inspection and installation

1 It is good practice to replace the piston rings when an engine is being overhauled. Before installing the new piston rings, the ring end gaps must be checked.
2 Lay out the pistons and the new ring sets so the rings will be matched with the same piston and cylinder during the end gap measurement procedure and engine assembly.

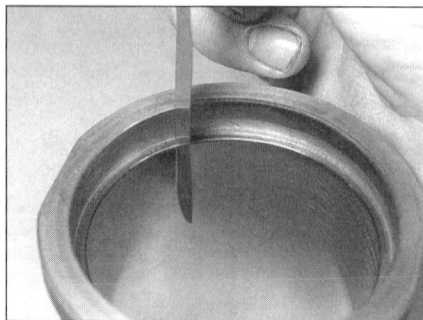

16.3 Measuring piston ring end gap

3 Insert the top ring into the top of the front cylinder and square it up with the cylinder walls by pushing it in with the top of the piston. The ring should be about 20 mm below the top edge of the cylinder. To measure the end gap, slip a feeler gauge between the ends of the ring and compare the measurement to the specifications at the beginning of the Chapter **(see illustration)**.
4 If the gap is larger or smaller than specified, double check to make sure that you have the correct rings before proceeding.
5 If the gap is too small, it must be enlarged or the ring ends may come in contact with each other during engine operation, which can cause serious damage. The end gap can be increased by filing the ring ends very carefully with a fine file. When performing this operation, file only from the outside in **(see illustration)**.
6 Excess end gap is not critical unless it is greater than 1 mm. Again, double check to

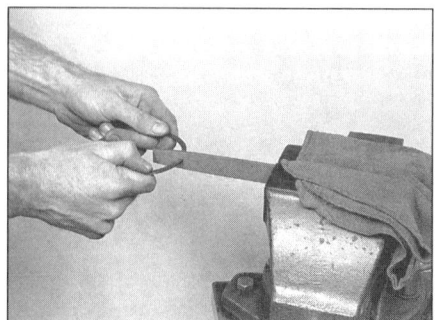

16.5 End gap can be enlarged by clamping a file in a vice and filing the ring ends

16.9a Install the oil ring expander
in its groove . . .

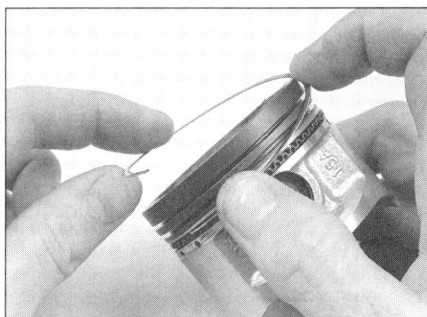

16.9b . . . and fit the side rails each side of
it. The oil ring must be installed by hand

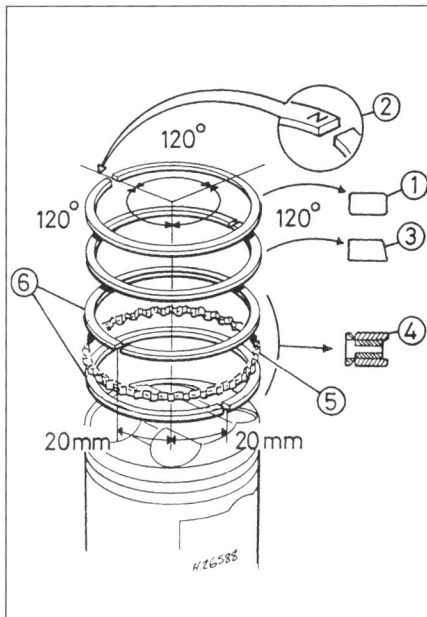

16.13 Arrange the ring end gaps like this

1   Top compression ring
2   Compression ring top marking (N or R)
3   Second compression ring
4   Oil ring complete
5   Expander ring
6   Side rails

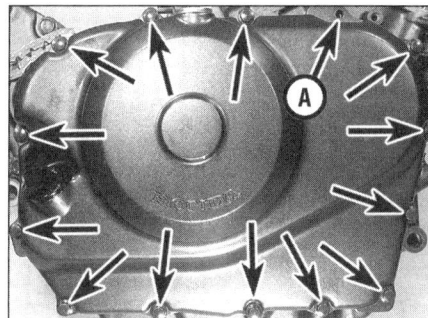

17.5 Right side crankcase cover bolts
(arrows). Note the location of the cable
bracket (A) (shown removed)

17.6 Note the position of the two dowels
(arrows) and remove them
if they are loose

make sure you have the correct rings for your engine and check that the bore is not worn.

7 Repeat the procedure for each ring that will be installed in the front cylinder and for each ring in the rear cylinder. Remember to keep the rings, pistons and cylinders matched up.

8 Once the ring end gaps have been checked/corrected, the rings can be installed on the pistons.

9 The oil control ring (lowest on the piston) is installed first. It is composed of three separate components. Slip the expander into the groove, then install the upper side rail. Do not use a piston ring installation tool on the oil ring side rails as they may be damaged. Instead, place one end of the side rail into the groove between the expander and the ring land. Hold it firmly in place and slide a finger around the piston while pushing the rail into the groove. Next, install the lower side rail in the same manner (see illustrations).

10 After the three oil ring components have been installed, check to make sure that both the upper and lower side rails can be turned smoothly in the ring groove.

11 Install the second (middle) ring next. It can be readily distinguished from the top ring by its cross-section shape (see illustration 16.13). To avoid breaking the ring, use a piston ring installation tool and make sure that the identification letter (an "N" on 600 cc engines and an "R" on 650 cc engines) near the end gap is facing up. Fit the ring into the middle groove on the piston. Do not expand

the ring any more than is necessary to slide it into place.

12 Finally, install the top ring in the same manner. The top ring can be distinguished from the second ring by its cross-section shape (see illustration 16.13). Make sure the identification letter (an "N" on 600 cc engines and an "R" on 650 cc engines) near the end gap is facing up.

13 Once the rings are correctly installed, check they move freely without snagging and stagger their end gaps as shown (see illustration).

17 Clutch - removal, inspection and installation

Note: The clutch can be removed with the engine in the frame. If the engine has already been removed, ignore the preliminary steps which don't apply.

Removal

1 Drain the engine oil as described in Chapter 1.

2 Detach the clutch cable from the lever on the crankcase cover (see Section 18).

3 Remove the rear cylinder exhaust pipe (see Chapter 4).

4 On J and K models, unscrew the external oil pipe lower bolt from the right-hand side crankcase cover, and the pipe holder bolt

from the crankcase. Discard the lower bolt sealing washers as new ones must be used.

5 Working in a criss-cross pattern, evenly slacken the right-hand side crankcase cover retaining bolts, noting the position of the clutch cable bracket (see illustration). Lift the cover away from the engine, being prepared to catch any residual oil which may be released as the cover is removed.

6 Remove the gasket and discard it. Note the positions of the two locating dowels fitted to the crankcase and remove them for safe-keeping if they are loose (see illustration). On J and K models, remove the oil orifice, noting which way round it fits, and discard its O-ring as a new one must be used.

7 Working in a criss-cross pattern, gradually slacken the clutch release plate retaining bolts until spring pressure is released, then remove the bolts, plate and springs (see illustrations).

8 To remove the clutch nut the mainshaft must be locked. This can be done in several ways. If the engine is in the frame, engage 1st gear and have an assistant hold the rear brake on hard with the rear tyre in firm contact with the ground. Alternatively, the Honda service tool (Pt. No. 07923-KE10000) can be used to stop the clutch centre from turning whilst the nut is slackened. If the engine has been removed from the frame (and the Honda tool is not available), install the universal joint onto the output driven shaft and engage 5th gear, then fit a suitable spanner onto the flats of the

2

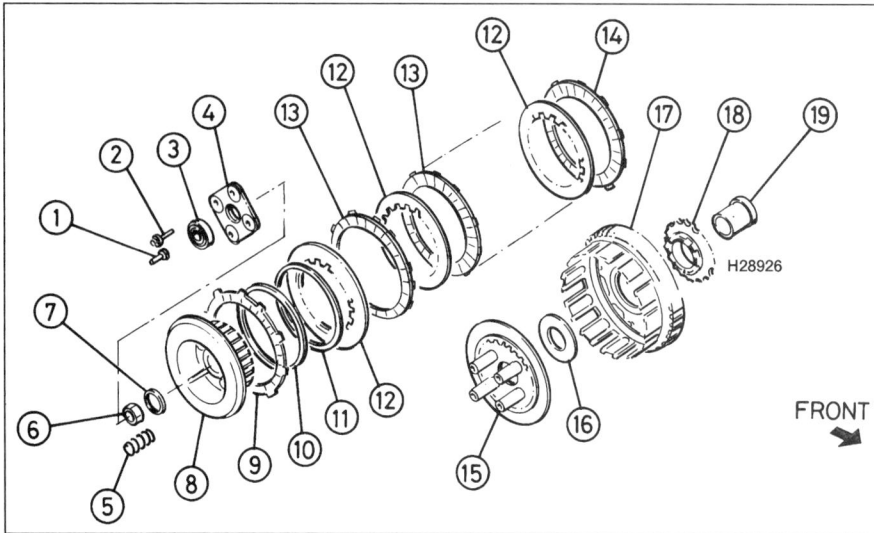

17.7a Clutch components

1	Release rod	8	Clutch centre	15	Pressure plate
2	Release plate bolts	9	Friction plate - type A	16	Thrust washer
3	Release bearing	10	Spring seat	17	Clutch housing
4	Release plate	11	Anti-judder spring	18	Oil pump drive sprocket
5	Springs	12	Plain plates	19	Clutch housing guide
6	Clutch nut	13	Friction plates - type B		
7	Washer	14	Friction plate - type C		

17.7b Remove the four bolts to free the release plate

universal joint and secure it against the work surface (see illustration). This locks the mainshaft and allows the clutch nut to be removed. Whilst the shaft is locked, also slacken the oil pump driven sprocket bolt (see illustration). Unscrew the clutch nut and remove the washer from the mainshaft, noting how it fits (see illustration).

9 Grasp the clutch centre with the complete set of clutch plates and the pressure plate and remove them as a pack (see illustration). Unless the plates are being replaced with new ones, keep them in their original order. Note that of the eight friction plates, there are three types, identified as A, B and C (see illustration). The outermost (type A) plate has a slightly larger internal diameter allowing it to fit over the anti-judder spring and spring seat, and its tangs fit into the shallow slots in the clutch housing. It is also slightly thicker than the rest. The innermost (type C) plate has different tang ends to the rest. The six middle plates are type B. Take care not to mix them up.

10 Remove the thrust washer from the shaft.

11 Remove the clutch housing (see illustration).

12 Note the tabs on the oil pump drive sprocket behind the clutch housing which must locate in the slots in the back of the housing on reassembly. Unscrew the oil pump driven sprocket bolt and remove the sprocket

17.8a Using a spanner on the universal joint to lock the mainshaft

17.8b Slacken the oil pump sprocket bolt (arrow) whilst the shaft is locked

17.8c Remove the clutch nut , noting how it is staked to the mainshaft (arrow)

17.9a Remove the clutch centre and plates as a pack

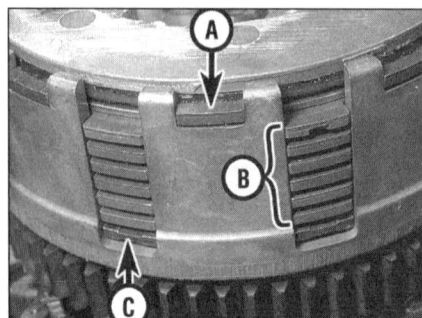

17.9b Clutch friction plates - type A, type B, type C

17.11 Remove the clutch housing

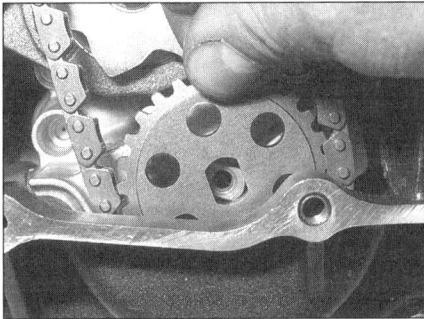

17.12a Slip the oil pump sprocket off the pump shaft . . .

17.12b . . . and disengage the chain from the drive sprocket

17.12c Remove the oil pump drive sprocket

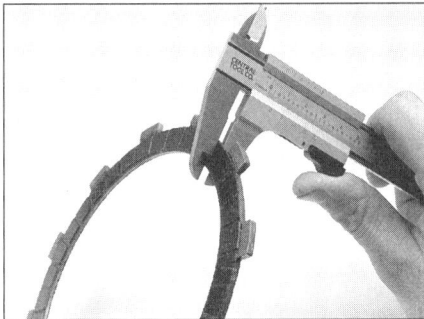

17.13 Measure the thickness of the friction plates

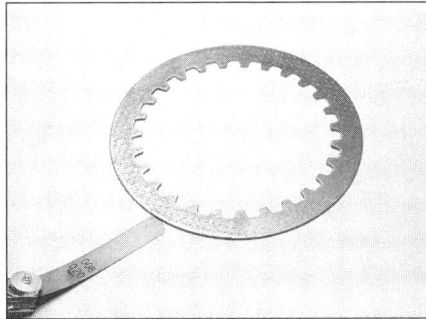

17.14 Check the plain plates for warpage

from the pump, then disengage the pump drive chain and withdraw the drive sprocket from the mainshaft **(see illustrations)**. Note the "IN" mark on the back of the oil pump driven sprocket which must face inwards. Remove the clutch housing guide from the mainshaft.

Inspection

13 After an extended period of service the clutch friction plates will wear and promote clutch slip. Measure the thickness of each friction plate using a vernier caliper **(see illustration)**. If any plate has worn to or beyond the service limit given in the Specifications at the beginning of the Chapter, the friction plates must be replaced as a set. Also, if any of the plates smell burnt or are glazed, they must be replaced as a set.

14 The plain plates should not show any signs of excess heating (bluing). Check for warpage using a flat surface and feeler gauges **(see illustration)**. If any plate exceeds the maximum permissible amount of warpage, or shows signs of bluing, all plain plates must be replaced as a set.

15 Measure the free length of each clutch spring using a vernier caliper **(see illustration 13.17a)**. If any spring is below the service limit specified, replace all the springs as a set.

16 Inspect the clutch assembly for burrs and indentations on the edges of the protruding tangs of the friction plates and/or slots in the edge of the housing with which they engage. Similarly check for wear between the inner tongues of the plain plates and the slots in the clutch centre. Wear of this nature will cause

clutch drag and slow disengagement during gear changes, since the plates will snag when the pressure plate is lifted. With care a small amount of wear can be corrected by dressing with a fine file, but if this is excessive the worn components should be replaced.

17 Using a vernier caliper, measure the diameter of the mainshaft where the clutch housing guide fits over it. Also measure the

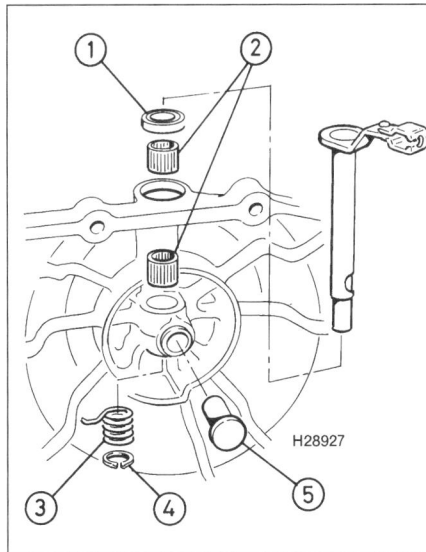

17.21a Clutch release mechanism

1 Dust seal   4 Circlip
2 Needle bearings   5 Release rod
3 Spring

internal and external diameter of the housing guide, and the internal diameter of the clutch housing and the oil pump drive sprocket. Compare the measurements to the specifications at the beginning of the Chapter and replace any components that are worn beyond their service limit. Also check all the above components for signs of damage or scoring, and replace if necessary.

18 Check the pressure plate and thrust washer for signs of roughness, wear or damage, and replace any parts as necessary.

19 Check the clutch release plate for signs of damage. Check that the bearing outer race is a tight fit in the centre of the plate, and that the inner race rotates freely without any rough spots. Replace the bearing if necessary.

20 Check the clutch anti-judder spring and spring seat for distortion, wear or damage, and replace them if necessary.

21 Check the clutch release mechanism in the clutch cover for smooth operation **(see illustration)**. Check the shaft and release rod for signs of damage. If necessary, prise off the circlip and withdraw the shaft from the cover, noting how the return spring fits **(see illustration)**. Check the two needle roller bearings for roughness, wear or damage, or looseness in the cover. If they need to be replaced, heat the cover in very hot water to ease removal and drift them out. If the shaft is removed, lever out the dust seal and replace it with a new one. Check the shaft return spring for fatigue or damage and replace it if necessary. Clean all components and lubricate the seal and bearings with grease.

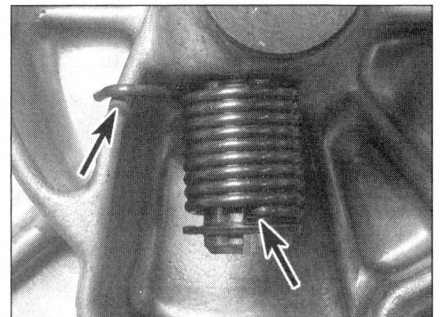

17.21b Note how the ends of the return spring locate (arrows)

2

17.23 Install the clutch housing guide

17.24a Note the "IN" mark on the driven sprocket (arrow) which must face inwards

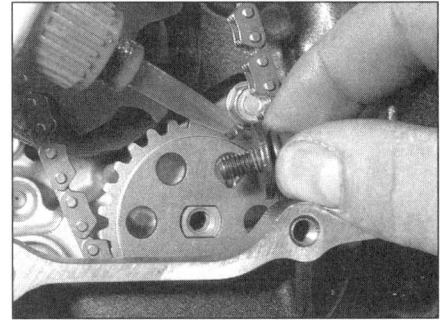
17.24b Apply a thread locking compound to the oil pump sprocket bolt

TOOL TiP

Insert a screwdriver through one of the holes in the sprocket and lock it against the crankcase to prevent the sprocket from turning whilst tightening the bolt.

Installation

22 Remove all traces of old gasket from the crankcase and clutch cover surfaces.

23 Smear the outside of the clutch housing guide with molybdenum disulphide grease, then install the guide onto the mainshaft **(see illustration)**.

24 Install the oil pump drive chain onto its drive and driven sprockets, then install the sprockets and chain as an assembly onto the clutch housing guide and oil pump, making sure that the "IN" mark on the driven sprocket faces the engine **(see illustration)** and that the tabs on the drive sprocket face out **(see illustration 17.12b)**. Apply a suitable non-permanent thread locking compound to the sprocket bolt **(see illustration)** and tighten it to the torque setting specified at the

17.25 Make sure the tabs (A) engage in the slots (B) in the back of the clutch housing, and that the teeth (C) mesh with those on the primary drive gear (D)

beginning of the chapter (see **Tool Tip**). Alternatively, tighten the bolt when tightening the clutch nut (see Step 29).

17.26a Install the thrust washer . . .

25 Install the clutch housing onto the housing guide on the mainshaft, making sure the tabs on the oil pump drive sprocket engage with the slots in the rear of the housing, and the teeth of the clutch housing engage with those of the primary drive gear **(see illustration)**.

26 Install the thrust washer onto the shaft, followed by the clutch pressure plate **(see illustrations)**.

27 Coat each clutch plate with engine oil, then build up the plates in the housing, starting with the type C friction plate, then a plain plate and alternating type B friction and plain plates until all are installed **(see illustrations)**. Finally install the type A friction plate, locating its tangs in the shallow slots in the clutch housing rather than in the deep slots of the type B and C plates **(see illustration)**.

28 Install the anti-judder spring seat onto the clutch centre, followed by the anti-judder spring; note that the inner edge of the spring faces outwards **(see illustration)**.

17.26b . . . followed by the pressure plate

17.27a Fit the type C friction plate, identified by indents on its tangs (arrow) . . .

17.27b . . . followed by a plain plate . . .

17.27c . . . then alternating type B friction plates and plain plates . . .

17.27d . . . and finally install the type A friction plate, the tangs of which locate in the shallow slots in the housing (arrows)

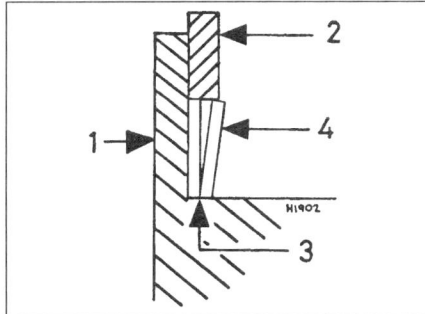

17.28 Correct fitting of anti-judder spring

1 Clutch centre   3 Spring seat
2 Type A plate   4 Anti-judder spring

17.29a Install the clutch centre . . .

17.29b . . . followed by the washer and clutch nut

17.29c Stake the clutch nut against the indent in the end of the mainshaft using a suitable punch

17.30a Install the clutch springs . . .

17.30b . . . followed by the release plate and its bolts

17.31 The release rod must locate in the cutout in the shaft (arrow)

17.32 Install the crankcase cover

29 Install the clutch centre onto the mainshaft splines, then install the washer and the clutch nut **(see illustrations)**. Using the method employed on removal to lock the mainshaft, tighten the nut to the torque setting specified at the beginning of the Chapter. Stake the rim of the nut into the indent in the end of the mainshaft using a suitable punch **(see illustration)**. Whilst the clutch is locked, and if not already done (see Step 24), also tighten the oil pump driven sprocket bolt to the specified torque setting, having first applied a suitable non-permanent thread locking compound to its threads. **Note:** *Check that the clutch centre rotates freely after tightening.*

30 Install the clutch springs, release plate and release plate bolts and tighten them evenly in a criss-cross sequence **(see illustrations)**.
31 If disassembled, install the clutch release mechanism in the clutch cover **(see illustrations 17.21a and 17.21b)**. Align the shaft so that the release rod fits into its recess in the shaft **(see illustration)**.
32 If removed, insert the dowels in the crankcase **(see illustration 17.6)**. On J and K models, fit a new O-ring onto the oil orifice, then install the orifice into the crankcase with its larger diameter hole facing out. Install the crankcase cover using a new gasket, making sure it locates correctly over the dowels **(see**

illustration). Tighten the cover bolts evenly in a criss-cross sequence, making sure the clutch cable bracket is in its correct position **(see illustration 17.5)**.
33 On J and K models, install the external oil pipe lower bolt, using new sealing washers, and the pipe holder bolt, and tighten them to the specified torque setting.
34 Install the clutch cable onto the lever on the crankcase cover (see Section 18).
35 Install the rear cylinder exhaust pipe (see Chapter 4).
36 Refill the engine with oil (see Chapter 1).
37 Check the clutch lever freeplay and adjust if necessary (see Chapter 1).

2

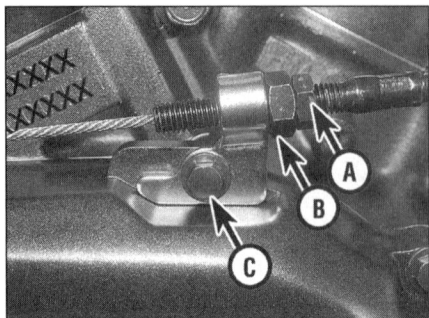

18.1a Clutch cable adjuster locknut (A), adjuster nut (B), and bracket bolt (C)

18.1b Detach the cable end from the lever . . .

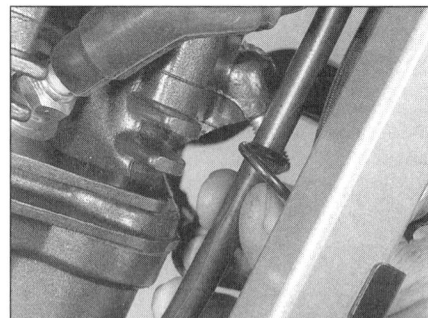

18.1c . . . and release the cable from its guide

18.4a Detach cable from the adjuster . . .

18.4b . . . and from the lever

If this work is being carried out with the engine already removed, ignore the preliminary steps.

Removal

1 Drain the engine oil (see Chapter 1).

2 Unscrew the gearchange linkage arm pinch bolt and remove the linkage arm from the shaft. Note the punch marks on the arm and the shaft which must be aligned on installation **(see illustration)**.

3 Remove the clutch (see Section 17).

4 Note how the gearchange selector arm claw fits onto the selector drum pins, and how the gearchange shaft centralising spring ends fit on each side of the locating pins **(see illustration)**. Lift the selector arm claw off the dowel pins in the selector drum and withdraw the gearchange shaft from the engine **(see illustrations)**.

5 Unscrew the bolt securing the selector drum stopper arm to the crankcase, then lift

18 Clutch cable -
removal and installation

1 Fully slacken the cable adjuster locknut and adjuster nut from the cable bracket mounted to the right-hand side crankcase cover **(see illustration)**. Disconnect the cable end from the clutch release mechanism lever, noting how it fits and release the adjuster from the bracket **(see illustration)**. Release the cable from the guide on the right-hand side frame downtube **(see illustration)**.

2 If necessary, unscrew the bolt securing the cable bracket to the crankcase and remove the bracket **(see illustration 18.1a)**.

3 Pull back the rubber cover from the clutch adjuster at the handlebar end of the cable (J and K models only). Fully slacken the lockwheel then screw the adjuster nut fully in. This resets it to the beginning of its adjustment span.

4 Align the slots in the adjuster and lockwheel with that in the lever bracket, then pull the outer cable end from the socket in the adjuster and release the inner cable from the lever **(see illustrations)**. Take note of the exact routing of the cable before withdrawing it - incorrect installation could result in poor steering movement.

5 Installation is the reverse of removal. Adjust the amount of clutch lever freeplay (see Chapter 1).

19 Gearchange mechanism -
removal, inspection and installation

Note: *The gearchange mechanism can be removed with the engine in the frame.*

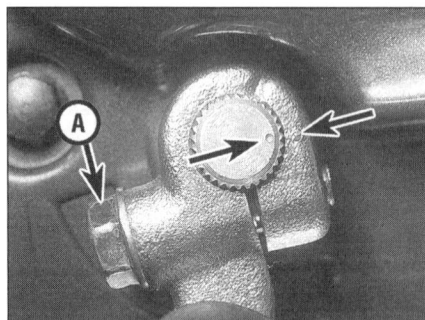

19.2 Unscrew the gearchange lever pinch bolt (A). Note the punch marks (arrows)

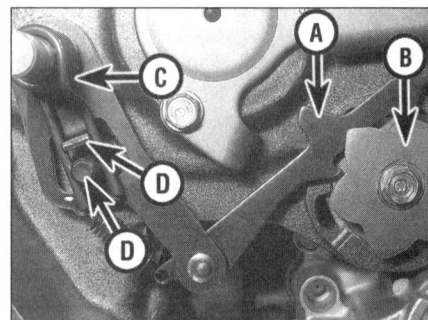

19.4b Lift the selector arm claw off the drum pins . . .

19.4a Selector arm claw (A), selector drum (B), centralising spring (C), pins (D)

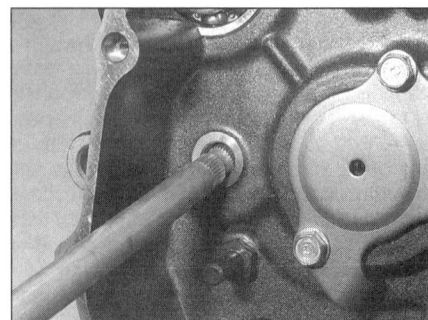

19.4c . . . and withdraw the shaft

19.5 Stopper arm (A), stopper arm bolt (B), stopper plate (C)

19.11 Install the stopper arm assembly

19.12 Make sure the centralising spring ends locate correctly over the pins (arrows)

the stopper arm off the stopper plate on the selector drum and remove the arm with its collar and return spring, noting how they fit **(see illustration)**.

6 If necessary, unscrew the bolt securing the stopper plate to the selector drum, then remove the plate, taking care not to lose any of the pins as you do. Remove the pins for safekeeping.

Inspection

7 Inspect the selector arm and the stopper arm return springs and the shaft centralising spring. If they are fatigued, worn or damaged they must be replaced.

8 Check the gearchange shaft for straightness and damage to the splines. If the shaft is bent you can attempt to straighten it, but if the splines are damaged the shaft must be replaced.

9 Inspect the selector arm claw and the pins, and the stopper arm roller and the stopper plate. If they are worn or damaged they must be replaced.

Installation

10 If removed, install the pins into the end of the selector drum, then install the stopper plate, making sure it locates correctly on the pins. Apply a suitable thread locking compound to the threads of the stopper plate bolt, then install the bolt and tighten it to the specified torque setting.

11 Install the stopper arm bolt with its washer through the stopper arm, the return spring and the collar, then install the assembly onto the crankcase. Position the stopper arm roller on the stopper plate and locate the spring ends correctly over the stopper arm and against the crankcase **(see illustration)**. Tighten the bolt securely. Make sure the stopper arm is free to move and is returned by the pressure of the spring.

12 Install the gearchange shaft assembly into its hole in the engine, lifting the selector arm claw into position on the selector drum pins. Ensure the centralising spring ends are correctly located on each side of the pins on the shaft and the crankcase **(see illustration)**.

13 Install the gearchange linkage arm onto the end of the shaft on the left-hand side of the engine, aligning the punch marks on the

arm and shaft, and check that the mechanism works correctly **(see illustration 19.2)**. Tighten the pinch bolt to the specified torque.

14 Install the clutch (see Section 17). Replenish the engine with oil (see Chapter 1).

20 Starter clutch and gear assembly - removal, inspection and installation

Note: *The starter clutch and idle gear assembly can be removed with the engine in the frame.*

Removal

1 Working in a criss-cross pattern, evenly slacken the left-hand side crankcase front cover retaining bolts **(see illustration)**. Lift the cover away from the engine, being prepared to catch any residual oil which may be

20.1a Left side crankcase front cover bolt locations (arrows)

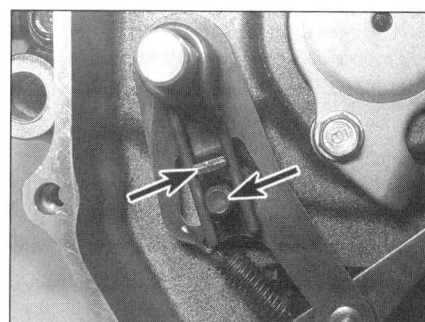

20.2 Starter drive gear (A), idle/reduction gear (B)

released as the cover is removed. Remove the gasket and discard it. Note the positions of the two locating dowels fitted to the crankcase and remove them for safe-keeping if they are loose **(see illustration)**.

2 Remove the starter drive gear and the idle/reduction gear along with their shafts **(see illustration)**. Note the "OUT" mark on the starter drive gear which must face outwards. Note also that the drive gear shaft is shorter than the idle/reduction gear shaft.

3 Remove the alternator rotor (see Chapter 9). If the starter driven gear does not come away with the rotor, remove it from the crankshaft along with the needle roller bearing. The starter clutch is secured to the back of the rotor by six Torx bolts.

Inspection

4 Install the starter driven gear into the starter clutch (if removed) **(see illustration)** and, with

20.1b Note the positions of the two dowels (arrows) - remove them if loose

20.4 Insert the driven gear into the starter clutch

2

20.6 Check the condition of the sprags in the starter clutch

20.7 Measure the driven gear hub diameter

20.10 The starter clutch is secured to the alternator rotor by six Torx bolts (arrows)

20.11a Fit the needle roller bearing into the starter driven gear . . .

20.11b . . . then fit the driven gear onto the end of the crankshaft

20.12 Make sure the thrust washer is installed in the starter clutch

20.13a Install the idle/reduction gear . . .

20.13b . . . and the starter drive gear with its "OUT" mark facing out

the rotor face down on a workbench, check that the gear rotates freely in an anti-clockwise direction and locks against the rotor in a clockwise direction. If it doesn't, replace the starter clutch.

5 Withdraw the starter driven gear from the starter clutch. If it appears stuck, rotate it anti-clockwise as you withdraw it to free it from the starter clutch.

6 Check the bearing surface of the starter driven gear hub and the condition of the sprags inside the clutch body (see illustration). If the bearing surface shows signs of excessive wear or the sprags are damaged, marked or flattened at any point, they should be replaced.

7 Measure the external diameter of the driven gear hub and compare it to the specifications at the beginning of the Chapter (see illustration). Replace the gear if it is worn beyond the service limit.

8 Check the needle roller bearing for signs of wear or damage and replace it if necessary.

9 Examine the teeth of the starter idle/reduction gear and the corresponding teeth of the starter driven gear and starter drive gear. Replace the gears as a set if worn or chipped teeth are discovered.

10 To replace the starter clutch sprag assembly, undo the six Torx bolts securing the clutch to the rotor (see illustration). Remove the clutch from the back of the rotor and separate the sprag assembly from the clutch body, noting how it fits. Install the new sprag assembly with its flanged side facing the alternator, then install the clutch assembly back onto the rotor. Apply a suitable thread locking compound to the bolts and tighten them to the torque setting specified at the beginning of the Chapter. Lubricate the starter clutch sprags with new engine oil.

Installation

11 Install the needle roller bearing into the starter driven gear, then install the starter driven gear over the bearing with the gear hub facing outwards (see illustrations).

12 Install the alternator rotor (see Chapter 9), making sure the thrust washer is installed in the back of the starter clutch (see illustration).

13 Install the idle/reduction gear and the starter drive gear with their shafts, making sure the longer shaft is installed with idle/reduction gear and the shorter shaft with the drive gear. Make sure the "OUT" mark on the drive gear faces outwards and that the smaller pinion on the idle/reduction gear faces inwards and meshes correctly with the teeth of the starter driven gear (see illustrations).

20.14a Fit a new gasket then install the cover

20.14b Apply thread-locking compound to the top right cover bolt

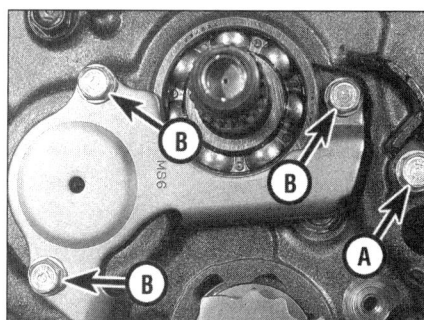

21.3 Cam chain tensioner set plate bolt (A), transmission shaft bearing set plate bolts (B) - later model type shown

14 If removed, insert the dowels in the crankcase **(see illustration 20.1b)**. Install the crankcase cover using a new gasket, making sure it locates correctly onto the dowels **(see illustration)**. Apply a suitable thread-locking compound to the top right-hand cover bolt **(see illustration)**, then tighten the cover bolts evenly in a criss-cross sequence.

21 Crankcase - separation and reassembly

Separation

1 To access the crankshaft and connecting rods, bearings, oil pump and transmission components, the crankcase must be split into two parts.
2 To enable the crankcases to be separated, the engine must be removed from the frame (see Section 5). Before the crankcases can be separated, the camshafts, cam chain tensioners, cylinder heads, cylinder blocks, ignition pulse generator coils, cam chains, clutch, gearchange mechanism, oil filter,

water pump, starter motor, alternator, starter clutch and starter idle/reduction gears must be removed. See the relevant Sections or Chapters for details.
3 Unscrew the bolt securing the cam chain tensioner set plate to the right-hand crankcase half and remove the set plate, noting how it fits **(see illustration)**. On J and K models the bolt for the plate on the right-hand side crankcase half also secures the right-hand end of the transmission shaft bearing set plate (see Step 4).
4 Unscrew the bolts securing the transmission shaft bearing set plate to the right-hand side crankcase half and remove the set plate, noting how it fits **(see illustration 21.3)**. On J and K models the right-hand bolt also secures the cam chain tensioner set plate and will already have been removed (see Step 3), and the mainshaft bearing has another retainer plate secured by one bolt on the right-hand side of the bearing.
5 Starting with the left-hand side crankcase half, unscrew the two 6 mm bolts followed by the four 8 mm bolts **(see illustration)**. Slacken each bolt 1/2 a turn at a time in a criss-cross pattern until they are all loose, then remove

the bolts. **Note:** *As each bolt is removed, store it in its relative position in a cardboard template of the crankcase halves. This will ensure all bolts are installed in the correct location on reassembly.*
6 Moving to the right-hand side crankcase half, unscrew the three 6 mm bolts followed by the eleven 8 mm bolts **(see illustration)**. Slacken each bolt 1/2 a turn at a time in a criss-cross pattern until they are all loose, then remove the bolts. Note the copper sealing washer on the top 8 mm bolt in between the cylinders. **Note:** *As each bolt is removed, store it in its relative position in a cardboard template of the crankcase halves. This will ensure all bolts are installed in the correct location on reassembly.*
7 Now the output driven shaft must be locked in order for the output drive shaft bolt to be removed **(see illustration 21.6)**. Honda provide a special tool (Pt. No. 07923-6890101) for locking the shaft, or alternatively install the universal joint onto the output drive shaft and engage 5th gear, then fit a suitable spanner onto the flats of the universal joint and secure it against the work surface **(see illustration 17.8a)**. This

2

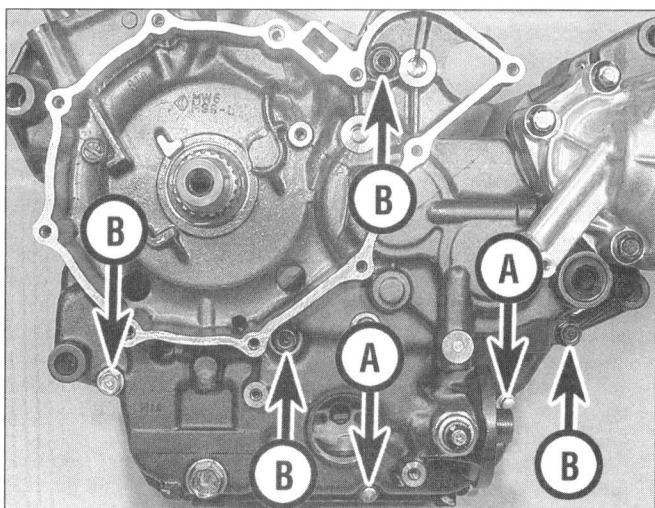

21.5 Left-hand side crankcase bolts - 6 mm (A), 8 mm (B)

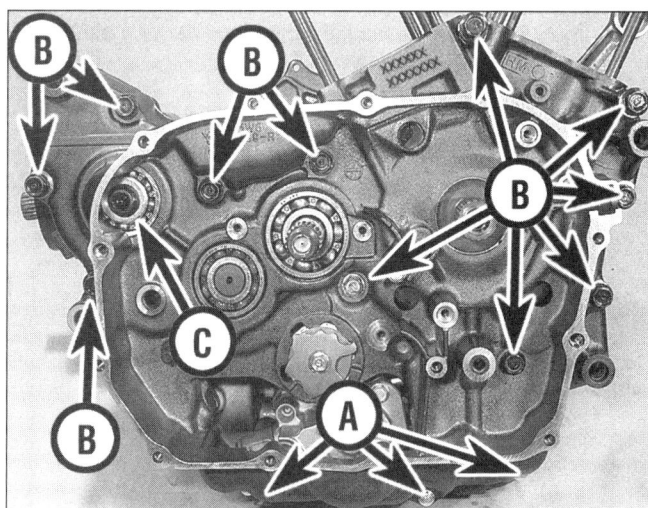

21.6 Right-hand side crankcase bolts - 6 mm (A), 8 mm (B) - and output drive shaft bolt (C)

21.7 With the transmission locked, remove the output drive shaft bolt

21.8a Rotate the selector drum stopper plate until the arms match the holes in the crankcase

21.8b Use a screwdriver on the leverage point (arrow) if necessary

21.9 Remove the two dowels (arrows) if they are loose

21.12 Lubricate all components, especially around the bearings, with oil

Reassembly

10 Remove all traces of sealant from the crankcase mating surfaces.

11 Ensure that all components and their bearings are in place in the right and left-hand crankcase halves. If the oil pump and its T-pipe have not been removed, install a new O-ring, with its tapered side facing out, onto the exposed end of the pipe T-piece. Check that the thrust washer is installed on the right-hand end of the transmission countershaft.

12 Generously lubricate the transmission shafts, selector drum and forks, and the crankshaft, particularly around the bearings, with clean engine oil, then use a rag soaked in high flash-point solvent to wipe over the gasket surfaces of both halves to remove all traces of oil (see illustration).

13 Install the two locating dowels in the left-hand crankcase half (see illustration 21.9).

14 If installed, make sure the stopper plate is positioned as on removal to allow the right-hand crankcase half to fit over it (see illustration 21.8a).

15 Apply a small amount of suitable sealant to the mating surface of the right-hand crankcase half (see illustration).

Caution: Do not apply an excessive amount of sealant, as it will ooze out when the case halves are assembled and may obstruct oil passages.

16 Check again that all components are in position, then carefully install the right-hand crankcase half down onto the left-hand crankcase half (see illustration). Make sure the dowels and shaft ends all locate correctly into the right-hand crankcase half.

17 Check that the right-hand crankcase half is correctly seated. Note: The crankcase halves should fit together without being forced. If the casings are not correctly seated, remove the right-hand crankcase half and investigate the problem. Do not attempt to pull them together using the crankcase bolts as the casing will crack and be ruined.

18 Lift the engine off its left-hand side and position it upright. Apply a suitable thread-locking compound to the threads of the output drive shaft bolt, then, using the method employed in Step 7 to lock the output driven

21.15 Apply sealant to the mating surface of the right-hand crankcase half

21.16 Fit the right-hand crankcase half down onto the left

locks the transmission and allows the output drive shaft bolt to be removed (see illustration).

8 Carefully turn the engine onto its side with the left-hand side crankcase half facing down. If the gear selector drum stopper plate has not been removed (see Section 19), rotate it so that its outline shape matches the hole in the right-hand crankcase half, otherwise it will snag on the case when it is lifted (see illustration). Carefully lift the right-hand crankcase half off the left-hand half, using a screwdriver on the leverage point and a soft hammer to tap around the joint to initially separate the halves if necessary (see illustration). Note: If the halves do not separate easily, make sure all fasteners have been removed. Do not try and separate the halves by levering against the crankcase

mating surfaces as they are easily scored and will leak oil. Use only the special leverage point. The right-hand side crankcase half will come away by itself, leaving the oil pump, crankshaft, transmission shafts, selector drum and selector forks in the left-hand crankcase half.

9 Remove the two locating dowels from the crankcase if they are loose (they could be in either crankcase half), noting their locations (see illustration). If the oil pump and its T-pipe are not being disturbed, remove the exposed O-ring from the oil pipe T-piece, noting which way up it fits, and discard it as a new one must be used. Check that the thrust washer is on the right-hand end of the transmission countershaft; if not, it is probably stuck to the bearing in the right-hand crankcase half.

21.18 Apply thread-locking compound to the output drive shaft bolt threads and tighten it to the specified torque setting

21.20 Make sure the copper sealing washer is installed with the top bolt between the cylinders

shaft, tighten the bolt to the torque setting specified at the beginning of the Chapter **(see illustration)**.

19 Check that the transmission shafts rotate freely and independently in neutral, then rotate the selector drum by hand and select each gear in turn whilst rotating the mainshaft. Check that all gears can be selected and that the shafts rotate freely in every gear.

20 Clean and oil the threads of the right-hand crankcase bolts and insert them in their original locations **(see illustration 21.6)**. Make sure the copper sealing washer is installed with the top 8 mm bolt in between the cylinders **(see illustration)**. Secure all bolts hand-tight at first, then tighten the eleven 8 mm bolts followed by the three 6 mm bolts 1/2 a turn at a time in a criss-cross pattern to the torque setting specified at the beginning of the Chapter. When torquing the bolts, be sure to distinguish correctly between the 8 mm bolts and the 6 mm bolts.

21 Clean and oil the threads of the left-hand crankcase bolts and install them in their original locations **(see illustration 21.5)**. Secure all bolts hand-tight at first, then tighten the four 8 mm bolts followed by the two 6 mm bolts 1/2 a turn at a time in a criss-cross pattern to the torque setting specified at the beginning of the Chapter. When torquing the bolts, be sure to distinguish correctly between the 8 mm bolts and the 6 mm bolts.

22 With all crankcase fasteners tightened, check that the crankshaft and transmission shafts rotate smoothly and easily. Check the operation of the transmission in each gear (see Step 19). If there are any signs of undue stiffness, tight or rough spots, or of any other problem, the fault must be rectified before proceeding further.

23 Install all other removed assemblies in the reverse of the sequence given in Steps 2 to 4. Apply a suitable thread-locking compound to the transmission shaft bearing set plate bolts.

22 Crankcase - inspection and servicing

1 After the crankcases have been separated and the crankshaft, oil pump and transmission components have been removed, the crankcases should be cleaned thoroughly with solvent and dried with compressed air.

2 Remove the oil jet from each crankcase half, and check the condition of their O-rings, replacing them if necessary **(see illustrations)**. All oil passages should be blown out with compressed air. Apply clean engine oil to the oil jet O-rings before installing them back in the engine.

3 All traces of old gasket sealant should be removed from the mating surfaces. Minor damage to the surfaces can be cleaned up with a fine sharpening stone or grindstone. **Caution:** *Be very careful not to nick or gouge the crankcase mating surfaces or oil leaks will result. Check both crankcase halves very carefully for cracks and other damage.*

4 Small cracks or holes in aluminium castings may be repaired with an epoxy resin adhesive as a temporary measure. Permanent repairs can only be effected by argon-arc welding, and only a specialist in this process is in a

position to advise on the economy or practical aspect of such a repair. If any damage is found that can't be repaired, replace the crankcase halves as a set.

5 Damaged threads can be economically reclaimed by using a diamond section wire insert, of the Helicoil type, which is easily fitted after drilling and re-tapping the affected thread. Most motorcycle dealers and small engineering firms offer a service of this kind.

6 Sheared studs or screws can usually be removed with screw extractors, which consist of a tapered, left-hand thread screw of very hard steel. These are inserted into a pre-drilled hole in the stud or screw, and usually succeed in dislodging the most stubborn stud or screw. If a problem arises which seems beyond your scope, it is worth consulting an engineering firm before condemning an otherwise sound casing. Many of these firms advertise regularly in the motorcycle press.

7 Check that all the cylinder studs are tight in the crankcase halves. If any are loose, remove them, then clean their threads and apply a suitable non-permanent thread locking compound and tighten them to the torque setting specified at the beginning of the Chapter. When torquing the studs, be sure to distinguish correctly between the 8 mm stud and the 10 mm studs.

2

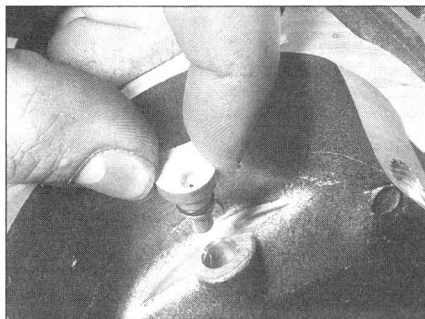

22.2a Remove the oil jet . . .

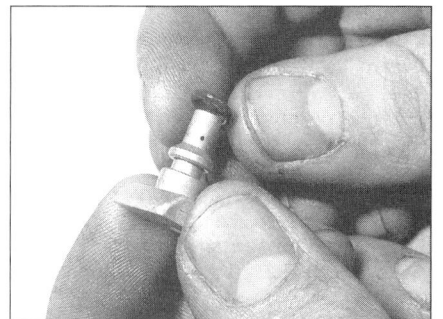

22.2b . . . renew the O-ring if necessary

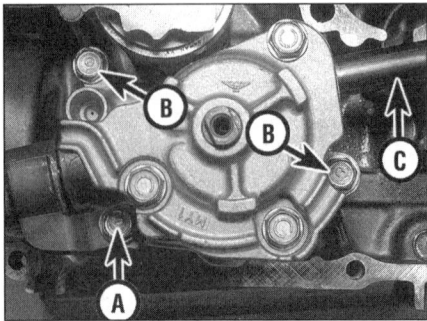

23.2a Pressure relief valve cover bolt (A), pump mounting bolts (B), T-pipe (C)

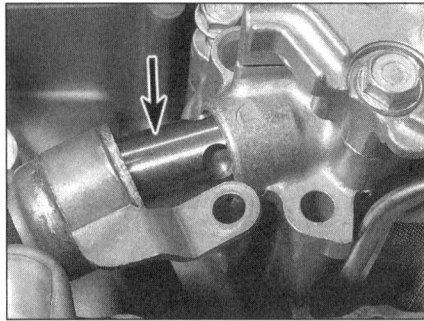

23.2b Remove the pressure relief valve cover and withdraw the valve (arrow) from the pump

23.3 Remove the dowels and discard their O-rings

23.5a Unscrew the three bolts (arrows)

23.5b Remove the two dowels if they are loose

23.9 Measure the rotor tip clearance as shown

23 Oil pump and pressure relief valve - removal, inspection, installation and pressure check

Removal

1 Separate the crankcase halves (Section 21).
2 Unscrew the bolt securing the pressure relief valve cover to the pump, then remove the cover from the end of the relief valve and withdraw the valve from the pump (see illustrations). Discard the valve O-ring as a new one must be used.
3 Unscrew the two bolts securing the pump assembly to the crankcase, then remove the pump along with its T-pipe (see illustration 23.2a). Remove the two large pump dowels from the crankcase and discard their O-rings as new ones must be used (see illustration). Remove the small pump dowel if it is loose.

Inspection

4 Remove the T-pipe from the pump and discard its O-rings as new ones must be used.
5 Unscrew the three bolts securing the pump body to the cover and separate the body from the cover (see illustration). Remove the dowels from either the body or the cover if they are loose (see illustration).
6 Remove the oil strainer and its seal from the pump cover. Discard the seal as a new one must be used.
7 Withdraw the pump drive shaft along with its thrust washer, and the inner and outer

23.10 Measure the outer rotor to body clearance as shown

rotors from the pump body. Note how the pin locates through the shaft and in the notches in the inner rotor, and how the punch mark on the outer rotor faces the pump cover. Clean all the components in solvent.
8 Inspect the pump body and rotors for scoring and wear. If any damage, scoring or uneven or excessive wear is evident, replace the pump (individual components are not available).
9 Measure the clearance between the inner rotor tip and the outer rotor with a feeler gauge and compare it to the maximum clearance listed in the specifications at the beginning of the Chapter (see illustration). If the clearance measured is greater than the maximum listed, replace the pump.
10 Measure the clearance between the outer rotor and the pump body with a feeler gauge and compare it to the maximum clearance listed in the specifications at the beginning of

23.11 Measure the rotor end float as shown

the Chapter (see illustration). If the clearance measured is greater than the maximum listed, replace the pump.
11 Lay a straightedge across the rotors and the pump body and, using a feeler gauge, measure the rotor end float (the gap between the rotors and the straightedge) (see illustration). If the clearance measured is greater than the maximum listed, replace the pump.
12 Remove the circlip from the end of the relief valve body and withdraw the washer, spring and valve plunger. Clean all the components in solvent. Check that the plunger moves freely in the body and inspect it for wear or damage. If the valve is good, install the plunger into the body, followed by the spring and the washer, and secure them in place with the circlip. Note that apart from the O-ring, none of the relief valve components are available separately.

23.14a Install the outer rotor . . .

23.14b . . . followed by the inner rotor

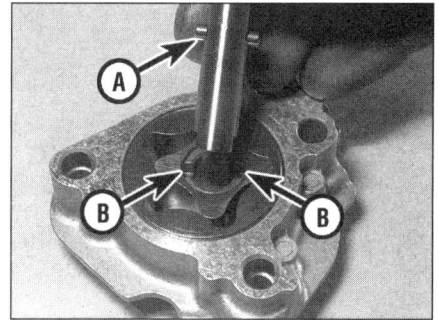

23.14c The pin (A) must locate in the notches (B) in the inner rotor

23.14d Install the thrust washer over the shaft and onto the inner rotor

23.15a Fit a new seal to the strainer . . .

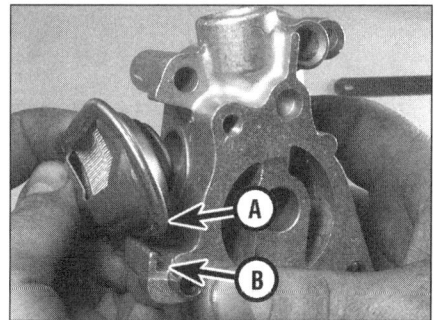

23.15b . . . then install the strainer with its rim (A) fitting into the slot (B) in the cover

23.16a Fit the two dowels (arrows), then install the cover onto the pump . . .

23.16b . . . and secure it with its bolts

2

13 Check the pump drive chain and sprockets for wear or damage, and replace them as a set if necessary.

14 If the pump is good, make sure all the components are clean, then lubricate them with new engine oil. Install the outer rotor into the pump body with the punch mark facing out, towards the pump cover **(see illustration)**. Install the inner rotor into the outer rotor so that its notches face outwards **(see illustration)**. Fit the pin into the pump drive shaft and install the shaft into the inner rotor, making sure the pin fits into the notches in the inner rotor **(see illustration)**. Install the thrust washer over the shaft and onto the inner rotor **(see illustration)**.

15 Make sure the strainer is clean and free of any debris, then install it onto the pump cover using a new seal, making sure its rim fits into the slot in the cover **(see illustrations)**.

16 Install the dowels into the pump body, then install the cover, making sure it locates correctly over the dowels **(see illustration)**. Install the three bolts into the pump body and tighten them securely **(see illustration)**.

17 Fit new O-rings, with their tapered side facing out, to each end of the pump T-pipe, then install the pipe into the pump **(see illustrations)**.

23.17a Fit new O-rings to the pump T-pipe with their tapered side facing out . . .

23.17b . . . then install the pipe into the pump

23.18a Fit new O-rings around the two large dowels

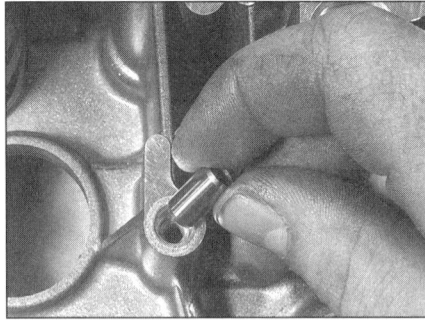
23.18b Install the small pump dowel if removed

23.20a Make sure the pump locates onto the dowels . . .

23.20b . . . and the T-pipe fits into its hole

23.20c Secure the pump with its mounting bolts

Installation

18 Install the two large pump dowels into the crankcase and fit new O-rings around them **(see illustration)**. If removed, also install the small pump dowel **(see illustration)**.

19 Before installing the pump, prime it by pouring oil into the outlet and turning the shaft by hand. This ensures that oil is being pumped as soon as the engine is turned over.

20 Install the pump with its T-pipe onto the crankcase, making sure the pump locates correctly onto the dowels and the pipe is properly inserted into its hole **(see**

illustrations)**. Install the pump assembly bolts and tighten them securely **(see illustration)**.

21 Fit a new O-ring onto the pressure relief valve, then install the valve into the pump **(see illustration)**. Install the valve cover over the end of the valve and secure it with its bolt **(see illustration)**.

Pressure check

22 To check the oil pressure, a suitable gauge and adapter piece (which screws into the oil pressure switch thread) will be needed.

23 Warm the engine up to normal operating temperature then stop it.

24 Unscrew the gearchange linkage arm pinch bolt and remove the linkage arm from the shaft **(see illustration 5.16)**. Note the punch marks on the arm and the shaft which must be aligned on installation.

25 Unscrew the bolts securing the left-hand side crankcase rear cover and remove the cover **(see illustration 5.17a)**. The oil pressure switch is located between the water pump and oil filter. Pull back the rubber boot, then remove the screw securing the wiring connector to the switch **(see illustration 5.17c)**.

23.21a Install the pressure relief valve with a new O-ring . . .

23.21b . . . then fit the valve cover

26 Unscrew the switch and swiftly screw the adapter into the crankcase threads. Connect the gauge to the adapter.

27 Start the engine and increase the engine speed to 6000 rpm whilst watching the gauge reading. The oil pressure should be similar to that given in the Specifications at the start of this Chapter.

28 If the pressure is significantly lower than the standard, either the relief valve is stuck open, the oil pump is faulty, the oil pump pick-up strainer is blocked or there is other engine damage. Begin diagnosis by checking the oil pump pick-up strainer and relief valve, then the oil pump. If those items check out okay, chances are the bearing oil clearances are excessive and the engine needs to be overhauled.

29 If the pressure is too high, the relief valve is stuck closed. To check it, see above.

30 Stop the engine and unscrew the gauge and adapter from the crankcase.

31 Having applied a smear of sealant to its threads, install the oil pressure switch and tighten it securely. Reconnect its wire terminal and fit the dust cover over the switch. Check the oil level (see Chapter 1).

32 Install the crankcase rear cover. Align the punch marks on the gearchange linkage arm and shaft when installing the arm on the shaft **(see illustration 5.28)**, and tighten the pinch bolt to the specified torque setting.

24 Transmission shafts - removal and installation

Mainshaft and countershaft

Removal

1 Separate the crankcase halves (Section 21).

2 Remove the thrust washer, driven gear and its bushing from the end of the output drive shaft **(see illustrations)**. Note how the driven gear locates onto the damper cam on the shaft.

3 Grasp the mainshaft and countershaft and the selector drum and forks as an assembly and withdraw them from the crankcase as a unit, noting their relative positions in the crankcase and how they fit. With the assembly on a bench, separate the mainshaft, countershaft and selector drum and forks, noting how the selector forks engage in the grooves on the gear pinions and the tracks in the selector drum.

4 Note that each selector fork is marked for identification. The left-hand shift fork is marked with an "L", the middle shift fork is marked with a "C", and the right-hand shift fork is marked with an "R", all of which must face the right-hand crankcase. If removed, install the forks back on the shaft in their correct positions as a reminder for installation.

5 Check whether the thrust washer for the countershaft end is on the shaft or in the crankcase (probably lying loose on the bearing). Install the washer onto the left-hand end of the shaft as a reminder for installation. Also check that the thrust washer is in position on the right-hand end of the countershaft.

6 If necessary, the mainshaft and counter-shaft can be disassembled and inspected for wear or damage as described in Section 25.

Installation

7 Lay the mainshaft and countershaft side by side on the bench so that the pinions for each gear are meshed together. Make sure that the shafts are the correct way round, in which case the smallest pinion on the mainshaft is on the right-hand end and meshes with the second largest pinion on the countershaft, which is the second pinion from the right. Also make sure that the thrust washer is installed on each end of the countershaft. Install the selector forks in position with their identification marks positioned as described in Step 4. Engage the forks in their grooves in the pinions on the shafts.

8 The mainshaft and countershaft and the selector drum and forks must be installed as a complete assembly. To achieve this without the entire assembly falling apart as it is installed, it is advisable to strap the shafts and selector forks together using cable ties **(see illustrations)**.

24.2a Remove the thrust washer . . .

24.2b . . . the driven gear . . .

24.2c . . . and the bushing from the output drive shaft

2

24.8a Transmission shafts and selector forks shown strapped as an assembly with the right-hand end upwards

24.8b Transmission shafts and selector forks shown strapped as an assembly with the left-hand end facing

24.9a Engage the selector drum tracks with the guide pins on the selector forks . . .

24.9b . . . and install the assembly into the crankcase

9 Engage the forks with the selector drum so that their guide pins locate in the selector drum tracks **(see illustration)**. Grasp the mainshaft and countershaft and the selector drum and forks and install them into the left-hand crankcase, making sure that both mainshaft and countershaft ends engage in their bearings and the selector fork shaft end and the selector drum end engage in their holes in the crankcase. If cable ties were used, cut them and slip them out of position.
10 Check that both the mainshaft and countershaft, the selector drum and selector forks all rotate or move freely.
11 Install the driven gear bushing, driven gear pinion and thrust washer on the end of the output drive shaft **(see illustrations 24.2c, 24.2b and 24.2a)**.
12 Reassemble the crankcase halves (see Section 21).

Output shafts

Removal

13 Separate the crankcase halves and remove the mainshaft, countershaft and selector drum (see Section 21 and Steps 2 to 5 above).
14 Unscrew the three bolts securing the output shaft housing assembly to the left-hand

crankcase, noting the locations of the different length bolts, and remove the assembly **(see illustration)**. Discard the housing O-ring as a new one must be used.
15 Remove the oil orifice from the crankcase or the housing **(see illustration)**. Discard its O-rings as new ones must be used.

Installation

16 Make sure the oil orifice is clear, using compressed air to blow through it if available. Fit new O-rings to the orifice and install it into the output shaft housing.

24.14 The output shaft housing assembly is secured to the crankcase by three bolts (arrows)

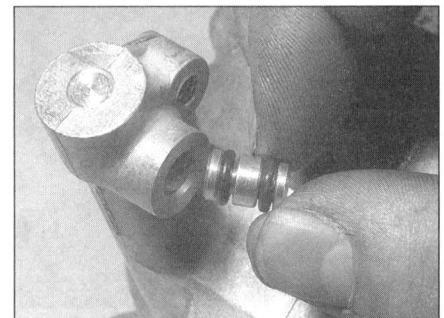

24.15 Remove the oil orifice and replace its O-rings with new ones

17 Fit a new O-ring to the output shaft housing assembly **(see illustration)**. Install the housing into the crankcase, making sure the locating pin on the mating surface of the housing fits into its hole in the crankcase **(see illustrations)**. Install the three housing bolts, making sure they are installed in their correct locations **(see illustration 24.14)**, and tighten them to the specified torque setting.
18 Install the mainshaft, countershaft and selector drum assembly, then reassemble the crankcase halves (see Steps 7 to 11 above and Section 21).

24.17a Fit a new O-ring to the housing

24.17b Make sure the locating pin (arrow) . . .

24.17c . . . fits into its hole in the crankcase (arrow)

25 Transmission shafts - disassembly, inspection and reassembly

1 Remove the transmission shafts from the left crankcase half (see Section 24). Always disassemble the transmission shafts separately to avoid mixing up the components.

Mainshaft

Disassembly

2 Remove the thrust washer from the left-hand end of the shaft, followed by the 2nd gear pinion **(see illustration)**.

> **HAYNES HiNT**
> *When disassembling the transmission shafts, place the parts on a long rod or thread a wire through them to keep them in order and facing the proper direction.*

3 Remove the circlip from the shaft. Slide the splined washer and the 5th gear pinion off the shaft, followed by the 5th gear splined bush and splined washer.
4 Remove the circlip securing the 3rd gear pinion, then slide the pinion off the shaft.
5 Remove the circlip securing the 4th gear pinion, then slide the splined washer and the pinion off the shaft, followed by the 4th gear bush and the thrust washer.
6 The 1st gear pinion is integral with the shaft.

Inspection

7 Wash all of the components in clean solvent and dry them off.
8 Check the gear teeth for cracking chipping, pitting and other obvious wear or damage. Any pinion that is damaged as such must be replaced.
9 Inspect the dogs and the dog holes in the gears for cracks, chips, and excessive wear especially in the form of rounded edges. Make sure mating gears engage properly. Replace the paired gears as a set if necessary.
10 Check for signs of scoring or blueing on the pinions, bushes and shaft. This could be caused by overheating due to inadequate

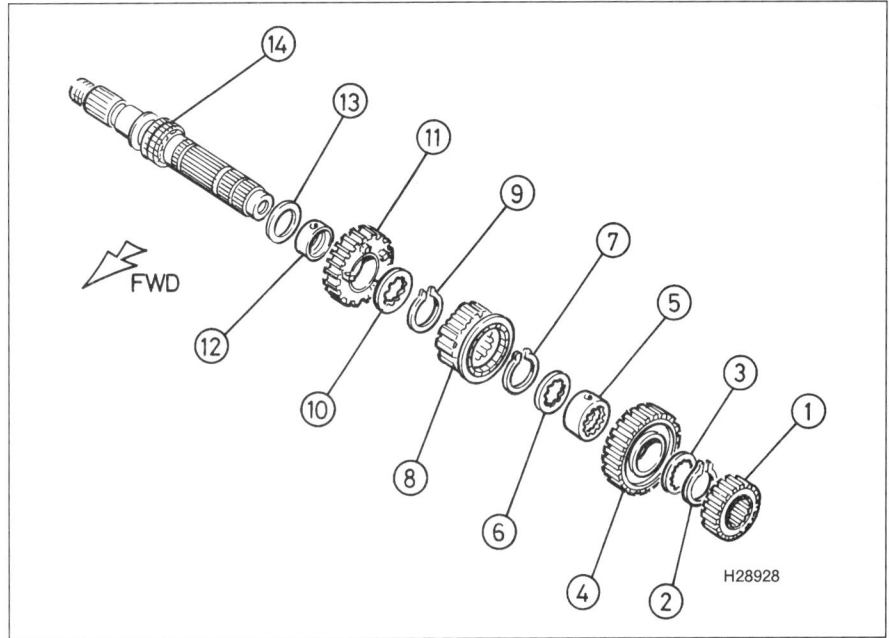

25.2 Mainshaft components

1 2nd gear pinion	6 Splined washer	11 4th gear pinion
2 Circlip	7 Circlip	12 4th gear bush
3 Splined washer	8 3rd gear pinion	13 Thrust washer
4 5th gear pinion	9 Circlip	14 1st gear pinion (integral
5 5th gear splined bush	10 Splined washer	with shaft)

lubrication. Check that all the oil holes and passages are clear. Replace any damaged pinions or bushes.
11 Check that each pinion moves freely on the shaft or bush but without undue freeplay. Check that each bush moves freely on the shaft but without undue freeplay. Measure the internal diameter of all gears which run on bushes and the external diameter of the bushes which they run on **(see illustrations)**. If either component has worn to beyond its service limit it must be replaced. Using the above measurements calculate the gear-to-bush clearance and compare the results to the specifications listed at the beginning of the Chapter. If the clearance exceeds the specified limit replace the relevant gear and bush as a pair. Also measure the internal diameters of the bushes and their

corresponding shaft external diameter, and calculate the shaft-to-bush clearance.
12 The shaft is unlikely to sustain damage unless the engine has seized, placing an unusually high loading on the transmission, or the machine has covered a very high mileage. Check the surface of the shaft, especially where a pinion turns on it, and replace the shaft if it has scored or picked up, or if there are any cracks. Place the shaft on V-blocks and check the runout at the shaft centre using a dial gauge. Damage of any kind can only be cured by replacement.
13 Check the bearings for play or roughness, and that they are a tight fit in the crankcase **(see illustration)**. Replace any bearing that is worn. To remove the bearings, heat the crankcase half to loosen their fit in the casing. If all other components have been removed

2

25.11a Measure the internal diameter of the gear . . .

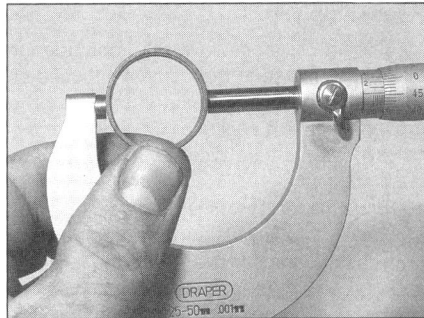

25.11b . . . and the external diameter of its bush

25.13 Check the transmission shaft bearings in the crankcase

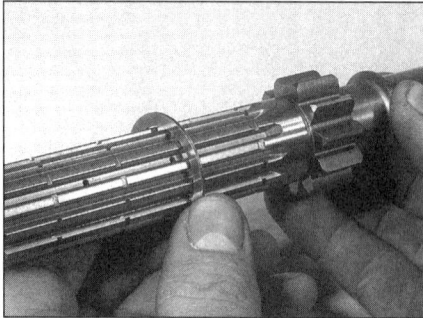

25.16a Install the thrust washer . . .

25.16b . . . followed by the
4th gear bush . . .

25.16c . . . and the 4th gear pinion

25.16d Install the splined washer . . .

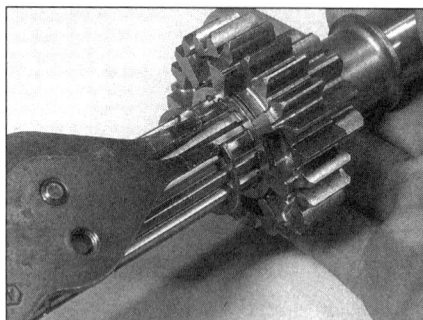

25.16e . . . followed by the circlip

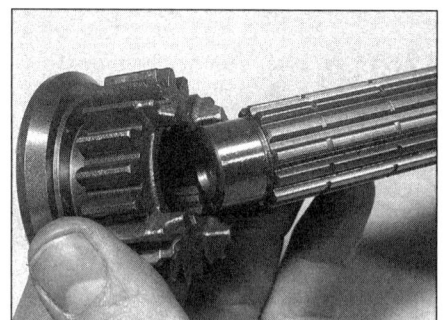

25.17a Install the 3rd gear pinion . . .

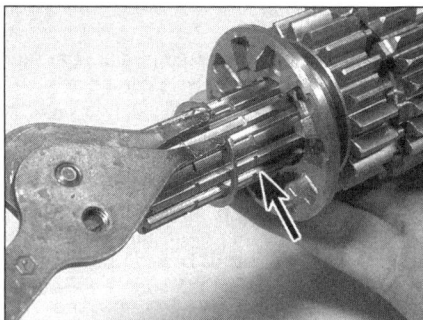

25.17b . . . and the circlip, making sure it
locates in its groove (arrow)

25.18a Install the splined washer . . .

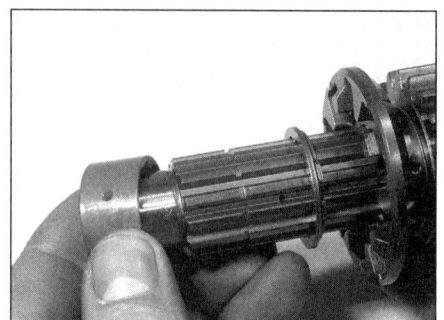

25.18b . . . followed by the 5th gear
splined bush . . .

from the casing, the best way to do this is to immerse the casing in boiling water for a few minutes (taking care not to scald your hands), then tap the casing face down on a wooden work surface - this should jar them free. If stubborn, the bearings in the right-hand half can be drifted from position, although be careful to support the area of casing around the bearing housing. The bearings in the left-hand half are fitted into blind holes, necessitating a knife-edged bearing puller with slide-hammer attachment to remove them. Note that the set plate behind each of the bearings in the left-hand half must be replaced with a new one on installation. Install all bearings using a hammer and drift (such as a socket) which only bears on the outer race of the bearing. Apply clean engine oil to the bearings.

14 Check the circlips and thrust washers and replace any that are bent or appear weakened or worn. It is a good idea to use new circlips as a matter of course.

Reassembly

15 During reassembly, apply molybdenum disulphide grease to the inside and outside of the bushes, and lubricate all the other components with engine oil. Make sure the oil holes in the shaft are aligned with those on the bush or pinion.

16 Slide the thrust washer, 4th gear bush and 4th gear pinion, with its dogs facing away from the integral 1st gear, onto the left-hand end of the shaft (see illustrations). Install the splined washer and circlip, making sure that the circlip locates in the groove in the shaft (see illustrations).

17 Install the 3rd gear pinion onto the shaft with its selector fork groove facing away from the 4th gear pinion and secure it in place with the circlip, making sure it locates properly in its groove (see illustrations).

18 Install the splined washer, the 5th gear splined bushing, the 5th gear pinion, with its dogs facing the 3rd gear pinion, and the splined washer, then secure them in place with the circlip, making sure that the circlip locates in the groove in the shaft (see illustrations).

19 Install the 2nd gear pinion (see illustrations).

Countershaft

Disassembly

20 Remove the thrust washer from the left-hand end of the shaft, then slide the 2nd gear

25.18c . . . the 5th gear pinion . . .

25.18d . . . the splined washer . . .

25.18e . . . and the circlip

pinion, the 2nd gear bushing, the thrust washer and the 5th gear pinion off the shaft **(see illustration)**.

21 Remove the thrust washer from the right-hand end of the shaft, then slide the output drive gear, the 1st gear pinion, the 1st gear splined bushing and the splined washer off the shaft.

22 Remove the circlip securing the 4th gear pinion, then slide the pinion off the shaft.

23 Remove the circlip securing the 3rd gear pinion, then slide the splined washer, the 3rd gear bush, the 3rd gear pinion and the thrust washer off the shaft.

Inspection

24 Wash all of the components in clean solvent and dry them off.

25 Check the gear teeth for cracking chipping, pitting and other obvious wear or damage. Check that the rivets in the output drive gear are tight and secure. Any pinion that is damaged as such must be replaced.

26 Inspect the dogs and the dog holes in the gears for cracks, chips, and excessive wear especially in the form of rounded edges. Make sure mating gears engage properly. Replace the paired gears as a set if necessary.

27 Check for signs of scoring or blueing on the pinions, bushes and shaft. This could be caused by overheating due to inadequate lubrication. Check that all the oil holes and passages are clear. Replace any damaged pinions or bushes.

28 Check that each pinion moves freely on the shaft or bush but without undue freeplay. Check that each bush moves freely on the shaft but without undue freeplay. Measure the internal diameter of all gears which run on bushes and the external diameter of the bushes which they run on **(see illustrations 25.11a and 25.11b)**. If either component has worn to beyond its service limit it must be replaced. Using the above measurements calculate the gear-to-bushing clearance and compare the results to the specifications listed at the beginning of the Chapter. If the clearance exceeds the specified limit replace the relevant gear and bushing as a pair. Also measure the internal diameters of the bushes and their corresponding shaft external diameter, and calculate the shaft-to-bushing clearance.

25.19a Install the 2nd gear pinion

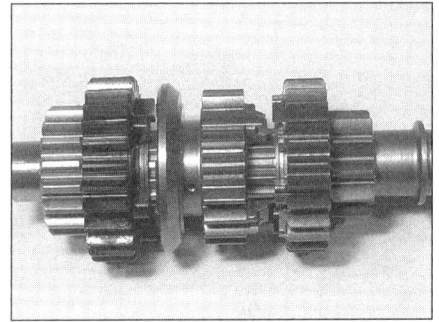

25.19b The assembled mainshaft should look like this

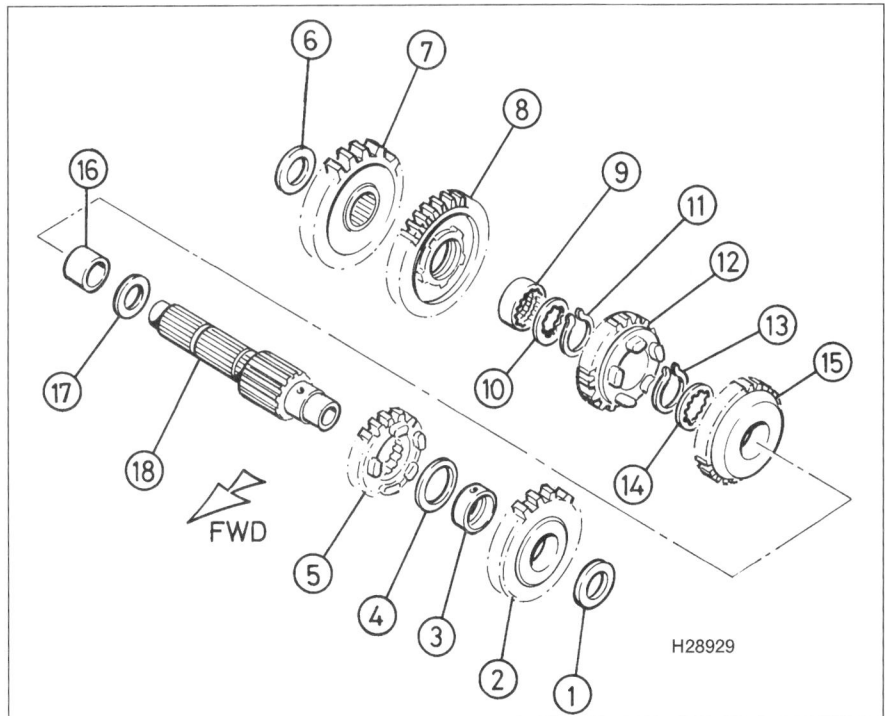

25.20 Countershaft components

1 Thrust washer	7 Output drive gear	13 Circlip
2 2nd gear pinion	8 1st gear pinion	14 Splined washer
3 2nd gear bush	9 1st gear splined bush	15 3rd gear pinion
4 Thrust washer	10 Splined washer	16 3rd gear bush
5 5th gear pinion	11 Circlip	17 Thrust washer
6 Thrust washer	12 4th gear pinion	18 Countershaft

H28929

FWD

2

25.33a Install the thrust washer . . .

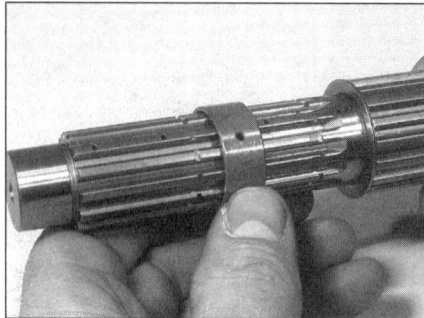

25.33b . . . then the 3rd gear bush . . .

25.33c . . . the 3rd gear pinion . . .

25.33d . . . the splined washer . . .

25.33e . . . and the circlip

25.34a Install the 4th gear pinion . . .

29 The shaft is unlikely to sustain damage unless the engine has seized, placing an unusually high loading on the transmission, or the machine has covered a very high mileage. Check the surface of the shaft, especially where a pinion turns on it, and replace the shaft if it has scored or picked up, or if there are any cracks. Place the shaft on V-blocks and check the runout at the shaft centre using a dial gauge. Damage of any kind can only be cured by replacement.

30 Check the bearings for play or roughness, and that they are a tight fit in the crankcase **(see illustration 25.13)**. Replace any bearing that is worn. To remove the bearings, heat the crankcase half and drift the bearing out using a suitable drift, or by using a bearing remover. Discard the bearing set plate from the left-hand side crankcase and install a new one. Install the new bearings using a suitable bearing driver. Apply clean oil to the bearings before installation.

31 Check the circlips and thrust washers and replace any that are bent or appear weakened or worn. It is a good idea to use new circlips as a matter of course.

Reassembly

32 During reassembly, apply molybdenum disulphide grease inside and outside of the bushes, and lubricate all the other parts with engine oil. Make sure the oil holes in the shaft are aligned with those on the bush or pinion.

33 Install the thrust washer onto the narrow end of the shaft, followed by the 3rd gear bush, the 3rd gear pinion, with its dog holes facing out, and the splined washer, and secure them in place with the circlip, making

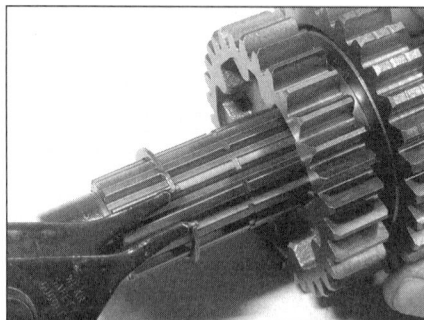

25.34b . . . and the circlip . . .

25.34c . . . making sure it is correctly seated in its groove (arrow)

25.35a Install the splined washer . . .

25.35b . . . followed by the 1st gear splined bush . . .

sure it is properly seated in its groove **(see illustrations)**.

34 Install the 4th gear pinion onto the shaft with its selector fork groove facing the 3rd gear pinion and secure it in place with the circlip, making sure it is properly seated in its groove **(see illustrations)**.

35 Install the splined washer, followed by the 1st gear splined bushing, the 1st gear pinion, the output drive gear and the thrust washer **(see illustrations)**.

36 Install the 5th gear pinion onto the wide end of the shaft with its dogs facing away from the 3rd gear pinion, followed by the

25.35c . . . the 1st gear pinion . . .

25.35d . . . the output drive gear . . .

25.35e . . . and the thrust washer

25.36a Install the 5th gear pinion . . .

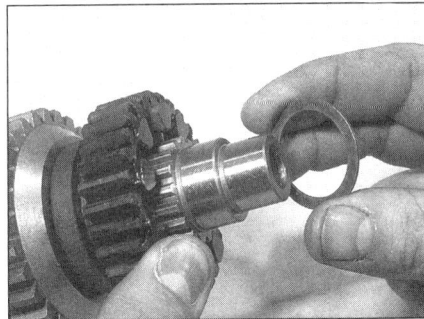
25.36b . . . then the thrust washer . . .

25.36c . . . the 2nd gear bush . . .

25.36d . . . the 2nd gear pinion . . .

25.36e . . . and the thrust washer

25.36f The assembled countershaft
should look like this

2

thrust washer, the 2nd gear bush, the 2nd gear pinion and the thrust washer **(see illustrations)**.

Output shafts

Disassembly

37 During the normal course of events the output shaft assemblies should last throughout the life of the motorcycle without the need for overhaul or component replacement. If the bearings or any other components need to be removed or replaced, the whole housing assembly should be taken to a Honda dealer as specialised equipment and skills are needed to replace the bearings. If either of the bevel gear shafts become worn or damaged, they are only available, and must be replaced, as a matched pair, and again this should be carried out by a Honda dealer.

38 For access to the drive shaft bevel gear and shim, unscrew the two bolts securing the

drive shaft bearing housing to the main housing and remove the bearing housing and shaft as an assembly **(see illustration)**. Discard the bearing housing O-ring as a new one must be used.

39 For access to the driven shaft bevel gear and shim, unscrew the four bolts securing the driven shaft bearing housing to the main housing and remove the bearing housing and shaft as an assembly. Discard the bearing housing O-ring as a new one must be used.

Inspection

40 Inspect the drive shaft bevel gear for signs of wear or damage and check that the shaft rotates freely in the bearing housing. If any wear or damage is evident, or if the bearing shows signs of roughness or play, replace the gear and/or bearing as necessary (see Step 37).

41 Inspect the driven shaft bevel gear for signs of wear or damage and check that the

shaft rotates freely in the bearing. If any wear or damage is evident, or if the bearing shows signs of roughness or play, replace the gear and/or bearing as necessary (see Step 37).

42 Check the drive shaft damper assembly for signs of wear or damage. In particular, check the damper spring and the damper cam surfaces. Using a spring compressor (Honda special tool Pt. No. 07964-ME90000 or the commercial equivalent), and using a spacer in between the compressor bolt and the shaft end to avoid damaging the shaft's internal threads, compress the damper spring and remove the circlip from the end of the shaft. Slowly release the compressor, and remove the damper cam and the spring. Measure the spring free length and compare it to the specifications. If the spring is shorter than the service limit, it must be replaced. Install the damper spring with its closer-wound coils facing the housing.

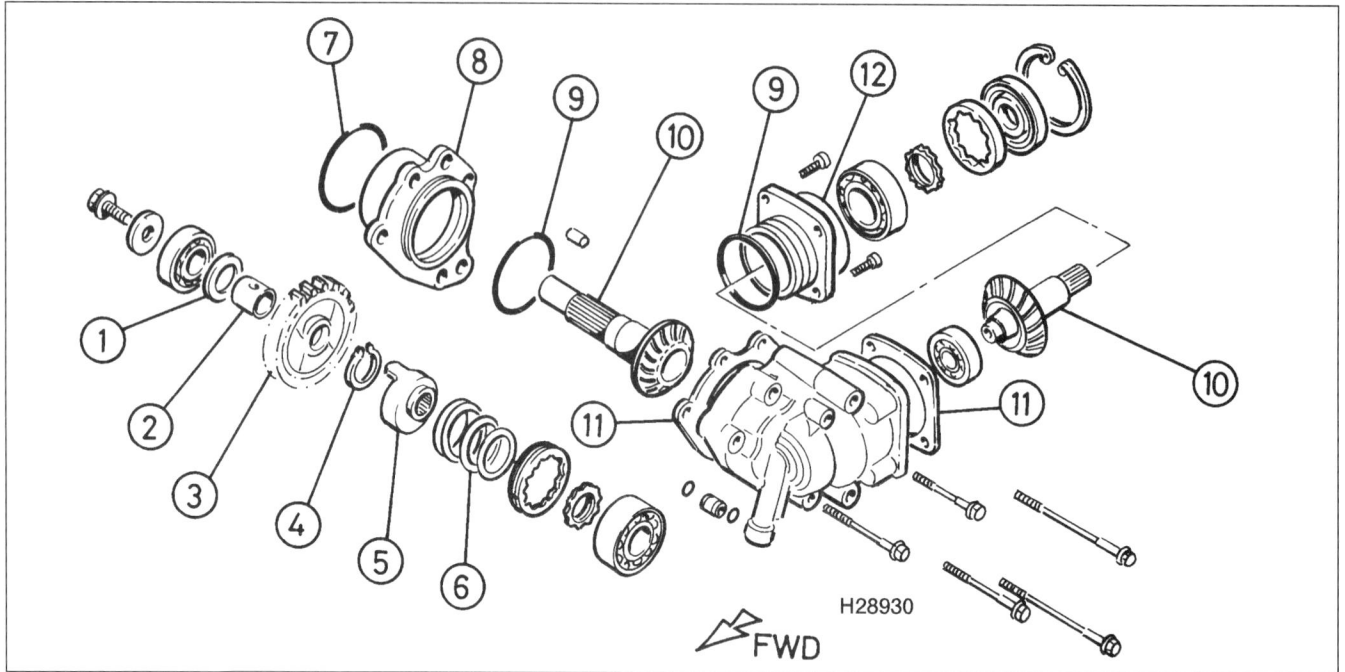

25.38 Output shaft assembly components

1 Thrust washer
2 Output driven gear bush
3 Output driven gear pinion
4 Circlip

5 Damper cam
6 Damper spring
7 O-ring
8 Output drive shaft bearing housing

9 O-ring
10 Output drive and driven bevel gear pair
11 Shim
12 Output driven shaft bearing housing

43 Measure the internal diameter of the output driven gear and the external diameter of its bush **(see illustrations)**. If either component has worn to or beyond its service limit it must be replaced. Using the above measurements calculate the gear-to-bush clearance and compare the results to the specifications listed at the beginning of the Chapter. If the clearance exceeds the specified limit replace the relevant gear and bush as a pair. Also measure the internal diameter of the bush and the corresponding shaft external diameter, and calculate the shaft-to-bush clearance **(see illustrations)**.

44 Check the amount of backlash by clamping the housing in a vice equipped with soft jaws, and positioning a dial gauge mounted on a stand adjacent to the drive shaft. A method of securing the driven shaft so that it does not rotate is required. Honda provide a special tool (Pt. No. 07923-6890101) for locking the shaft, or alternatively install the universal joint onto the output driven shaft and engage 5th gear, then fit a suitable spanner onto the flats of the universal joint and secure it against the work surface **(see illustration 17.8a)**.

45 Set up the dial gauge, using the stand to position the gauge end against the shaft. With the driven shaft locked, rotate the drive shaft gently back and forward between the extremes of its free movement. Note the reading on the gauge, then release the driven shaft and rotate the drive shaft through 120° and repeat the process. Repeat once more so that three readings are obtained at three symmetrical points on the shaft.

46 If the amount of backlash measured differs from the standard specified at the beginning of the Chapter, the drive shaft must

25.43a Measure the internal diameter of the output driven gear . . .

25.43b . . . and the external diameter of its bush

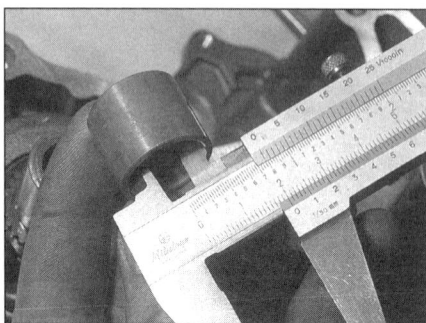

25.43c Measure the internal diameter of the bush . . .

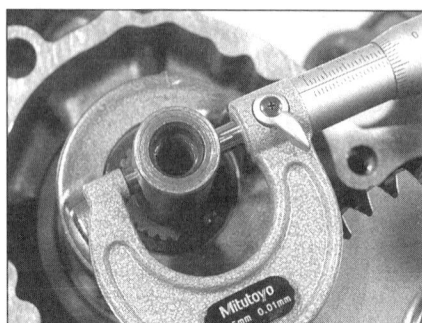

25.43d . . . and the external diameter of the shaft

be re-shimmed to bring it back within limits. If the difference between the three readings exceeds the specified limit, the bearings have not been installed squarely and must be removed and installed correctly (see Step 37).

47 If the amount of backlash exceeds the standard specified, the drive shaft shim must be replaced with a thinner one. If the amount of backlash is less than the standard specified, the drive shaft shim must be replaced with a thicker one. Replacement shims are available in 0.05 mm increments from 0.20 to 0.60 mm. A change of 0.05 mm in the thickness of the shim will result in a change of 0.015 mm in the amount of backlash.

48 For access to the drive shaft shim, unscrew the two bolts securing the drive shaft bearing housing to the main housing and remove the bearing housing and shaft as an assembly. Install the correct shim(s), then install the bearing housing using the original O-ring and tighten the bolts to the torque setting specified at the beginning of the Chapter. Re-check the backlash.

49 Check the gear tooth contact pattern using Prussian blue applied to the teeth of the driven shaft bevel gear. For access to the driven shaft bevel gear, unscrew the four bolts securing the driven shaft bearing housing to the main housing and remove the bearing housing and shaft as an assembly. Apply the Prussian blue, then install the bearing housing using the original shim and O-ring and tighten the bolts to the torque setting specified at the beginning of the Chapter. Rotate the drive shaft several turns in the normal direction of rotation, then remove the drive shaft bearing housing (see Step 38) and check the pattern of the Prussian blue that has been transferred from the driven gear to the drive gear.

50 Contact between the bevel gears is correct if the Prussian blue has been transferred to the middle of each tooth. If the blue is either too high or too low on the teeth, the driven shaft must be re-shimmed to restore the pattern to the correct height.

51 If the contact pattern is too high, the driven shaft shim must be replaced with a thinner one. If the contact pattern is too low, the driven shaft shim must be replaced with a thicker one. Replacement shims are available in 0.05 mm increments from 0.40 to 0.60 mm.

A change of 0.10 mm in the thickness of the shim will result in a change of 1.5 to 2.0 mm in the height of the contact pattern.

52 For access to the driven shaft shim, unscrew the four bolts securing the driven shaft bearing housing to the main housing and remove the bearing housing and shaft as an assembly. Install the correct shim(s), then install the bearing housing using the original O-ring and tighten the bolts to the specified torque setting. Re-check the contact pattern. When the contact pattern is correct, re-check the backlash (see Steps 44 to 48).

Reassembly

53 When the amount of backlash and the contact pattern are correct, remove both bearing housings and discard their O-rings. Fit new O-rings to the bearing housings, then install them with their correct shims onto the main housing and tighten their bolts to the specified torque setting.

26 Selector drum and forks - removal, inspection and installation

Note: *Access can be gained to the stopper plate, stopper arm and selector arm with the engine in the frame and the clutch removed (see Section 19). All other operations require the crankcases to be separated.*

Removal

1 Remove the transmission shafts (see Section 24).

2 Note that each selector fork is marked for identification. The left-hand fork is marked with an "L", the middle fork is marked with a "C", and the right-hand fork is marked with an "R", all of which must face the right-hand crankcase half **(see illustration)**. Remove the outer selector forks from the fork shaft. Bend back the tabs on the centre fork lockwasher, then unscrew the bolt and remove the lockwasher; slide the fork off the shaft, noting how it fits **(see illustration)**.

Inspection

3 Inspect the selector forks for any signs of wear or damage, especially around the fork ends where they engage with the groove in the pinion. Check also that the forks fit correctly in their pinion groove. Measure the thickness of the fork ends and compare the readings to the specifications at the beginning of the Chapter **(see illustration)**. Check closely to see if the forks are bent. If the forks are in any way damaged or worn beyond the service limit, they must be replaced.

4 Check that the forks fit correctly on their shaft. They should move freely with a light fit but no appreciable freeplay. Measure the internal diameter of each fork bore and the diameter of the fork shaft where each fork fits on it **(see illustrations)**. Compare the readings to the specifications, and replace any components that are worn beyond the service limit. Check that the fork shaft holes in the crankcases are not worn or damaged.

5 The selector fork shaft can be checked for trueness by rolling it along a flat surface. A bent shaft will cause difficulty in selecting

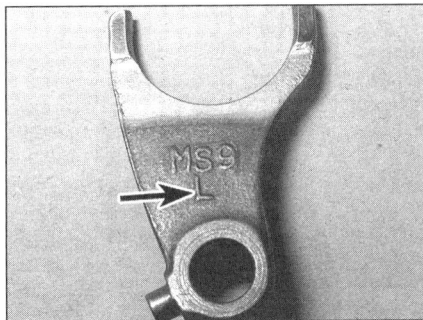
26.2a Note the identification letter on the fork (arrow)

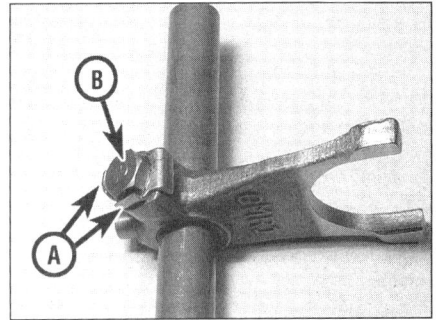
26.2b Bend back the lockwasher tabs (A) and remove the bolt (B)

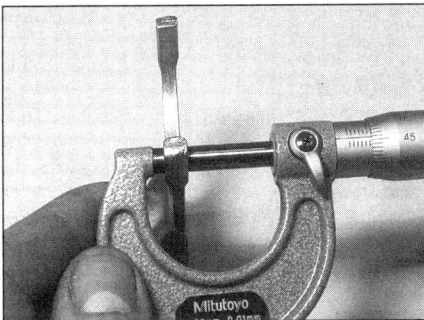
26.3 Measure the selector fork end thickness

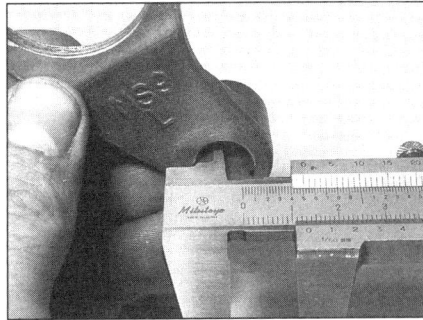
26.4a Measure the internal diameter of each fork bore . . .

26.4b . . . and the external diameter of its location on the shaft

2

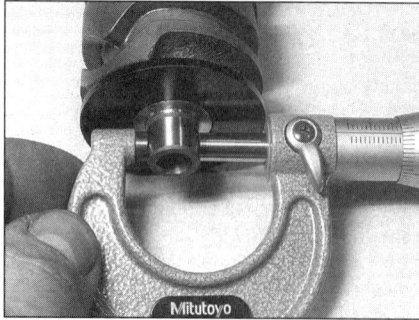

26.7 Measure the selector drum journal diameter

28.4 Blow through the crank oil passages with compressed air

gears and make the gearshift action heavy. Replace the shaft if it is bent.

6 Inspect the selector drum grooves and selector fork guide pins for signs of wear or damage. If either component shows signs of wear or damage the gearshift fork(s) and drum must be replaced.

7 Check that the selector drum bearing rotates freely and has no sign of freeplay between its inner and outer race. Replace the bearing if necessary. It is retained by the stopper plate which is secured by a single central screw. Measure the diameter of the journal on the left-hand end of the drum and compare the measurement to the specifications (see illustration). If it is worn beyond the service limit, replace the selector drum. Also check the drum journal hole in the crankcase for wear or damage.

Installation

8 Install the middle selector fork marked "C" on the fork shaft so that the "C" faces the right-hand end of the shaft. Install the lockwasher and bolt, then tighten the bolt securely and bend back the tabs of the lockwasher to secure it in place.

9 Install the selector fork marked "L" onto the left-hand end of the shaft so that the "L" faces right. Install the fork marked "R" onto the right-hand end of the shaft so that the "R" faces right.

10 Install the transmission shafts (see Section 24).

27 Main and connecting rod bearings - general information

1 Even though main and connecting rod bearings are generally replaced with new ones during the engine overhaul, the old bearings should be retained for close examination as they may reveal valuable information about the condition of the engine.

2 Bearing failure occurs mainly because of lack of lubrication, the presence of dirt or other foreign particles, overloading the engine and/or corrosion. Regardless of the cause of bearing failure, it must be corrected before the

engine is reassembled to prevent it from happening again.

3 When examining the connecting rod bearings, remove them from the connecting rods and caps and lay them out on a clean surface in the same general position as their location on the crankshaft journals. This will enable you to match any noted bearing problems with the corresponding crankshaft journal.

4 Dirt and other foreign particles get into the engine in a variety of ways. It may be left in the engine during assembly or it may pass through filters or breathers. It may get into the oil and from there into the bearings. Metal chips from machining operations and normal engine wear are often present. Abrasives are sometimes left in engine components after reconditioning operations, especially when parts are not thoroughly cleaned using the proper cleaning methods. Whatever the source, these foreign objects often end up imbedded in the soft bearing material and are easily recognised. Large particles will not imbed in the bearing and will score or gouge the bearing and journal. The best prevention for this cause of bearing failure is to clean all parts thoroughly and keep everything spotlessly clean during engine reassembly. Frequent and regular oil and filter changes are also recommended.

5 Lack of lubrication or lubrication breakdown has a number of interrelated causes. Excessive heat (which thins the oil), overloading (which squeezes the oil from the bearing face) and oil leakage or throw off (from excessive bearing clearances, worn oil pump or high engine speeds) all contribute to lubrication breakdown. Blocked oil passages will also starve a bearing and destroy it. When lack of lubrication is the cause of bearing failure, the bearing material is wiped or extruded from the steel backing of the bearing. Temperatures may increase to the point where the steel backing and the journal turn blue from overheating.

6 Riding habits can have a definite effect on bearing life. Full throttle low speed operation, or labouring the engine, puts very high loads on bearings, which tend to squeeze out the oil film. These loads cause the bearings to flex,

which produces fine cracks in the bearing face (fatigue failure). Eventually the bearing material will loosen in pieces and tear away from the steel backing. Short trip riding leads to corrosion of bearings, as insufficient engine heat is produced to drive off the condensed water and corrosive gases produced. These products collect in the engine oil, forming acid and sludge. As the oil is carried to the engine bearings, the acid attacks and corrodes the bearing material.

7 Incorrect bearing installation during engine assembly will lead to bearing failure as well. Tight fitting bearings which leave insufficient bearing oil clearances result in oil starvation. Dirt or foreign particles trapped behind a bearing insert result in high spots on the bearing which lead to failure.

8 To avoid bearing problems, clean all parts thoroughly before reassembly, double check all bearing clearance measurements and lubricate the new bearings with clean engine oil during installation.

28 Crankshaft and main bearings - removal, inspection and installation

Removal

1 Separate the crankcase halves (refer to Section 21).

2 Lift the crankshaft out of the left-hand crankcase half. If it appears stuck, tap it gently using a soft-faced mallet.

3 If required, remove the connecting rods from the crankshaft (see Section 29).

Inspection

4 Clean the crankshaft with solvent, using a rifle-cleaning brush to scrub out the oil passages. If available, blow the crank dry with compressed air, and also blow through the oil passages (see illustration). Check the cam chain sprockets for wear or damage. If any of the sprocket teeth are excessively worn, chipped or broken, the crankshaft must be replaced.

5 Refer to Section 27 and examine the main bearings. If they are scored, badly scuffed or

28.9 Measure the crankshaft main bearing journal OD

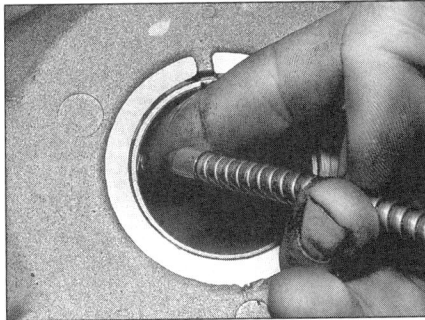

28.13a Apply oil to the main bearings . . .

28.13b . . . then install the crankshaft

appear to have been seized, new bearings must be installed. Always replace the main bearings as a set. If they are badly damaged, check the corresponding crankshaft journal. Evidence of extreme heat, such as discoloration, indicates that lubrication failure has occurred. Be sure to thoroughly check the oil pump and pressure relief valve as well as all oil holes and passages before reassembling the engine.

6 The crankshaft journals should be given a close visual examination, paying particular attention where damaged bearings have been discovered. If the journals are scored or pitted in any way a new crankshaft will be required. Note that undersizes are not available, precluding the option of re-grinding the crankshaft.

7 Place the crankshaft on V-blocks and check the runout at the main bearing journals using a dial gauge. Compare the reading to the maximum specified at the beginning of the Chapter. If the runout exceeds the limit, the crankshaft must be replaced.

Oil clearance check

8 Whether new bearing shells are being fitted or the original ones are being re-used, the main bearing oil clearance should be checked prior to reassembly.

9 Using a vernier caliper, measure the diameter of the crankshaft main bearing journals and the corresponding internal diameter of the main bearing **(see illustration)**. Calculate the difference between the two to determine the main bearing oil

clearance and compare the results to the specifications at the beginning of the Chapter. If the oil clearance exceeds the service limit, new main bearings must be selected and installed.

Bearing selection

10 Replacement main bearings are supplied on a selected fit basis. Selection of the bearings requires very accurate measurements to be taken using specialist measuring equipment. As the old bearings will have to be removed and the new ones installed by a Honda dealer using specialist tools, it is advised that bearing selection is also entrusted to the dealer.

Bearing replacement

11 Replacement of the main bearings requires the use of specialist tools, equipment and skills in order to avoid damaging either the crankcase or the new bearings. It is therefore advised that replacement is undertaken by a Honda dealer.

Installation

12 If removed, install the connecting rods onto the crankshaft (see Section 29).

13 Apply clean engine oil to the main bearings, then lower the crankshaft into position in the left-hand crankcase **(see illustrations)**.

14 Reassemble the crankcase halves (see Section 21).

29 Connecting rods - removal, inspection and installation

Removal

1 Remove the crankshaft (see Section 28).

2 Before removing the rods from the crankshaft, measure the side clearance on each rod with a feeler gauge **(see illustration)**. If the clearance on any rod is greater than the service limit listed in this Chapter's Specifications, that rod will have to be replaced with a new one.

3 Using paint or a felt marker pen, mark the relevant cylinder identity on each connecting rod and bearing. Mark across the cap-to-connecting rod join to ensure that the cap is fitted the correct way around on reassembly.

4 Unscrew the big-end cap nuts and separate the connecting rod, cap and both bearing shells from the crankpin **(see illustration)**. Keep the rod, cap, nuts and (if they are to be re-used) the bearing shells together in their correct positions to ensure correct installation.

Inspection

5 Check the connecting rods for cracks and other obvious damage.

6 If not already done (see Section 15), apply clean engine oil to the piston pin, insert it into the connecting rod small-end and check for any freeplay between the two **(see illustration)**. Measure the pin OD and the

2

29.2 Measure the connecting rod side clearance

29.4 Unscrew the connecting rod big-end cap nuts

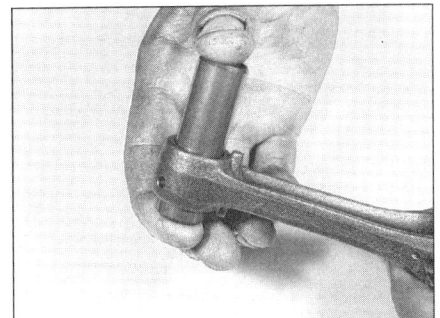

29.6 Slip the piston pin into the rod's small-end and rock it back and forth to check for looseness

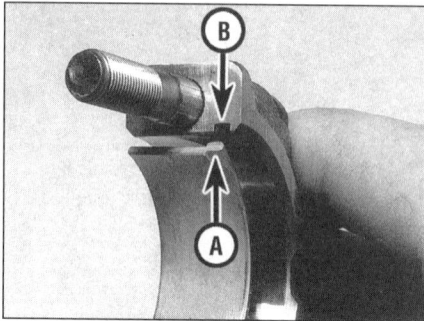

29.11 Make sure the tab (A)
locates in the notch (B)

29.12 Place a strip of Plastigauge on each
bearing journal

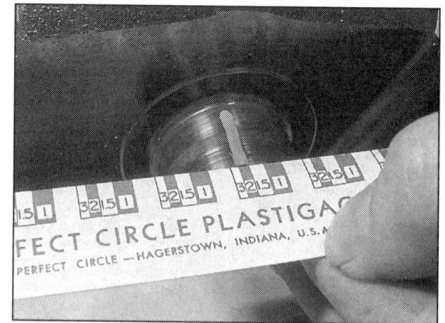

29.13 Measure the crushed Plastigauge
using the scale on the pack to obtain the
oil clearance

small-end bore ID and compare the measurements to the specifications at the beginning of the Chapter (see illustrations 15.13b and 15.13d). Calculate the difference between the measurements taken to obtain the piston pin-to-small end clearance and compare the result to the specifications. Replace components that are worn beyond the specified limits.

7 Refer to Section 27 and examine the connecting rod bearing shells. If they are scored, badly scuffed or appear to have seized, new shells must be installed. Always replace the shells in the connecting rods as a set. If they are badly damaged, check the corresponding crankpin. Evidence of extreme heat, such as discoloration, indicates that lubrication failure has occurred. Be sure to thoroughly check the oil pump and pressure relief valve as well as all oil holes and passages before reassembling the engine.

8 Have the rods checked for twist and bend by a Honda dealer if you are in doubt about their straightness.

Oil clearance check

9 Whether new bearing shells are being fitted or the original ones are being re-used, the connecting rod bearing oil clearance should be checked prior to reassembly.

10 Clean the backs of the bearing shells and the bearing locations in both the connecting rod and cap.

11 Press the bearing shells into their locations, ensuring that the tab on each shell engages the notch in the connecting rod/cap (see illustration). Make sure the bearings are fitted in the correct locations and take care not to touch any shell's bearing surface with your fingers.

12 Cut two lengths of the appropriate size Plastigauge (they should be slightly shorter than the width of the crankpin). Place a strand of Plastigauge on each (cleaned) crankpin journal and fit the (clean) connecting rod assemblies, shells and caps (see illustration). Make sure the cap is fitted the correct way around so the previously made markings align and tighten the bearing cap nuts to the torque setting specified at the beginning of the Chapter whilst ensuring that the connecting

rod does not rotate. Slacken the cap nuts and remove the connecting rod assemblies, again taking great care not to rotate the crankshaft.

13 Compare the width of the crushed Plastigauge on each crankpin to the scale printed on the Plastigauge envelope to obtain the connecting rod bearing oil clearance (see illustration).

14 If the clearance is not within the specified limits, the bearing shells may be the wrong grade (or excessively worn if the original shells are being re-used). Before deciding that different grade shells are needed, make sure that no dirt or oil was trapped between the bearing shells and the connecting rod or cap when the clearance was measured. If the clearance is excessive, even with new shells (of the correct size), the crankpin is worn and the crankshaft should be replaced.

15 On completion carefully scrape away all traces of the Plastigauge material from the crankpin and bearing shells using a fingernail or other object which is unlikely to score the shells.

Bearing shell selection

16 Replacement bearing shells for the big-end bearings are supplied on a selected fit basis. Codes stamped on the crankshaft and rod are used to identify the correct replacement bearings. The crankpin journal size number is stamped on the crankshaft middle web adjacent to the crankpin and will be either an A or a B (see illustration). The

connecting rod size code is marked on the flat face of the connecting rod and cap and will be either a 1 or a 2.

17 A range of bearing shells is available. Select the correct bearing shells for a particular connecting rod in accordance with the table below. The bearings themselves are identified by a letter and a corresponding colour (see table). The dimensions relating to the particular codes are given in the specifications at the beginning of the Chapter.

Crankpin journal code	Connecting rod code	Replacement bearing code
1	A	C - Brown
1	B	B - Black
2	A	B - Black
2	B	A - Blue

Connecting rod selection

18 If a connecting rod needs to be replaced, the weight of the replacement rod needs to be matched to the other rod being re-used. If both rods are being replaced, they need to be matched together. The connecting rod weight code is marked on the flat face of the connecting rod and cap and will be either an A, B, C or a D (650 cc engines only) (see illustration 29.16).

19 Select the rod in accordance with the table (see illustration).

Installation

20 Install the bearing shells in the connecting rods and caps, aligning the notch in the bearing with the groove in the rod or cap (see illustration 29.11). Lubricate the shells with molybdenum disulphide grease and assemble

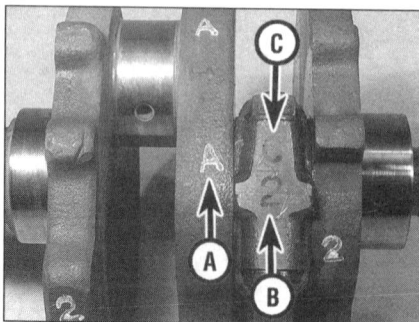

29.16 Crankpin journal size coding (A),
connecting rod size coding (B), and
connecting rod weight coding (C)

Rear cyl.	Front cyl.			
	A	B	C	D*
A	Yes	Yes	No	No
B	Yes	Yes	Yes	No
C	No	Yes	Yes	Yes
D*	No	No	Yes	Yes

*D marking only applies to 650 cc engine

29.19 Connecting rod weight
selection table

29.20 Install the connecting rods onto the crankshaft

29.21 Tighten the connecting rod nuts to the specified torque setting

31 Recommended running-in procedure

1 Treat the machine gently for the first few miles to make sure oil has circulated throughout the engine and any new parts installed have started to seat.

2 Even greater care is necessary if the engine has been rebored or a new crankshaft has been installed. In the case of a rebore, the bike will have to be run in as when new. This means greater use of the transmission and a restraining hand on the throttle until at least 600 miles (1000 km) have been covered. There's no point in keeping to any set speed limit - the main idea is to keep from labouring the engine and to gradually increase performance up to the 600 mile (1000 km) mark. These recommendations can be lessened to an extent when only a new crankshaft is installed. Experience is the best guide, since it's easy to tell when an engine is running freely. The accompanying table of maximum engine speed limitations, which Honda provide for new motorcycles, can be used as a guide.

3 If a lubrication failure is suspected, stop the engine immediately and try to find the cause. If an engine is run without oil, even for a short period of time, severe damage will occur.

---

the components on the crankpin **(see illustration)**. Install the bolts and tighten the nuts finger-tight at this stage. Check to make sure that all components have been returned to their original locations using the marks made on disassembly.

21 The connecting rod nuts must be tightened evenly and in several stages to the torque setting specified at the beginning of the Chapter **(see illustration)**.

22 Check that the rods rotate smoothly and freely on the crankpin. If there are any signs of roughness or tightness, remove the rods and re-check the bearing clearance.

23 Install the crankshaft (see Section 28).

30 Initial start-up after overhaul

1 Make sure the engine oil and coolant levels are correct (see *Daily (pre-ride) checks*), then remove the spark plugs from the engine. Place the engine kill switch in the OFF position.

2 Turn on the ignition switch and crank the engine over with the starter until the oil pressure indicator light goes off (which indicates that oil pressure exists). Reinstall the spark plugs, connect the plug caps and turn the kill switch to RUN.

3 Make sure there is fuel in the tank, then turn the fuel tap to the ON position and operate the choke.

4 Start the engine and allow it to run at a moderately fast idle until it reaches operating temperature.

⚠ *Warning: If the oil pressure light doesn't go off, or it comes on while the engine is running, stop the engine immediately.*

5 Check carefully for oil and coolant leaks and make sure the transmission and controls, especially the brakes, function properly before road testing the machine. Refer to Section 31 for the recommended running-in procedure.

6 Upon completion of the road test, and after the engine has cooled down completely, recheck the valve clearances and check the engine oil and coolant levels (see *Daily (pre-ride) checks*).

Mileage	Max engine speed	Considerations
Up to 600 miles (1000 km)	4000 rpm max	Vary throttle position/speed
600 to 1000 miles (1000 to 1600 km)	6000 rpm max	Vary throttle position/speed. Use full throttle for short bursts
Over 1000 miles (1600 km)	8500 rpm max	Do not exceed tachometer red line

2

Notes

Chapter 3
Cooling system

Contents

Degrees of difficulty

Easy, suitable for novice with little experience	**Fairly easy,** suitable for beginner with some experience	**Fairly difficult,** suitable for competent DIY mechanic	**Difficult,** suitable for experienced DIY mechanic	**Very difficult,** suitable for expert DIY or professional

Specifications

Coolant
Mixture type and capacity .... see Chapter 1

Radiator
Cap valve opening pressure .... 13 to 18 psi (0.9 to 1.3 Bar)

Thermostat
Opening temperature .... 80 to 84°C
Valve lift .... 8 mm (min) @ 95°C (for five minutes)

Fan switch
Cooling fan cut-in temperature .... 93 to 97°C

Temperature gauge sender
Resistance
  @ 50°C .... 130 to 180 ohms
  @ 100°C .... 25 to 30 ohms

Torque setting
Fan switch .... 18 Nm

3

1 General information

The cooling system uses a water/antifreeze coolant to carry away excess energy in the form of heat. The cylinders are surrounded by a water jacket from which the heated coolant is circulated by thermo-syphonic action in conjunction with a water pump, driven off the oil pump. The hot coolant passes upwards to the thermostat and through to the radiator. The coolant then flows across the radiator core, where it is cooled by the passing air, down to the water pump and back up to the engine where the cycle is repeated.

A thermostat is fitted in the system to prevent the coolant flowing through the radiator when the engine is cold, therefore accelerating the speed at which the engine reaches normal operating temperature. A thermostatically-controlled cooling fan is also fitted to aid cooling in extreme conditions.

The complete cooling system is partially sealed and pressurised, the pressure being controlled by a valve contained in the spring-loaded radiator cap. By pressurising the coolant the boiling point is raised, preventing premature boiling in adverse conditions. The overflow pipe from the system is connected to a reservoir tank into which excess coolant is expelled under pressure. The discharged coolant automatically returns to the radiator when the engine cools.

⚠ *Warning: Do not remove the pressure cap from the radiator when the engine is hot. Scalding hot coolant and steam may be blown out under pressure, which could cause serious injury. When the engine has* cooled, place a thick rag, like a towel over the pressure cap; slowly rotate the cap anti-clockwise to the first stop. This procedure allows any residual pressure to escape. When the steam has stopped escaping, press down on the cap while turning it anti-clockwise and remove it.

⚠ *Warning: Do not allow antifreeze to come in contact with your skin or painted surfaces of the motorcycle. Rinse off any spills immediately with plenty of water. Antifreeze is highly toxic if ingested. Never leave antifreeze lying around in an open container or in puddles on the floor; children and pets are attracted by its sweet smell and may drink it. Check with the local authorities about disposing of used antifreeze. Many communities will have collection centres which will see that antifreeze is disposed of safely.*

Caution: At all times use the specified type of antifreeze, and always mix it with distilled water in the correct proportion. The antifreeze contains corrosion inhibitors which are essential to avoid damage to the cooling system. A lack of these inhibitors could lead to a build-up of corrosion which would block the coolant passages, resulting in overheating and severe engine damage. Distilled water must be used as opposed to tap water to avoid a build-up of scale which would also block the passages.

2 Radiator pressure cap - check

1 If problems such as overheating or loss of coolant occur, check the entire system as described in Chapter 1. The radiator cap opening pressure should be checked by a Honda dealer with the special tester required to do the job. If the cap is defective, replace it with a new one.

3 Coolant reservoir - removal and installation

Removal

1 Remove the rear shock absorber (see Chapter 6).
2 Place a suitable container underneath the reservoir, then release the clamp securing the inlet/outlet hose (see illustration). Detach the hose and allow the coolant to drain into the container.
3 Release the clamp securing the overflow hose to the reservoir and detach the hose (see illustration).
4 Unscrew the two reservoir mounting bolts and remove the reservoir from the bike (see illustrations).

Installation

5 Installation is the reverse of removal. Make sure the hoses are correctly installed and secured with their clamps. On completion refill the reservoir as described in Chapter 1.

4 Cooling fan and cooling fan switch - check and replacement

Cooling fan

Check

1 If the engine is overheating and the cooling fan isn't coming on, first check the cooling fan circuit fuse (see Chapter 9) and then the fan switch as described in Steps 8 to 12 below.
2 If the fan does not come on (and the fan switch is good), the fault lies in either the

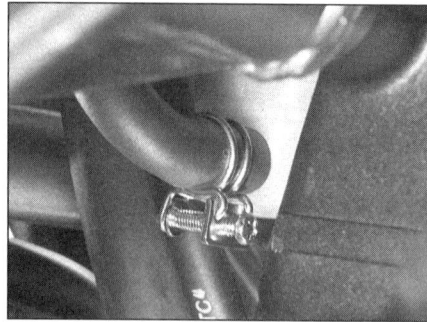
3.2 The reservoir inlet/outlet hose is secured by a screw type clamp

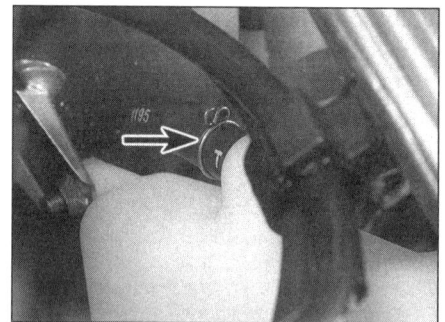
3.3 The overflow hose is secured by a spring type clamp (arrow)

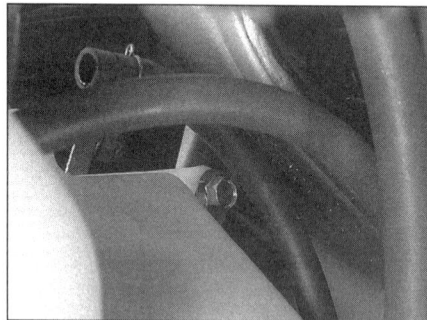
3.4a The reservoir is secured . . .

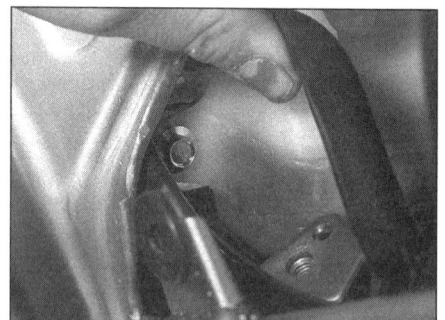
3.4b . . . by two mounting bolts

cooling fan motor or the relevant wiring. Test all the wiring and connections (see Chapter 9).
3 To test the cooling fan motor, separate the two-pin fan wiring connector behind the radiator (see illustration). Using a 12 volt battery and two jumper wires, connect the blue/black fan wire to the battery positive (+ve) lead and the black/blue fan wire to the battery negative (-ve) lead. Once connected the fan should operate. If it does not, and the wiring checks out OK, then the fan motor is faulty and must be replaced with a new unit.

Replacement

Warning: The engine must be completely cool before carrying out this procedure.

4 Remove the radiator (see Section 7).
5 Unscrew the three bolts securing the fan shroud and fan assembly to the radiator, noting that the lower bolt also secures the

earth cable (see illustration). Unscrew the three nuts on the front of the fan which secure the fan assembly to the shroud and remove the shroud. The fan blade can be released from the fan motor by removing its central retaining nut.
6 Installation is the reverse of removal. Tighten all mounting bolts and nuts securely.
7 Install the radiator (see Section 7).

Cooling fan switch

Check

8 If the engine is overheating and the cooling fan isn't coming on, first check the cooling fan circuit fuse (see Chapter 9). If the fuse is blown, check the fan circuit for a short to earth (see *Fault Finding Equipment* and the wiring diagram at the end of this book).
9 If the fuse is good, remove the screws securing the radiator left-hand end cover and

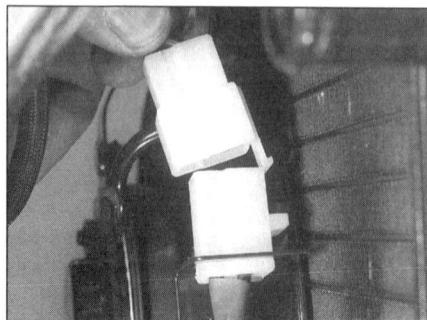
4.3 Disconnect the fan wiring connector

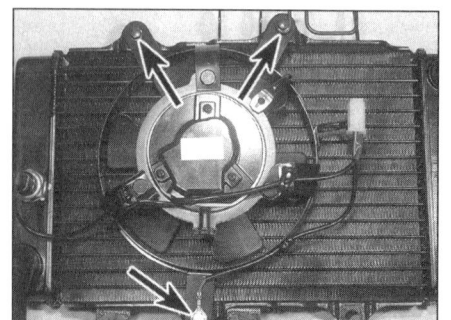
4.5 Fan assembly mounting bolts (arrows). Note earth cable attached to the lower bolt

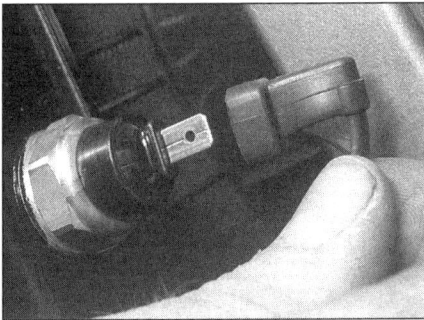

4.9 Disconnect the fan switch wiring connector

remove it from the radiator **(see illustration 7.3a)**. Disconnect the black/blue wire from the fan switch fitted to the left-hand side of the radiator **(see illustration)**. Using a jumper wire if necessary, connect the wire to earth and switch the ignition ON. The fan should come on. If it does, the fan switch is defective and must be replaced. Switch the ignition OFF. If it does not come on, the fan should be tested as described in Step 3 above.

10 If the fan works but is suspected of cutting in at the wrong temperature, a more comprehensive test of the switch can be made as follows.

11 Remove the switch from the radiator as described in Steps 13 and 14 below. Fill a small heatproof container with coolant and place it on a stove. Connect the positive (+ve) probe of an ohmmeter to the terminal of the switch and the meter negative (-ve) probe to the switch body, and using some wire or other support suspend the switch in the coolant so that just the sensing portion and the threads are submerged. Also place a thermometer capable of reading temperatures up to 110°C in the coolant so that its bulb is close to the switch. The testing set-up is similar to that used for the temperature gauge sender unit **(see illustration 5.7)**. *Note: None of the components should be allowed to directly touch the container.*

⚠️ *Warning: This must be done very carefully to avoid the risk of personal injury.*

12 Initially the ohmmeter reading should be very high, indicating that the switch is open (OFF). Heat the coolant, stirring it gently. When the temperature reaches around 93 to 97°C the meter reading should drop to around zero ohms, indicating that the switch has closed (ON). Now turn the heat off. As the temperature falls below 93 to 97°C the meter reading should show infinite (very high) resistance, indicating that the switch has opened (OFF). If the meter readings obtained are different, or they are obtained at different temperatures, then the switch is faulty and must be replaced.

Replacement

⚠️ *Warning: The engine must be completely cool before carrying out this procedure.*

13 Drain the cooling system (see Chapter 1).

4.14 The fan switch is located in the left-hand side of the radiator

14 Remove the screws securing the radiator left-hand end cover and remove it from the radiator **(see illustration 7.3a)**. The fan switch is located in the left-hand side of the radiator **(see illustration)**. Disconnect the wiring, then unscrew the switch and withdraw it from the radiator. Discard the O-ring as a new one must be used.

15 Fit a new O-ring and apply a suitable sealant to the switch threads, then install the switch in the radiator and tighten it to the torque setting specified at the beginning of the Chapter.

16 Reconnect the switch wiring and slip the dust cover into place. Install the radiator side cover.

17 Refill the cooling system (see Chapter 1).

5 Coolant temperature gauge and sender - check and replacement

Coolant temperature gauge

Check

1 The circuit consists of the sender mounted in the bottom of the thermostat housing and the gauge assembly mounted in the instrument panel. If the system malfunctions check first that the battery is fully charged and that the fuses are all good.

2 If the gauge is not working, remove the fuel tank (see Chapter 4) to access the sender unit. Disconnect the wire from the sender and turn the ignition switch ON **(see illustration)**. The temperature gauge needle should be on

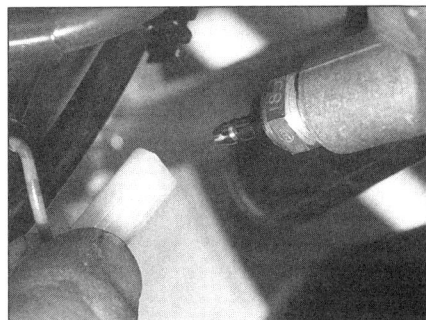

5.2 Disconnect the temperature gauge sender wiring from the thermostat housing

the "C" on the gauge. Now earth the sender wire on the engine. The needle should swing immediately over to the "H" on the gauge. If the needle moves as described above, the sender is proven defective and must be replaced.

Caution: Do not earth the wire for any longer than is necessary to take the reading, or the gauge may be damaged.

3 If the needle movement is still faulty, or if it does not move at all, the fault lies in the wiring or the gauge itself. Check all the relevant wiring and wiring connectors. If all appears to be well, the gauge is defective and must be replaced.

Replacement

4 See Chapter 9.

Temperature gauge sender

Check

5 Remove the fuel tank (see Chapter 4). The sender is fitted to the bottom of the thermostat housing **(see illustration 5.10)**.

6 Disconnect the sender wiring. Using a continuity tester, check for continuity between the sender body and earth. There should be continuity (zero ohms). If there is no continuity (infinite resistance), check that the thermostat housing mounting is secure.

7 Remove the sender (see Steps 9 to 11 below). Fill a small heatproof container with coolant and place it on a stove. Using an ohmmeter, connect the positive (+ve) probe of the meter to the terminal on the sender, and the meter negative (-ve) probe to the body of the sender. Using some wire or other support suspend the sender in the coolant so that just the sensing portion and the threads are submerged. Also place a thermometer capable of reading temperatures up to 110°C in the water so that its bulb is close to the sender **(see illustration)**. *Note: None of the components should be allowed to directly touch the container.*

⚠️ **3** *Warning: This must be done very carefully to avoid the risk of personal injury.*

8 Heat the coolant, stirring it gently. When the temperature reaches around 50°C the meter should read between 130 and 180 ohms. When the temperature reaches around 100°C the

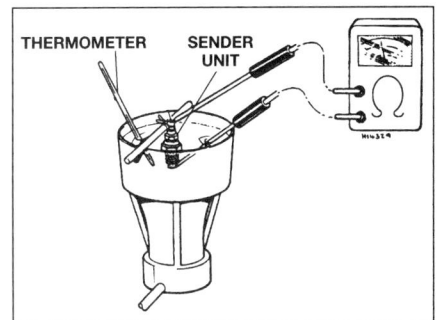

5.7 Temperature gauge sender testing set-up

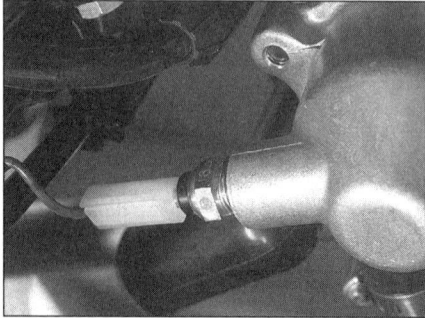

5.10 Temperature gauge sender location

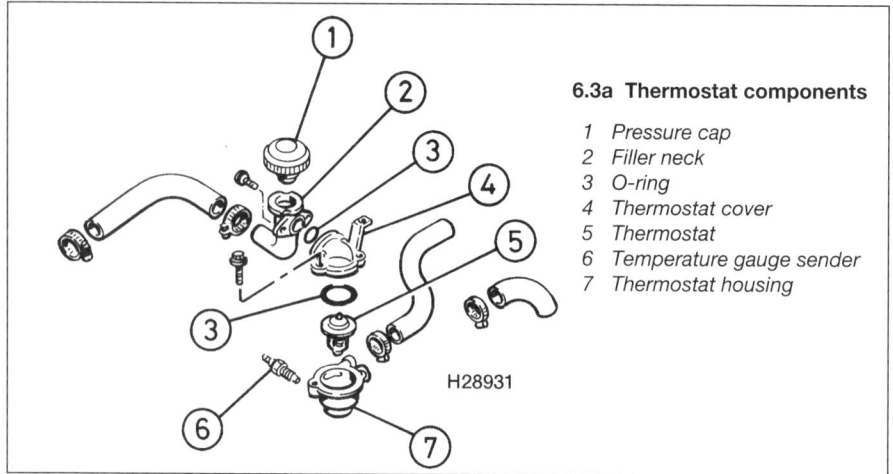

6.3a Thermostat components

1 Pressure cap
2 Filler neck
3 O-ring
4 Thermostat cover
5 Thermostat
6 Temperature gauge sender
7 Thermostat housing

H28931

meter should read between 25 and 30 ohms. If the meter readings obtained are different, or they are obtained at different temperatures, then the sender is faulty and must be replaced.

Replacement

Warning: The engine must be completely cool before carrying out this procedure.

9 Drain the cooling system (see Chapter 1).
10 If not already done, remove the fuel tank (see Chapter 4) to gain access to the sender which is fitted to the bottom of the thermostat housing **(see illustration)**. Disconnect the sender wiring.
11 Unscrew the sender and remove it from the thermostat housing.
12 Apply a smear of sealant to the threads of the new sender unit, then install it into the thermostat housing and tighten it securely. Connect the sender wiring.
13 Refill the cooling system (see Chapter 1), then install the fuel tank (see Chapter 4).

6 Thermostat - removal, check and installation

Removal

Warning: The engine must be completely cool before carrying out this procedure.

1 The thermostat is automatic in operation and should give many years service without requiring attention. In the event of a failure, the valve will probably jam open, in which case the engine will take much longer than normal to warm up. Conversely, if the valve jams shut, the coolant will be unable to circulate and the engine will overheat. Neither condition is acceptable, and the fault must be investigated promptly.
2 Remove the fuel tank and the air filter housing (see Chapter 4) and drain the cooling system (see Chapter 1).
3 The thermostat is located in the thermostat housing adjacent to the filler neck pressure cap **(see illustration)**. Unscrew the two bolts

securing the thermostat cover to the filler neck, and the two bolts securing the thermostat cover to the thermostat housing **(see illustration)**. Remove the cover, then withdraw the thermostat, noting how it fits. Discard the O-rings as new ones must be fitted.

Check

4 Examine the thermostat before carrying out the test. If it remains in the open position at room temperature, it should be replaced.
5 Suspend the thermostat by a piece of wire in a container of cold water. Place a thermometer in the water so that the bulb is close to the thermostat **(see illustration)**. Heat the water, noting the temperature when the thermostat opens, and compare the result with the specifications given at the beginning of the Chapter. Also check the amount the valve opens after it has been heated at 95°C for five minutes and compare the measurement to the specifications. If the readings obtained differ from those given, the thermostat is faulty and must be replaced.

6.3b Thermostat cover-to-filler neck bolts (A) and cover-to-housing bolts (B)

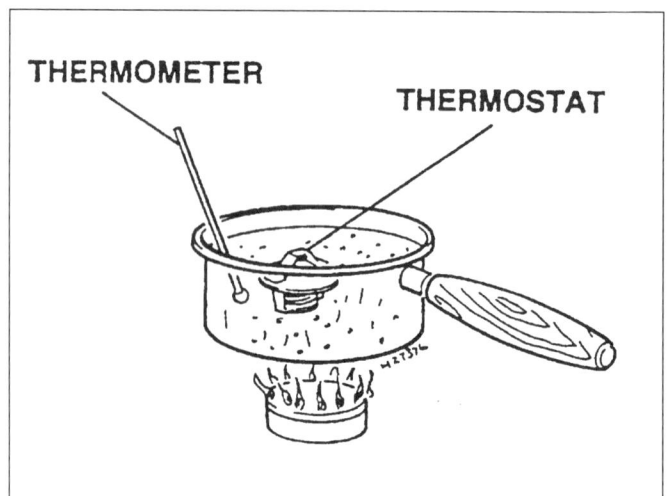

THERMOMETER   THERMOSTAT

6.5 Thermostat opening check

6 In the event of thermostat failure, as an emergency measure only, it can be removed and the machine used without it. **Note**: *Take care when starting the engine from cold as it will take much longer than usual to warm up. Ensure that a new unit is installed as soon as possible.*

Installation

7 Fit the thermostat into the housing, making sure that it slots into the grooves in the housing.

8 Fit new O-rings to the thermostat housing and the filler neck, then install the thermostat cover. Install the four cover bolts and tighten them securely.

9 Refill the cooling system (see Chapter 1).

10 Install the air filter housing and the fuel tank (see Chapter 4).

7 Radiator -
removal and installation

Removal

⚠ **Warning: The engine must be completely cool before carrying out this procedure.**

1 Drain the cooling system (see Chapter 1).

2 Trace the cooling fan wiring back from the fan and disconnect it at its connector **(see illustration 4.3)**.

3 Remove the screws securing each radiator end cover and remove them from the radiator **(see illustration)**. The ends of the stone guard slot into the end covers **(see illustration)**. Remove the guard with the covers.

4 Slacken the clamps securing the top and bottom radiator hoses and detach them from the radiator **(see illustrations)**.

5 Unscrew the two bolts securing the bottom of the radiator to the mounting bracket **(see illustration)**. Note the arrangement of the collar and rubber grommet.

6 If fitted, remove the split pin from the radiator top mounting bolt and discard it as a new one must be used. Make sure the radiator is supported, then remove the top mounting nut, bolt and collar and carefully remove the radiator assembly **(see illustration)**. Note how the wiring harness fits in the guide on the top of the radiator **(see illustration)**.

7 If necessary, remove the cooling fan (see Section 4) from the radiator.

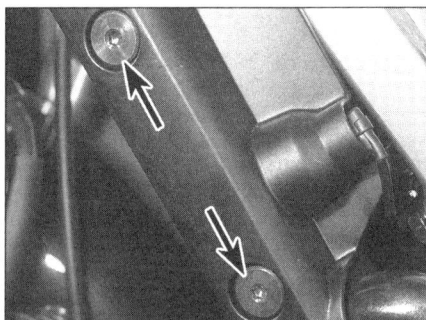
7.3a Each radiator end cover is secured by two screws (arrows)

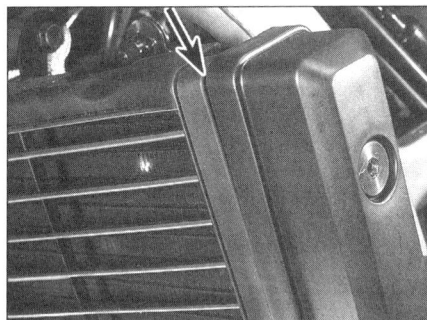
7.3b The ends of the stone guard (arrow) slot into the end covers

7.4a Slacken the top . . .

7.4b . . . and bottom radiator hose clamps

7.5a Radiator bottom mounting bolts (arrows)

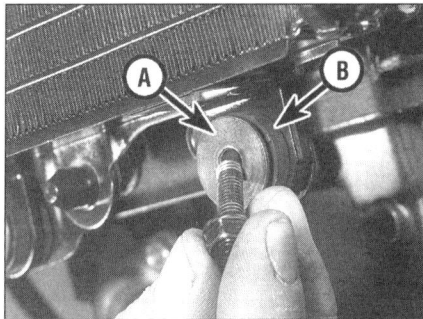
7.5b Note the arrangement of the collar (A) and rubber grommet (B)

7.6a Radiator top mounting bolt

7.6b Note the wiring harness guide on the top of the radiator

3

8 Check the stone guard and the radiator for signs of damage and clear any dirt or debris that might obstruct air flow and inhibit cooling. If the radiator fins are badly damaged or broken the radiator must be replaced. Also check the rubber mounting grommets, and replace them if necessary.

Installation

9 Installation is the reverse of removal, noting the following.

a) *Install the radiator top mounting bolt first, but do not fully tighten it. Install the bottom mounting bolts then tighten all the bolts.*

b) *Make sure that the fan wiring is correctly connected, and the wiring harness is located in its guide on the top of the radiator.*

c) *Ensure the coolant hoses are securely retained by their clamps, and use new ones if necessary.*

d) *On completion refill the cooling system as described in Chapter 1.*

8 Water pump - check, removal and installation

Check

1 The water pump is located on the lower left-hand side of the engine. To access the pump, unscrew the gearchange linkage arm pinch bolt and remove the linkage arm from the shaft. Unscrew the bolts securing the left-hand side crankcase rear cover and remove the cover **(see illustration 5.17a in Chapter 2)**. Visually check the area around the pump for signs of leakage.

2 To prevent leakage of water from the cooling system to the lubrication system and vice versa, two seals are fitted on the pump shaft. On the underside of the pump body there is also a drainage hole **(see illustration)**. If either seal fails, this hole should allow the coolant or oil to escape and prevent the oil and coolant mixing.

3 The seal on the water pump side is of the mechanical type which bears on the rear face of the impeller. The second seal, which is mounted behind the mechanical seal is of the normal feathered lip type. However, neither seal is available as a separate item as the pump is sold as an assembly. Therefore, if on inspection the drainage hole shows signs of leakage, the pump must be removed and replaced.

Removal

4 Drain the coolant and the engine oil (see Chapter 1). Remove the crankcase rear cover as described in Step 1.

5 Unscrew the bolt securing the coolant pipe to the front of the left-hand side crankcase **(see illustration)**.

6 Unscrew the bolts securing the pump cover to the pump and the pump to the crankcase and remove the cover (on J, K and M models the drain/cover bolt will already have been removed) **(see illustration)**. Discard the cover O-ring as a new one must be used. Remove the two dowels from the pump or the cover if they are loose, noting their locations. If required, unscrew the bolt securing the water pipe to the cover and remove the pipe **(see illustration)**. Discard the pipe O-ring if the pipe is removed as a new one must be used.

7 Release the clamp securing the coolant hose to the water pump and detach the hose. Carefully remove the pump from the crankcase, noting how it fits. Remove the O-ring from the rear of the pump body and discard it as a new one must be used.

8 Wiggle the water pump impeller back-and-forth and in-and-out. If there is excessive movement the pump must be replaced. Also check for corrosion or a build-up of scale in the pump body and clean or replace the pump as necessary.

Installation

9 Apply a smear of engine oil to the new pump body O-ring and install it onto the rear of the pump body **(see illustration)**. Install the pump into the crankcase, aligning the slot in the impeller shaft with the tab on the oil pump shaft **(see illustration)**.

10 Attach the coolant hose to the pump and secure it with its clamp.

11 Apply a smear of engine oil to the new cover O-ring and install it into its groove in the pump. Install the two pump dowels into their holes in the pump.

8.2 Check the pump drainage hole (arrow) for signs of leakage

8.5 Unscrew the coolant pipe bracket bolt

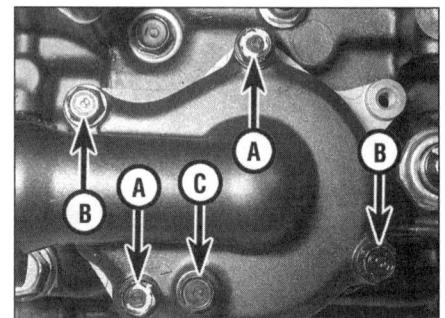

8.6a Pump cover bolts (A), pump mounting bolts (B), drain bolt (C) (P, S & T models). On J, K & M models, the drain bolt is the lower cover bolt (A)

8.6b Water pipe-to-cover securing bolt

8.9a Fit a new O-ring to the pump

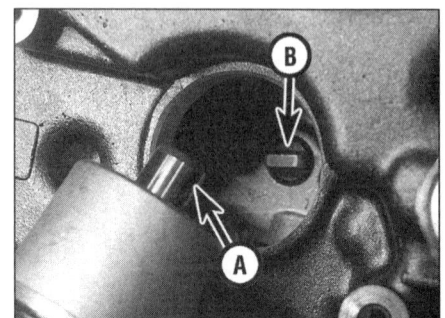

8.9b Align the slot (A) with the tab (B)

8.12a Fit a new O-ring to the pipe . . .

8.12b . . . and install it into the pump

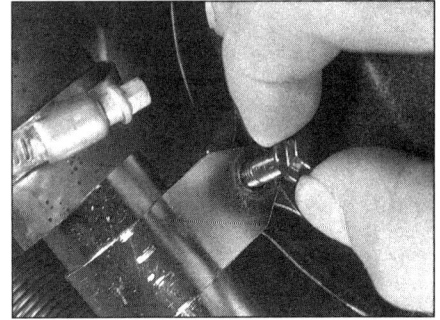

8.14 Secure the pipe to the crankcase

12 If the coolant pipe was detached from the pump cover, apply a smear of coolant to the new pipe O-ring, then install the pipe into the cover and tighten its bolt securely **(see illustrations)**.

13 Install the cover onto the pump, then install the four bolts and tighten them securely, using a new sealing washer on the coolant drain bolt.

14 Install the bolt securing the coolant pipe to the crankcase **(see illustration)**.

15 Refill the cooling system (see Chapter 1).

16 Refill the engine with oil (see Chapter 1).

17 Install the crankcase rear cover and gearchange linkage arm - align the punch marks on the arm and shaft **(see illustration 5.28c in Chapter 2)**.

9 Coolant hoses - removal and installation

Removal

1 Before removing a hose, drain the coolant as described in Chapter 1.

2 Use a screwdriver to slacken the hose clamps, then slide them back along the hose and clear of the union spigot. The smaller-bore hoses are secured by spring clamps which can be expanded by squeezing their ears together with pliers.

3 If a hose proves stubborn, release it by rotating it on its union before working it off. If all else fails, cut the hose with a sharp knife then slit it at each union so that it can be peeled off in two pieces. Whilst this is expensive it is preferable to buying a new radiator.

Caution: The radiator unions are fragile. Do not use excessive force when attempting to remove the hoses

4 The water pipe inlet union to the front cylinder block can be removed by unscrewing the two retaining bolts. If it is removed, the O-ring must be replaced. The outlet pipe from each cylinder head can be removed by unscrewing the bolt which retains it. If they are removed, their O-rings must be replaced.

5 Refer to Chapter 2, Section 14 for the coolant joint collar between the two cylinder blocks.

Installation

6 Slide the clips onto the hose and then work it on to its respective union.

> **HAYNES HiNT** *If the hose is difficult to push on its union, it can be softened by soaking it in very hot water, or alternatively a little soapy water can be used as a lubricant.*

7 Rotate the hose on its unions to settle it in position before sliding the clamps into place and tightening them securely.

8 If either the inlet union to the front cylinder block or the outlet pipes from the cylinder heads have been removed, fit a new O-ring, then install the union or pipes and tighten the mounting bolts securely.

3

Chapter 4
Fuel and exhaust systems

Contents

Degrees of difficulty

Easy, suitable for novice with little experience	Fairly easy, suitable for beginner with some experience	Fairly difficult, suitable for competent DIY mechanic	Difficult, suitable for experienced DIY mechanic	Very difficult, suitable for expert DIY or professional

Specifications

Fuel
Grade .... Unleaded, minimum 91 RON (Research Octane Number)
Fuel tank capacity .... 19 litres
Fuel tank reserve capacity .... 2.5 litres

Carburettors
Type
   600 cc engine .... 34.0 mm CV
   650 cc engine .... 36.5 mm CV

Carburettor adjustments
Pilot screw setting (turns out)
   600 cc engine
      J and K models 1 3/4
      M models 1 7/8
   650 cc engine
      P models 2 1/2
      S and T models 2 1/4
Float height
   600 cc engine .... 7.0 mm
   650 cc engine .... 9.2 mm
Idle speed .... see Chapter 1
Synchronisation vacuum range .... see Chapter 1

4

Jet sizes

Pilot jet
    600 cc engine 38
    650 cc engine 42
Main jet
    600 cc engine
        J and K models
            Front cylinder 135
            Rear cylinder 130
        M models (both cylinders) 128
    650 cc engine
        P models
            Front cylinder 132
            Rear cylinder 128
        S and T models (both cylinders) 125

Torque settings

Fuel tank mounting bolts
    Front .... 12 Nm
    Rear .... 22 Nm
Exhaust system
    Downpipe nuts .... 27 Nm
    Clamp bolts .... 27 Nm
    Silencer bolts .... 27 Nm

---

1 General information and precautions

General information

The fuel system consists of the fuel tank, the fuel tap and filter, the fuel pump, the carburettors, fuel hoses and control cables.

The fuel tap is of the gravity type with an integral filter inside the fuel tank.

The carburettors used on all models are Keihin CV types. On all models there is a carburettor for each cylinder. For cold starting, a choke lever mounted on the left-hand handlebar and connected by a cable, controls an enrichment circuit in the carburettor.

Air is drawn into the carburettors via an air filter which is housed under the fuel tank.

The exhaust system is a two-into-one design.

Many of the fuel system service procedures are considered routine maintenance items and for that reason are included in Chapter 1.

Precautions

⚠️ *Warning: Petrol is extremely flammable, so take extra precautions when you work on any part of the fuel system. Don't smoke or allow open flames or bare light bulbs near the work area, and don't work in a garage where a natural gas-type appliance is present. If you spill any fuel on your skin, rinse it off immediately with soap and water. When you perform any kind of work on the fuel system, wear safety glasses and have a fire extinguisher suitable for a class B type fire (flammable liquids) on hand.*

Always perform service procedures in a well-ventilated area to prevent a build-up of fumes.

Never work in a building containing a gas appliance with a pilot light, or any other form of naked flame. Ensure that there are no naked light bulbs or any sources of flame or sparks nearby.

Do not smoke (or allow anyone else to smoke) while in the vicinity of petrol or of components containing it. Remember the possible presence of vapour from these sources and move well clear before smoking.

Check all electrical equipment belonging to the house, garage or workshop where work is being undertaken (see the Safety First! section of this manual). Remember that certain electrical appliances such as drills, cutters etc create sparks in the normal course of operation and must not be used near petrol or any component containing it. Again, remember the possible presence of fumes before using electrical equipment.

Always mop up any spilt fuel and safely dispose of the rag used.

Any stored fuel that is drained off during servicing work must be kept in sealed containers that are suitable for holding petrol, and clearly marked as such; the containers themselves should be kept in a safe place. Note that this last point applies equally to the fuel tank if it is removed from the machine; also remember to keep its cap closed at all times.

Note that the fuel system consists of the fuel tank and tap, with its cap and related hoses.

Read the Safety first! section of this manual carefully before starting work.

Owners of machines used in the US, particularly California, should note that their machines must comply at all times with Federal or State legislation governing the permissible levels of noise and of pollutants such as unburnt hydrocarbons, carbon monoxide etc. that can be emitted by those machines. All vehicles offered for sale must comply with legislation in force at the date of manufacture and must not subsequently be altered in any way which will affect their emission of noise or of pollutants.

In practice, this means that adjustments may not be made to any part of the fuel, ignition or exhaust systems by anyone who is not authorised or mechanically qualified to do so, or who does not have the tools, equipment and data necessary to properly carry out the task. Also if any part of these systems is to be replaced it must be replaced with only genuine Honda components or by components which are approved under the relevant legislation. The machine must never be used with any part of these systems removed, modified or damaged.

2 Fuel tank and tap - removal and installation

⚠️ *Warning: Refer to the precautions given in Section 1 before starting work.*

Fuel tank

Removal

1 Make sure the fuel tap is turned to the OFF position and the fuel cap is secure.

2 Remove the seat and the left-hand side panel (see Chapter 8), then disconnect the battery, negative (-ve) terminal first.

2.3 Release the clamp and detach the fuel hose from the tap

2.4a Unscrew the tank rear mounting bolt . . .

2.4b . . . then the front mounting bolt . . .

2.5 . . . and remove the tank

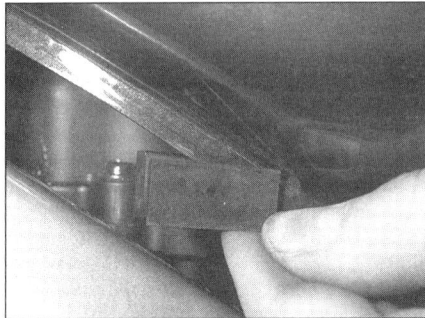

2.7 Do not forget the rubber mounts on each side of the tank

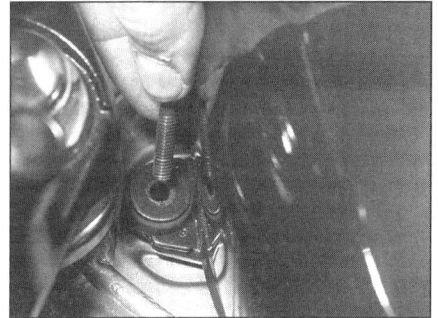

2.8a Install the front mounting bolt . . .

2.8b . . . then the rear mounting bolt

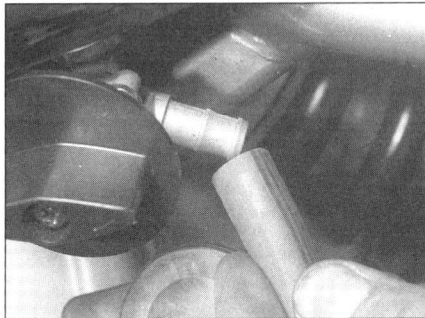

2.9 Connect the fuel hose to the tap

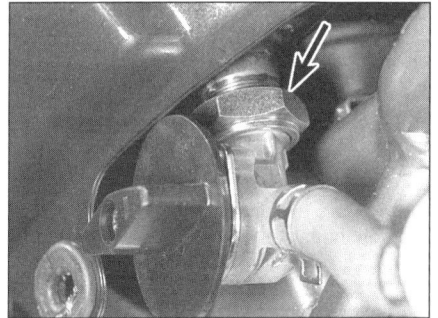

2.14 The tap is secured to the tank by a nut (arrow)

3 Release the fuel hose clamp and detach the hose from the tap, noting its routing **(see illustration)**.

4 Unscrew the fuel tank rear mounting bolt first, then the front mounting bolt, and remove the bolts with their collars, noting how they fit **(see illustrations)**.

5 Remove the tank by carefully drawing it back and away from the bike **(see illustration)**. Take care not to lose the mounting rubbers from the front and rear of the tank, and from between the sides of the tank and the frame, noting how they fit. On all except J models, note the routing of the overflow drain hose into the drain tray.

6 Check the tank mounting rubbers for damage or deterioration and replace them if necessary.

Installation

7 If removed, install the tank mounting rubbers **(see illustration)**. Carefully lower the fuel tank into position, making sure the rubbers remain in place and that the overflow drain hose is correctly routed. Check that the tank is properly seated and is not pinching any control cables or wires.

8 Install the front mounting bolt and its collar first, and tighten it to the torque setting specified at the beginning of the Chapter **(see illustration)**. Next install the rear mounting bolt and its collar, and tighten it to the specified torque setting **(see illustration)**.

9 Reconnect the fuel hose to the tap, making sure it is correctly fitted and routed, and secure it with its clamp **(see illustration)**.

10 Connect the battery, fitting the negative (-ve) terminal last, then install the seat and the left-hand side panel (see Chapter 8).

11 Turn the fuel tap to the ON or RES position and check that there is no sign of fuel leakage. Start the engine and check again that there is no sign of fuel leakage, then shut if off.

Fuel tap

Removal

12 The tap should not be removed unnecessarily otherwise there is a danger of damaging the O-ring or the filter.

13 Remove the fuel tank as described above. Connect a drain hose to the fuel tap stub and insert its end in a container suitable and large enough for storing the petrol. Turn the fuel tap to the RES position, and allow the tank to fully drain.

14 Unscrew the nut securing the tap to the tank and withdraw the tap assembly **(see illustration)**. Check the condition of the O-ring. If it is in good condition it can be re-used. If it is in any way deteriorated or damaged it must be replaced.

15 Clean the gauze filter to remove all traces of dirt and fuel sediment. Check the gauze

4

6.5 Release the fuel hose clamp and detach the hose from the union (arrow)

6.6 Slacken the clamps securing the carburettors to the inlet adapters

6.7 Carburettor drain screw (arrow)

for holes. If any are found, a new filter should be fitted.

16 Apart from the tap control knob, filter and O-ring, internal components are not available for the fuel tap. If the tap is leaking, unscrew the screw securing the knob to the tap and remove the control knob. Tighten the screws securing the tap cover to the tap body. If leakage persists, the tap should be replaced with a new unit, however nothing is lost by dismantling the tap for further inspection. Remove the screws and disassemble the tap, noting how the components fit.

Installation

17 Installation is the reverse of removal.

3 Fuel tank -
cleaning and repair

1 All repairs to the fuel tank should be carried out by a professional who has experience in this critical and potentially dangerous work. Even after cleaning and flushing of the fuel system, explosive fumes can remain and ignite during repair of the tank.

2 If the fuel tank is removed from the bike, it should not be placed in an area where sparks or open flames could ignite the fumes coming out of the tank. Be especially careful inside garages where a natural gas-type appliance is located, because the pilot light could cause an explosion.

4 Idle fuel/air mixture
adjustment - general
information

1 Due to the increased emphasis on controlling motorcycle exhaust emissions, certain governmental regulations have been formulated which directly affect the carburation of this machine. In order to comply with the regulations, the carburettors on some models are sealed so they can't be tampered with. The pilot screws on other models are accessible, but the use of an exhaust gas analyser is the only accurate way to adjust the idle fuel/air mixture and be sure

the machine doesn't exceed the emissions regulations.

2 The pilot screws are set to their correct position by the manufacturer and should not be adjusted unless it is necessary to do so for a carburettor overhaul. If the screws are renewed, they should be set to the position specified at the beginning of the Chapter.

3 If the engine runs extremely rough at idle or continually stalls, and if a carburettor overhaul does not cure the problem, take the motorcycle to a Honda dealer equipped with an exhaust gas analyser. They will be able to properly adjust the idle fuel/air mixture to achieve a smooth idle and restore low speed performance.

5 Carburettor overhaul -
general information

1 Poor engine performance, hesitation, hard starting, stalling, flooding and backfiring are all signs that major carburettor maintenance may be required.

2 Keep in mind that many so-called carburettor problems are really not carburettor problems at all, but mechanical problems within the engine or ignition system malfunctions. Try to establish for certain that the carburettors are in need of maintenance before beginning a major overhaul.

3 Check the fuel filter, the fuel hoses, the intake manifold joint clamps, the air filter, the ignition system, the spark plugs and carburettor synchronisation before assuming that a carburettor overhaul is required.

4 Most carburettor problems are caused by dirt particles, varnish and other deposits which build up in and block the fuel and air passages. Also, in time, gaskets and O-rings shrink or deteriorate and cause fuel and air leaks which lead to poor performance.

5 When overhauling the carburettors, disassemble them completely and clean the parts thoroughly with a carburettor cleaning solvent and dry them with filtered, unlubricated compressed air. Blow through the fuel and air passages with compressed air to force out any dirt that may have been

loosened but not removed by the solvent. Once the cleaning process is complete, reassemble the carburettor using new gaskets and O-rings.

6 Before disassembling the carburettors, make sure you have a carburettor rebuild kit (which will include all necessary O-rings and other parts), some carburettor cleaner, a supply of clean rags, some means of blowing out the carburettor passages and a clean place to work. It is recommended that only one carburettor be overhauled at a time to avoid mixing up parts.

6 Carburettors -
removal and installation

> **Warning:** *Refer to the precautions given in Section 1 before starting work.*

Removal

1 Remove the fuel tank (see Section 2).
2 Remove the air filter housing (refer to Section 12).
3 Detach the throttle cables from the carburettors (see Section 10).
4 Detach the choke cables from the carburettors (see Section 11).
5 Release the clamp securing the main fuel hose to the carburettors and detach the hose **(see illustration)**.
6 Slacken the clamps securing the carburettors to the cylinder head inlet adapters and ease the carburettors off the adapters, noting how they fit **(see illustration)**. **Note:** *Keep the carburettors upright to prevent fuel spillage from the float chambers and the possibility of the piston diaphragms being damaged.*
7 Place a suitable container below the float chambers, then slacken the drain screws and drain all the fuel from the carburettors **(see illustration)**. Once all the fuel has been drained, tighten the drain screws securely.
8 If necessary, release the clamps securing the inlet adapters to the cylinder heads and remove the adapters, noting how they fit **(see illustration)**.

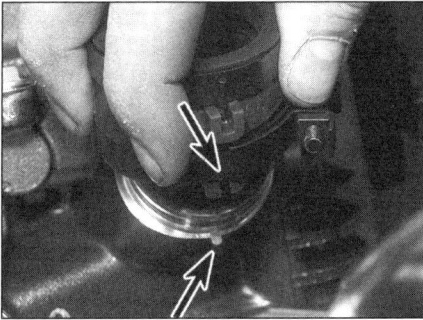

6.8 Note the fitting of the inlet adapters as they must be correctly installed (arrows)

Installation

9 Installation is the reverse of removal, noting the following.

  a) *Check for cracks or splits in the cylinder head inlet adapters. If they have been removed from the cylinder head, make sure they are installed with the slotted tab on the adapter aligning with the raised lip on the underside of the cylinder head stub (see illustration 6.8).*

  b) *Make sure the air filter housing and the cylinder head inlet adapters are fully engaged with the carburettors and their retaining clamps are securely tightened.*

  c) *Make sure all hoses are correctly routed and secured and not trapped or kinked.*

  d) *Check the operation of the choke and throttle cables and adjust them as necessary (see Chapter 1).*

  e) *Check idle speed and carburettor synchronisation; adjust as necessary (Chapter 1).*

7 Carburettors - disassembly, cleaning and inspection

Warning: Refer to the precautions given in Section 1 before starting work.

Disassembly

1 Remove the carburettors from the machine as described in the previous Section. **Note:** *Do not separate the carburettors unless absolutely necessary; each carburettor can be dismantled sufficiently for all normal cleaning and adjustments while in place on the mounting brackets. Dismantle the carburettors separately to avoid interchanging parts* **(see illustration)**.

2 Unscrew and remove the four top cover retaining screws **(see illustration)**. Lift off the cover and remove the spring from inside the piston.

3 Carefully peel the diaphragm away from its sealing groove in the carburettor and withdraw the diaphragm and piston assembly. **Caution:** *Do not use a sharp instrument to displace the diaphragm as it is easily damaged.* Note how the tab on the diaphragm fits in the recess in the carburettor body.

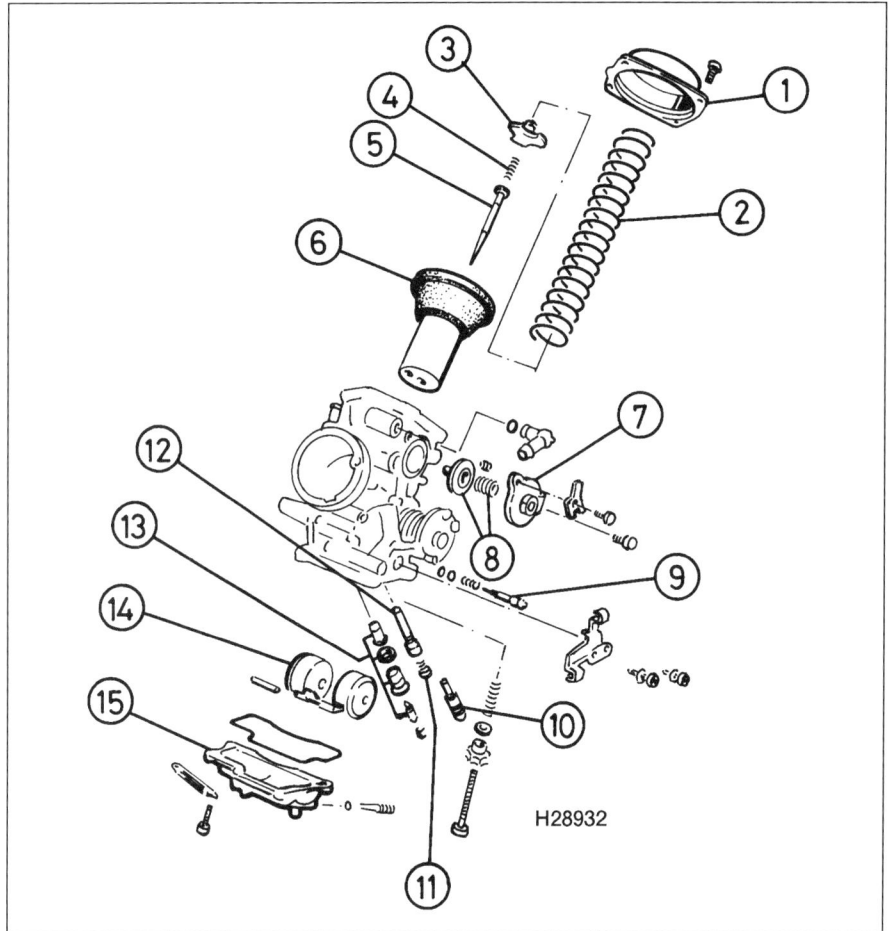

7.1 Carburettor components

1 Top cover	9 Pilot screw assembly
2 Spring	10 Pilot jet
3 Jet needle retainer	11 Main jet
4 Spring	12 Needle jet
5 Jet needle	13 Float needle valve assembly
6 Diaphragm/piston assembly	14 Float
7 Air cut-off valve cover	15 Float chamber
8 Air cut-off valve assembly	

4 If necessary, push down on the jet needle retainer using a Phillips screwdriver and rotate it until its tabs are released from the protrusions inside the piston **(see illustration)**. Push the needle up from the bottom of the piston and withdraw it from the top. Take care not to lose the spring and other components and note how they fit.

5 Unscrew the screws securing the float chamber to the base of the carburettor and

7.2 The carburettor top cover is secured by four screws (arrows)

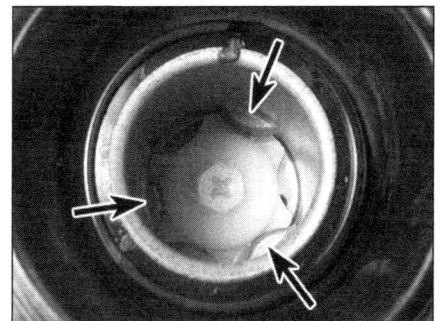

7.4 The jet needle retainer locates under three tabs in the piston (arrows)

7.5 The float chamber is secured by four screws (arrows)

7.6a Withdraw the float pin (arrow) and remove the float

7.6b Unscrew the float valve seat (arrow)

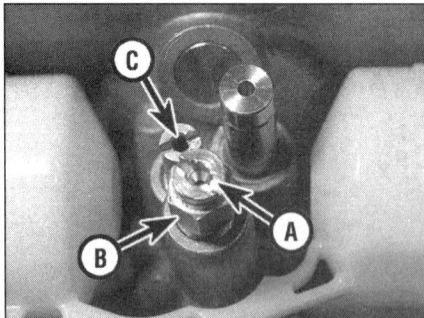

7.7 Main jet (A), needle jet (B), pilot jet (C)

7.10 Pilot screw (arrow)

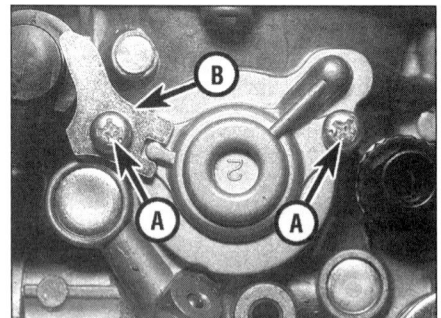

7.11a Air cut-off valve screws (A). Note the fitting of the plate (B)

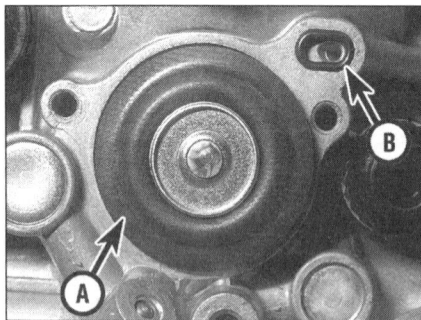

7.11b Air cut-off valve diaphragm (A) and O-ring (B)

7.12 Choke plunger (arrow)

remove the float chamber **(see illustration)**. Remove the gasket and discard it as a new one must be fitted.

6 Using a pair if thin-nose pliers, carefully withdraw the float pin **(see illustration)**. If necessary, displace the pin using a small punch or a nail. Remove the float and unhook the float needle valve, noting how it fits onto the tab on the float. Unscrew and remove the float needle valve seat, taking care not to damage its gauze filter **(see illustration)**.

7 Unscrew and remove the main jet from the needle jet **(see illustration)**.

8 Unscrew and remove the needle jet **(see illustration 7.7)**.

9 Unscrew and remove the pilot jet, next to the needle jet bore **(see illustration 7.7)**.

10 The pilot screw can be removed from the carburettor, but note that its setting will be disturbed (see **Haynes Hint**). Unscrew and

remove the pilot screw along with its spring, washer and O-ring **(see illustration)**.

> **HAYNES HINT** *To record the pilot screw's current setting, turn the screw in until it seats lightly, counting the number of turns necessary to achieve this, then fully unscrew it. On installation, the screw is simply backed out the number of turns you've recorded.*

11 Remove the two screws securing the air cut-off valve cover and its plate, noting that it is under spring pressure **(see illustration)**. Carefully release the cover and remove the spring and cut-off valve diaphragm, noting how they fit **(see illustration)**. Also remove the O-ring.

12 If the choke plungers were reinstalled into the carburettor following cable removal (see Section 11), unscrew the choke plunger nut and withdraw the spring and the plunger from the carburettor body **(see illustration)**.

Cleaning

Caution: Use only a petroleum-based solvent for carburettor cleaning. Don't use caustic cleaners.

13 Submerge the metal components in the solvent for approximately thirty minutes (or longer, if the directions recommend it).

14 After the carburettor has soaked long enough for the cleaner to loosen and dissolve most of the varnish and other deposits, use a brush to remove the stubborn deposits. Rinse it again, then dry it with compressed air.

15 Use a jet of compressed air to blow out all of the fuel and air passages in the main and upper body.

Caution: Never clean the jets or passages with a piece of wire or a drill bit, as they will be enlarged, causing the fuel and air metering rates to be upset.

Inspection

16 Check the operation of the choke plunger in the carburettor. If it doesn't move smoothly, inspect the needle on the end of the choke plunger and the plunger itself. Replace the plunger assembly if worn or bent.

17 Check the tapered portion of the pilot screw and the spring for wear or damage. Replace them if necessary.

18 Check the carburettor body, float chamber and top cover for cracks, distorted sealing surfaces and other damage. If any defects are found, replace the faulty component, although replacement of the entire carburettor will probably be necessary (check with a Honda dealer on the availability of separate components).

19 Check the piston and diaphragm for splits, holes and general deterioration. Holding it up to a light will help to reveal problems of this nature.

20 Insert the piston in the carburettor body and check that the it moves up-and-down smoothly. Check the surface of the piston for wear. If it's worn excessively or doesn't move smoothly, replace it.

21 Check the jet needle for straightness by rolling it on a flat surface (such as a piece of glass). Replace it if it's bent or if the tip is worn.

22 Check the tip of the float needle valve and the valve seat. If either has grooves or scratches in it, or is in any way worn, they must be replaced as a set. Also check the condition of the valve seat filter.

23 Operate the throttle shaft to make sure the throttle butterfly valve opens and closes smoothly. If it doesn't, replace the carburettor.

24 Check the floats for damage. This will usually be apparent by the presence of fuel inside one of the floats. If the floats are damaged, they must be replaced.

25 Check the air cut-off valve assembly components and O-ring for wear or damage and replace the assembly if necessary (individual components are not available).

8 Carburettors - separation and joining

> **Warning: Refer to the precautions given in Section 1 before proceeding**

Separation

1 The carburettors do not need to be separated for normal overhaul. If you need to separate them (to replace a carburettor body, for example), refer to the following procedure.

2 Remove the carburettors from the machine (see Section 6). Mark the body of each carburettor with its cylinder location to ensure that it is positioned correctly on reassembly.

3 Make a note of how the throttle return springs, linkage assembly and carburettor synchronisation springs are arranged to ensure that they are fitted correctly on reassembly **(see illustration)**. Also note the arrangement of the various hoses and their unions **(see illustrations)**.

4 Unscrew the two screws securing the carburettors together and carefully separate the carburettors **(see illustration)**. Retrieve the synchronisation springs. On J, K and M models, if the air hose connection elbow is removed, replace the elbow O-ring.

Joining

5 Assembly is the reverse of the disassembly procedure, noting the following.

 a) Make sure the fuel and air hoses and elbows are correctly and securely inserted into the carburettors **(see illustrations 8.3b and 8.3c)**.

 b) Install the synchronisation spring after the carburettors are joined together. Make sure it is correctly and squarely seated **(see illustration 8.3a)**.

 c) Check the operation of both the choke and throttle linkages ensuring that both operate smoothly and return quickly under spring pressure before installing the carburettors on the machine.

 d) Install the carburettors (see Section 6) and check carburettor synchronisation and idle speed (see Chapter 1).

8.3a Synchronisation spring arrangement

8.3b Carburettor hose arrangement

8.3c Carburettor hose arrangement

8.4 Carburettor joining screw

4

9 Carburettors - reassembly and float height check

Warning: Refer to the precautions given in Section 1 before proceeding.

Note: *When reassembling the carburettors, be sure to use the new O-rings, seals and other parts supplied in the rebuild kit. Do not overtighten the carburettor jets and screws as they are easily damaged.*

1 Install the air cut-off valve O-ring, using a new one if necessary, into its recess, followed by the air cut-off valve diaphragm, making sure it is properly seated **(see illustrations)**. Fit the spring against the diaphragm, then install the cover with its plate and tighten its screws securely **(see illustrations)**.

2 Install the pilot screw (if removed) along with its spring, washer and O-ring, turning it in until it seats lightly **(see illustration 7.10)**. Now, turn the screw out the number of turns previously recorded, or as specified at the beginning of the Chapter.

3 Screw the pilot jet into the body of the carburettor **(see illustration)**.

4 Install the needle jet into the body of the carburettor **(see illustration)**. Screw the main jet into the end of the needle jet **(see illustration)**.

5 If removed, install the float needle valve seat, making sure its filter is attached **(see illustration)**.

6 Hook the float needle valve onto the float tab, then position the float assembly in the carburettor and install the pin, making sure it is secure **(see illustrations)**.

7 To check the float height, hold the carburettor so the float hangs down, then tilt it back until the needle valve is just seated, but not so far that the needle's spring-loaded tip is compressed. Measure the distance between the gasket face (with the gasket removed) and the bottom of the float with an accurate ruler **(see illustration)**. The correct setting should be as given in the Specifications at the beginning of the Chapter. If it is incorrect, adjust the float height by carefully bending the float tab a little at a time until the correct height is obtained.

9.1a Install the air cut-off valve O-ring . . .

9.1b . . . followed by the diaphragm . . .

9.1c . . . the spring . . .

9.1d . . . and the cover with its plate

9.3 Install the pilot jet

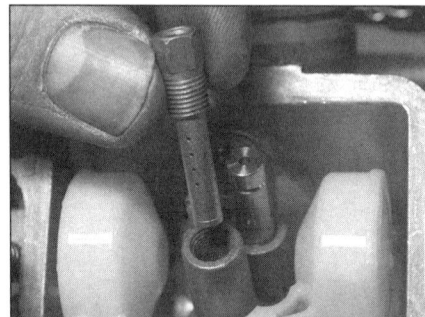
9.4a Install the needle jet

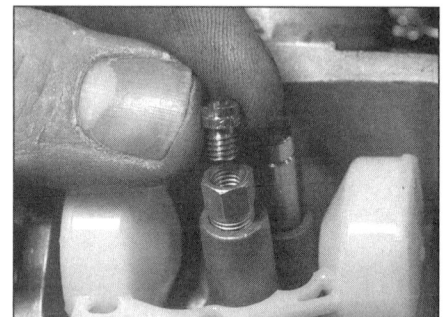
9.4b Install the main jet into the end of the needle jet

9.5 Install the float needle valve seat

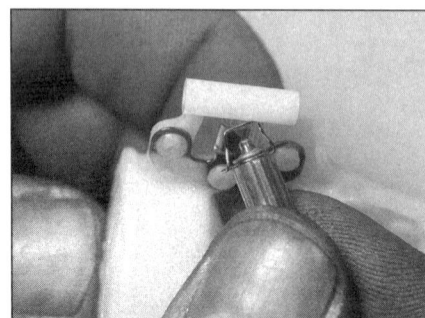
9.6a Fit the needle valve onto the tab on the float . . .

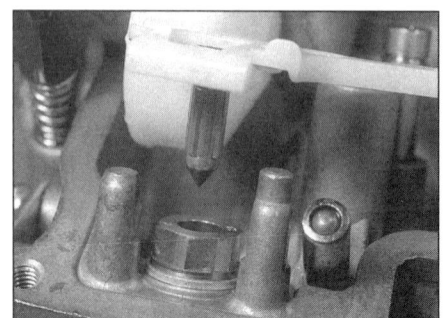
9.6b . . . then install the float assembly

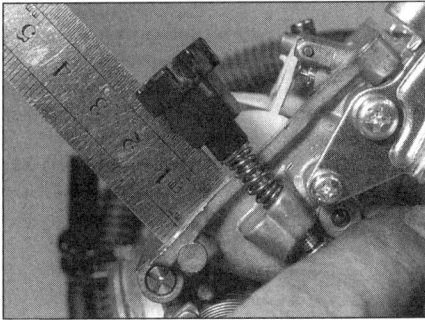

9.7 Measuring the float height

9.8 Install the float chamber
using a new gasket

9.9a Install the jet needle
into the piston . . .

9.9b . . . and secure it with its retainer,
making sure the spring sits properly
between the needle and the retainer

9.10a Install the piston assembly . . .

9.10b . . . making sure the diaphragm tab
is correctly positioned and seated (arrow)

9.11a Install the spring . . .

9.11b . . . and the cover, making sure it is
correctly aligned (arrows) . . .

9.11c . . . and secure it with its screws

4

8 With the float height checked, fit a new gasket to the float chamber, making sure it is seated properly in its groove, and install the chamber on the carburettor **(see illustration)**.

9 If removed, carefully install the jet needle, spring and retainer into the piston, making sure all the components are correctly fitted, then push down on the needle retainer using a Phillips screwdriver and rotate it until its tabs lock under the protrusions in the piston **(see illustrations)**.

10 Insert the piston assembly into the body and lightly push it down, ensuring the jet needle is correctly aligned with the needle jet

(see illustration). Align the tab on the diaphragm with the recess in the carburettor body, then press the diaphragm outer edge into its groove, making sure it is correctly seated and that the tab locates in the recess **(see illustration)**. Check the diaphragm is not creased, and that the piston moves smoothly up and down in its guide.

11 Install the spring into the piston **(see illustration)**. Fit the top cover to the carburettor, aligning the mark with the tab on the diaphragm, and tighten its screws securely **(see illustrations)**.

12 Install the carburettors (see Section 6).

10 Throttle cables -
removal and installation

Warning: Refer to the precautions given in Section 1 before proceeding.

Removal

1 Remove the fuel tank (see Section 2), and, if access is too restricted, also remove the air filter housing (see Section 12).

2 Slacken the locknuts securing the cable lower ends to their mounting brackets and

10.2a Release the throttle cable ends from their brackets . . .

10.2b . . . and detach the nipples from the throttle cam

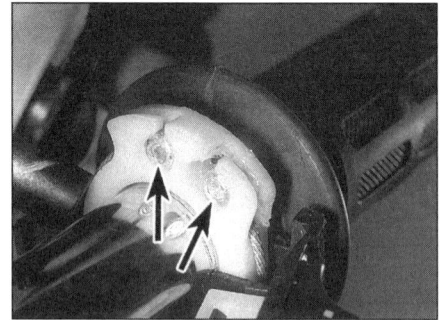

10.3a Detach the nipples from the throttle grip pulley (arrows) . . .

10.3b . . . then unscrew the elbow nuts and remove the cables

10.8a Attach the nipples to the throttle cam . . .

10.8b . . . then secure the cables in the bracket

release each outer cable from its bracket **(see illustration)**. Detach the inner cables from the throttle cam **(see illustration)**. Mark each cable according to its location.

3 Unscrew the two right-hand handlebar switch/throttle pulley housing screws, and separate the two halves. Detach the cable nipples from the pulley, then unscrew each cable elbow retaining nut and remove each cable and elbow from the housing, noting how they fit **(see illustrations)**. Mark each cable to ensure it is connected correctly on installation.

4 Remove the cables from the machine noting the correct routing of each cable.

Installation

5 Install the cables making sure they are correctly routed. The cables must not interfere with any other component and should not be kinked or bent sharply.

6 Install the cable elbows into the lower half of the switch/throttle pulley housing, making sure each cable is installed into its correct position, and tighten their retaining nuts securely. Lubricate the cable nipples with multi-purpose grease and install them into the throttle pulley **(see illustrations 10.3a and 10.3b)**

7 Fit the two halves of the housing onto the handlebar, making sure the pin in the lower half of the housing locates in the hole in the underside of the handlebar, and install the screws, tightening them securely.

8 Lubricate the cable lower end nipples with multi-purpose grease and attach them to the carburettor throttle cam **(see illustration)**. Install the outer cable ends into the mounting brackets, making sure each cable is installed in its correct position, and tighten their locknuts securely **(see illustration)**.

9 Operate the throttle to check that it opens and closes freely.

10 Check and adjust the throttle cables (Chapter 1). Turn the handlebars back and forth to make they don't cause the steering to bind.

11 Install the air filter housing if removed (see Section 12), and the fuel tank (see Section 2).

12 Start the engine and check that the idle speed does not rise as the handlebars are turned. If it does, the throttle cables are routed incorrectly. Correct the problem before riding the motorcycle.

11.1a Choke plunger assembly nut (arrow)

11 Choke cable -
removal and installation

Removal

1 Remove the fuel tank (see Section 2). Unscrew each choke plunger assembly nut from the carburettors and withdraw the assembly from each carburettor body **(see illustration)**. Compress the spring and detach the cable end from the choke plunger, noting how it fits **(see illustration)**. Withdraw the cable from the assembly. If the carburettor is not being disassembled for cleaning, it is advisable to reinstall the choke plunger assembly into the carburettor to avoid losing any of the components.

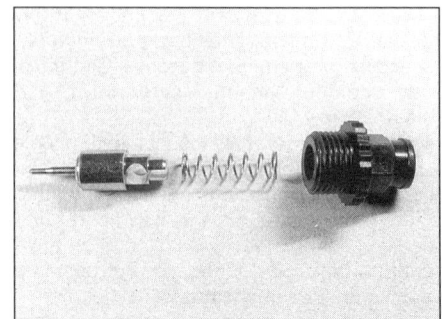

11.1b Choke plunger assembly components

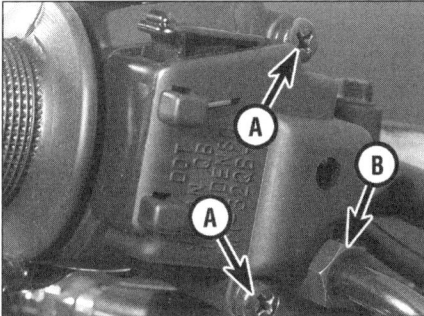
11.2a Handlebar switch screws (A), choke cable elbow nut (B)

11.2b Detach the cable nipple from the lever (arrow)

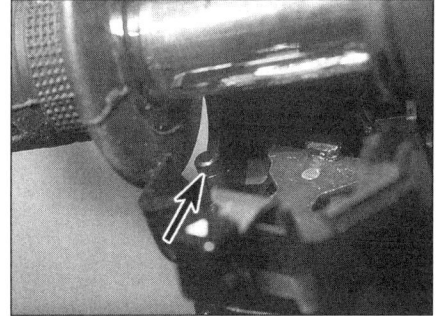
11.5 The pin on the lower switch housing (arrow) locates in a hole in the handlebar

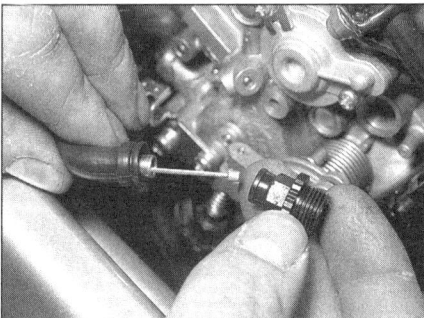
11.6a Install the plunger assembly nut onto the cable . . .

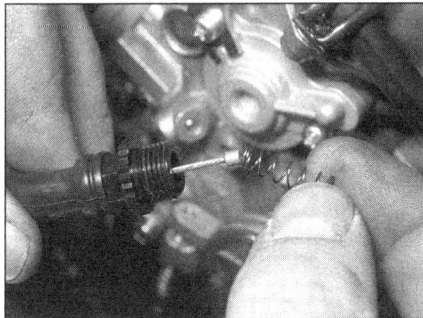
11.6b . . . followed by the spring . . .

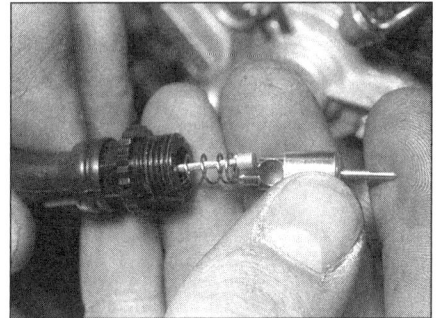
11.6c . . . and the plunger

11.6d Install the plunger assembly into the carburettor

11.7 Fit the cable into its guide

12.2 Slacken the clamp screws securing the housing to the carburettor inlets

4

2 Unscrew the two left-hand handlebar switch/choke lever housing screws and separate the two halves **(see illustration)**. Detach the cable nipple from the choke lever **(see illustration)**, then unscrew the cable elbow retaining nut and withdraw the cable and elbow from the housing.
3 Remove the cable from the machine noting its correct routing.

Installation

4 Install the cable making sure it is correctly routed. The cable must not interfere with any other component and should not be kinked or bent sharply.
5 Lubricate the upper cable nipple with multi-purpose grease. Install the cable elbow

in the switch/choke lever housing lower half and attach the nipple to the choke lever. Tighten the cable elbow retaining nut securely. Fit the two halves of the housing onto the handlebar, making sure the pin in the lower half of the housing locates in the hole in the underside of the handlebar **(see illustration)**, and install the screws, tightening them securely.
6 Pass the lower end of each inner cable through its plunger assembly nut and spring, then attach the nipple to the plunger, making sure it is secure **(see illustrations)**. Install each plunger assembly into the carburettor body and tighten its nut securely **(see illustration)**.

7 Fit the cable in its guide **(see illustration)**. Check the operation of the choke cable as described in Chapter 1.

12 Air filter housing - removal and installation

Removal

1 Remove the fuel tank (see Section 2).
2 Slacken the clamp screws securing the air filter housing to the carburettor intakes **(see illustration)**.
3 Release the air filter drain hose clamp at the air filter housing end and detach the hose

12.3a Detach the drain hose . . .

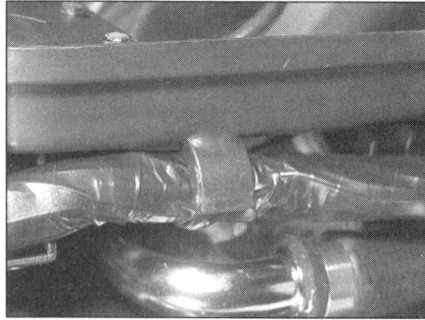
12.3b . . . and release the wiring loom from its clip

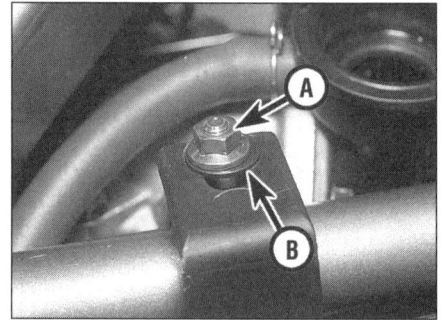
12.4a Air filter housing nut (A) and collar (B)

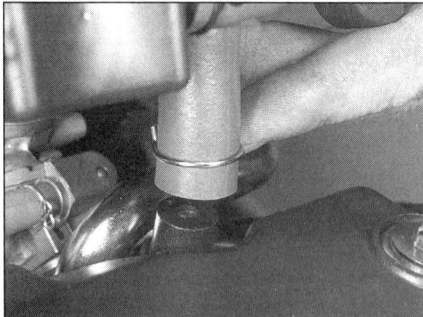
12.4b Detach the crankcase breather hose . . .

12.4c . . . and the sub-air filter hoses as the housing is lifted away

12.5 Do not forget to install the collar

from the housing **(see illustration)**. Also release the wiring loom from its clip on the side of the housing **(see illustration)**.

4 Unscrew the nut and remove the collar securing the front of the air filter housing to the frame, then carefully lift the housing up off the carburettors, noting how it fits **(see illustration)**. Release the crankcase breather hose from the rear cylinder valve cover and the sub-air filter hoses from the carburettors as they become accessible **(see illustrations)**.

Installation

5 Installation is the reverse of removal. Make sure all the hoses are correctly installed and secured by their clamps. Do not forget to fit the collar with the filter housing nut **(see illustration)**.

13 Exhaust system -
removal and installation

⚠️ **Warning: If the engine has been running the exhaust system will be very hot. Allow the system to cool before carrying out any work.**

Silencer

Removal

1 Slacken the clamp bolts securing the silencer/collector box to the exhaust downpipes **(see illustration)**.

2 Unscrew and remove the silencer mounting nut and bolt, noting the spacer (S and T models only), and the collector box mounting bolt, then carefully pull the silencer/collector box from the downpipes **(see illustrations)**.

13.1 Silencer clamp bolts (arrows)

13.2b Note the spacer (arrow) on S and T models only

Note that the seals between the downpipes and the silencer/collector box are easily damaged and should be checked following removal of the silencer and replaced if necessary.

13.2a Silencer mounting bolt

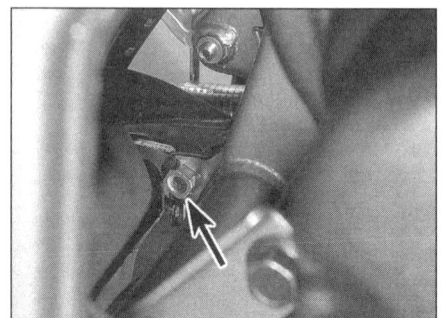
13.2c The collector box has a captive nut (arrow) for its mounting bolt

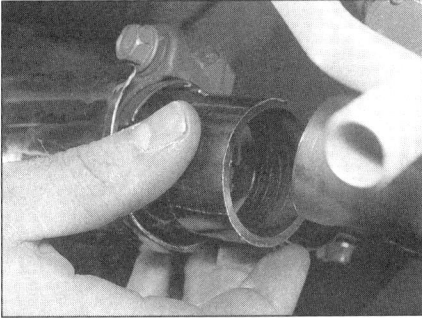

13.4 Check the condition of the seals as they are easily damaged

13.6 Front downpipe nuts (arrows)

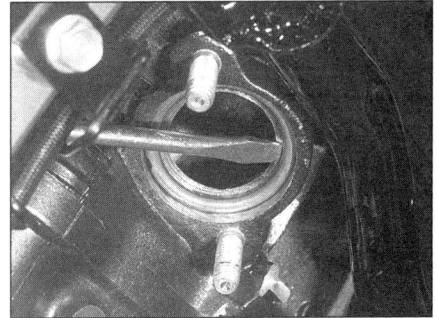

13.8 Lever out the old exhaust gaskets and discard them

3 If necessary, unscrew the three screws securing the heat guard to the silencer/collector box and remove the guard.

Installation

4 Installation is the reverse of removal. Make sure the seals between the silencer/collector box and the downpipes are in good condition and correctly installed **(see illustration)**. Tighten the silencer/collector box mounting bolt and clamp bolt to the torque settings specified at the beginning of the Chapter.

Complete system

Removal

5 Remove the silencer (see above).
6 Unscrew the front downpipe flange retaining nuts from the cylinder head studs and carefully remove the pipe **(see illustration)**.
7 Unscrew the rear downpipe flange retaining nuts from the cylinder head studs and carefully remove the pipe.
8 Remove the gasket from each cylinder head, noting that the rear gasket is a smaller diameter than that of the front, and discard them as new ones must be fitted **(see illustration)**.

13.10 Fit a new gasket into each cylinder head

9 Note that the seals between the downpipes and the silencer/collector box are easily damaged and should be checked following removal of the downpipes and replaced if necessary **(see illustration 13.4)**.

Installation

10 Fit a new gasket into each of the cylinder head ports with the flanged side inwards, making sure that the smaller diameter gasket is fitted to the rear cylinder head **(see illustration)**. Apply a smear of grease to the gaskets to keep them in place whilst fitting the downpipe.

13.11 Fit the flange over the studs

11 Install the rear downpipe, and slide the flange onto the cylinder head studs and fit the nuts **(see illustration)**. Tighten the downpipe nuts evenly to the torque setting specified at the beginning of the Chapter.
12 Install the front downpipe, and slide the flange onto the cylinder head studs and fit the nuts. Tighten the downpipe nuts evenly to the torque setting specified at the beginning of the Chapter.
13 Install the silencer (see above).
14 Run the engine and check the system for leaks.

4

Notes

Chapter 5
Ignition system

Contents

Degrees of difficulty

Easy, suitable for novice with little experience		Fairly easy, suitable for beginner with some experience		Fairly difficult, suitable for competent DIY mechanic		Difficult, suitable for experienced DIY mechanic		Very difficult, suitable for expert DIY or professional	

Specifications

General information

Firing order	Front (232°), Rear (488°)
Spark plugs	see Chapter 1

Ignition timing

At idle

J and K models	10° BTDC
All other models	8° BTDC
Full advance	31° BTDC @ 7000 rpm

Pulse generator coils

Resistance	450 to 550 ohms at 20°C

Ignition HT coils

Primary winding resistance	2.2 to 2.6 ohms at 20°C

Secondary winding resistance

With plug leads	30 to 36 K ohms at 20°C
Without plug leads	20 to 25 K ohms at 20°C

Torque settings

Timing mark inspection cap	10 Nm
Primary drive gear/timing rotor bolt	90 Nm

External oil pipe (J and K models only)

Upper bolts	10 Nm
Lower bolt	23 Nm
Crankcase cover bolts (right side)	10 Nm

5

1 General information

All models are fitted with a fully transistorised electronic ignition system, which due to its lack of mechanical parts is totally maintenance free. The system comprises a rotor, pulse generator coils, ignition control unit and ignition HT coils (refer to the wiring diagram at the end of Chapter 8 for details).

The triggers on the rotor, fitted to the right-hand end of the crankshaft, magnetically operate the pulse generator coils as the crankshaft rotates. The pulse generator coils send a signal to the ignition control unit which then supplies the ignition HT coils with the power necessary to produce a spark at the plugs.

The system uses two coils, the front coil supplying the front cylinder spark plugs and the rear coil supplying the rear cylinder plugs.

The ignition control unit has an electronic advance function in order to advance the ignition in line with increased engine speeds.

Because of their nature, the individual ignition system components can be checked but not repaired. If ignition system troubles occur, and the faulty component can be isolated, the only cure for the problem is to replace the part with a new one. Keep in mind that most electrical parts, once purchased, cannot be returned. To avoid unnecessary expense, make very sure the faulty component has been positively identified before buying a replacement part.

2 Ignition system - check

⚠ **Warning: The energy levels in electronic systems can be very high. On no account should the ignition be switched on whilst the plugs or plug caps are being held. Shocks from the HT circuit can be most unpleasant. Secondly, it is vital that the engine is not turned over or run with any of the plug caps removed, and that the plugs are soundly earthed when the system is checked for sparking. The ignition system components can be seriously damaged if the HT circuit becomes isolated.**

1 As no means of adjustment is available, any failure of the system can be traced to failure of a system component or a simple wiring fault. Of the two possibilities, the latter is by far the most likely. In the event of failure, check the system in a logical fashion, as described below. Before testing, check that the battery is in good condition and fully charged (see *Fault Finding Equipment* in the Reference section of this Manual).

2 Disconnect one HT lead from both cylinder spark plugs. Connect each lead to a spare spark plug and lay each plug on the engine

with the threads contacting the engine. If necessary, hold each spark plug with an insulated tool.

⚠ **Warning: Do not remove any of the spark plugs from the engine to perform this check - atomised fuel being pumped out of the open spark plug hole could ignite, causing severe injury!**

3 Having observed the above precautions, check that the kill switch is in the RUN position, turn the ignition switch ON and turn the engine over on the starter motor. If the system is in good condition a regular, fat blue spark should be evident at each plug electrode. If the spark appears thin or yellowish, or is non-existent, further investigation will be necessary. Before proceeding further, turn the ignition off and remove the key as a safety measure.

4 The ignition system must be able to produce a spark which is capable of jumping a particular size gap. Whilst Honda do not specify the size of this gap, a healthy system should produce a spark capable of jumping at least 6 mm. A simple testing tool can be made to test the minimum gap across which the spark will jump (see *Tool Tip*).

5 Connect one of the spark plug HT leads from one coil to the protruding electrode on the test tool, and clip the tool to a good earth on the engine or frame. Check that the kill switch is in the RUN position, turn the ignition switch ON and turn the engine over on the starter motor. If the system is in good condition a regular, fat blue spark should be seen to jump the gap between the nail ends. Repeat the test for the other coil. If the test results are good the entire ignition system can be considered good. If the spark appears thin or yellowish, or is non-existent, further investigation will be necessary.

6 Ignition faults can be divided into two categories, namely those where the ignition system has failed completely, and those

A simple spark gap testing tool can be made from a block of wood, a large alligator clip and two nails, one of which is fashioned so that a spark plug cap or bare HT lead end can be connected to its end. Make sure the gap between the two nail ends is the same as specified.

which are due to a partial failure. The likely faults are listed below, starting with the most probable source of failure. Work through the list systematically, referring to the subsequent sections for full details of the necessary checks and tests. **Note:** *Before checking the following items ensure that the battery is fully charged and that all fuses are in good condition.*

  a) *Loose, corroded or damaged wiring connections, broken or shorted wiring between any of the component parts of the ignition system (see Chapter 9).*
  b) *Faulty HT lead or spark plug cap, faulty spark plug, dirty, worn or corroded plug electrodes, or incorrect gap between electrodes.*
  c) *Faulty ignition switch or engine kill switch (see Chapter 9).*
  d) *Faulty neutral or side stand switch (see Chapter 9).*
  e) *Faulty pulse generator coils or damaged rotor.*
  f) *Faulty ignition HT coil(s).*
  g) *Faulty ignition control unit.*

7 If the above checks don't reveal the cause of the problem, have the ignition system tested by a Honda dealer. Honda produce a tester which can perform a complete diagnostic analysis of the ignition system.

3 Ignition HT coils - check, removal and installation

Check

1 In order to determine conclusively that the ignition coils are defective, they should be tested by a Honda dealer equipped with the special diagnostic tester.

2 However, the coils can be checked visually (for cracks and other damage) and the primary and secondary coil resistance can be measured with a multimeter. If the coils are undamaged, and if the resistance readings are as specified at the beginning of the Chapter, they are probably capable of proper operation.

3 Remove the seat (see Chapter 8) and disconnect the battery negative (-ve) lead. To gain access to the coils, remove the fuel tank (see Chapter 4). The front coil is mounted on the frame behind the steering head, and the rear coil is mounted on the frame behind the rear cylinder valve cover **(see illustrations)**.

4 Disconnect the primary circuit electrical connectors from the coil being tested and the HT leads from the spark plugs. Mark the locations of all wires and leads before disconnecting them.

5 Set the meter to the ohms x 1 scale and measure the resistance between the primary circuit terminals **(see illustration)**. This will give a resistance reading of the primary windings and should be consistent with the

3.3a The front coil is mounted behind the steering head

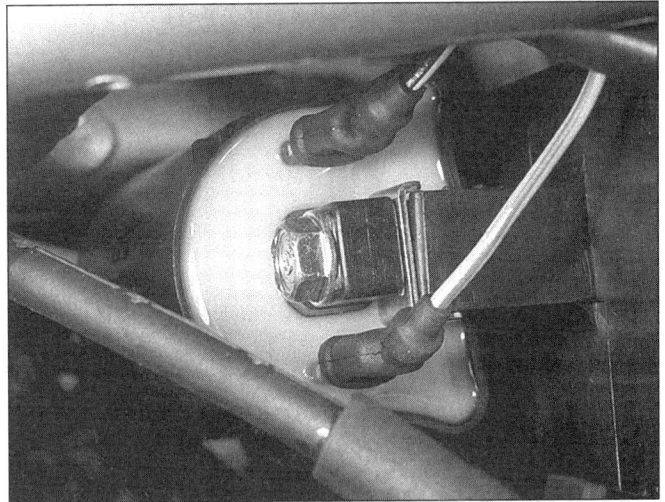

3.3b The rear coil is mounted behind the rear cylinder valve cover

value given in the Specifications at the beginning of the Chapter.

6 To check the condition of the secondary windings, set the meter to the K ohm scale. Connect one meter probe to each HT lead socket **(see illustration 3.5)**. If the reading obtained is not within the range shown in the Specifications, unscrew the plug lead connectors from the coil and measure the resistance between the HT terminals. If both values differ greatly from those specified it is likely that the coil is defective, whereas if only the first reading obtained is suspect then it can be assumed that the fault lies in the plug leads or caps rather than the coil itself.

7 Should any of the above checks not produce the expected result, have your

findings confirmed on the diagnostic tester (see Step 1). If the coil is confirmed to be faulty, it must be replaced; the coil is a sealed unit and cannot therefore be repaired. Note that the HT leads can be removed from the coils and replaced separately.

Removal

8 Remove the seat (see Chapter 8) and disconnect the battery negative (-ve) lead. Remove the fuel tank (see Chapter 4).

9 The front coil is mounted on the frame behind the steering stem, and the rear coil is mounted on the frame behind the rear cylinder valve cover. Disconnect the primary circuit electrical connectors from the coils and disconnect the HT leads from the spark

plugs. Mark the locations of all wires and leads before disconnecting them.

10 Unscrew the two bolts securing each coil to the frame and remove the coils **(see illustrations 3.3a and 3.3b)**. Note the routing of the HT leads.

Installation

11 Installation is the reverse of removal. Make sure the wiring connectors and HT leads are securely connected.

4 Pulse generator coils - check, removal and installation

Check

1 Remove the seat (see Chapter 8) and disconnect the battery negative (-ve) lead.

2 Trace the pulse generator coil wiring back from the right-hand side crankcase cover and disconnect it at the white 4-pin connector. Using a multimeter set to the ohms x 100 scale, measure the resistance between the white/yellow and yellow wires (for the front cylinder coil) and then between the white/blue and blue wires (for the rear cylinder coil) on the pulse generator coil side of the connector.

3 Compare the reading obtained with that given in the Specifications at the beginning of this Chapter. The pulse generator coils must be replaced if the reading obtained differs greatly from that given, particularly if the meter indicates a short circuit (no measurable resistance) or an open circuit (infinite, or very high resistance).

4 If one or both pulse generator coils are thought to be faulty, first check that this is not due to a damaged or broken wire from the coil to the connector; pinched or broken wires can usually be repaired. Note that the pulse generator coils are not available individually but come as a pair.

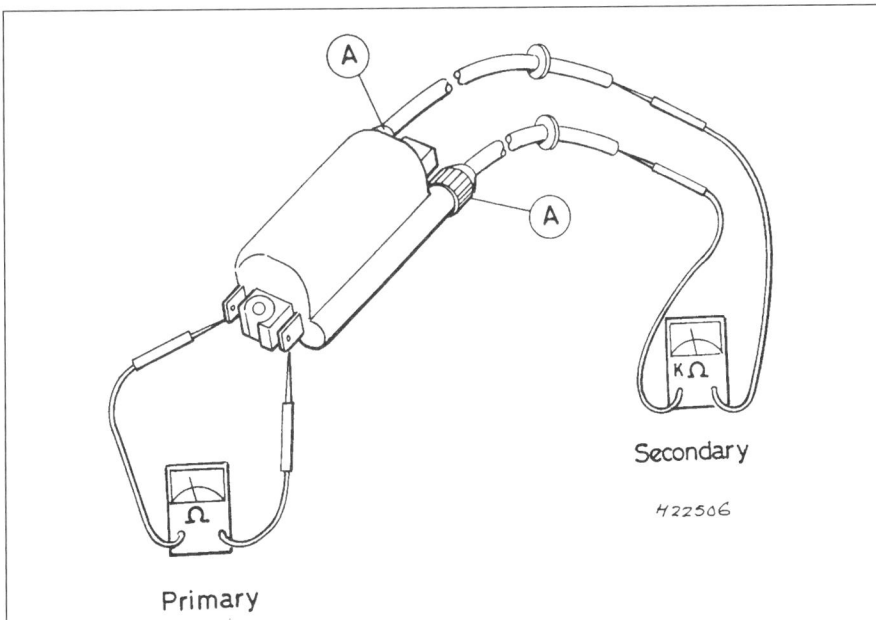

3.5 Ignition HT coil test connections

Release connectors (A) to make secondary winding test without plug leads

5

Removal

5 Remove the seat (see Chapter 8) and disconnect the battery negative (-ve) lead.

6 Trace the pulse generator coil wiring back from the right-hand side crankcase cover and disconnect it at the white 4-pin connector. Free the wiring from its guide on the right-hand frame downtube.

7 On J and K models, unscrew the external oil pipe lower bolt from the right-hand side crankcase cover, and the pipe holder bolt from the crankcase. Discard the lower bolt sealing washers as new ones must be used.

8 Working in a criss-cross pattern, evenly slacken the right-hand side crankcase cover retaining bolts, noting the position of the clutch cable bracket **(see illustration)**. Lift the cover away from the engine, being prepared to catch any residual oil which may be released as the cover is removed.

9 Remove the gasket and discard it. Note the positions of the two locating dowels fitted to the crankcase and remove them for safe-keeping if they are loose **(see illustration)**. On J and K models, remove the oil orifice, noting which way round it fits, and discard its O-ring as a new one must be used.

10 Unscrew the two bolts securing each coil, noting the position of the wiring guide plate on the lower coil **(see illustration)**. Remove the rubber wiring grommet from its recess in the crankcase and remove the coil assembly.

11 Examine the rotor for signs of damage and replace if necessary (see Chapter 2).

Installation

12 Install the pulse generator coil assembly onto the crankcase, making sure the wiring guide is correctly installed, and tighten the coil bolts securely **(see illustration)**.

13 Apply a smear of sealant to the rubber wiring grommet before fitting it in its recess in the crankcase **(see illustration)**.

14 Insert the dowels in the crankcase **(see illustration 4.9)**. On J and K models, fit a new O-ring onto the oil orifice, then install the orifice into the crankcase with its larger diameter hole facing out. Install the crankcase cover using a new gasket and tighten its bolts evenly in a criss-cross sequence, making sure the clutch cable bracket is in its correct position **(see illustration 4.8)**.

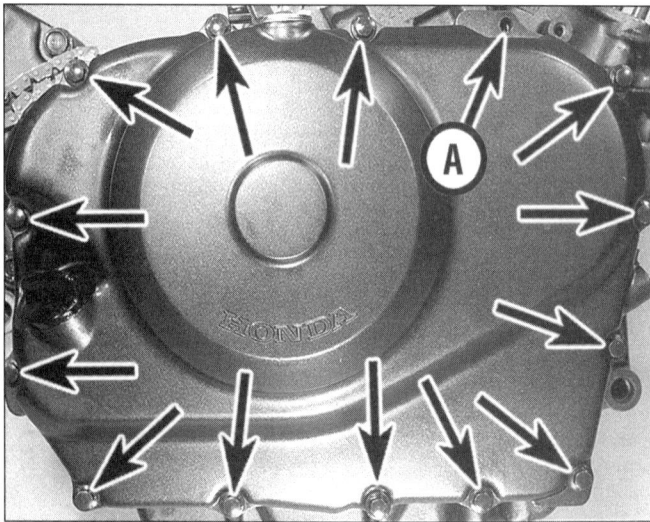

4.8 Right-hand crankcase cover bolts (arrows). Note the location of the cable bracket (A) (shown removed)

4.9 Note the position of the two dowels (arrows) and remove them if they are loose

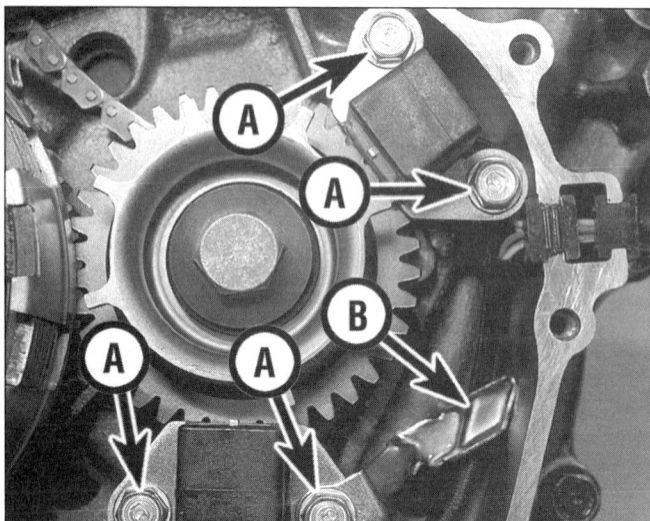

4.10 Pulse generator coil mounting bolts (A). Note the wiring guide (B)

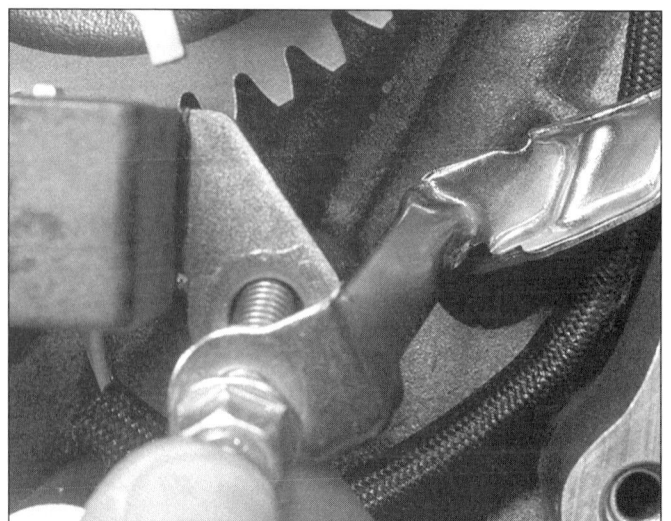

4.12 Install the wiring guide as shown

4.13 Fit the rubber wiring grommet as shown

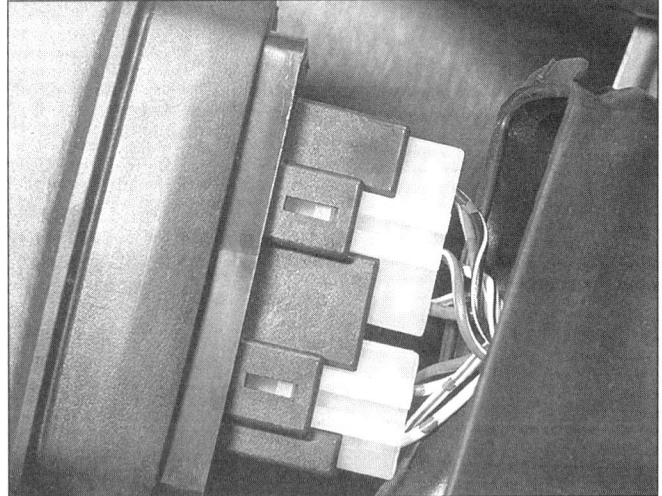

5.2 Pull back the rubber boot and disconnect the connectors from the ignition control unit

15 On J and K models, install the external oil pipe lower bolt, using new sealing washers, and the pipe holder bolt, and tighten them to the specified torque setting.

16 Route the wiring up to the connector and reconnect it. Secure the wiring in its guide on the right-hand frame downtube.

17 Reconnect the battery negative (-ve) lead and install the seat (see Chapter 8).

5 Ignition control unit - removal, check and installation

Removal

1 Remove the seat (see Chapter 8) and disconnect the battery negative (-ve) lead.

2 Remove the rear cowl (see Chapter 8). Pull back the rubber boot covering the ignition control unit wiring connector and disconnect the connectors **(see illustration)**.

3 Either withdraw the ignition control unit from its rubber sleeve, or remove the sleeve from its locating tabs with the unit inside **(see illustration)**.

Check

4 If the tests shown in the preceding Sections have failed to isolate the cause of an ignition fault, it is likely that the ignition control unit itself is faulty. No test details are available with which the unit can be tested on home workshop equipment. Take the machine to a Honda dealer for testing on the diagnostic tester.

Installation

5 Installation is the reverse of removal. Make sure the wiring connector is securely connected and its rubber boot is in place.

6 Ignition timing - general information and check

General information

1 Since no provision exists for adjusting the ignition timing and since no component is subject to mechanical wear, there is no need for regular checks; only if investigating a fault

such as a loss of power or a misfire, should the ignition timing be checked.

2 The ignition timing is checked dynamically (engine running) using a stroboscopic lamp. The inexpensive neon lamps should be adequate in theory, but in practice may produce a pulse of such low intensity that the timing mark remains indistinct. If possible, one of the more precise xenon tube lamps should be used, powered by an external source of the appropriate voltage. **Note:** *Do not use the machine's own battery as an incorrect reading may result from stray impulses within the machine's electrical system.*

Check

3 Warm the engine up to normal operating temperature then stop it.

4 Unscrew the timing mark inspection cap from the left-hand side crankcase cover **(see illustration)**.

5 The timing mark on the rotor is an "F" which indicates the firing point at idle speed (note that each cylinder has its own "F" mark, that for the front cylinder being adjacent to the "FT" mark, that for the rear cylinder being adjacent to the "RT" mark) **(see illustration)**. The static

5.3 The ignition control unit rubber sleeve attaches to tabs on the frame

6.4 Timing mark inspection hole

6.5 Front cylinder timing mark is represented by the scribed line next to the single F

timing mark with which this should align is a notch in the top of the inspection hole.

HAYNES HiNT *The rotor timing mark can be highlighted with white paint to make it more visible under the stroboscope light.*

6 Connect the timing light to the front cylinder HT lead as described in the manufacturer's instructions.

7 Start the engine and aim the light at the static timing mark.

8 With the machine idling at the specified speed, the timing F mark should align with the static timing mark.

9 Slowly increase the engine speed whilst observing the timing mark. The timing mark should move anti-clockwise, increasing in relation to the engine speed until it reaches the full advance point (no identification letter).

10 As already stated, there is no means of adjustment of the ignition timing on these machines. If the ignition timing is incorrect, or suspected of being incorrect, one of the ignition system components is at fault, and the system must be tested as described in the preceding Sections of this Chapter.

11 When the check is complete, examine the condition of the timing mark inspection cap O-ring, replacing it if necessary, then smear some molybdenum disulphide grease onto the cap threads. Install the cap and tighten it to the torque setting specified at the beginning of the Chapter.

Chapter 6
Frame, suspension and final drive

Contents

Degrees of difficulty

Easy, suitable for novice with little experience	Fairly easy, suitable for beginner with some experience	Fairly difficult, suitable for competent DIY mechanic	Difficult, suitable for experienced DIY mechanic	Very difficult, suitable for expert DIY or professional

Specifications

Front forks

Oil level*
  J model . . . . 182 mm
  K, M and P models . . . . 123 mm
  S and T models . . . . 106 mm
Oil capacity
  J model . . . . 405 cc
  K, M and P models . . . . 466 cc
  S and T models . . . . 482 cc
Oil type . . . . ATF
Fork spring free length
  J model
    Standard . . . . Not available
    Service limit . . . . 321 mm
  K, M and P models
    Standard . . . . 320 mm
    Service limit . . . . 314 mm
  S and T models
    Standard . . . . 371 mm
    Service limit . . . . Not available
Fork tube runout limit . . . . 0.2 mm

*Oil level is measured from the top of the tube with the fork spring removed and the leg fully compressed.

6

Rear shock absorber

Spring free length

J model

Standard	151 mm
Service limit	148 mm

All other models

Standard	175 mm
Service limit	171 mm

Final drive

Oil type	Hypoid gear oil SAE 80
Oil capacity	
After draining	0.11 litres
After disassembly	0.12 litres

Torque settings

Footrest bracket bolts	27 Nm
Gearchange lever pivot bolt	12 Nm
Centre stand pinch bolts	25 Nm
Side stand pivot bolt	38 Nm
Handlebar mounting bolts	30 Nm
Front brake master cylinder assembly clamp bolts	12 Nm
Clutch lever assembly clamp bolts	12 Nm
Top yoke fork clamp bolts	23 Nm
Bottom yoke fork clamp bolts	50 Nm
Fork top bolt	23 Nm
Fork damper rod bolt	20 Nm
Steering head bearing adjuster nut	
J model	22 Nm
All other models	28 Nm
Steering stem nut	105 Nm
Rear shock absorber	
J model	
Upper mounting bolt	95 Nm
Lower mounting bolt	45 Nm
All other models	
Upper mounting bolt	110 Nm
Lower mounting bolt	45 Nm
Swingarm pivot bolts	
Left-hand pivot bolt	100 Nm
Right-hand pivot bolt	
Pre-load setting	12 Nm
Normal setting	10 Nm
Right-hand pivot bolt locknut (using special tool)	90 Nm
Final drive housing nuts	65 Nm

1 General information

All models use a lightweight twin hexagonal-section tube frame.

Front suspension is by a pair of conventional oil-damped telescopic forks.

At the rear, a single-sided swingarm acts on a single shock absorber which is adjustable for pre-load and rebound damping (pre-load only on J models).

The drive to the rear wheel is by shaft, rather than the more commonly-found chain, and the shaft is housed inside the longitudinal section of the swingarm. The final drive housing turns the drive through 90° to the rear wheel.

2 Frame - inspection and repair

1 The frame should not require attention unless accident damage has occurred. In most cases, frame replacement is the only satisfactory remedy for such damage. A few frame specialists have the jigs and other equipment necessary for straightening the frame to the required standard of accuracy, but even then there is no simple way of assessing to what extent the frame may have been over stressed.
2 After the machine has accumulated a lot of miles, the frame should be examined closely for signs of cracking or splitting at the welded joints. Loose engine mount bolts can cause ovaling or fracturing of the mounting tabs.

Minor damage can often be repaired by welding, depending on the extent and nature of the damage.
3 Remember that a frame which is out of alignment will cause handling problems. If misalignment is suspected as the result of an accident, it will be necessary to strip the machine completely so the frame can be thoroughly checked.

3 Footrests and brackets - removal and installation

Rider's footrests

Removal

1 Remove the split pin and washer from the bottom of the footrest pivot pin, then

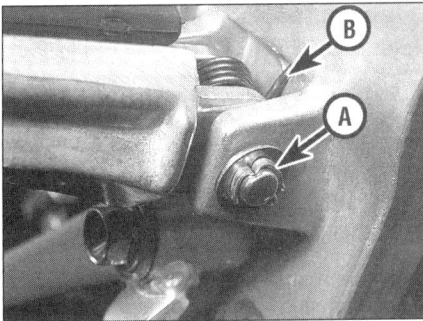

3.1 Remove the split pin (A) and withdraw the pivot pin from the front. Note the fitting of the return spring (B)

3.2 The rubber is secured to the footrest by two bolts

3.4 Remove the split pin and withdraw the pivot pin from the front to free the passenger footrest

withdraw the pivot pin and remove the footrest, noting how the return spring is located (see illustration). Discard the split pin as a new one must be used.

2 If necessary, the footrest rubber can be separated from the footrest by unscrewing the two bolts on the underside of the footrest (see illustration).

Installation

3 Installation is the reverse of removal, using a new split pin to secure the pivot pin. Make sure the return spring is correctly located.

Passenger's footrests

Removal

4 Remove the split pin and washer from the bottom of the footrest pivot pin, then withdraw the pivot pin and remove the footrest (see illustration). Discard the split pin as a new one must be used.

5 If necessary, the footrest rubber can be separated from the footrest by removing the washer from the inner end of the footrest and sliding the rubber off the footrest.

Installation

6 Installation is the reverse of removal, using a new split pin to secure the pivot pin.

Footrest brackets

Right-hand bracket

Removal

7 Remove the rider's footrest (see Step 1).

8 Unscrew the bolt securing the silencer to the bracket (see illustration 13.2a in Chapter 4), noting the spacer (S and T models only), and the two bolts securing the bracket to the frame. Carefully manoeuvre the bracket to provide access to the rear brake pedal and master cylinder which are mounted on the back of the bracket. Take care not to twist the brake hose.

9 Unhook the brake pedal return spring from the bracket and the brake light switch spring from the brake pedal (see illustration). Remove the circlip securing the brake pedal to its pivot shaft. Remove the split pin and clevis pin from the master cylinder pushrod link, then separate the brake pedal from the

master cylinder. Slip the brake pedal and its washer off the pivot. Depress the retaining tabs on the underside of the brake light switch adjuster nut and remove the switch from its bracket. Free the switch wiring from its clamp.

10 Unscrew the two bolts securing the master cylinder to the bracket and remove the bracket (see illustration). Support the master cylinder so that no strain is placed on its hoses.

Installation

11 Installation is the reverse of removal. Use a new split pin to secure the pushrod clevis pin. Tighten the footrest bracket mounting bolts to the torque setting specified at the beginning of the Chapter.

Left-hand bracket

Removal

12 Remove the rider's footrest (see Step 1).

13 Unscrew the bolt securing the gearchange lever to the bracket (see illustration). Remove the lever from the bracket but leave it attached to its linkage arm.

6

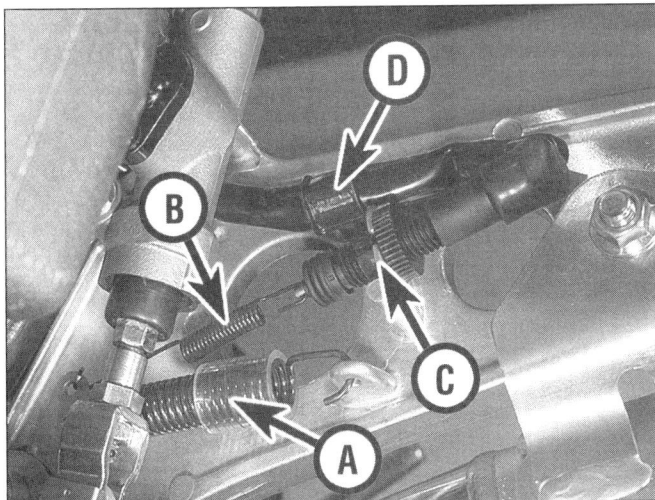

3.9 Brake pedal return spring (A), brake light switch spring (B), brake light switch adjuster nut retaining tabs (C), wiring clamp (D)

3.10 The master cylinder is secured to the back of the footrest bracket by two bolts (arrows)

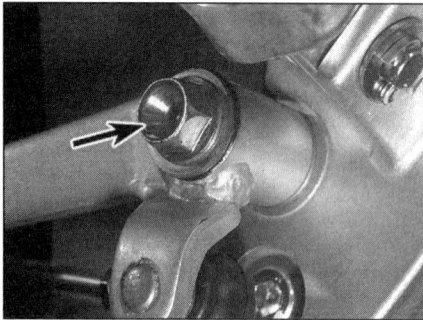

3.13 Gearchange lever bolt (arrow)

14 Unscrew the two bolts securing the bracket to the frame and remove the bracket.

Installation

15 Installation is the reverse of removal. Tighten the gearchange lever pivot bolt and the footrest bracket mounting bolts to the specified torque setting.

4 Stands - removal and installation

Centre stand - J, K and M models only

1 The centre stand is secured in the frame by a pivot shaft which is held in lugs on the frame by two pinch bolts. Support the bike on its side stand and free one end of the centre stand return spring. Remove the split pin from the left-hand end of the pivot shaft, then slacken both shaft pinch bolts and, supporting the stand, withdraw the shaft. Remove the stand. Discard the shaft split pin as a new one must be used.

2 Inspect the stand and shaft for signs of wear and replace if necessary. Apply a smear of grease to the shaft and fit the stand back on the bike, tightening the pinch bolts to the torque setting specified at the beginning of the Chapter. Use a new split pin on the pivot shaft end. Reconnect the return spring.

3 Make sure the return spring is in good condition and is capable of holding the stand up when not in use. A broken or weak spring is an obvious safety hazard.

Side stand

4 The side stand is attached to a bracket on the frame. An extension spring anchored to the bracket ensures that the stand is held in the retracted position. The side stand incorporates a switch which cuts out the ignition if the side stand is extended when the engine is running and in gear.

5 Support the bike on its centre stand (if fitted), or on an auxiliary stand.

6 Free the stand spring and unscrew the nut from the pivot bolt. Withdraw the pivot bolt to free the stand from its bracket.

7 On installation apply grease to the pivot bolt shank and tighten the nut to the torque setting specified at the beginning of the Chapter. Reconnect the side stand spring and check that it holds the stand securely up when not in use - an accident is almost certain to occur if the stand extends while the machine is in motion.

8 For check and replacement of the side stand switch see Chapter 9.

5 Handlebars - removal and installation

J, K and M models

Right-hand handlebar

Note: *If required, the handlebar can be displaced for access to the fork top bolt or the top yoke without removing the switch housing and the front brake master cylinder assembly.*

1 Remove the right-hand handlebar switch housing (see Chapter 9).

2 Remove the front brake master cylinder assembly (see Chapter 7).

3 Unscrew the two bolts securing the instrument cluster and displace the cluster to provide access to the handlebar mounting bolts. There is no need to disconnect the instrument cluster wiring or speedometer cable.

4 Prise out the caps from the bolts securing the handlebar to the top yoke, then unscrew the bolts and remove the handlebar.

5 If necessary, unscrew the handlebar end-weight retaining screw, then remove the weight from the end of the handlebar and slide off the throttle twistgrip. If replacing the grip, it may be necessary to slit it using a sharp knife as it is adhered to the throttle twist.

6 Installation is the reverse of removal, noting the following:

a) *If a new grip is being fitted, secure it to the throttle twist using a suitable adhesive (Honda bond A).*

b) *If removed, apply a smear of grease to the inside of the throttle twistgrip and a suitable non-permanent locking compound to the handlebar end-weight retaining screw.*

c) *Tighten the handlebar mounting bolts to the torque setting specified at the beginning of the Chapter.*

d) *Make sure the front brake master cylinder assembly clamp is installed with its "UP" mark facing up and with the clamp mating surfaces aligned with the punch mark on the handlebar (see illustrations 5.19a and 5.19b). Tighten the upper bolt first, then the lower bolt, to the torque setting specified at the beginning of the Chapter.*

Left-hand handlebar

Note: *If required, the handlebar can be displaced for access to the fork top bolt or the top yoke without removing the switch housing and the clutch lever assembly.*

7 Remove the left-hand handlebar switch (see Chapter 9).

8 Unscrew the two bolts securing the clutch lever assembly clamp to the handlebar and remove the assembly, noting the "UP" mark on the clamp face and the punch mark on the handlebar which must align with the clamp mating surfaces on installation.

9 Unscrew the two bolts securing the instrument cluster and displace the cluster to provide access to the handlebar mounting bolts. There is no need to disconnect the instrument cluster wiring or speedometer cable.

10 Prise out the caps from the bolts securing the handlebar to the top yoke, then unscrew the bolts and remove the handlebar.

11 If necessary, unscrew the handlebar end-weight retaining screw, then remove the weight from the end of the handlebar. If replacing the grip, it may be necessary to slit it using a sharp knife as it is adhered to the handlebar.

12 Installation is the reverse of removal, noting the following:

a) *If a new grip is being fitted, secure it to the handlebar using a suitable adhesive (Honda bond A).*

b) *If removed, apply a suitable non-permanent locking compound to the handlebar end-weight retaining screw.*

c) *Tighten the handlebar mounting bolts to the torque setting specified at the beginning of the Chapter.*

d) *Make sure the clutch lever assembly clamp is installed with its "UP" mark facing up and with the clamp mating surfaces aligned with the punch mark on the handlebar (see illustrations 5.19a and 5.19b). Tighten the upper bolt first, then the lower bolt, to the torque setting specified at the beginning of the Chapter.*

P, S and T models

Removal

Note: *If required, the handlebars can be displaced for access to the fork top bolts or the top yoke without removing the switch housings, the front brake master cylinder assembly and the clutch lever assembly.*

13 Remove both left and right-hand handlebar switches (see Chapter 9).

14 Remove the front brake master cylinder assembly (see Chapter 7).

15 Unscrew the two bolts securing the clutch lever assembly clamp to the handlebar and remove the assembly, noting the "UP" mark on the clamp face and the punch mark on the handlebar which must align with the clamp mating surfaces on installation **(see illustrations 5.19a and 5.19b).**

5.16a Remove the handlebar clamp bolt caps . . .

5.16b . . . then unscrew the bolts and remove the clamps

16 Prise out the caps from the bolts securing the handlebar clamps to the top yoke, then unscrew the bolts and remove the clamps and the handlebars **(see illustrations)**.

17 If necessary, unscrew the handlebar end-weight retaining screws, then remove the weights from the end of the handlebars. If replacing the grips, it may be necessary to slit them using a sharp knife as they are adhered to the throttle twistgrip (right-hand) and the handlebar (left-hand).

Installation

18 Installation is the reverse of removal. Align the handlebars so that the ridges are central in the clamp mounts **(see illustration)**. Fit the clamps with the punch mark facing forward **(see illustration)**. Tighten the handlebar mounting bolts to the torque setting specified at the beginning of the Chapter.

19 If removed, apply a suitable non-permanent locking compound to the handlebar end-weight retaining screws. If new grips are being fitted, secure them using a suitable adhesive (Honda bond A). Make sure

the front brake master cylinder and clutch lever assembly clamps are installed with their "UP" mark facing up and with the clamp mating surfaces aligned with the punch mark on the handlebar **(see illustrations)**. Tighten the upper bolt first, then the lower bolt, to the torque setting specified at the beginning of the Chapter.

6 Forks - removal and installation

Removal

1 Remove the front wheel (see Chapter 7).
2 Remove the front mudguard (Chapter 8).
3 On J, K and M models, displace the handlebars (see Section 5). Support the right-hand handlebar so the master cylinder is upright and no strain is placed on the hose. On P, S and T models, displace the handlebars only if the forks are being dismantled. This provides access to the fork top bolt (not necessary if the forks are not being disassembled).
4 Slacken, but do not remove, the fork clamp bolts in the top yoke **(see illustration)**. If the

5.18a The ridged areas on the handlebar must be central in the clamps

5.18b The punch mark on each clamp must face forward (arrow)

5.19a Fit the clamp with the "UP" mark facing up . . .

5.19b . . . and with the mating surfaces aligned with the punch mark (arrows)

6.4 Top yoke fork clamp bolt

6

6.5 Bottom yoke fork clamp bolt

6.6 Install the forks through the bottom yoke and the turn signal bracket

forks are to be disassembled, it is advisable to slacken the fork top bolts at this stage.

> **HAYNES HiNT** *Slackening the fork pinch bolts in the top yoke before slackening the fork top bolt releases pressure on the top bolt. This makes it much easier to remove and helps to preserve the threads.*

5 Note the position of fork tubes relative to the top yoke so that they are installed in the same position. Slacken but do not remove the fork clamp bolts in the bottom yoke, and remove the forks by twisting them and pulling

them downwards **(see illustration)**. Note how the forks pass through the turn signal brackets.

> **HAYNES HiNT** *If the fork legs are seized in the yokes, spray the area with penetrating oil and allow time for it to soak in before trying again.*

Installation

6 Remove all traces of corrosion from the fork tubes and the yokes and slide the forks back into place **(see illustration)**. On J, K and M

models align the groove in the fork tube with the underside of the top yoke. On P, S and T models, align the upper edge of the fork tube with the top surface of the top yoke **(see illustration 6.4)**.

7 Tighten the bottom yoke pinch bolts to the torque setting specified at the beginning of the Chapter **(see illustration 6.5)**. If the fork legs have been dismantled, the fork tube top bolts should now be tightened to the specified torque setting. Now tighten the top yoke pinch bolts to the specified torque setting **(see illustration 6.4)**.

8 Install the front mudguard (see Chapter 8), the front wheel (see Chapter 7) and the handlebars if removed (see Section 5).

9 Check the operation of the front forks and brake before taking the bike out on the road.

7 Forks - disassembly, inspection and reassembly

Disassembly

1 Always dismantle the fork legs separately to avoid interchanging parts and thus causing an accelerated rate of wear. Store all components in separate, clearly marked containers **(see illustration)**.

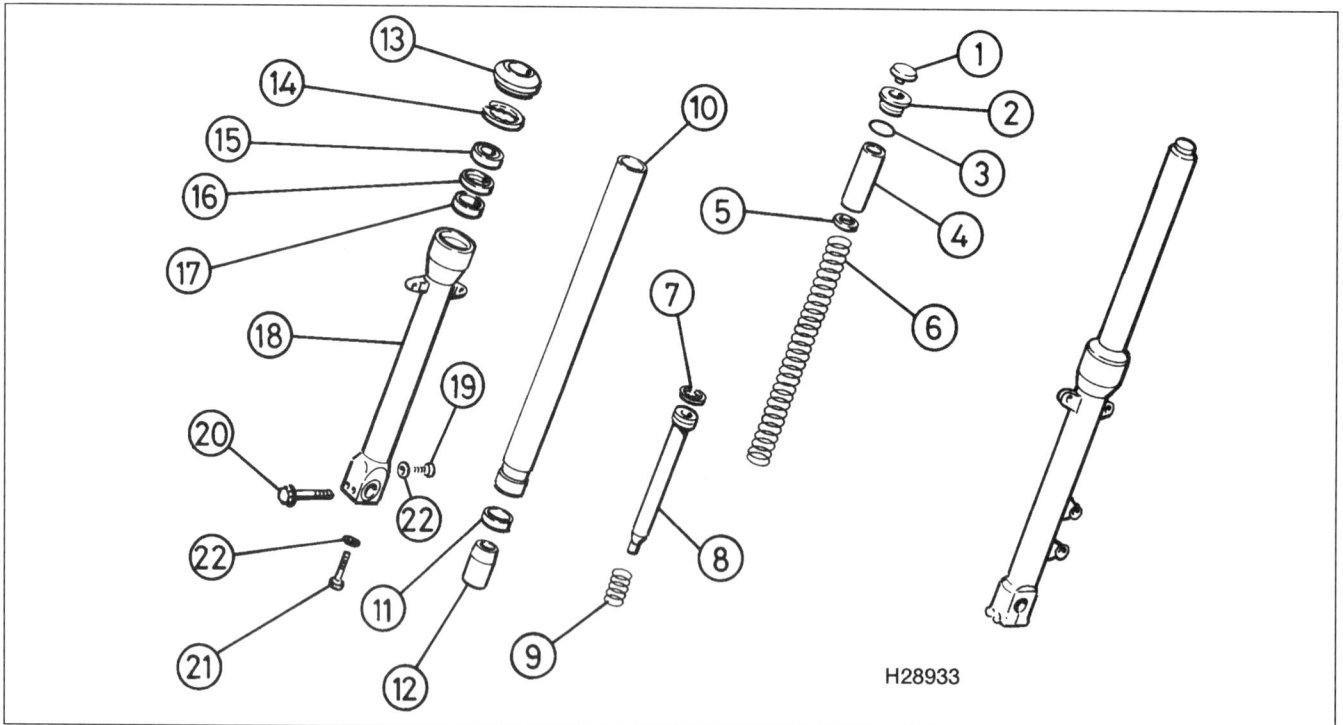

H28933

7.1 Front fork components

1	Top bolt cap	6	Spring	11	Bottom bush
2	Top bolt	7	Piston ring	12	Damper rod seat
3	O-ring	8	Damper rod	13	Dust seal
4	Spacer	9	Rebound spring	14	Retaining clip
5	Spring seat	10	Fork tube	15	Oil seal

16	Washer	20	Axle clamp bolt
17	Top bush	21	Damper rod bolt
18	Fork slider	22	Sealing washer
19	Drain screw		

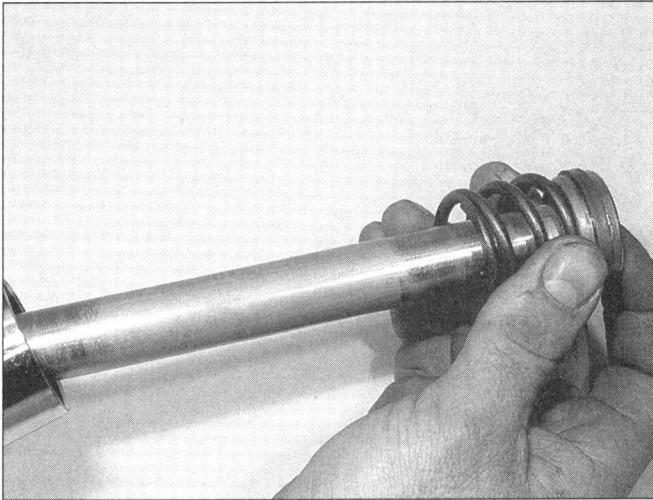

7.8 Withdraw the damper rod and rebound spring from the tube

7.9 Prise out the dust seal using a flat-bladed screwdriver

2 Before dismantling the fork, it is advised that the damper rod bolt be slackened at this stage. Compress the fork tube in the slider so that the spring exerts maximum pressure on the damper rod head, then have an assistant slacken the damper rod bolt in the base of the fork slider.

3 If the fork top bolt was not slackened with the fork in situ, carefully clamp the fork tube in a vice, taking care not to overtighten or score its surface, then slacken the fork top bolt.

4 Unscrew the fork top bolt from the top of the fork tube.

⚠️ *Warning: The fork spring is pressing on the fork top bolt with considerable pressure. Unscrew the bolt very carefully, keeping a downward pressure on it and release it slowly as it is likely to spring clear. It is advisable to wear some form of eye and face protection when carrying out this operation.*

5 Slide the fork tube down into the slider and withdraw the spacer, spring seat and the spring from the tube, noting which way up they fit.

6 Invert the fork leg over a suitable container and pump the fork vigorously to expel as much fork oil as possible.

7 Remove the previously slackened damper rod bolt and its copper sealing washer from the bottom of the slider. Discard the washer as a new one must be used on reassembly. If the damper rod bolt was not slackened before dismantling the fork, it may be necessary to re-install the spring, spring seat, spacer and top bolt to prevent the damper rod from turning. Alternatively, a broom handle or tapered length of wooden dowel passed down through the fork tube, can be pressed hard into the damper rod head and held to stop it turning.

8 Withdraw the damper rod from the fork tube, and remove the rebound spring **(see illustration)**.

9 Carefully prise out the dust seal from the top of the slider to gain access to the oil seal retaining clip **(see illustration)**. Discard the dust seal as a new one must be used.

10 Carefully remove the retaining clip, taking care not to scratch the surface of the tube **(see illustration)**.

11 To separate the tube from the slider it will be necessary to displace the top bush and oil seal. The bottom bush should not pass through the top bush, and this can be used to good effect. Push the tube gently inwards until it stops against the damper rod seat. Take care not to do this forcibly or the seat may be damaged. Then pull the tube sharply outwards until the bottom bush strikes the top bush. Repeat this operation until the top bush and seal are tapped out of the slider **(see illustration)**.

7.10 Prise out the retaining clip using a flat-bladed screwdriver

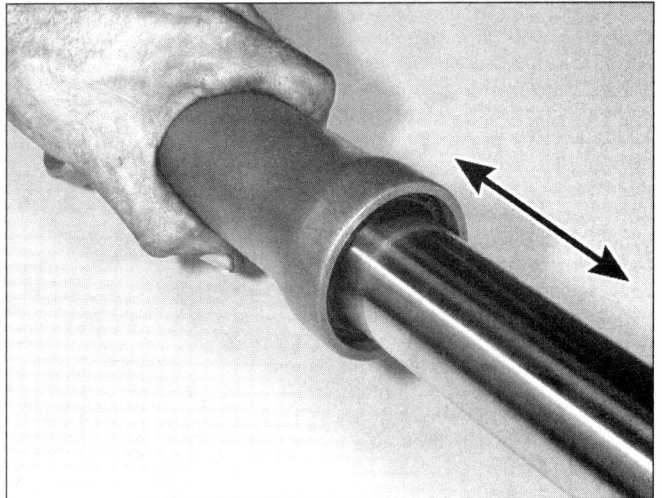

7.11 To separate the slider and fork tube, pull them apart firmly several times - the slide-hammer effect will pull them apart

6

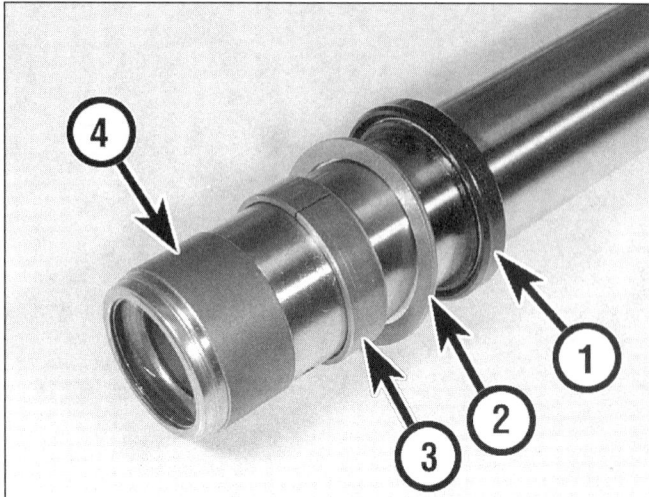

7.12 The oil seal (1), washer (2), top bush (3) and bottom bush (4) will come out with the fork tube

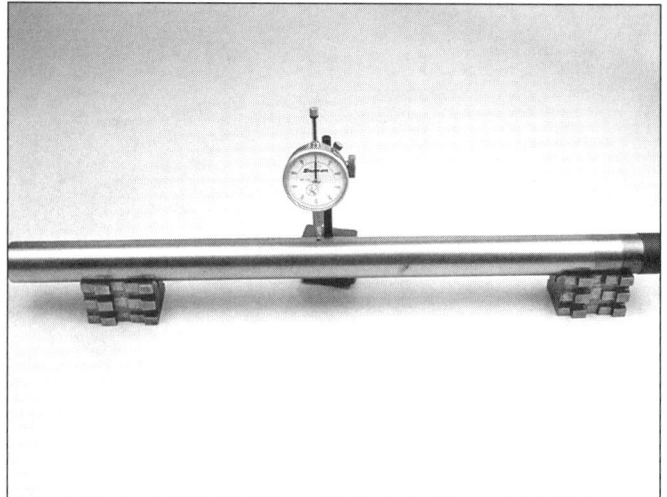

7.15 Check the fork tube for runout using V-blocks and a dial indicator

12 With the tube removed, slide off the oil seal and its washer, noting which way up they fit **(see illustration)**. Discard the oil seal as a new one must be used. The top bush can then also be slid off its upper end. Do not remove the bottom bush from the tube unless it is to be replaced.

13 Tip the damper rod seat out of the slider, noting which way up it fits.

Inspection

14 Clean all parts in solvent and blow them dry with compressed air, if available. Check the fork tube for score marks, scratches, flaking of the chrome finish and excessive or abnormal wear. Look for dents in the tube and replace the tube in both forks if any are found. Check the fork seal seat for nicks, gouges and scratches. If damage is evident, leaks will occur.

15 Check the fork tube for runout using V-blocks and a dial gauge, or have it done at a dealer service department or other repair shop **(see illustration)**.

⚠️ *Warning: If it is bent, it should not be straightened; replace it with a new one.*

16 Check the spring for cracks and other damage. Measure the spring free length and compare the measurement to the specifications at the beginning of the Chapter. If it is defective or sagged below the service limit, replace the springs in both forks with new ones. Never replace only one spring.

17 Examine the working surfaces of the two bushes; if worn or scuffed they must be replaced. To remove the bottom bush from the fork tube, prise it apart at the slit using a screwdriver and slide it off **(see illustration)**. Make sure the new one seats properly.

18 Check the damper rod assembly components for damage and wear, and replace any that are defective **(see illustration)**.

Reassembly

19 Install the rebound spring and piston ring (if removed) onto the damper rod **(see illustration)**. Insert the damper rod into the fork tube and slide it into place so that it projects fully from the bottom of the tube, then install the seat on the bottom of the damper rod **(see illustration)**.

20 Oil the fork tube and bottom bush with the specified fork oil and insert the assembly into the slider **(see illustration)**. Fit a new copper sealing washer to the damper rod bolt and apply a few drops of a suitable thread locking compound to its threads then install the bolt into the bottom of the slider **(see illustration)**. Tighten the bolt to the specified torque setting. If the damper rod rotates inside the tube, temporarily install the fork spring and top bolt (see Steps 26 and 27) and compress the fork to hold the damper rod. Alternatively, a broom handle pressed hard into the damper rod head quite often suffices.

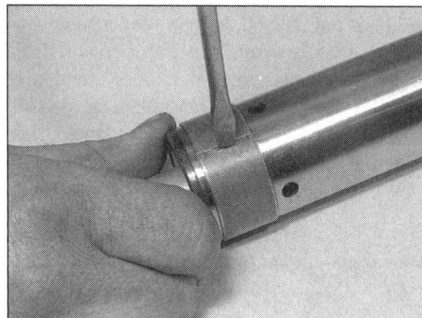

7.17 Prise off the bottom bush using a flat-bladed screwdriver

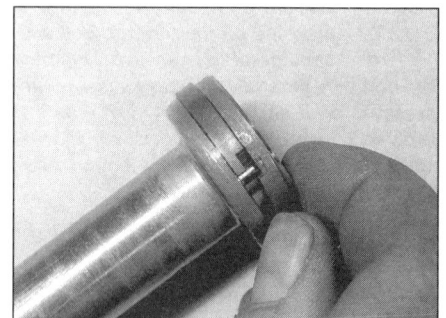

7.18 Replace the damper rod piston ring if it is worn or damaged

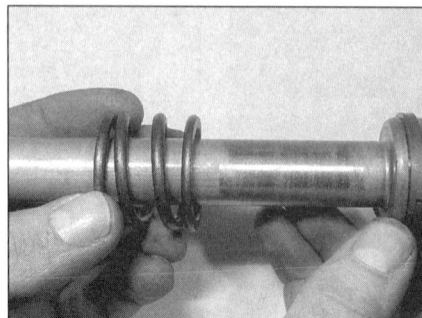

7.19a Slide the rebound spring onto the damper rod

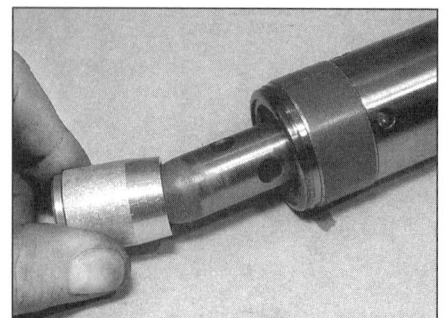

7.19b Fit the seat to the bottom of the damper rod

7.20a Slide the tube into the slider

7.20b Apply a thread-locking compound to the damper rod bolt and use a new sealing washer

7.21a Install the top bush . . .

7.21b . . . followed by the washer

7.22 Make sure the oil seal is the correct way up

7.23 Install the retaining clip . . .

7.24 . . . followed by the dust seal

7.25a Pour the oil into the top of the tube

7.25b Measure the oil level with the fork held vertical

21 Push the fork tube fully into the slider, then oil the top bush and slide it down over the tube **(see illustration)**. Press the bush squarely into its recess in the slider as far as possible, then install the washer **(see illustration)**. Either use the service tool (Pt. Nos. 07947-KA50100 and 07947-KF00100) or a suitable piece of tubing to tap the bush fully into place; the tubing must be slightly larger in diameter than the fork tube and slightly smaller in diameter than the bush recess in the slider. Take care not to scratch the fork tube during this operation; it is best to make sure that the fork tube is pushed fully into the slider so that any accidental scratching is confined to the area above the oil seal.

22 When the bush is seated fully and squarely in its recess in the slider (remove the washer to check, wipe the recess clean, then reinstall the washer), install the new oil seal. Smear the seal's lips with fork oil and slide it over the tube so that its markings face upwards. Drive the seal into place as described in Step 21 until the retaining clip groove is visible above the seal.**(see illustration)**.

23 Once the seal is correctly seated, fit the retaining clip, making sure it is correctly located in its groove **(see illustration)**.

24 Lubricate the lips of the new dust seal then slide it down the fork tube and press it into position **(see illustration)**.

25 Slowly pour in the specified quantity and grade of fork oil **(see illustration)** and pump

the fork to distribute the oil evenly. The oil level should also be measured and adjustment made by adding or subtracting oil. Fully compress the fork tube into the slider and measure the fork oil level from the top of the tube **(see illustration)**. Add or subtract fork oil until the oil is at the level specified in the Specifications Section of this Chapter.

26 Pull the fork tube out of the slider as far as possible then install the spring, with its closer-wound coils at the bottom, followed by the spring seat and the spacer **(see illustrations)**.

27 Fit a new O-ring to the fork top bolt and thread the bolt into the top of the fork tube **(see illustration)**. Wipe off any excess oil before starting to prevent the possibility of the fork tube slipping whilst it is being held. Keep the

6

7.26a Install the spring with its closer-wound coils at the bottom

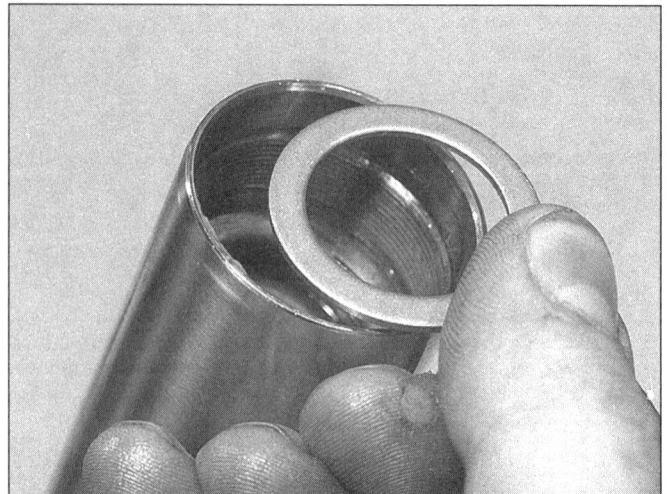

7.26b Install the spring seat . . .

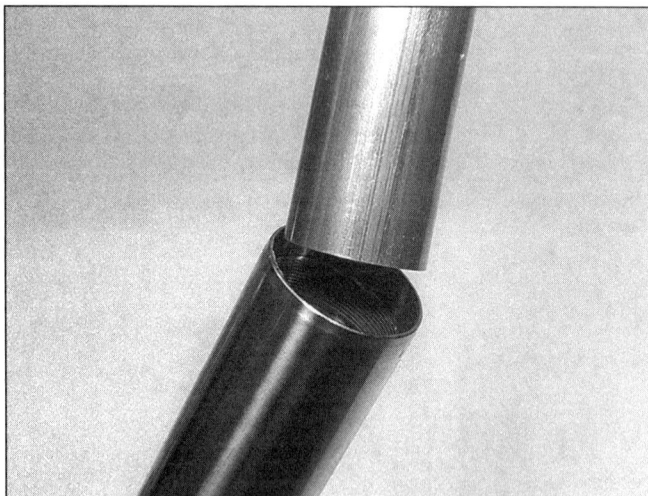

7.26c . . . followed by the spacer

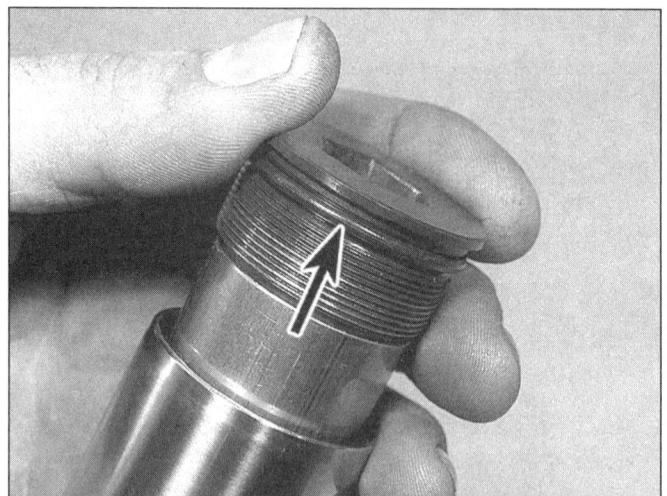

7.27 Fit a new O-ring (arrow) onto the top bolt and thread the bolt into the fork tube

fork tube fully extended whilst pressing on the spring. Screw the top bolt carefully into the fork tube making sure it is not cross-threaded.

⚠ **Warning: It will be necessary to compress the spring by pressing it down using the top bolt to engage the threads of the top bolt with the fork tube. This is a potentially dangerous operation and should be performed with care, using an assistant if necessary.**

28 The top bolt can be tightened to the specified torque setting at this stage if the tube is held between the padded jaws of a vice, but do not risk distorting the tube by doing so. A better method is to tighten the top bolt when the fork has been installed in the bike and is securely held in the yokes **(see Tool Tip)**.

29 Install the forks as described in Section 6.

TOOL TiP *Use a ratchet-type tool when installing the fork top bolt. This makes it unnecessary to remove the tool from the bolt whilst threading it in, making it easier to maintain a downward pressure on the spring.*

8 Steering stem - removal and installation

Caution: Although not strictly necessary, before removing the steering stem it is recommended that the fuel tank be removed. This will prevent accidental damage to the paintwork.

Removal

1 Remove the front forks (see Section 6).
2 On J, K and M models, unscrew the fuse box cover retaining screws and remove the cover, then unscrew the screws securing the fuse box to the top yoke and move the fuse box aside, leaving its wiring connected and noting its routing.
3 On P, S and T models, unscrew the bolts securing the instrument cluster to the top yoke and move the cluster aside to allow the top yoke to be removed. There is no need to disconnect the instrument cluster wiring or speedometer cable. Also displace the handlebars (see Section 5) if not already done.
4 Disconnect the horn wires, then unscrew the horn mounting bolt/nut and remove the horn(s)

8.4a Disconnect the horn wires and remove the horn mounting bolt

8.4b Release the brake hose from its clamps

from the bottom yoke (see illustration). Also release the brake hose from its clamps on the bottom yoke (see illustration).

5 If the top yoke is to be removed from the bike altogether, disconnect the ignition switch wiring at its connector in the headlight housing (see Chapter 9).

6 Remove the steering stem nut and washer and lift the top yoke off the steering stem (see illustration). Support the headlight as the top yoke is removed, and note how the prongs on the top of the headlight bracket frame fit into the holes in the underside of the yoke. Lift the headlight and its frame out of the holes in the

bottom yoke, taking care not to lose the rubbers on the prongs of the frame and noting how it fits, and support the assembly carefully.

7 Bend back the tabs of the steering stem lockwasher to release it from the locknut, then unscrew and remove the locknut using a suitable C-spanner (see illustration). Remove the lockwasher and discard it as a new one must be used.

8 Supporting the bottom yoke, unscrew and remove the adjuster nut and the bearing cover from the steering stem.

9 Gently lower the bottom yoke and steering stem out of the frame.

10 Remove the upper bearing and its inner race from the top of the steering head. Remove all traces of old grease from the bearings and races and check them for wear or damage as described in Section 9. **Note:** *Do not attempt to remove the races from the frame or the lower bearing from the steering stem unless they are to be replaced.*

Installation

11 Smear a liberal quantity of grease on the bearing outer races in the frame. Work the grease well into both the upper and lower bearings.

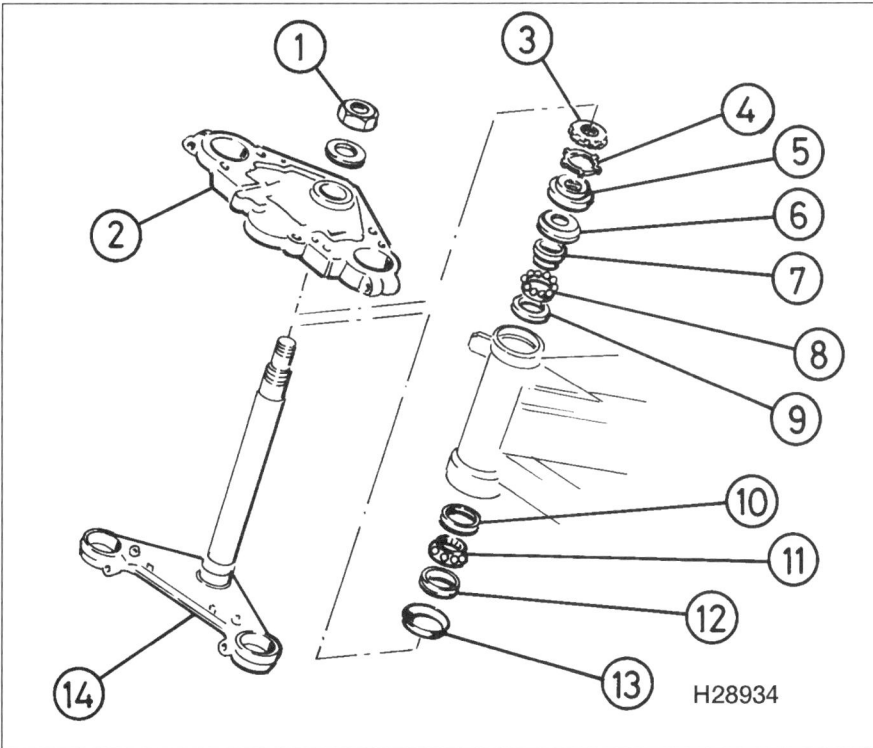

8.6 Steering stem components

1 Steering stem nut	6 Bearing cover	9 Upper bearing outer race	12 Lower bearing inner race
2 Top yoke	7 Upper bearing inner race	10 Lower bearing outer race	13 Dust seal
3 Locknut	8 Upper bearing	11 Lower bearing	14 Bottom yoke and steering stem
4 Lockwasher			
5 Adjuster nut			

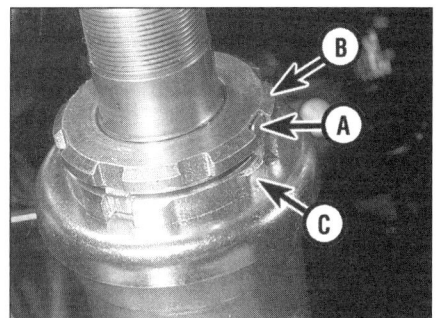

8.7 Steering stem lockwasher (A), locknut (B), adjuster nut (C)

6

12 Carefully lift the steering stem/bottom yoke up through the frame. Install the upper bearing and its inner race in the top of the steering head. Install the bearing cover and thread the adjuster nut on the steering stem. Tighten the adjuster nut to the torque setting specified at the beginning of the Chapter, then turn the steering stem through its full lock four or five times and tighten the adjuster nut again to the specified setting. If it is not possible to apply a torque wrench to the adjuster nut, tighten the nut sufficiently to remove freeplay (yet still allowing free steering movement) and adjust the bearings as described in Chapter 1.
Caution: Take great care not to apply excessive pressure because this will cause premature failure of the bearings.
13 When the bearings are correctly adjusted, install the new lockwasher onto the adjuster nut and bend down two of its opposite tabs. Install the locknut and tighten it finger-tight, then tighten it further (to a maximum of 90°) until its slots align with the remaining tabs on the lockwasher. Hold the adjuster nut to prevent it from moving if necessary. Bend up the lockwasher tabs to secure the locknut.
14 Install the headlight frame bottom prongs into their holes in the bottom yoke, making sure the rubbers are in place **(see illustration)**, then install the top yoke onto the steering stem, making sure the top prongs of the headlight frame fit into the holes in the underside of the top yoke and their rubbers are in place. Install the steering stem nut and its washer and tighten it finger-tight at this stage. Temporarily install one of the forks to align the top and bottom yokes, and secure it by tightening the bottom yoke clamp bolt only.
15 Tighten the steering stem nut to the specified torque setting. If disconnected, reconnect the ignition switch wiring connector.
16 Install the fork legs (see Section 6).
17 Install the horn(s) on the bottom yoke and tighten the retaining bolt/nut securely, then fit the horn wires **(see illustration 8.4a)**. Secure the brake hose in its clamps on the bottom yoke **(see illustration 8.4b)**.

8.14 Make sure the headlight frame prongs fit into their holes (arrow)

18 On P, S and T models install the handlebars (see Section 5) and the instrument panel.
19 On J, K and M models, install the fuse box, making sure its wiring is correctly routed.
20 Carry out a check of the steering head bearing freeplay as described in Chapter 1, and if necessary re-adjust.

9 Steering head bearings - inspection and replacement

Inspection

1 Remove the steering stem as described in Section 8.
2 Remove all traces of old grease from the bearings and races and check them for wear or damage. Also check the condition of the dust seal beneath the lower bearing.
3 The races should be polished and free from indentations. Inspect the bearing balls for signs of wear, damage or discoloration, and examine their retainer cage for signs of cracks or splits. Spin the bearings by hand. They should spin freely and smoothly. If there are any signs of wear on any of the above components both upper and lower bearing assemblies must be replaced as a set.

Replacement

4 The races are an interference fit in the steering head and can be tapped from position with a suitable drift. Tap firmly and evenly around each race to ensure that it is driven out squarely. It may prove advantageous to curve the end of the drift slightly to improve access.
5 Alternatively, the races can be removed using a slide-hammer type bearing extractor; these can often be hired from tool shops.
6 The new outer races can be pressed into the head using a drawbolt arrangement **(see illustration)**, or by using a large diameter tubular drift which bears only on the outer edge of the race. Ensure that the drawbolt washer or drift (as applicable) bears only on the outer edge of the race and does not contact the working surface. Alternatively, have the races installed by a Honda dealer equipped with the bearing race installing tools.

> **HAYNES HiNT** *Installation of new head bearing races is made much easier if the races are left overnight in the freezer. This causes them to contract slightly making them a looser fit.*

7 To remove the lower bearing inner race from the steering stem, use two screwdrivers placed on opposite sides of the race to work it free. If the bearing is firmly in place it will be necessary to use a bearing puller, or in extreme circumstances to split the bearing's inner section.

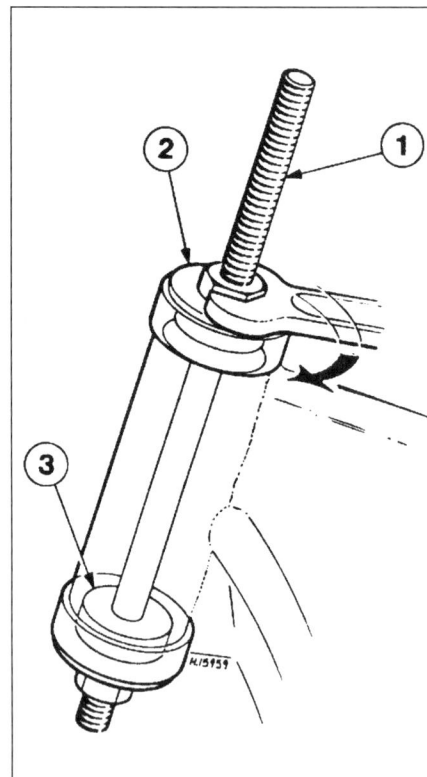

9.6 Drawbolt arrangement for fitting steering stem bearing races

1 Long bolt or threaded bar
2 Thick washer
3 Guide for lower race

8 Fit the new lower bearing inner race onto the steering stem. A length of tubing with an internal diameter slightly larger than the steering stem will be needed to tap the new bearing into position. Ensure that the drift bears only on the inner edge of the bearing and does not contact its working surface.
9 Install the steering stem as described in Section 8.

10 Rear shock absorber - removal, inspection and installation

Removal

1 Place the machine on the centre stand (if fitted), or support it using an auxiliary stand so that the rear wheel is raised off the ground.
2 Remove the seat and side panels (see Chapter 8).
3 Remove the rear wheel (see Chapter 7).
4 On all except J models, unscrew the bolt securing the shock absorber pre-load adjuster to the frame **(see illustration)**. Pull the adjuster hose clip from its hole in the battery case **(see illustration)**.

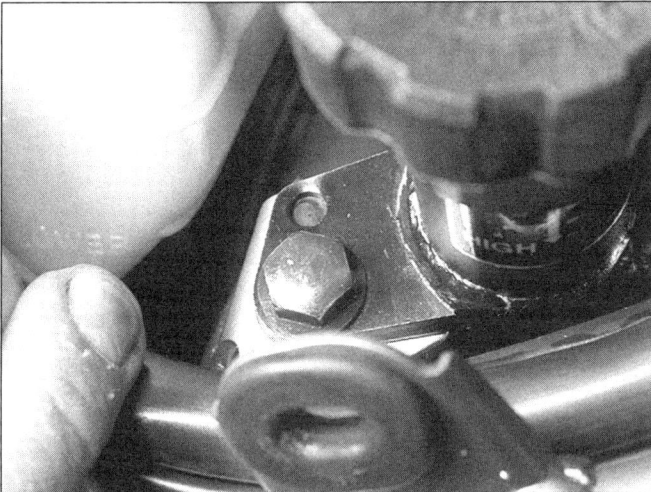

10.4a Shock absorber pre-load adjuster mounting bolt

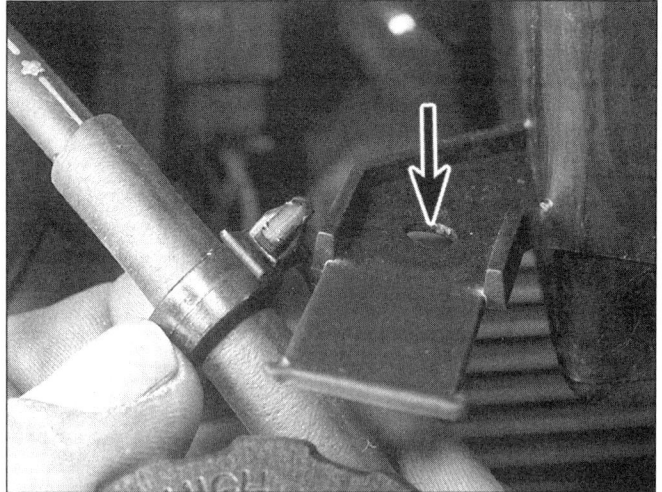

10.4b Pull the hose clip out of its hole (arrow)

5 Unscrew the shock absorber lower mounting bolt nut, then support the swingarm and withdraw the bolt **(see illustrations)**.
6 Unscrew the upper mounting bolt nut, then support the shock absorber and withdraw the bolt **(see illustrations)**.
7 Manoeuvre the shock absorber and its remote pre-load adjuster (except J models) out of the back of the frame, noting how it fits **(see illustration)**. Do not attempt to separate

the adjuster from the shock absorber. Note the routing of the drain tube.

Inspection

8 Inspect the shock absorber for obvious physical damage and the coil spring for looseness, cracks or signs of fatigue.
9 Inspect the damper rod for signs of bending, pitting and oil leakage.
10 Inspect the pivot hardware at the top and bottom of the shock for wear or damage.

11 If the shock absorber on J, K, M and P models is in any way damaged or worn, it can be disassembled and the damaged or worn components replaced. Disassembly of the shock absorber requires the use of an hydraulic press or spring compressor. It is therefore advised that the unit is taken to a Honda dealer or specialist repair shop. On S and T models replacement parts are not available for the shock absorber.

10.5a Unscrew the shock absorber
lower mounting bolt nut . . .

10.5b . . . and remove the bolt

10.6a Unscrew the shock absorber
upper mounting bolt nut . . .

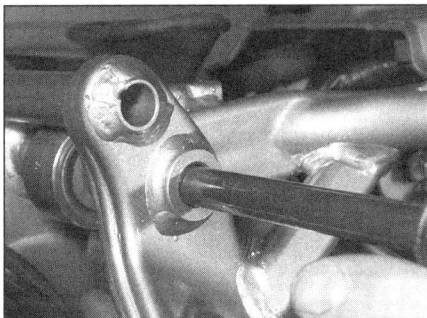

10.6b . . . and remove the bolt

10.7 Remove the shock absorber
from the back of the frame

6

10.12 Shock absorber disposal drilling point

Refer to text for details

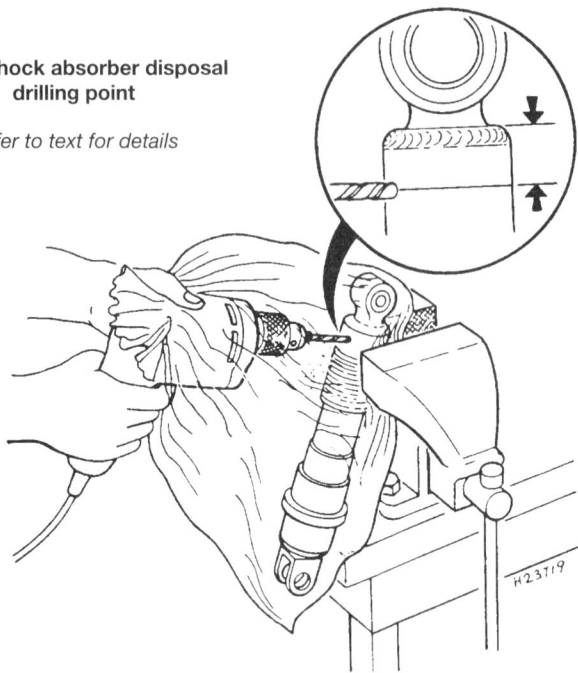

10.13 Make sure the pin (A) on the pre-load adjuster locates in the hole (B)

11 Suspension - adjustments

Front forks

1 The front forks are not adjustable.

Rear shock absorber

J models

2 The rear shock absorber is adjustable for spring pre-load. Adjustment is made by rotating the numbered collar at the bottom of the shock absorber.

3 There are seven positions. Position 1 is the softest setting, position 7 is the hardest. Adjustment is made using a suitable C-spanner (one is provided in the toolkit) in the cutouts of the collar. Align the setting number required with the adjustment stopper.

4 To increase the pre-load, turn the spring seat clockwise. To decrease the pre-load, turn the spring seat anti-clockwise.

All other models

5 The rear shock absorber is adjustable for spring pre-load and rebound damping.

6 Spring pre-load adjustment is made by turning the adjuster knob on the remote adjuster located behind the left-hand side panel **(see illustration)**. There are six positions indicated by lines marked on the adjuster. Align the position required with the lip on the adjuster body. The standard position is the second line and is marked "STD" on the adjuster **(see illustration)**.

12 Honda specifies releasing the nitrogen gas pressure before discarding the shock absorber. To do this a 2 to 3 mm hole must be drilled 20 mm from the top of the shock absorber **(see illustration)**. If in doubt, take the shock to a dealer for disposal.

⚠️ **Warning: Wear eye protection while drilling to prevent possible injury from escaping gas or flying metal chips. Honda specify that the drill and damper be placed inside a plastic bag during the operation as protection against the escaping gas. Do not drill the hole any farther down the body than specified otherwise you may drill into the oil chamber, causing oil to be expelled under pressure. Also ensure that the drill bit is sharp; a blunt drill bit could cause an excessive build-up of heat which could lead to an explosion and severe personal injury.**

Installation

13 Installation is the reverse of removal, noting the following.

a) *Apply multi-purpose lithium grease to the pivot points and engine oil to the threads of the mounting bolts.*
b) *Install the shock absorber with the drain tube facing forward. Make sure it is correctly routed and secured.*
c) *Install the upper mounting bolt first, but do not tighten it until the lower bolt is installed.*
d) *On all except J models, make sure the pre-load adjuster is correctly installed with the pin on its base located in the hole in the frame* **(see illustration)**.
e) *Tighten the mounting bolts to the torque setting specified at the beginning of the Chapter.*
f) *Secure the adjuster hose with its clip (except J models)* **(see illustration 10.4b)**.
g) *If the shock absorber has been disassembled, adjust the settings as required (see Section 11).*

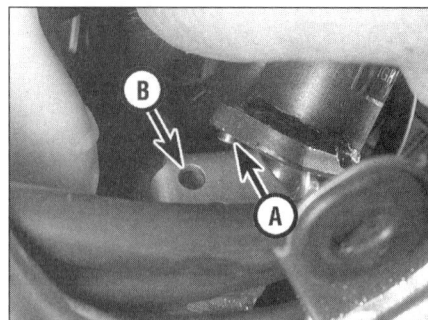

11.6a Spring pre-load adjuster

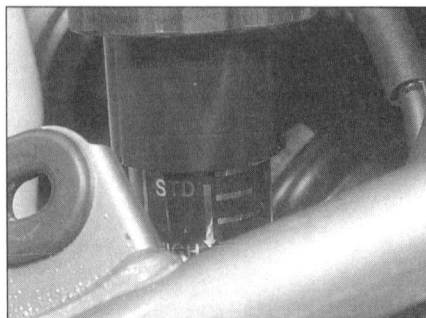

11.6b "STD" denotes the standard pre-load setting

11.9 Rebound damping adjuster

7 To increase the pre-load, turn the adjuster knob clockwise.

8 To decrease the pre-load, turn the adjuster knob anti-clockwise.

9 Rebound damping adjustment is made by turning the adjuster on the bottom left-hand side of the shock absorber using a flat-bladed screwdriver **(see illustration)**. There are three positions. The standard position is with the dot on the adjuster screw aligned with the dot on the adjuster body.

10 To increase the damping force turn the adjuster clockwise. To go from the standard to the second position, turn the adjuster 180°. To go from the standard to the third position, turn the adjuster 270°. To go from the second to the third position, turn the adjuster 90°.

11 To reduce the damping force turn the adjuster anti-clockwise. To go from the third to the second position, turn the adjuster 90°. To go from the third to the standard position, turn the adjuster 270°. To go from the second to the standard position, turn the adjuster 180°.

12 Swingarm - removal and installation

Removal

1 Remove the rear wheel (see Chapter 7).

2 Remove the brake hose clamps from the swingarm and final drive housing **(see illustrations)**. Support the caliper so that no strain is placed on the hose.

3 Remove the rear brake caliper from the final drive housing, but do not disconnect the brake hose (see Chapter 7).

4 Although it is not essential to separate the final drive housing and driveshaft from the swingarm in order to remove the swingarm, it is advisable to do so as the weight of the final drive housing makes it difficult to manoeuvre the swingarm out of and into the frame (see Section 14).

5 Remove the rear shock absorber lower mounting bolt (see Section 10 if necessary).

6 Prise off the swingarm pivot caps on both sides of the swingarm **(see illustration)**.

7 Counter-hold the pivot bolt on the right-hand side and slacken the locknut **(see illustration)**. This requires the use of a Honda service tool (Pt. No. 07908-ME90000), which is a special wrench that fits the locknut **(see illustration)**. There is no alternative to the use of this tool; if you do not have access to it, the swingarm pivot locknut must be unscrewed and later tightened by a dealer service department.

8 With the aid of an assistant to support the swingarm, unscrew the pivot bolts on both

12.2a Unscrew the brake hose clamps (arrows) to release the hose from the swingarm . . .

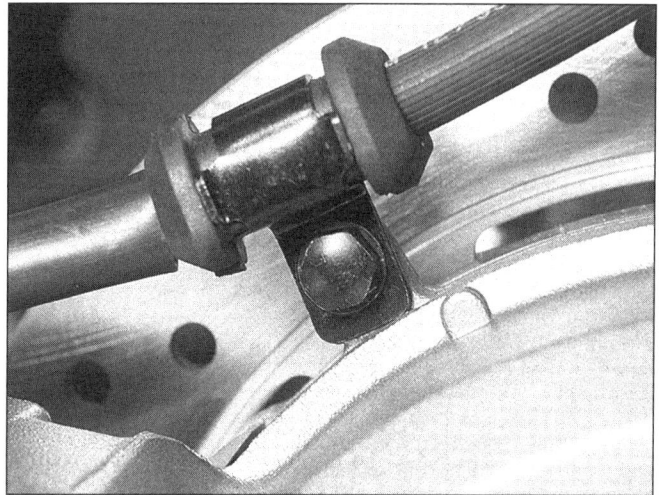

12.2b . . . and from the final drive housing

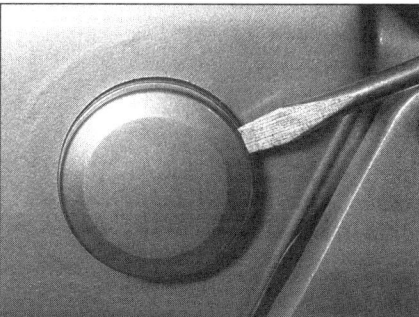

12.6 Prise off the swingarm pivot caps using a flat-bladed screwdriver inserted into the notch

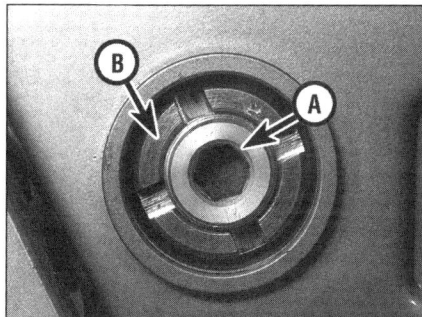

12.7a Swingarm right-hand pivot bolt (A) and locknut (B)

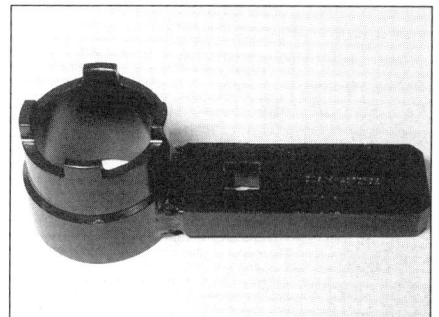

12.7b This Honda service tool is essential for removing and installing the swingarm

6

12.8 Swingarm left-hand pivot bolt

12.12a Tighten the left-hand pivot bolt to the specified torque setting

12.12b Tighten the locknut to the specified torque setting using the special tool and counter-holding the pivot bolt

sides and then carefully withdraw the swingarm from the frame **(see illustration)**. Note the positions of any breather and drain pipes and move them aside if necessary. If the driveshaft has not been removed and the universal joint does not come away with the swingarm, remove it from the output driven shaft.

9 Inspect all components for wear or damage as described in Section 13.

Installation

10 If removed, install the driveshaft into the swingarm (see Section 14). Fit the rubber gaiter to the output driven shaft with the "UP" mark facing up.

11 If the driveshaft has not been removed, make sure that the universal joint is installed in the swingarm and engaged correctly with the splines on the driveshaft. Manoeuvre the swingarm into position in the frame, making sure the universal joint engages correctly with the splines on the output driven shaft, and install the pivot bolts.

12 Tighten the left-hand side pivot bolt to the torque setting specified at the beginning of the Chapter **(see illustration)**. Tighten the right-hand side pivot bolt to the pre-load torque setting specified, then slacken it off and tighten it to the normal setting specified. Move the swingarm up and down several times to settle the bearings, then check that the right-hand side pivot bolt is tightened to the normal torque setting specified and adjust if necessary. Install the locknut onto the right-hand pivot bolt and tighten it to the specified torque setting using a torque wrench applied to the socket in the arm of the special tool (see Step 7) **(see illustration)**. **Note:** *The specified torque setting takes into account the extra leverage provided by the service tool and cannot be duplicated without it.* Counter-hold the pivot bolt to prevent it from turning whilst tightening the locknut. Install the pivot bolt caps.

13 If removed, install the final drive housing onto the swingarm (see Section 14).

14 Install the shock absorber lower mounting bolt and tighten it to the specified torque setting (see Section 10 if necessary).

15 Install the rear brake caliper and secure the brake hose with its clamps (refer to Chapter 7).

16 Install the rear wheel (see Chapter 7).

17 Make sure the rubber gaiter is correctly fitted over the ends of both the swingarm and the output driven shaft housing and that any drain and breather hoses are correctly routed.

18 Check the operation of the rear suspension before taking the machine on the road.

13 Swingarm - inspection and bearing replacement

Inspection

1 Thoroughly clean all components, removing all traces of dirt, corrosion and grease **(see illustration)**.

2 Inspect all components closely, looking for obvious signs of wear such as heavy scoring, and cracks or distortion due to accident damage. Any damaged or worn component must be replaced.

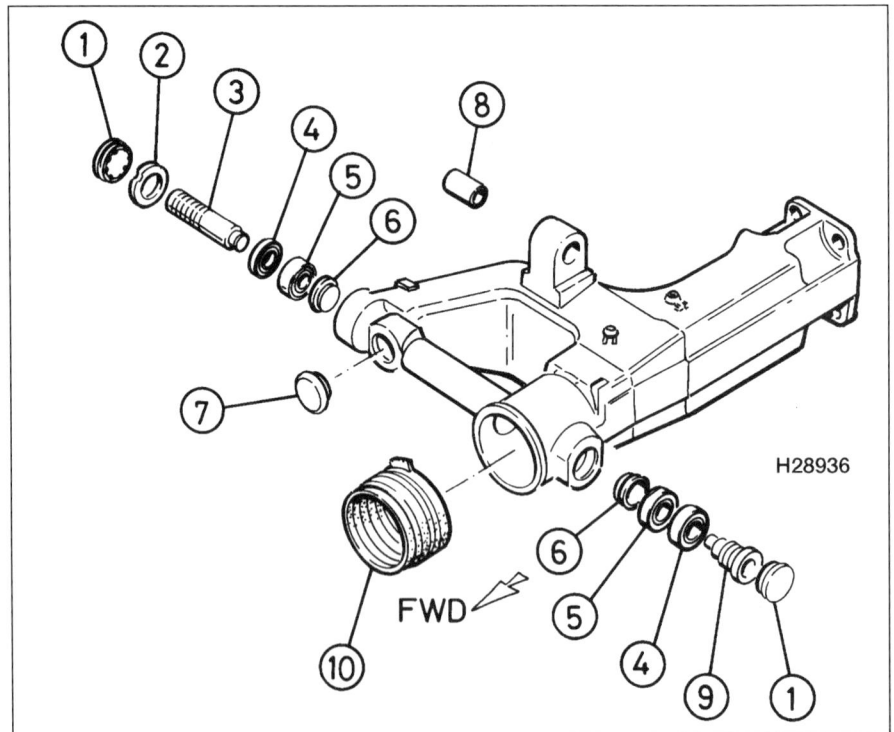

H28936

13.1 Swingarm components

1 Pivot caps	5 Bearing	8 Shock absorber bush
2 Locknut	6 Grease retainer plate	9 Pivot bolt
3 Pivot bolt	7 Grommet	10 Rubber gaiter
4 Grease seal		

Bearing replacement

3 Lever out the grease seals with a screwdriver and discard them as new ones must be used.

4 Remove the bearings, then clean them and inspect them for wear or damage. If the bearings do not run smoothly and freely or if there is excessive freeplay, they must be replaced. Inspect the bearing races in the swingarm for signs of pitting or other damage.

5 The bearings and races must be replaced as a set. Remove the races from the swingarm using an internal puller attached to a slide-hammer, and install them using a suitable tubular drift which only bears on the outer edge of the bearings, not their working surfaces. The grease retainer plates that sit behind the races should be discarded and new ones used if they are removed. Lubricate the bearings and grease seal lips using a waterproof lithium wheel bearing grease and press in the new seals.

14 Driveshaft and final drive - removal, inspection and installation

Removal

1 Drain the final drive gear oil (see Chapter 1).

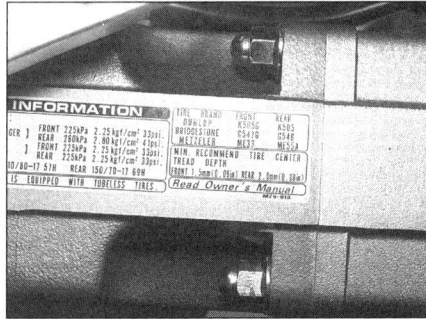

14.4a Unscrew the nuts securing the final drive housing to the swingarm

14.4b Remove the final drive housing from the swingarm

2 Remove the rear wheel (see Chapter 6).

3 If necessary, remove the rear brake disc from the final drive housing (see Chapter 7).

4 Support the final drive housing and unscrew the four nuts securing it to the swingarm **(see illustration)**. Remove the housing from the swingarm **(see illustration)**. The driveshaft is a push fit into both the final drive housing and the universal joint, and therefore will either come away with the final drive housing or detach from it and remain attached to the universal joint - it is more likely to come away with the housing. The universal joint is a sliding fit onto both the driveshaft and the output driven shaft, and therefore will either detach from the output shaft and come away with the driveshaft, or detach from the driveshaft and remain in the swingarm. Withdraw the driveshaft from either the swingarm or the final drive housing as required, and slide the universal joint off the driveshaft or remove it from the swingarm (using the driveshaft to draw it out) as required. If the driveshaft is withdrawn from the final drive housing, discard the oil seal and spring clip as new ones must be used **(see illustration)**.

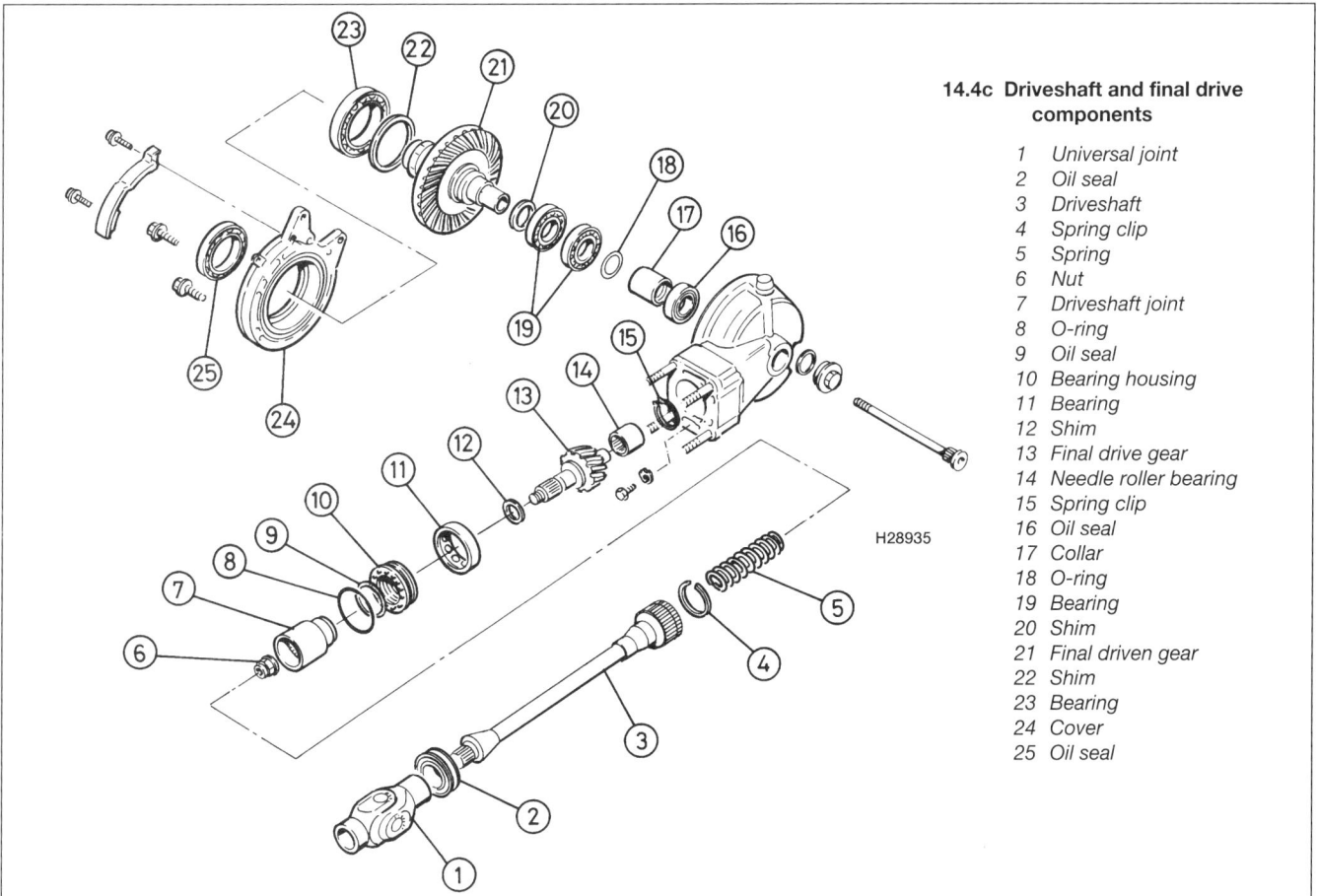

14.4c Driveshaft and final drive components

1 Universal joint
2 Oil seal
3 Driveshaft
4 Spring clip
5 Spring
6 Nut
7 Driveshaft joint
8 O-ring
9 Oil seal
10 Bearing housing
11 Bearing
12 Shim
13 Final drive gear
14 Needle roller bearing
15 Spring clip
16 Oil seal
17 Collar
18 O-ring
19 Bearing
20 Shim
21 Final driven gear
22 Shim
23 Bearing
24 Cover
25 Oil seal

H28935

6

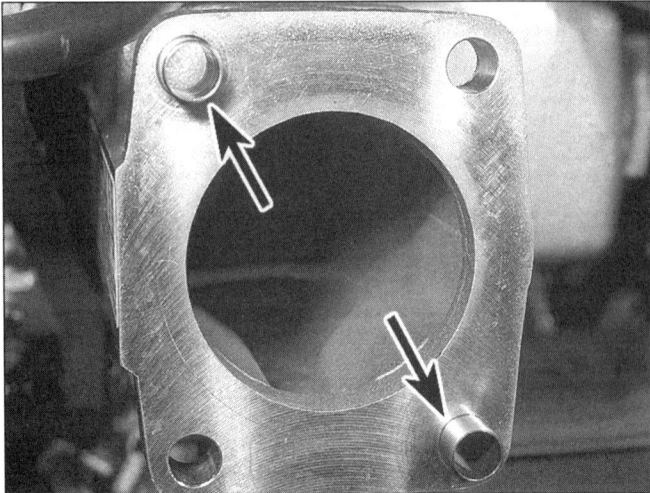

14.5 Remove the dowels if they are loose (arrows)

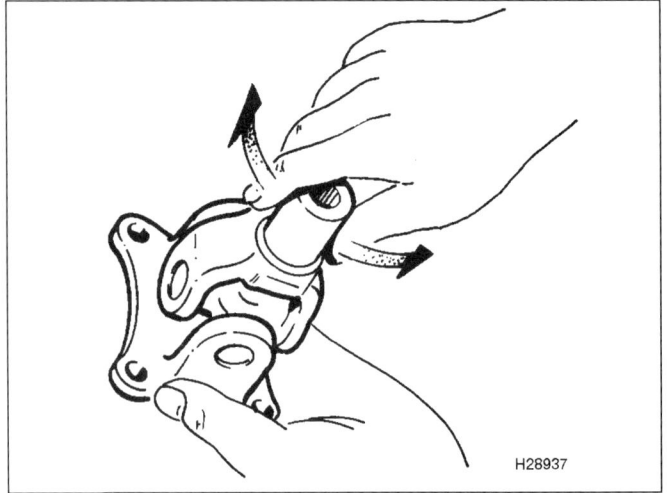

14.7 Checking the universal joint for play in the bearings

5 Note the positions of the two dowels and remove them if they are loose **(see illustration)**.

Inspection

6 Inspect the driveshaft splines for wear or damage. If wear is evident and there is excessive clearance between the driveshaft and either the final drive housing or the universal joint, the shaft must be replaced.

7 Inspect the universal joint for signs of wear or damage **(see illustration)**. There should be no noticeable play in the bearings, and the joint should move smoothly and freely with no signs of roughness or notchiness. If any wear or damage is evident, the universal joint must be replaced.

8 Install the driveshaft into the final drive housing and rotate the shaft. Check that the shaft is able to rotate smoothly and freely and that the power is transmitted correctly through the bevel gear assembly to the output boss. If there are any signs of roughness or notchiness, any evidence of wear on the input and output boss splines, or any evidence of oil leakage from the seals, the unit must be disassembled and examined further.

9 If attention to the final drive housing is required, the complete unit should be taken to a Honda dealer who will have the necessary special tools and expertise to carry out the rather complicated inspection and overhaul procedure.

Installation

10 If the driveshaft has been separated from the final drive housing, fit a new oil seal and spring clip **(see illustration)**. Lubricate the splines on both ends of the driveshaft, on the universal joint and on the final drive housing input boss with molybdenum disulphide grease.

11 Slide the universal joint onto the front end of the driveshaft. Check that the spring is in position in the end of the driveshaft and install the driveshaft into the final drive housing, making sure it is pressed fully home so that the spring clip locates in the groove in the splines in the housing **(see illustrations)**.

12 If removed, fit the two dowels into the end of the swingarm **(see illustration 14.5)**.

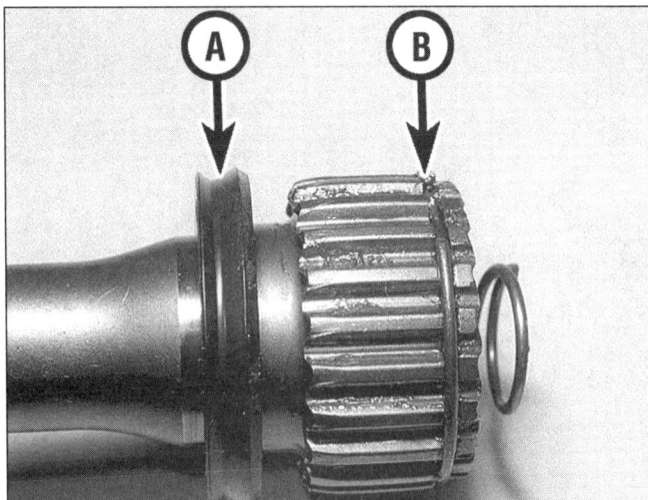

14.10 Fit a new oil seal (A) and spring clip (B)

14.11a Make sure the spring (arrow) is in position . . .

14.11b . . . then install the driveshaft into the final drive housing . . .

14.11c . . . making sure it is pressed fully home

14.13a Install the assembly into the swingarm . . .

14.13b . . . making sure the final drive housing
fits correctly over the dowels

13 Install the final drive housing, driveshaft and universal joint as an assembly into the swingarm, making sure the universal joint fits correctly over the splines of the output driven shaft (peel back the rubber gaiter to expose the end of the output shaft) **(see illustrations)**.

Tighten the housing nuts evenly and in a criss-cross pattern to the torque setting specified at the beginning of the Chapter. Make sure the rubber gaiter is correctly fitted over the ends of both the swingarm and the output driven shaft housing.

14 If removed, install the rear brake disc (see Chapter 7).
15 Install the rear wheel (see Chapter 6).
16 Finally, fill the final drive housing with the correct grade and quantity of oil (refer to Chapter 1).

6

Chapter 7
Brakes, wheels and tyres

Contents

Degrees of difficulty

Easy, suitable for novice with little experience	**Fairly easy,** suitable for beginner with some experience	**Fairly difficult,** suitable for competent DIY mechanic	**Difficult,** suitable for experienced DIY mechanic	**Very difficult,** suitable for expert DIY or professional

Specifications

Brakes

Brake fluid type	DOT 4
Disc minimum thickness	
J model (front and rear)	
Standard	5.0 mm
Service limit	4.0 mm
All other models	
Front	
Standard	6.0 mm
Service limit	5.0 mm
Rear	
Standard	5.0 mm
Service limit	4.0 mm
Disc maximum runout (front and rear, all models)	0.3 mm

7

Brakes (continued)

Caliper bore ID
  J, K, M and P models
    Front

Standard	30.230 to 30.280 mm
Service limit	30.29 mm

    Rear

Standard	38.180 to 38.230 mm
Service limit	38.24 mm

  S and T models
    Front

Standard	27.000 to 27.050 mm
Service limit	27.06 mm

    Rear

Standard	38.180 to 38.230 mm
Service limit	38.24 mm

Caliper piston OD
  J, K, M and P models
    Front

Standard	30.148 to 30.198 mm
Service limit	30.14 mm

    Rear

Standard	38.115 to 38.148 mm
Service limit	38.11 mm

  S and T models
    Front

Standard	26.935 to 26.968 mm
Service limit	26.93 mm

    Rear

Standard	38.115 to 38.148 mm
Service limit	38.11 mm

Master cylinder bore ID
  J, K, M and P models (front and rear)

Standard	12.700 to 12.743 mm
Service limit	12.76 mm

  S and T models
    Front

Standard	11.000 to 11.043 mm
Service limit	11.055 mm

    Rear

Standard	12.700 to 12.743 mm
Service limit	12.76 mm

Master cylinder piston OD
  J, K, M and P models (front and rear)

Standard	12.657 to 12.684 mm
Service limit	12.65 mm

  S and T models
    Front

Standard	10.957 to 10.984 mm
Service limit	10.945 mm

    Rear

Standard	12.657 to 12.684 mm
Service limit	12.65 mm

Wheels

Maximum wheel runout (front and rear)	
Axial (side-to-side)	2.0 mm
Radial (out-of-round)	2.0 mm
Maximum axle runout	0.2 mm

Tyres

	Front	Rear
Tyre pressures (cold)		
Rider	33 psi (2.3 Bar)	33 psi (2.3 Bar)
Rider and passenger	33 psi (2.3 Bar)	41 psi (2.8 Bar)
Tyre sizes*	110/80-17 57H	150/70-17 69H

Refer to the owners manual or the tyre information label on the swingarm for approved tyre brands.

Torque settings

Brake pad pin . . . .   17 Nm
Brake pad pin plug . . . .   2.5 Nm
Front brake caliper mounting bolts . . . .   27 Nm
Front brake disc retaining bolts . . . .   40 Nm
Front brake master cylinder clamp bolts . . . .   12 Nm
Rear brake caliper mounting bolt . . . .   27 Nm
Rear brake caliper slider bolt . . . .   22 Nm
Rear brake disc retaining bolts . . . .   27 Nm
Rear brake master cylinder mounting bolts . . . .   12 Nm
Brake caliper bleed valves . . . .   6 Nm
Brake hose banjo union bolts . . . .   30 Nm
Footrest bracket mounting bolts . . . .   27 Nm
Silencer mounting bolt . . . .   27 Nm
Front axle bolt . . . .   60 Nm
Front axle clamp bolts . . . .   22 Nm
Rear wheel nut . . . .   120 Nm

1 General information

All models covered in this manual are fitted with cast alloy wheels designed for tubeless tyres only. Both front and rear brakes are hydraulically operated disc brakes, the front having a single sliding caliper with dual pistons, the rear having a single sliding caliper with a single piston.
Caution: Disc brake components rarely require disassembly. Do not disassemble components unless absolutely necessary. If a hydraulic brake line is loosened, the entire system must be disassembled, drained, cleaned and then properly filled and bled upon reassembly. Do not use solvents on internal brake components. Solvents will cause the seals to swell and distort. Use only clean brake fluid or denatured alcohol for cleaning. Use care when working with brake fluid as it can injure your eyes and it will damage painted surfaces and plastic parts.

2 Front brake pads - replacement

Warning: The dust created by the brake system may contain asbestos, which is harmful to your health. Never blow it out with compressed air and don't inhale any of it. An approved filtering mask should be worn when working on the brakes.

1 Unscrew and remove the pad pin plug **(see illustration)**.

2 Unscrew and remove the pad pin, then withdraw the pads from the caliper, noting how they fit **(see illustration)**.

3 Inspect the surface of each pad for contamination and check that the friction material has not worn beyond its service limit. If either pad is worn down to, or beyond, the service limit wear groove (ie the grooves are no longer visible), fouled with oil or grease, or heavily scored or damaged by dirt and debris, both pads must be replaced as a set **(see illustration)**. Note that it is not possible to degrease the friction material; if the pads are contaminated in any way they must be replaced.

4 If the pads are in good condition clean them carefully, using a fine wire brush which is completely free of oil and grease to remove all traces of road dirt and corrosion. Using a pointed instrument, clean out the grooves in the friction material and dig out any embedded particles of foreign matter. Any areas of glazing may be removed using emery cloth.

5 Check the condition of the brake disc (see Section 4).

6 Remove all traces of corrosion from the pad pin. Inspect the pin for signs of damage and replace if necessary.

7 Push the pistons as far back into the caliper as possible using hand pressure only. Due to the increased friction material thickness of new pads, it may be necessary to remove the master cylinder reservoir cover and diaphragm and siphon out some fluid.

8 Smear the backs of the pads and the shank of the pad pin with copper-based brake grease, making sure that none gets on the front or sides of the pads. Do not use ordinary grease for this.

9 Installation of the pads and pad pin is the reverse of removal. Insert the pads into the caliper so that the friction material of each pad is facing the disc. Make sure that the

2.1 Remove the pad pin plug to reveal the pad pin

2.2 Withdraw the pads from the caliper

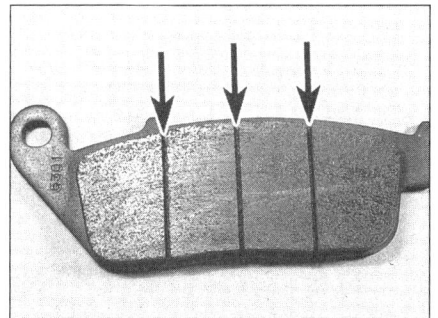

2.3 Front brake pad wear limit grooves (arrows)

7

2.9a Make sure that the pad spring (arrow) . . .

2.9b . . . and plate (arrow) are correctly positioned

2.9c Push up on the end of the pads to align the holes, then install the pad pin

3.1 Brake hose banjo bolt. Note the alignment of the hose with the lug (arrow)

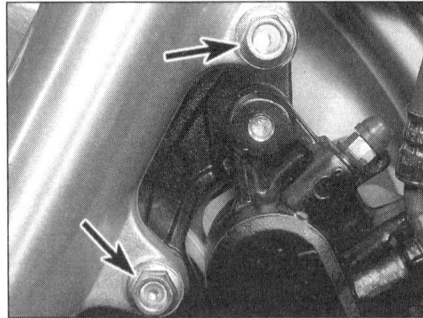

3.2 The front brake caliper is secured by two bolts (arrows)

pad spring and pad plate are correctly positioned **(see illustrations)**. Install the pads and push them up against the plate and spring to align the hole in the pads with that in the caliper, then install the pad pin **(see illustration)**. Tighten the pad pin and the pad pin plug to the torque settings specified at the beginning of the Chapter.

10 Top up the master cylinder reservoir if necessary (see Chapter 1), and replace the diaphragm and reservoir cover.

11 Operate the brake lever several times to bring the pads into contact with the disc. Check the master cylinder fluid level (see *Daily (pre-ride) checks*) and the operation of the brake before riding the motorcycle.

3 Front brake caliper - removal, overhaul and installation

⚠️ **Warning: If the caliper indicates the need for an overhaul (usually due to leaking fluid or sticky operation), all old brake fluid should be flushed from the system. Also, the dust created by the brake system may contain asbestos, which is harmful to your health. Never blow it out with compressed air and don't inhale any of it. An approved filtering mask should be worn when working on the brakes. Do not, under any circumstances, use petroleum-based solvents to clean brake parts. Use clean brake fluid, brake cleaner or denatured alcohol only.**

Removal

1 Remove the brake hose banjo bolt, noting its position on the caliper and separate the hose from the caliper **(see illustration)**. Plug the hose end or wrap a plastic bag tightly around it to minimise fluid loss and prevent dirt entering the system. Discard the sealing washers as new ones must be used on installation. **Note:** *If you are planning to overhaul the caliper and don't have a source of compressed air to blow out the pistons, just loosen the banjo bolt at this stage and retighten it lightly. The bike's hydraulic system can then be used to force the pistons out of the body once the pads have been removed. Disconnect the hose once the pistons have been sufficiently displaced.*

2 Unscrew the caliper mounting bolts, and slide the caliper away from the disc **(see illustration)**. Remove the brake pads as described in Section 2.

Overhaul

3 Clean the exterior of the caliper with denatured alcohol or brake system cleaner **(see illustration)**.

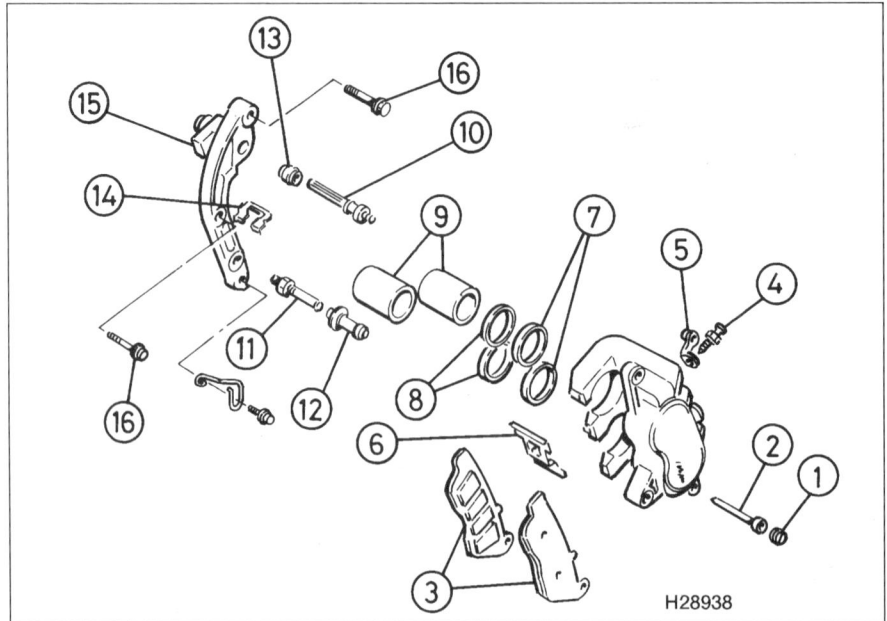

3.3 Front brake caliper components

1	Pad pin plug	5	Bleed valve cap	9	Piston	13	Rubber boot
2	Pad pin	6	Pad spring	10	Slider	14	Pad plate
3	Brake pads	7	Piston seal	11	Slider	15	Caliper bracket
4	Bleed valve	8	Dust seal	12	Rubber boot	16	Caliper bolts

H28938

4 Remove the pistons from the caliper body, either by pumping them out by operating the front brake lever until the pistons are displaced, or by forcing them out using compressed air. Mark each piston head and caliper body with a felt marker to ensure that the pistons can be matched to their original bores on reassembly. If the compressed air method is used, place a wad of rag between the pistons and the caliper to act as a cushion, then use compressed air directed into the fluid inlet to force the pistons out of the body. Use only low pressure to ease the pistons out and make sure both pistons are displaced at the same time. If the air pressure is too high and the pistons are forced out, the caliper and/or pistons may be damaged.

⚠ *Warning: Never place your fingers in front of the pistons in an attempt to catch or protect them when applying compressed air, as serious injury could result.*

5 Using a wooden or plastic tool, remove the dust seals from the caliper bores and discard them. New seals must be used on installation. If a metal tool is being used, take great care not to damage the caliper bores.

6 Remove and discard the piston seals in the same way.

7 Clean the pistons and bores with denatured alcohol, clean brake fluid or brake system cleaner. If compressed air is available, use it to dry the parts thoroughly (make sure it's filtered and unlubricated).

Caution: Do not, under any circumstances, use a petroleum-based solvent to clean brake parts.

8 Inspect the caliper bores and pistons for signs of corrosion, nicks and burrs and loss of plating. If surface defects are present, the caliper assembly must be replaced. If the necessary measuring equipment is available, compare the dimensions of the pistons and

3.13 Mount the caliper onto the disc

bores to those given in the Specifications Section of this Chapter, replacing any component that is worn beyond the service limit. Check that the caliper body is able to slide freely on the mounting bracket slider pins. If seized due to corrosion, separate the two components and clean off all traces of corrosion and hardened grease. Apply a smear of copper based grease to the mounting bracket slider pins and reassemble the two components. Replace the rubber boots if they are damaged or deteriorated. If the caliper is in bad shape the master cylinder should also be checked.

9 Lubricate the new piston seals with clean brake fluid and install them in their grooves in the caliper bores

10 Lubricate the new dust seals with clean brake fluid and install them in their grooves in the caliper bores.

11 Lubricate the pistons with clean brake fluid and install them closed-end first into the caliper bores. Using your thumbs, push the pistons all the way in, making sure they enter the bore squarely.

Installation

12 Install the brake pads (see Section 2).

13 Install the caliper on the brake disc making sure the pads sit squarely either side of the disc **(see illustration)**.

14 Apply a few drops of a suitable thread locking compound to the caliper mounting bolts, then install them in the caliper and tighten them to the torque setting specified at the beginning of this Chapter **(see illustrations)**.

15 Connect the brake hose to the caliper, using new sealing washers on each side of the fitting. Position the hose so that it butts up against its lug on the caliper **(see illustration 3.1)**. Tighten the banjo bolt to the torque setting specified at the beginning of the Chapter.

16 Fill the master cylinder with the recommended brake fluid (see Specifications) and bleed the hydraulic system as described in Section 11.

17 Check for leaks and thoroughly test the operation of the brake before riding the motorcycle.

---

4 Front brake disc - inspection, removal and installation

Inspection

1 Visually inspect the surface of the disc for score marks and other damage. Light scratches are normal after use and won't affect brake operation, but deep grooves and heavy score marks will reduce braking efficiency and accelerate pad wear. If a disc is badly grooved it must be machined or replaced.

2 To check disc runout, position the bike on its centre stand (or auxiliary stand) and support it so that the front wheel is raised off the ground. Mount a dial indicator to the fork slider, with the plunger on the indicator

3.14a Apply a thread locking compound to the caliper bolts . . .

3.14b . . . and tighten them to the specified torque setting

7

4.2 Set up a dial indicator to contact the brake disc, then rotate the wheel to check for runout

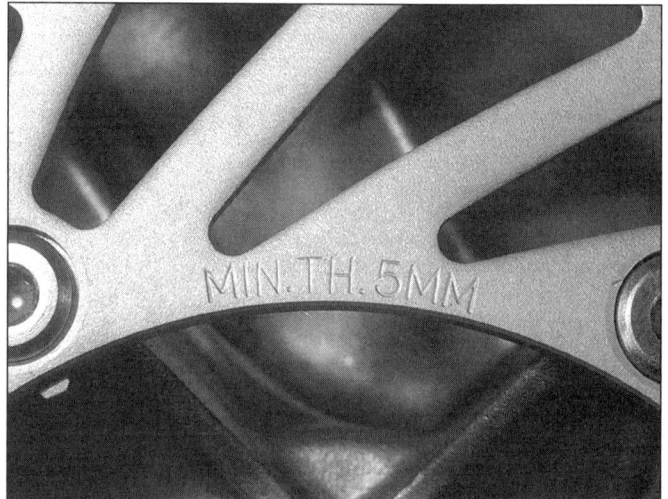

4.3a The minimum disc thickness is marked on the disc

4.3b Using a micrometer to measure disc thickness

4.5 The disc is secured by six bolts (arrows)

touching the surface of the disc about 10 mm (1/2 inch) from the outer edge (see illustration). Rotate the wheel and watch the indicator needle, comparing the reading with the limit listed in the Specifications at the beginning of the Chapter. If the runout is greater than the service limit, check the wheel bearings for play (see Chapter 1). If the bearings are worn, replace them (see Section 16) and repeat this check. If the disc runout is still excessive, it will have to be replaced, although machining by a competent engineering shop may be possible.

3 The disc must not be machined or allowed to wear down to a thickness less than the service limit as listed in this Chapter's Specifications and as marked on the disc itself (see illustration). The thickness of the disc can be checked with a micrometer (see illustration). If the thickness of the disc is less than the service limit, it must be replaced.

Removal

4 Remove the wheel (see Section 14).
Caution: Do not lay the wheel down and allow it to rest on the disc - the disc could become warped. Set the wheel on wood blocks so the disc doesn't support the weight of the wheel.

5 Mark the relationship of the disc to the wheel, so it can be installed in the same position. Unscrew the disc retaining bolts, loosening them a little at a time in a criss-cross pattern to avoid distorting the disc, then remove the disc from the wheel (see illustration).

Installation

6 Install the disc on the wheel, aligning the previously applied matchmarks (if you're reinstalling the original disc), and making sure the "Minimum thickness" specification stamped onto the disc is facing out.

7 Apply a suitable thread locking compound to the disc mounting bolt threads, then install the bolts and tighten them in a criss-cross pattern evenly and progressively to the torque setting specified at the beginning of the Chapter. Clean off all grease from the brake disc using acetone or brake system cleaner. If a new brake disc has been installed, remove any protective coating from its working surfaces.

8 Install the front wheel (see Section 14).

9 Operate the brake lever several times to bring the pads into contact with the disc. Check the operation of the brake carefully before riding the bike.

5 Front brake master cylinder - removal, overhaul and installation

1 If the master cylinder is leaking fluid, or if the lever does not produce a firm feel when

5.4 Slacken the reservoir cover screws (arrows)

5.5 Disconnect the brake light switch electrical connectors (arrows)

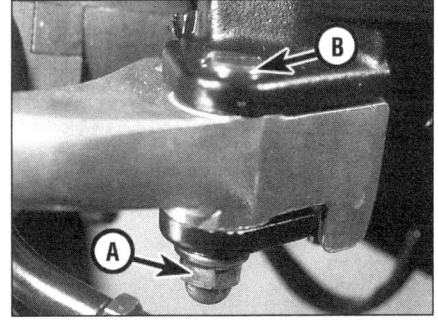

5.6 Remove the locknut (A), then unscrew the pivot bolt (B) and remove the lever

5.7 Brake hose banjo bolt. Note the alignment of the hose with the lug (arrow)

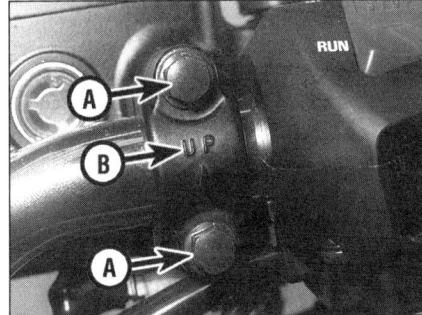

5.8 Front brake master cylinder mounting bolts (A). Note the "UP" mark (B)

the brake is applied, and bleeding the brakes does not help (see Section 11), and the hydraulic hoses are all in good condition, then master cylinder overhaul is recommended.

2 Before disassembling the master cylinder, read through the entire procedure and make sure that you have the correct rebuild kit. Also, you will need some new, clean brake fluid of the recommended type, some clean rags and internal circlip pliers. **Note:** *To prevent damage to the paint from spilled brake fluid, always cover the fuel tank when working on the master cylinder.*

Caution: Disassembly, overhaul and reassembly of the brake master cylinder must be done in a spotlessly clean work area to avoid contamination and possible failure of the brake hydraulic system components.

Removal

3 If required, remove the rear view mirror (see Chapter 8).

4 Loosen, but do not remove, the screws holding the reservoir cover in place **(see illustration)**.

5 Disconnect the electrical connectors from the brake light switch **(see illustration)**.

6 Remove the locknut from the underside of the brake lever pivot bolt, then unscrew the bolt and remove the brake lever **(see illustration)**.

7 Peel back the rubber boot from the top of the brake hose (if fitted), then unscrew the banjo bolt and separate the brake hose from the master cylinder **(see illustration)**. Note

the alignment of the hose. Discard the two sealing washers as these must be replaced with new ones. Wrap the end of the hose in a clean rag and suspend the hose in an upright position or bend it down carefully and place the open end in a clean container. The objective is to prevent excessive loss of brake fluid, fluid spills and system contamination.

8 Remove the master cylinder mounting bolts to free the clamp, noting the "UP" mark on the clamp and how the mating surfaces of the

clamp align with the punch mark on the handlebar **(see illustration)**. Lift the master cylinder and reservoir away from the handlebar. Do not tip the master cylinder upside down or brake fluid will run out.

Overhaul

9 Remove the reservoir cover retaining screws and lift off the cover, the diaphragm plate and the rubber diaphragm **(see illustration)**. Drain the brake fluid from the reservoir into a

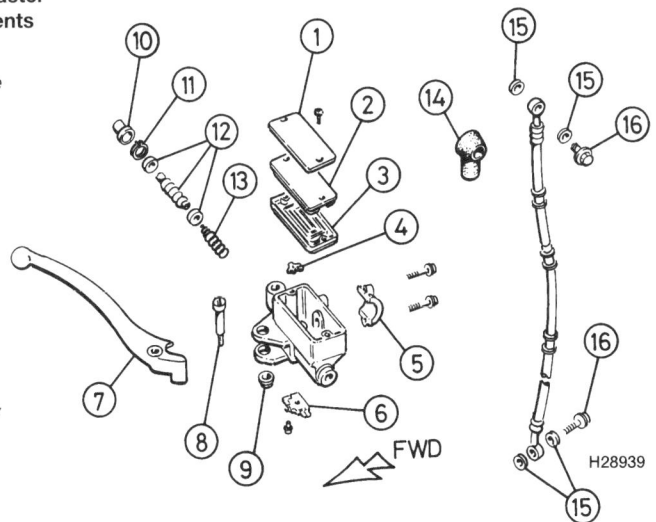

5.9 Front brake master cylinder components

1 Reservoir cover
2 Diaphragm plate
3 Rubber diaphragm
4 Protector
5 Clamp
6 Brake light switch
7 Brake lever
8 Lever pivot bolt
9 Pivot bolt locknut
10 Dust boot
11 Circlip
12 Piston assembly
13 Spring
14 Rubber boot
15 Sealing washer
16 Banjo bolt

FWD

H28939

7

5.21 Align the mating surfaces of the clamp with the punch mark (arrows)

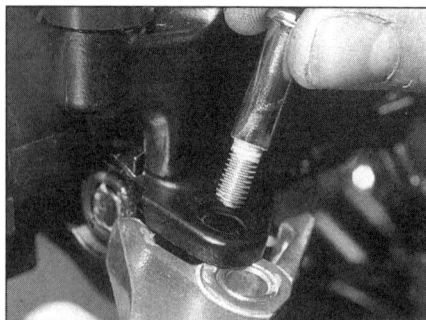

5.23a Install the brake lever and the pivot bolt

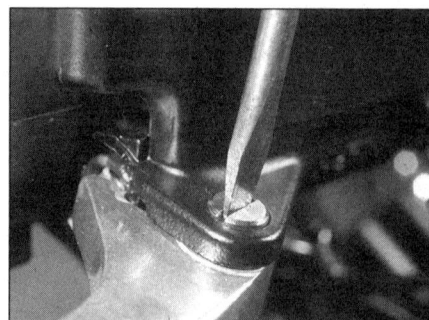

5.23b Tighten the pivot bolt . . .

5.23c . . . then fit the locknut

5.26 Install the rubber diaphragm, the diaphragm plate and the reservoir cover

suitable container. Wipe any remaining fluid out of the reservoir with a clean rag.

10 Remove the screw securing the brake light switch to the bottom of the master cylinder and remove the switch **(see illustration 5.5)**.

11 Carefully remove the dust boot from the end of the piston.

12 Using circlip pliers, remove the circlip and slide out the piston assembly and the spring, noting how they fit. Lay the parts out in the proper order to avoid confusion on reassembly.

13 Clean all parts with clean brake fluid or denatured alcohol. If compressed air is available, use it to dry the parts thoroughly (make sure it's filtered and unlubricated).
Caution: Do not, under any circumstances, use a petroleum-based solvent to clean brake parts.

14 Check the master cylinder bore for corrosion, scratches, nicks and score marks. If the necessary measuring equipment is available, compare the dimensions of the piston and bore to those given in the Specifications Section of this Chapter. If damage or wear is evident, the master cylinder must be replaced with a new one. If the master cylinder is in poor condition, then the caliper should be checked as well. Check that the fluid inlet and outlet ports in the master cylinder are clear.

15 The dust boot, piston assembly and spring are included in the rebuild kit. Use all of the new parts, regardless of the apparent condition of the old ones.

16 Install the spring in the master cylinder so that its tapered end faces the piston.

17 Lubricate the piston assembly components with clean hydraulic fluid and install the assembly into the master cylinder, making sure all the components are the correct way round. Make sure the lips on the cup seals do not turn inside out when they are slipped into the bore. Depress the piston and install the new circlip, making sure that it locates in the master cylinder groove.

18 Install the rubber dust boot, making sure the lip is seated correctly in the piston groove.

19 Install the brake light switch.

20 Inspect the reservoir cover rubber diaphragm and replace if damaged or deteriorated.

Installation

21 Attach the master cylinder to the handlebar and fit the clamp with its "UP" mark facing up **(see illustration 5.8)**. Align the mating surfaces of the clamp with the punch mark on the handlebar, then tighten the upper bolt first then the lower bolt **(see illustration)**.

22 Connect the brake hose to the master cylinder, using new sealing washers on each side of the union, and aligning the hose against the lug on the reservoir **(see illustration 5.7)**. Tighten the banjo bolt to the torque setting specified at the beginning of this Chapter. Fit the rubber boot over the union.

23 Install the brake lever into its bracket and secure it with its pivot bolt **(see**

illustrations). Tighten the bolt then install the pivot bolt locknut **(see illustration)**.

24 Connect the brake light switch wiring **(see illustration 5.5)** and install the rear view mirror (see Chapter 8).

25 Fill the fluid reservoir with the specified brake fluid (see Specifications). Refer to Section 11 of this Chapter and bleed the air from the system.

26 Fit the rubber diaphragm, making sure it is correctly seated, the diaphragm plate and the cover on the master cylinder reservoir **(see illustration)**.

6 Rear brake pads - replacement

⚠️ *Warning: The dust created by the brake system may contain asbestos, which is harmful to your health. Never blow it out with compressed air and don't inhale any of it. An approved filtering mask should be worn when working on the brakes.*

1 Unscrew and remove the pad pin plug, then slacken the pad pin **(see illustration)**.

2 Unscrew and remove the caliper rear slider bolt **(see illustration)**, then remove the pad pin. Pivot the caliper upwards on the front slider bolt and withdraw the pads from the caliper, noting how they fit **(see illustration)**. Note the anti-squeal shim fitted to the back of the outer pad.

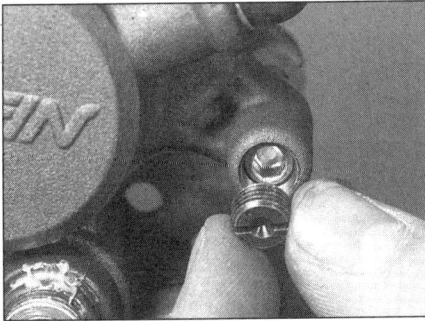

6.1 Remove the pad pin plug
to reveal the pad pin

6.2a Remove the rear slider bolt (arrow)

6.2b Pivot the caliper upwards and
withdraw the pads

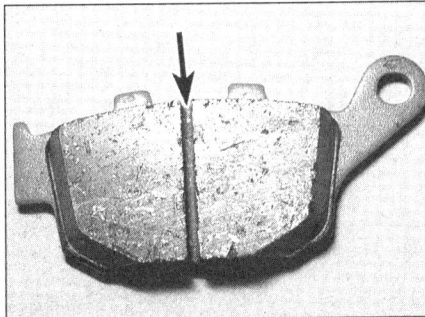

6.3 Rear brake pad wear limit groove
(arrow)

6.9a Bracket-mounted pad plate (arrow).
The pad spring is mounted
inside the caliper

6.9b Fit the anti-squeal shim
to the back of the outer pad

6.9c Push up on the end of the pads to
align the holes, then install the pad pin

6.9d Apply a thread locking compound
to the slider bolt . . .

6.9e . . . and tighten it to the
specified torque setting

3 Inspect the surface of each pad for contamination and check that the friction material has not worn beyond its service limit. If either pad is worn down to, or beyond, the service limit wear groove (i.e. the grooves are no longer visible), fouled with oil or grease, or heavily scored or damaged by dirt and debris, both pads must be replaced as a set (see illustration). Note that it is not possible to degrease the friction material; if the pads are contaminated in any way they must be replaced.
4 If the pads are in good condition clean them carefully, using a fine wire brush which is completely free of oil and grease to remove all traces of road dirt and corrosion. Using a pointed instrument, clean out the groove in the friction material and dig out any

embedded particles of foreign matter. Any areas of glazing may be removed using emery cloth.
5 Check the condition of the brake disc (see Section 8).
6 Remove all traces of corrosion from the pad pin and the slider bolt. Inspect them for signs of damage and replace them if necessary.
7 Push the piston as far back into the caliper as possible using hand pressure only. Due to the increased friction material thickness of new pads, it may be necessary to remove the master cylinder reservoir cover and diaphragm and siphon out some fluid.
8 Smear the backs of the pads and the shank of the pad pin with copper-based grease, making sure that none gets on the front or sides of the pads.

9 Installation of the pads and pad pin is the reverse of removal. Make sure the pad plate (see illustration) and spring are correctly positioned. Insert the pads into the caliper so that the friction material of each pad is facing the disc, and do not forget to fit the anti-squeal shim to the back of the outer pad (see illustration). Push the pads up against the spring to align the hole in the pads with that in the caliper, then install the pad pin (see illustration). Pivot the caliper down onto the disc, then apply a suitable thread locking compound to the threads of the slider bolt and install it in the caliper (see illustration). Tighten the slider bolt, the pad pin and the pad pin plug to the torque settings specified at the beginning of the Chapter (see illustration).

7

7.1 Brake hose banjo bolt. Note the alignment of the hose with the lug (arrow)

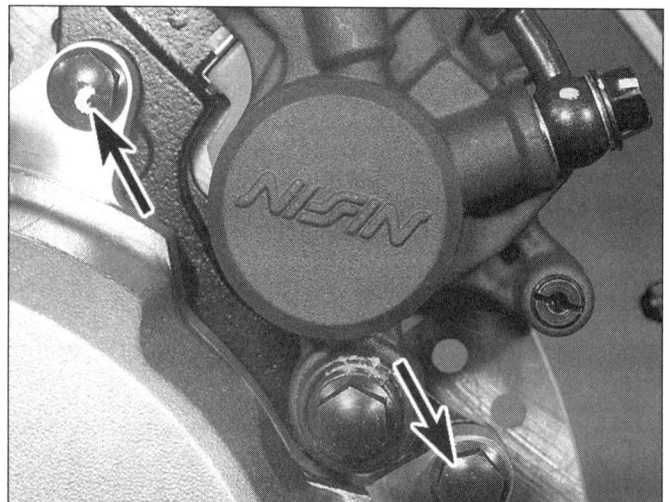

7.2 The rear brake caliper is secured by two bolts (arrows)

10 Top up the master cylinder reservoir with brake fluid (see Specifications), and replace the reservoir cover and diaphragm if removed.
11 Operate the brake pedal several times to bring the pads into contact with the disc. Check the master cylinder fluid level (see *Daily (pre-ride) checks*) and the operation of the brake before riding the motorcycle.

7 Rear brake caliper - removal, overhaul and installation

⚠️ *Warning: If a caliper indicates the need for an overhaul (usually due to leaking fluid or sticky operation), all old brake fluid should be flushed from the system. Also, the dust created by the brake system may contain asbestos, which is harmful to your health. Never blow it out with compressed air and don't inhale any of it. An approved filtering mask should be worn when working on the brakes. Do not, under any circumstances, use petroleum-based solvents to clean brake parts. Use clean brake fluid, brake cleaner or denatured alcohol only.*

Removal

1 Remove the brake hose banjo bolt, noting its position on the caliper, and separate the hose from the caliper **(see illustration)**. Plug the hose end or wrap a plastic bag tightly around it to minimise fluid loss and prevent dirt entering the system. Discard the sealing washers as new ones must be used on installation. **Note:** *If you are planning to overhaul the caliper and don't have a source of compressed air to blow out the piston, just loosen the banjo bolt at this stage and retighten it lightly. The bike's hydraulic system can then be used to force the piston out of the body once the pads have been removed. Disconnect the hose once the piston has been sufficiently displaced.*

2 Unscrew the caliper mounting bolts, and slide the caliper away from the disc **(see illustration)**. Remove the brake pads as described in Section 6.

Overhaul

3 Clean the exterior of the caliper with denatured alcohol or brake system cleaner **(see illustration)**.

4 Remove the piston from the caliper body, either by pumping it out by operating the rear brake pedal until the piston is displaced, or by forcing it out using compressed air. If the compressed air method is used, place a wad of rag between the piston and the caliper to act as a cushion, then use compressed air directed into the fluid inlet to force the piston out of the body. Use only low pressure to

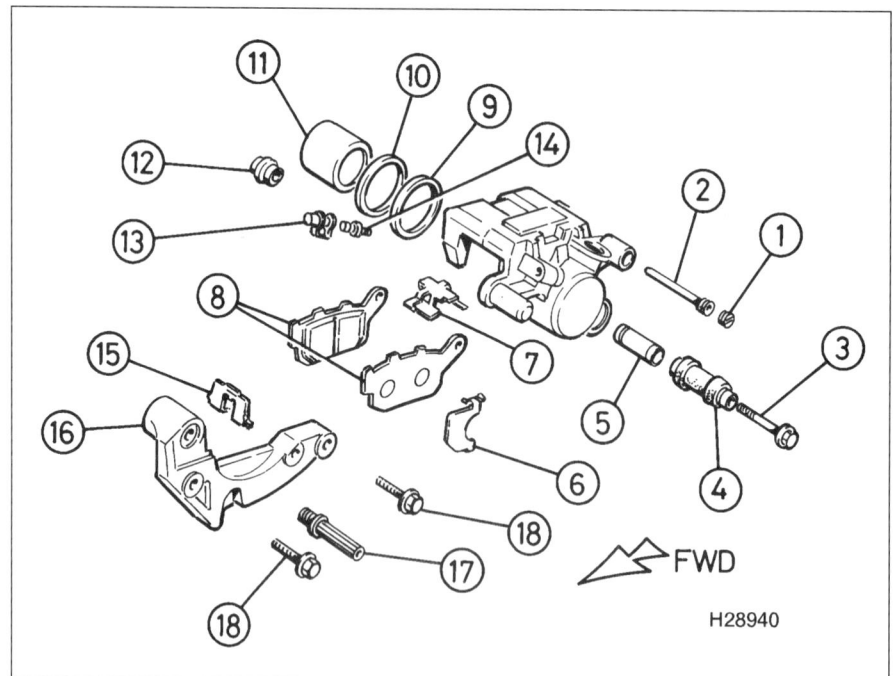

7.3 Rear brake caliper components

1	Pad pin plug	7	Pad spring	13	Bleed valve cap
2	Pad pin	8	Brake pads	14	Bleed valve
3	Slider bolt	9	Piston seal	15	Pad plate
4	Rubber boot	10	Dust seal	16	Caliper bracket
5	Sleeve	11	Piston	17	Slider bolt
6	Anti-squeal shim	12	Rubber boot	18	Caliper bolts

ease the piston out. If the air pressure is too high and the piston is forced out, the caliper and/or piston may be damaged.

⚠️ *Warning: Never place your fingers in front of the piston in an attempt to catch or protect it when applying compressed air, as serious injury could result.*

5 Using a wooden or plastic tool, remove the dust seal from the caliper bore and discard it. A new seal must be used on installation. If a metal tool is being used, take great care not to damage the caliper bore.

6 Remove and discard the piston seal in the same way.

7 Clean the piston and bore with denatured alcohol, clean brake fluid or brake system cleaner. If compressed air is available, use it to dry the parts thoroughly (make sure it's filtered and unlubricated).

Caution: Do not, under any circumstances, use a petroleum-based solvent to clean brake parts

8 Inspect the caliper bore and piston for signs of corrosion, nicks and burrs and loss of plating. If surface defects are present, the caliper assembly must be replaced. If the necessary measuring equipment is available, compare the dimensions of the piston and bore to those given in the Specifications Section of this Chapter, replacing any component that is worn beyond the service limit. Check that the caliper body is able to slide freely on the mounting bracket slider pins. If seized due to corrosion, unscrew the

rear slider bolt, then separate the two components and clean off all traces of corrosion and hardened grease. Apply a smear of copper-based grease to the mounting bracket slider pins and reassemble the two components. Replace the rubber boots if they are damaged or deteriorated. If the caliper is in bad shape the master cylinder should also be checked.

9 Lubricate the new piston seal with clean brake fluid and install it in its groove in the caliper bore.

10 Lubricate the new dust seal with clean brake fluid and install it in its groove in the caliper bore.

11 Lubricate the piston with clean brake fluid and install it closed-end first into the caliper bore. Using your thumbs, push the piston all the way in, making sure it enters the bore squarely.

Installation

12 Install the brake pads as described in Section 6.

13 Install the caliper on the brake disc making sure the pads sit squarely either side of the disc (see illustration).

14 Apply a few drops of a suitable thread locking compound to the caliper mounting bolts, then install them in the caliper and tighten them to the torque setting specified at the beginning of this Chapter (see illustrations).

15 Connect the brake hose to the caliper using new sealing washers on each side of the fitting. Position the hose so that it butts up

against its lug on the caliper (see illustration 7.1). Tighten the banjo bolt to the torque setting specified at the beginning of the Chapter.

16 Fill the master cylinder with the recommended brake fluid (see Specifications) and bleed the hydraulic system as described in Section 11.

17 Check for leaks and thoroughly test the operation of the brake before riding the motorcycle.

8 Rear brake disc - inspection, removal and installation

Inspection

1 Refer to Section 4 of this Chapter, noting that the dial indicator should be attached to the swingarm. Note the "DRIVE" mark and arrow on the disc which denotes the normal direction of rotation, and must therefore be fitted facing inwards (see illustration). Also note the minimum thickness mark.

Removal

2 Remove the rear wheel (see Section 15).

3 Mark the relationship of the disc to the final drive housing so it can be installed in the same position. Unscrew the disc retaining bolts, loosening them a little at a time in a criss-cross pattern to avoid distorting the disc, and remove the disc (see illustration).

7.13 Mount the caliper onto the disc

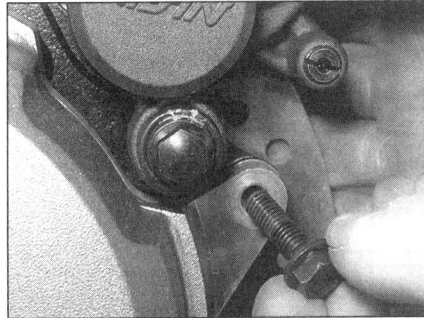
7.14a Apply a thread locking compound to the caliper bolts . . .

7.14b . . . and tighten them to the specified torque setting

8.1 Note the direction of drive arrow (A) and the minimum thickness mark (B)

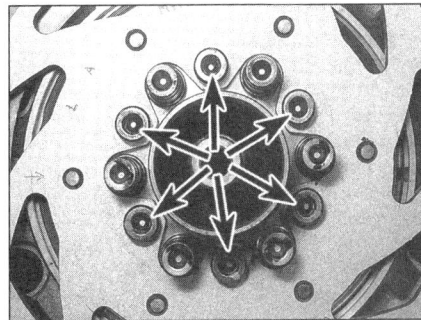
8.3 The rear disc is secured by six bolts (arrows)

7

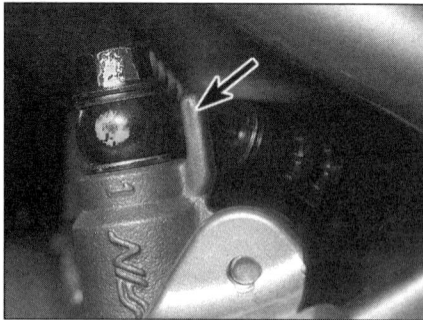

9.4 Brake hose banjo bolt. Note the alignment of the hose against the lug (arrow)

9.6 The master cylinder is secured to the back of the footrest bracket by two bolts (arrows)

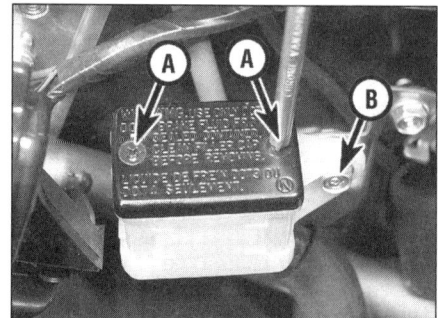

9.7 Master cylinder reservoir cover screws (A), and mounting bolt (B)

Installation

4 Position the disc on the final drive housing, aligning the previously applied matchmarks (if you're reinstalling the original disc) and making sure the direction of wheel rotation arrow faces to the right-hand side.

5 Apply a suitable thread locking compound to the disc mounting bolts, then install the bolts and tighten them in a criss-cross pattern evenly and progressively to the torque setting specified at the beginning of this Chapter. Clean off all grease from the brake disc using acetone or brake system cleaner. If a new brake disc has been installed, remove any protective coating from its working surfaces.

6 Install the rear wheel (see Section 15).

7 Operate the brake pedal several times to bring the pads into contact with the disc. Check the operation of the brake carefully before riding the motorcycle.

9 Rear brake master cylinder - removal, overhaul and installation

1 If the master cylinder is leaking fluid, or if the pedal does not produce a firm feel when the brake is applied, and bleeding the brakes does not help (see Section 11), and the hydraulic hoses are all in good condition, then master cylinder overhaul is recommended.

2 Before disassembling the master cylinder, read through the entire procedure and make sure that you have the correct rebuild kit. Also, you will need some new, clean brake fluid of the recommended type, some clean rags and internal circlip pliers.

Caution: Disassembly, overhaul and reassembly of the brake master cylinder must be done in a spotlessly clean work area to avoid contamination and possible failure of the brake hydraulic system components.

Removal

3 Remove the right-hand side panel (see Chapter 8).

4 Unscrew the brake hose banjo bolt and separate the brake hose from the master

cylinder **(see illustration)**. Note the alignment of the hose union. Discard the two sealing washers as these must be replaced with new ones. Wrap the end of the hose in a clean rag and suspend the hose in an upright position or bend it down carefully and place the open end in a clean container. The objective is to prevent excessive loss of brake fluid, fluid spills and system contamination.

5 Remove the split pin from the clevis pin securing the brake pedal to the master cylinder pushrod. Withdraw the clevis pin and separate the pedal from the pushrod. Discard the split pin as a new one must be used.

6 Unscrew the two bolts securing the master cylinder to the bracket **(see illustration)**.

7 Slacken the master cylinder fluid reservoir cover screws **(see illustration)**. Remove the bolt securing the reservoir to the bracket, then

remove the reservoir cover and pour the fluid into a container.

8 Separate the fluid reservoir hose from the elbow on the master cylinder by releasing the hose clamp.

Overhaul

9 If necessary, remove the spring pin (late K models onward) from the bottom of the pushrod, slacken the clevis locknut, then unscrew the clevis nut from the pushrod and withdraw the clevis **(see illustration)**.

10 Dislodge the rubber dust boot from the base of the master cylinder to reveal the pushrod retaining circlip.

11 Depress the pushrod and, using circlip pliers, remove the circlip. Slide out the piston assembly and spring. If they are difficult to remove, apply low pressure compressed air to

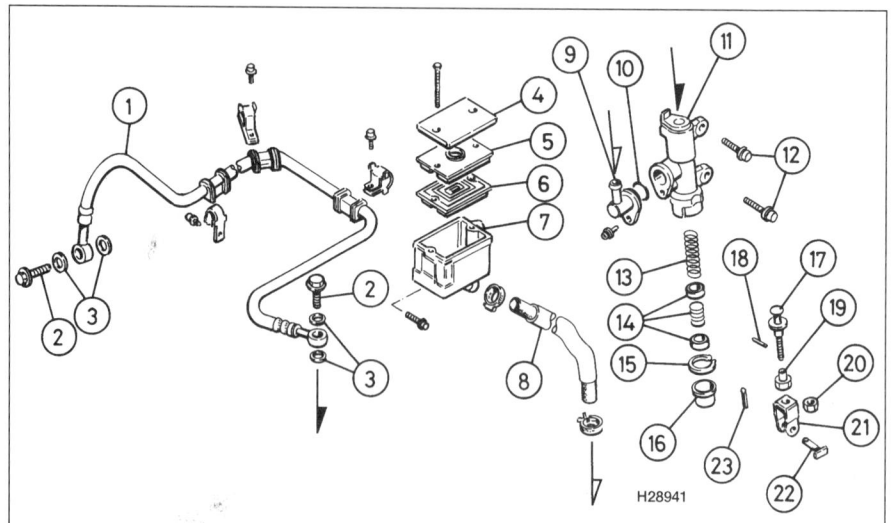

9.9 Rear brake master cylinder components

1	Brake hose	7	Reservoir	13	Spring	19	Locknut
2	Banjo bolt	8	Reservoir hose	14	Piston assembly	20	Clevis nut
3	Sealing washer	9	Hose elbow	15	Circlip	21	Clevis
4	Reservoir cover	10	O-ring	16	Dust boot	22	Clevis pin
5	Diaphragm plate	11	Master cylinder	17	Pushrod	23	Split pin
6	Rubber diaphragm	12	Master cylinder bolts	18	Spring pin		

9.22 Make sure the reservoir hose clamps (arrow) are secure

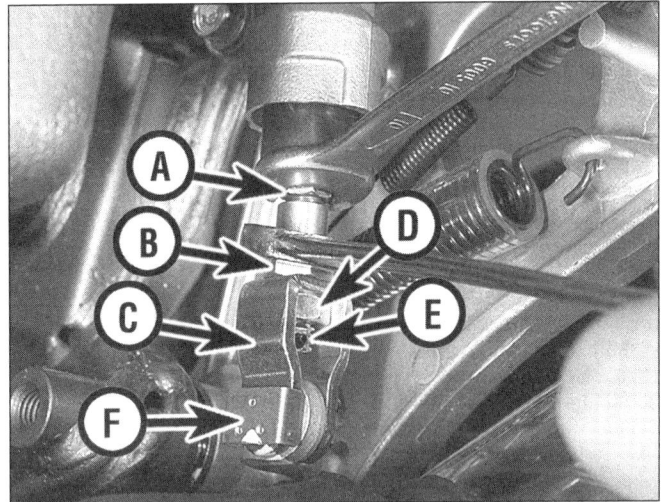

9.24 Pushrod adjuster nut (A), locknut (B), clevis (C), clevis nut (D), spring pin (E), clevis pin (F)

the fluid outlet. Lay the parts out in the proper order to prevent confusion during reassembly.
12 Clean all of the parts with clean brake fluid or denatured alcohol. If compressed air is available, use it to dry the parts thoroughly (make sure it's filtered and unlubricated).
Caution: Do not, under any circumstances, use a petroleum-based solvent to clean brake parts.
13 Check the master cylinder bore for corrosion, scratches, nicks and score marks. If the necessary measuring equipment is available, compare the dimensions of the piston and bore to those given in the Specifications Section of this Chapter. If damage is evident, the master cylinder must be replaced with a new one. If the master cylinder is in poor condition, then the caliper should be checked as well.
14 If required, unscrew the fluid reservoir hose elbow screw and detach the elbow from the master cylinder. Discard the O-ring as a new one must be fitted on installation. Inspect the reservoir hose for cracks or splits and replace if necessary.
15 The dust boot, piston assembly and spring are included in the rebuild kit. Use all of the new parts, regardless of the apparent condition of the old ones.
16 Install the spring in the master cylinder so that its tapered end faces the piston.
17 Lubricate the piston assembly components with clean hydraulic fluid and install the assembly into the master cylinder, making sure all the components are the correct way round. Make sure the lips on the cup seals do not turn inside out when they are slipped into the bore.
18 Install and depress the pushrod, then install a new circlip, making sure it is properly seated in the groove.
19 Install the rubber dust boot, making sure the lip is seated properly in the groove.

20 If removed, fit a new O-ring to the fluid reservoir hose elbow, then install the elbow onto the master cylinder and secure it with its screw. Reconnect the fluid reservoir hose and secure it with its clamp.

Installation

21 Install the master cylinder onto the footrest bracket and tighten the mounting bolts to the torque setting specified at the beginning of the Chapter.
22 Secure the fluid reservoir to the frame with its retaining bolt. Ensure that the hose is securely connected between the master cylinder and reservoir, correctly routed and secured by clamps at each end (see illustration). If the clamps have weakened, use new ones.
23 Connect the brake hose banjo bolt to the master cylinder, using a new sealing washer on each side of the banjo union. Ensure that

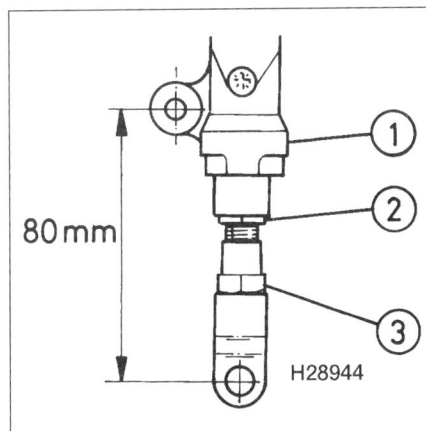

9.26 Brake pedal height adjustment

1 Master cylinder
2 Pushrod adjuster nut
3 Clevis locknut

the hose is positioned against the lug (see illustration 9.4) and tighten the banjo bolt to the specified torque setting.
24 If removed, install the clevis locknut, the clevis and the clevis nut onto the master cylinder pushrod end, but do not yet tighten the locknut (see illustration). Install the spring pin into the end of the pushrod (late K models onward).
25 If the clevis position on the pushrod was disturbed during overhaul, position it using the adjuster nut so that the distance between the hole in the clevis and the master cylinder lower mounting bolt hole is 80 mm (see illustration). Tighten the locknut against the clevis (see illustration 9.24).
26 Align the brake pedal arm with the pushrod clevis, then install the clevis pin and secure it using a new split pin.
27 Fill the fluid reservoir with the specified fluid (see Specifications) and bleed the system following the procedure in Section 11.
28 Check the operation of the brake carefully before riding the motorcycle.

10 Brake hoses and unions - inspection and replacement

Inspection

1 Brake hose condition should be checked regularly and the hoses replaced at the specified interval (see Chapter 1).
2 Twist and flex the rubber hoses while looking for cracks, bulges and seeping fluid. Check extra carefully around the areas where the hoses connect with the banjo fittings, as these are common areas for hose failure.
3 Inspect the metal banjo union fittings connected to the brake hoses. If the fittings are rusted, scratched or cracked, replace them.

7

Replacement

4 The brake hoses have banjo union fittings on each end. Cover the surrounding area with plenty of rags and unscrew the banjo bolt on each end of the hose. Detach the hose from any clips that may be present and remove the hose. Discard the sealing washers.

5 Position the new hose, making sure it isn't twisted or otherwise strained, and abut the tab on the hose union with the lug on the component casting. Install the banjo bolts, using new sealing washers on both sides of the unions, and tighten them to the torque setting specified at the beginning of this Chapter. Make sure they are correctly aligned and routed clear of all moving components.

6 Flush the old brake fluid from the system, refill with the recommended fluid (see Specifications) and bleed the air from the system (see Section 11). Check the operation of the brakes carefully before riding the motorcycle.

11 Brake system - bleeding

1 Bleeding the brakes is simply the process of removing all the air bubbles from the brake fluid reservoirs, the hoses and the brake calipers. Bleeding is necessary whenever a brake system hydraulic connection is loosened, when a component or hose is replaced, or when the master cylinder or caliper is overhauled. Leaks in the system may also allow air to enter, but leaking brake fluid will reveal their presence and warn you of the need for repair.

2 To bleed the brakes, you will need some new, clean brake fluid of the recommended type (see Specifications), a length of clear vinyl or plastic tubing, a small container partially filled with clean brake fluid, some rags and a spanner to fit the brake caliper bleed valve.

3 Cover the fuel tank and other painted components to prevent damage in the event that brake fluid is spilled.

4 If bleeding the rear brake, remove the right-hand side panel for access to the fluid reservoir.

5 Remove the reservoir cover, diaphragm plate and diaphragm and slowly pump the brake lever or pedal a few times, until no air bubbles can be seen floating up from the holes in the bottom of the reservoir. Doing this bleeds the air from the master cylinder end of the line. Loosely refit the reservoir cap/cover.

6 Pull the dust cap off the bleed valve (**see illustration**). Attach one end of the clear vinyl or plastic tubing to the bleed valve and submerge the other end in the brake fluid in the container.

7 Remove the reservoir cover and check the fluid level. Do not allow the fluid level to drop below the lower mark during the bleeding process.

11.6 Brake caliper bleed valve (arrow)

8 Carefully pump the brake lever or pedal three or four times and hold it in (front) or down (rear) while opening the caliper bleed valve. When the valve is opened, brake fluid will flow out of the caliper into the clear tubing and the lever will move toward the handlebar or the pedal will move down.

9 Retighten the bleed valve (note the torque setting in the Specifications of this Chapter), then release the brake lever or pedal gradually. Repeat the process until no air bubbles are visible in the brake fluid leaving the caliper and the lever or pedal is firm when applied. Disconnect the bleeding equipment and install the dust cap on the bleed valve.

10 Install the diaphragm and cover assembly, wipe up any spilled brake fluid and check the entire system for leaks.

> **HAYNES HINT** *If it's not possible to produce a firm feel to the lever or pedal the fluid my be aerated. Let the brake fluid in the system stabilise for a few hours and then repeat the procedure when the tiny bubbles in the system have settled out.*

12 Wheels - inspection and repair

1 In order to carry out a proper inspection of the wheels, it is necessary to support the bike upright so that the wheel being inspected is raised off the ground. Position the motorcycle on its centre stand or an auxiliary stand. Clean the wheels thoroughly to remove mud and dirt that may interfere with the inspection procedure or mask defects. Make a general check of the wheels and tyres as described in Chapter 1.

2 Attach a dial indicator to the fork slider or the swingarm and position its stem against the side of the rim (**see illustration**). Spin the wheel slowly and check the axial (side-to-side) runout of the rim. In order to accurately check radial (out of round) runout with the dial indicator, the wheel would have to be removed from the machine, and the tyre from the wheel. With the axle clamped in a vice and

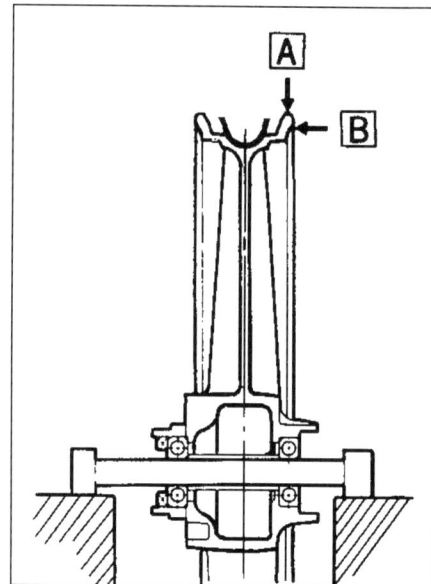
12.2 Check the wheel for radial (out-of-round) runout (A) and axial (side-to-side) runout (B)

the dial indicator positioned on the top of the rim, the wheel can be rotated to check the runout.

3 An easier, though slightly less accurate, method is to attach a stiff wire pointer to the fork slider or the swingarm and position the end a fraction of an inch from the wheel (where the wheel and tyre join). If the wheel is true, the distance from the pointer to the rim will be constant as the wheel is rotated. **Note:** *If wheel runout is excessive, check the wheel bearings carefully before replacing the wheel.*

4 The wheels should also be visually inspected for cracks, flat spots on the rim and other damage. Look very closely for dents in the area where the tyre bead contacts the rim. Dents in this area may prevent complete sealing of the tyre against the rim, which leads to deflation of the tyre over a period of time. If damage is evident, or if runout in either direction is excessive, the wheel will have to be replaced with a new one. Never attempt to repair a damaged cast alloy wheel.

13 Wheels - alignment check

1 Misalignment of the wheels, which may be due to a cocked rear wheel or a bent frame or fork yokes, can cause strange and possibly serious handling problems. If the frame or yokes are at fault, repair by a frame specialist or replacement with new parts are the only alternatives.

2 To check the alignment you will need an assistant, a length of string or a perfectly straight piece of wood and a ruler. A plumb bob or other suitable weight will also be required.

3 In order to make a proper check of the wheels it is necessary to support the bike in an upright position, either on its centre stand or on an auxiliary stand. Measure the width of both tyres at their widest points. Subtract the smaller measurement from the larger measurement, then divide the difference by two. The result is the amount of offset that should exist between the front and rear tyres on both sides.

4 If a string is used, have your assistant hold one end of it about halfway between the floor and the rear axle, touching the rear sidewall of the tyre.

5 Run the other end of the string forward and pull it tight so that it is roughly parallel to the floor. Slowly bring the string into contact with the front sidewall of the rear tyre, then turn the front wheel until it is parallel with the string. Measure the distance from the front tyre sidewall to the string.

6 Repeat the procedure on the other side of the motorcycle. The distance from the front tyre sidewall to the string should be equal on both sides.

7 As was previously pointed out, a perfectly straight length of wood may be substituted for the string. The procedure is the same.

8 If the distance between the string and tyre is greater on one side, or if the rear wheel appears to be cocked, refer to Chapter 1, *"Swingarm bearing check"*, and make sure the swingarm is tight.

9 If the front-to-back alignment is correct, the wheels still may be out of alignment vertically.

10 Using the plumb bob, or other suitable

weight, and a length of string, check the rear wheel to make sure it is vertical. To do this, hold the string against the tyre upper sidewall and allow the weight to settle just off the floor. When the string touches both the upper and lower tyre sidewalls and is perfectly straight, the wheel is vertical. If it is not, place thin spacers under one leg of the stand.

11 Once the rear wheel is vertical, check the front wheel in the same manner. If both wheels are not perfectly vertical, the frame and/or major suspension components are bent.

14 Front wheel - removal and installation

Removal

1 Position the motorcycle on its centre stand or on an auxiliary stand and support it under the crankcase so that the front wheel is off the ground. Always make sure the motorcycle is properly supported.

2 Remove the screw securing the speedometer cable on the left-hand side of the wheel hub and detach the cable from its drive unit **(see illustration)**.

3 Remove the brake caliper mounting bolts and slide the caliper off the disc **(see illustration 3.2)**. Support the caliper with a piece of wire or a bungee cord so that no strain is placed on its hydraulic hose. There is no need to disconnect the brake hose from the caliper.

4 Slacken the axle clamp bolts on the bottom of each fork, then unscrew the axle bolt from the right-hand side **(see illustrations)**.

5 Support the wheel, then withdraw the axle from the left-hand side and carefully lower the wheel **(see illustration)**. **Note**: *Do not operate the front brake lever with the wheel removed.*

6 Remove the spacer from the right-hand side of the wheel, noting which way round it fits, and the speedometer drive housing from the left-hand side **(see illustration)**.

Caution: Don't lay the wheel down and allow it to rest on the disc - the disc could become warped. Set the wheel on wood blocks so the disc doesn't support the weight of the wheel.

7 Check the axle for straightness by rolling it on a flat surface such as a piece of plate glass (first wipe off all old grease and remove any corrosion using fine emery cloth). If the equipment is available, place the axle in V-blocks and measure the runout using a dial indicator. If the axle is bent or the runout exceeds the limit specified, replace it.

8 Check the condition of the wheel bearings (see Section 16).

Installation

9 Apply a smear of lithium-based grease to the speedometer drive components. Fit the speedometer drive to the wheel's left-hand side, aligning its drive gear slots with the driveplate tabs **(see illustration)**.

10 Apply a smear of lithium-based grease to the outer surface of the spacer (where it contacts the grease seal) and install the spacer

14.2 Unscrew the speedometer cable retaining screw (arrow)

14.4a Axle clamp bolts (arrows)

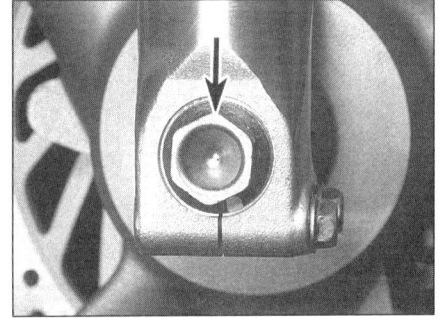

14.4b Axle bolt (arrow)

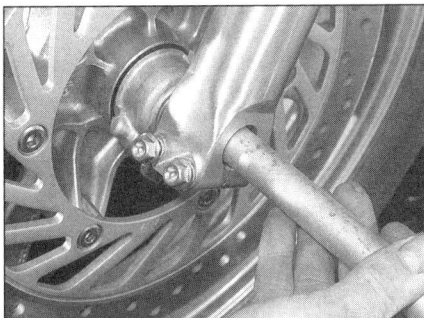

14.5 Withdraw the axle from the left side

14.6 Speedometer drive housing locates in wheel left-hand side

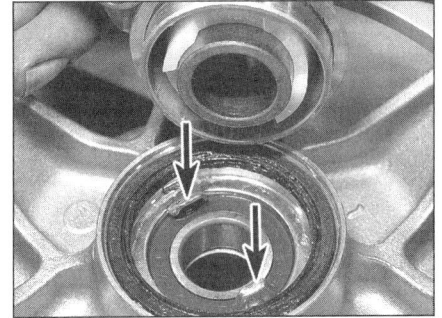

14.9 Align the driveplate tabs (arrows) with the slots in the drive gear

7

14.10 Install the spacer with its ridged end outwards (arrow)

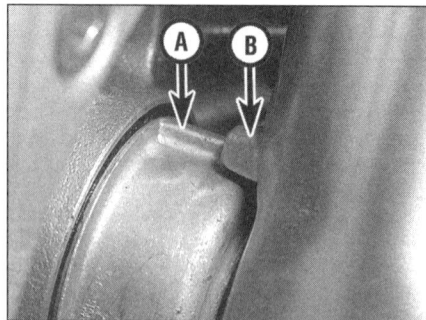
14.12 The lug on the speedometer drive housing (A) butts on the back of the lug on the fork slider (B)

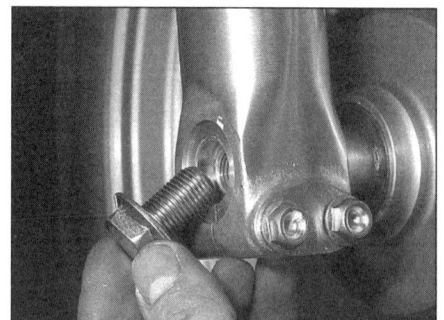
14.14a Install the axle bolt . . .

14.14b . . . and tighten it to the specified torque setting

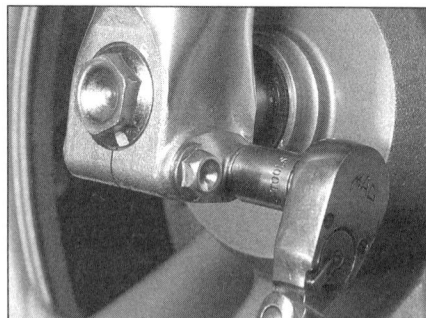
14.15 Tighten the axle clamp bolts to the specified torque setting

14.17a Fit the speedometer cable into its guide on the brake caliper . . .

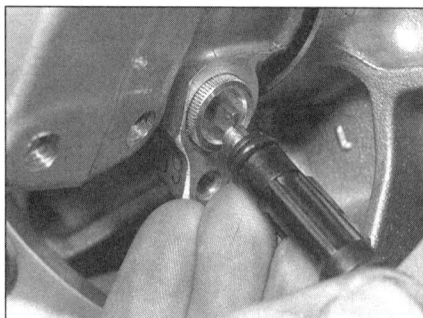
14.17b . . . then align the slot in the cable end with the drive tab . . .

14.17c . . . and secure it with its screw

in the right-hand side of the wheel, with its ridged end facing out (see illustration).

11 Manoeuvre the wheel into position. Apply a thin coat of grease to the axle.

12 Lift the wheel into position making sure the spacer remains in place. Make sure the lug on the speedometer drive housing fits against the back of the lug on the fork slider (see illustration).

13 Slide the axle into position from the left-hand side (see illustration 14.5).

14 Install the axle bolt (see illustration). Tighten the bolt to the specified torque setting (see illustration).

15 Tighten the axle clamp bolts on both forks to the specified torque setting (see illustration).

16 Install the brake caliper making sure the pads sit squarely on either side of the disc. Fit the caliper mounting bolts and tighten them to the torque setting specified at the beginning of the Chapter.

17 Pass the speedometer cable through its guides on the mudguard and the brake caliper (if withdrawn), then connect the cable to the drive housing, aligning the slot in the cable end with the drive tab, and securely tighten its screw (see illustrations).

18 Apply the front brake a few times to bring the pads back into contact with the disc. Move the motorcycle off its stand, apply the front brake and pump the front forks a few times to settle all components in position.

19 Check for correct operation of the front brake before riding the motorcycle.

15 Rear wheel - removal and installation

Removal

1 Position the motorcycle on its centre stand or on an auxiliary stand. Always make sure the bike is properly supported. It is advisable to place a block in front of the front wheel, or to tie the front brake lever back so that the front wheel is locked.

15.2a Prise off the wheel nut cap . . .

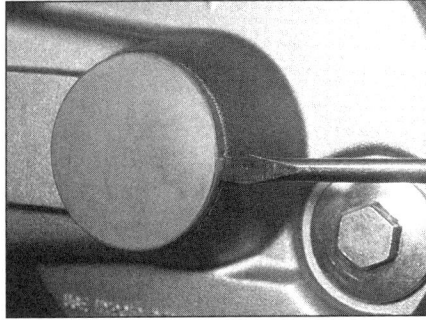

15.2b . . . and the axle cap

15.2c Remove the split pin from the axle and the wheel nut

15.3a Unscrew the wheel nut . . .

15.3b . . . and remove the axle spacer

15.7 Install the axle into the final drive housing

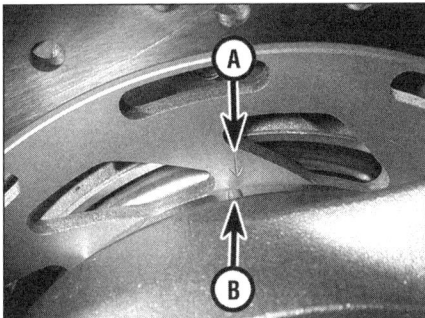

15.8a Align the arrows on the disc (A) with the index marks on the wheel (B) . . .

15.8b . . . then install the wheel

15.9 Tighten the axle nut to the specified torque setting

2 Prise off the wheel nut cap from the right-hand side of the wheel and the axle cap from the outside of the final drive housing **(see illustrations)**. Remove the split pin from the end of the axle, noting how it fits, and discard it as it is important that a new one be used **(see illustration)**.

3 Unscrew the wheel nut, then remove the axle spacer **(see illustrations)**. Grasp the wheel and draw it to the right until it is clear of the final drive housing, then manoeuvre it clear of the swingarm. Note the index marks on the wheel and the inside of the brake disc indicating the correct installation position.

4 Tap the axle from the inside using a soft-faced hammer and withdraw it from the final drive housing, noting how it fits.

5 Check the axle splines and threads for wear or damage. Check the axle for straightness by rolling it on a flat surface such as a piece of plate glass (first wipe off all old grease and remove any corrosion using fine emery cloth). If the equipment is available, place the axle in V-blocks and measure the runout using a dial indicator. If the axle is worn, damaged or bent, replace it.

6 Check the drive pin bolts on the final drive housing for tightness, wear or damage and tighten or replace any if necessary. If disturbed, apply a suitable thread locking compound to their threads and tighten them to the torque setting specified at the beginning of the Chapter. Check the corresponding drive pin holes in the wheel for wear or damage.

Installation

7 Apply a thin coat of lithium-based grease to the axle shaft and install it into the final drive housing, making sure the splines are correctly engaged **(see illustration)**. Tap it with a soft-faced hammer to make sure it is properly seated.

8 Align the arrows on the inside of the brake disc with the index marks on the wheel, then lift the wheel into position and install it onto the final drive housing, making sure the drive pins engage correctly in the wheel **(see illustrations)**.

9 Install the axle spacer **(see illustration 15.3b)**. Apply a thin coat of lithium-based grease to the threads on the end of the axle, then install the wheel nut and tighten it to the specified torque setting **(see illustration)**.

7

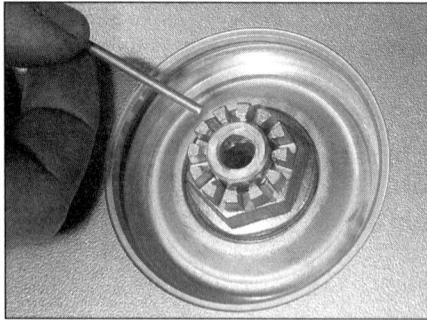

15.10a Fit a new split pin through the axle . . .

15.10b . . . then fit the wheel nut cap . . .

15.10c . . . and the axle cap

10 Fit a new split pin into the end of the axle and bend over its ends, then fit the wheel nut cap and the axle cap **(see illustrations)**.

16 Wheel bearings - removal, inspection and installation

Front wheel bearings

Note: *Always replace the wheel bearings in pairs. Never replace the bearings individually.*

Avoid using a high pressure cleaner on the wheel bearing area.

1 Remove the wheel as described in Section 14.

2 Set the wheel on blocks so the weight of the wheel does not rest on the brake disc.

3 Using a flat-bladed screwdriver, prise out the grease seals from both sides of the wheel **(see illustrations)**. Note the differences between the seals for installation. Discard the seals if they are worn or damaged as new ones should be used.

4 Withdraw the speedometer driveplate from the left-hand side of the wheel, noting how it fits **(see illustration)**.

5 Insert a finger through the bearing inner race and rotate it - if the bearing doesn't turn smoothly, has rough spots or is noisy, it must be replaced with a new one. **Note:** *Honda advise that the wheel bearings must be replaced with new ones if they are removed from the wheel hub.*

6 Using a metal rod (preferably a brass drift punch) inserted through the centre of the hub

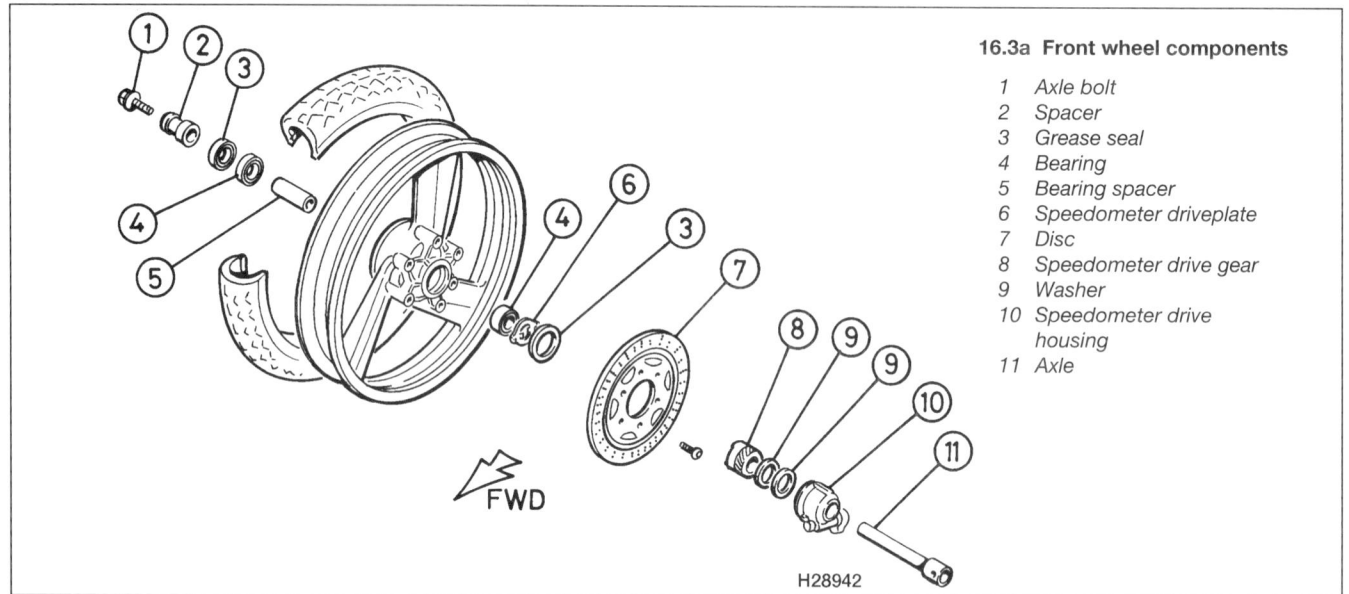

16.3a Front wheel components

1 Axle bolt
2 Spacer
3 Grease seal
4 Bearing
5 Bearing spacer
6 Speedometer driveplate
7 Disc
8 Speedometer drive gear
9 Washer
10 Speedometer drive housing
11 Axle

FWD

H28942

16.3b Prise out the left-hand grease seal . . .

16.3c . . . and the right-hand grease seal, noting their differences

16.4 Remove the speedometer driveplate

16.6 Using a drift to knock out the bearings

16.9 Using a bearing driver to drive in the bearings

bearing from the left-hand side, tap evenly around the inner race of the right-hand side bearing to drive it from the hub **(see illustration)**. The bearing spacer will also come out.

7 Lay the wheel on its other side and remove the other bearing using the same technique.

8 If the bearing is good and can be re-used, wash it in solvent once again and dry it, then pack the bearing with high-quality lithium-based grease.

9 Thoroughly clean the hub area of the wheel. Install the left-hand side bearing into its recess in the hub, with the marked or sealed side facing outwards. Using a bearing driver or a socket large enough to contact the outer race of the bearing, drive it in until it's completely seated **(see illustration)**.

10 Turn the wheel over and install the bearing spacer.

11 Drive the right-hand side bearing into place as described in Step 9.

12 Fit the speedometer driveplate to the left-hand side of the wheel, making sure its locating tangs are correctly located in the hub slots and the drive tabs face out **(see illustration)**.

13 Apply a smear of lithium-based grease to the lips of the grease seals, then install them using a seal driver, large socket or a flat piece of wood to drive them into place **(see illustrations)**. Make sure each seal is fitted to its correct side.

14 Clean off all grease from the brake disc using acetone or brake system cleaner then install the wheel as described in Section 14.

Rear wheel/final drive bearings

15 The rear wheel has no bearings. Refer to Chapter 6 for the procedure regarding the final drive bearings.

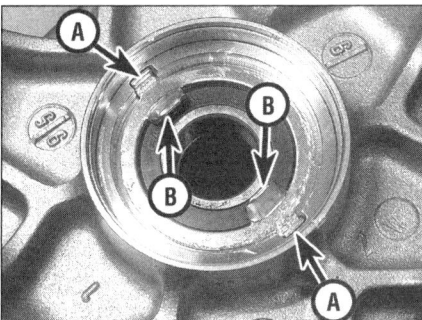
16.12 Fit the speedometer driveplate with its outer tangs located in the slots in the hub (A) and its drive tabs facing out (B)

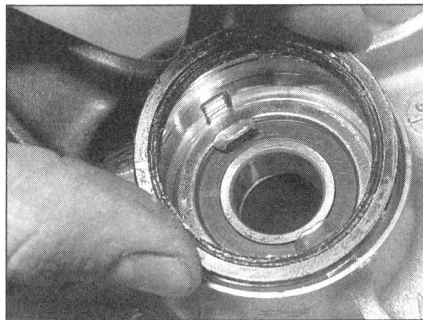
16.13a Fit the left-hand side . . .

17 Tyres -
general information and fitting

General information

1 The wheels fitted to all models are designed to take tubeless tyres only.

2 Refer to *Daily (pre-ride) checks* at the beginning of this manual, and to the scheduled checks in Chapter 1 for tyre and wheel maintenance.

Fitting new tyres

3 When selecting new tyres, refer to the tyre information label on the swingarm and the tyre options listed in the owners manual. Ensure that front and rear tyre types are compatible, the correct size and correct speed rating; if necessary seek advice from a Honda dealer or tyre fitting specialist **(see illustration)**.

16.13b . . . and the right-hand side grease seals . . .

16.13c . . . and drive them into place

7

MANUFACTURERS NAME
OR BRAND NAME

A COMMERCIAL NAME
OR IDENTITY

REAR TYRE
FITMENT

COUNTRY OF MANUFACTURE

TYRE CONSTRUCTION DETAILS
(NOT REQUIRED IN UK)

NORTH AMERICAN
TYRE IDENTIFICATION NUMBER

NORTH AMERICAN
DEPARTMENT OF TRANSPORT
COMPLIANCE SYMBOL

LOAD AND PRESSURE
MARKING REQUIREMENT
(NOT APPLICABLE IN UK)

BIAS BELTED TYRE SIZE

ARROW DENOTING
THE DIRECTION OF
WHEEL ROTATION

TYRE SIZE DESIGNATION

TYRE % PROFILE

SPEED SYMBOL

THE WORD TUBELESS
WHERE APPLICABLE

RADIAL CONSTRUCTION

MAX SPEED

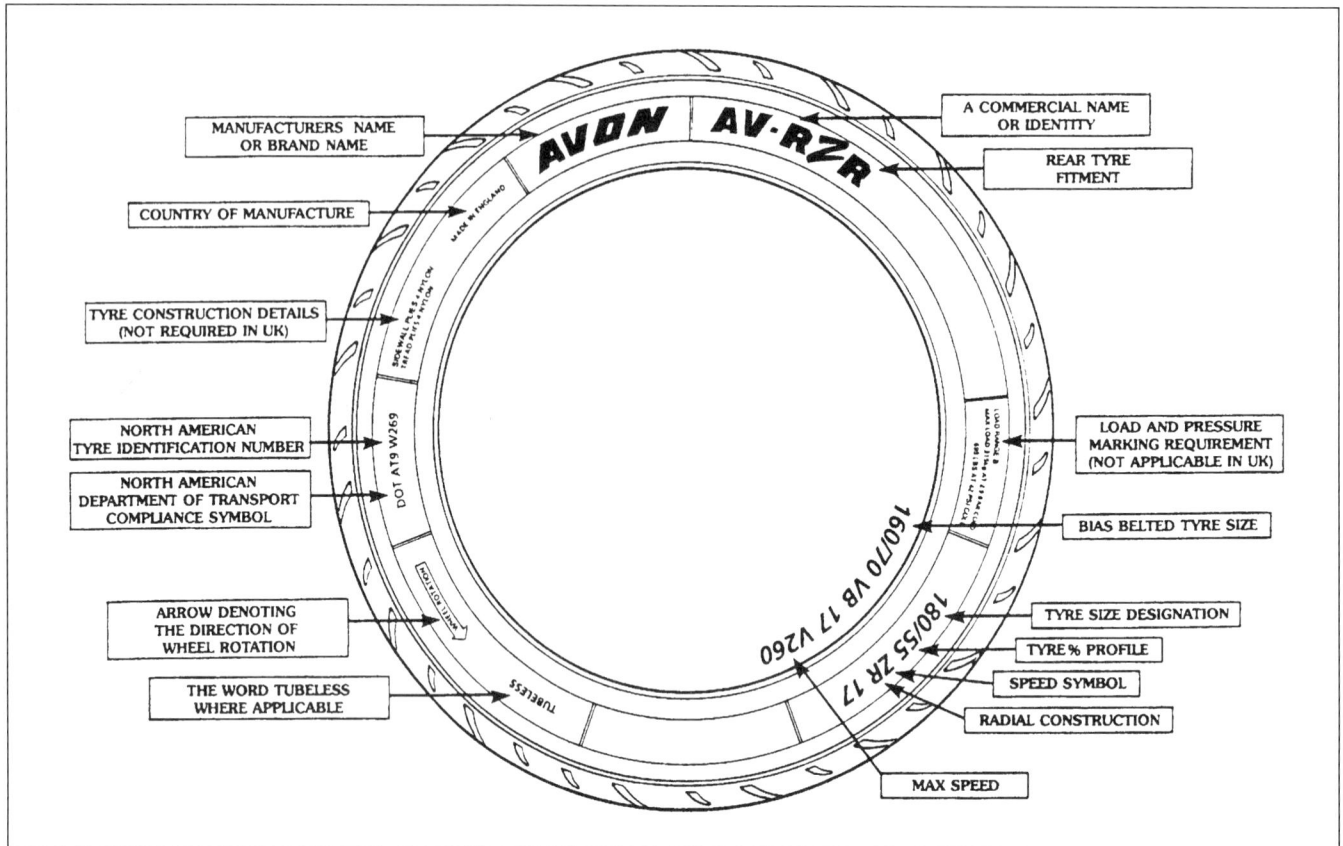

17.3 Common tyre sidewall markings

4 It is recommended that tyres are fitted by a motorcycle tyre specialist rather than attempted in the home workshop. The force required to break the seal between the wheel rim and tyre bead is substantial, and is usually beyond the capabilities of an individual working with normal tyre levers. Additionally, the specialist will be able to balance the wheels after tyre fitting.

5 Only certain types of puncture repair are suitable for tubeless motorcycle tyres. Refer to a tyre fitting specialist for advice and to your owners manual for details of the reduced speeds advised for a repaired tyre.

Chapter 8
Bodywork components

Contents

Degrees of difficulty

Easy, suitable for novice with little experience	Fairly easy, suitable for beginner with some experience	Fairly difficult, suitable for competent DIY mechanic	Difficult, suitable for experienced DIY mechanic	Very difficult, suitable for expert DIY or professional

1 General information

This Chapter covers the procedures necessary to remove and install the body parts. Since many service and repair operations on these motorcycles require the removal of the body parts, the procedures are grouped here and referred to from other Chapters.

In the case of damage to the body parts, it is usually necessary to remove the broken component and replace it with a new (or used) one. The material that the body panels are composed of doesn't lend itself to conventional repair techniques. There are however some shops that specialise in "plastic welding", so it may be worthwhile seeking the advice of one of these specialists before consigning an expensive component to the bin.

When attempting to remove any body panel, first study it closely, noting any fasteners and associated fittings, to be sure of returning everything to its correct place on installation. In some cases the aid of an assistant will be required when removing panels, to help avoid the risk of damage to paintwork. Once the evident fasteners have been removed, try to withdraw the panel as described but DO NOT FORCE IT - if it will not release, check that all fasteners have been removed and try again.

Where a panel engages another by means of tabs, be careful not to break the tab or its mating slot or to damage the paintwork. Remember that a few moments of patience at this stage will save you a lot of money in replacing broken fairing panels!

When installing a body panel, first study it closely, noting any fasteners and associated fittings removed with it, to be sure of returning everything to its correct place. Check that all fasteners are in good condition, including all trim nuts or clips and damping/rubber mounts; any of these must be replaced if faulty before the panel is reassembled. Check also that all mounting brackets are straight and repair or replace them if necessary before attempting to install the panel. Where assistance was required to remove a panel, make sure your assistant is on hand to install it.

Carefully settle the panel in place, following the instructions provided, and check that it engages correctly with its partners (where applicable) before tightening any of the fasteners. Where a panel engages another by means of tabs, be careful not to break the tab or its mating slot. Note that a small amount of lubricant (liquid soap or similar) applied to the mounting rubbers of the side panels will assist the panel retaining pegs to engage without the need for undue pressure.

Tighten the fasteners securely, but be careful not to overtighten any of them or the panel may break (not always immediately) due to the uneven stress.

2 Rear view mirrors - removal and installation

Removal

1 Unscrew the mirror from its mounting on the handlebar, using a suitable spanner on the lower nut to initially slacken it (see illustration).

Installation

2 Install the mirror into its mounting and screw it in until it is fully home. If the position of the mirror is not as required, counter-hold the lower nut on the stem and slacken the top nut. Adjust the mirror as required, then tighten the top nut whilst counter-holding the mirror.

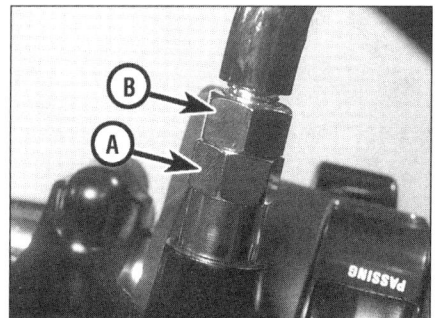

2.1 Mirror mounting nut (A) and locknut (B)

8

3.2a Side panel mounting points (arrows)

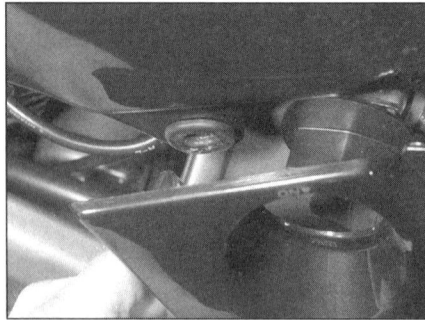

3.2b Release the panel from its pegs . . .

3.2c . . . draw it forward to release the tab

3.5a The rear cowl is secured by a bolt on each side . . .

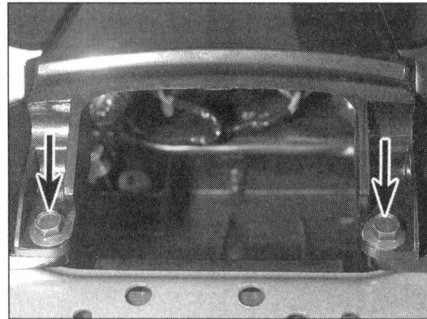

3.5b . . . and two at the rear (arrows)

3 Body panels - removal and installation

HAYNES HINT *A smear of liquid soap (washing-up liquid is ideal) applied to the mounting grommets will help the side panel pegs engage without the need for undue pressure.*

Side panels

Removal

1 Remove the seat (see Section 6).
2 The side panels are secured by two pegs at the front which fit into rubber grommets, and a tab at the rear which locates into the front of the rear cowl (see illustration). Gently pull the panel away from the frame to release the pegs, then draw it forwards to release the tab from the rear cowl (see illustrations). Do not force or bend the panel while removing it.

Installation

3 Installation is the reverse of removal.

Rear cowl

Removal

4 Remove the side panels (see above).
5 Unscrew the two side bolts and the two rear bolts securing the rear cowl to the frame, then carefully draw the cowl backwards until it is clear of the passenger grab-rail, noting how it fits (see illustrations).

Installation

6 Installation is the reverse of removal.

4 Front mudguard - removal and installation

Removal

1 Remove the front wheel (see Chapter 7).
2 Remove the screws securing the sides of the mudguard to the forks, noting the position of the brake hose clamp (see illustration). Withdraw the speedometer cable from its guide on the mudguard.
3 Carefully remove the mudguard by sliding it downwards until it clears the bottom of the forks.

Installation

4 Installation is the reverse of removal. Make sure the brake hose and speedometer cable are correctly routed and secured by their clamps (see illustrations).

4.2 Front mudguard mounting bolts

4.4a Note the fitting of the brake hose clamp (arrow)

4.4b Pass the speedometer cable through its guide

6.1 The seat lock is below the tail light

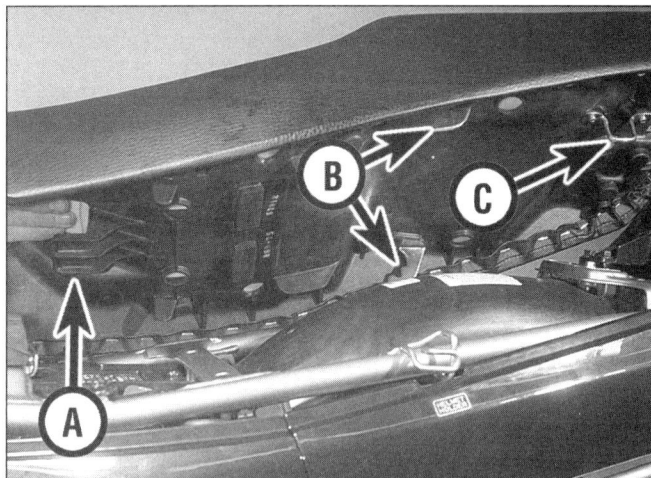

6.2 Note the tab (A), the side hooks (B), and the lock latch (C) which secure the seat

5 Rear mudguard - removal and installation

Removal

1 The rear mudguard comes in two sections. The front section is mounted to the frame rails under the seat and incorporates the battery case. The rear section is mounted to the end of the frame and incorporates the rear tail light assembly and the rear turn signal assemblies, and has the licence plate mounted to it.

2 Remove the seat (see Section 6), the battery (see Chapter 9), the rear cowl (see Section 3), the passenger grab-rail (see Section 7), the tail light assembly (see Chapter 9) and the rear turn signal assemblies (see Chapter 9). Also move aside all ancillary components such as the fuel pump and the various electrical components attached to the rear mudguard (see Chapter 9), the rear brake

fluid reservoir (see Chapter 7), and the ignition control unit (see Chapter 5).

3 Remove all clips and bolts securing the rear mudguard sections and remove them from the frame.

Installation

4 Installation is the reverse of removal.

6 Seat - removal and installation

Removal

1 Insert the ignition key into the seat lock which is located below the tail light assembly and turn it clockwise to unlock the seat **(see illustration)**.

2 Lift the rear of the seat and draw it back and away from the bike. Note how the tab at the front of the seat locates under the fuel

tank mounting bracket, and how the seat locates onto the frame rail **(see illustration)**.

Installation

3 Locate the tab at the front of the seat under the fuel tank mounting bracket. Align the seat at the rear and push down on it to engage the latches **(see illustration)**.

7 Passenger grab-rail - removal and installation

Removal

1 Remove the seat (see Section 6).

2 Remove the rear cowl (see Section 3).

3 Unscrew the four bolts securing the grab-rail to the frame and remove the grab-rail **(see illustration)**.

Installation

4 Installation is the reverse of removal.

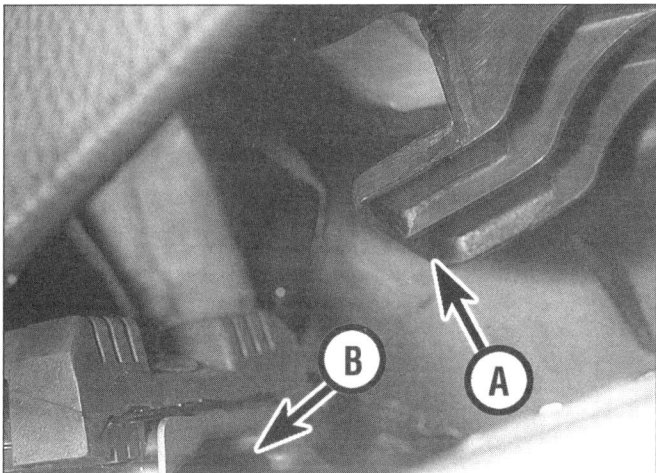

6.3 Locate the tab (A) under the fuel tank bracket (B)

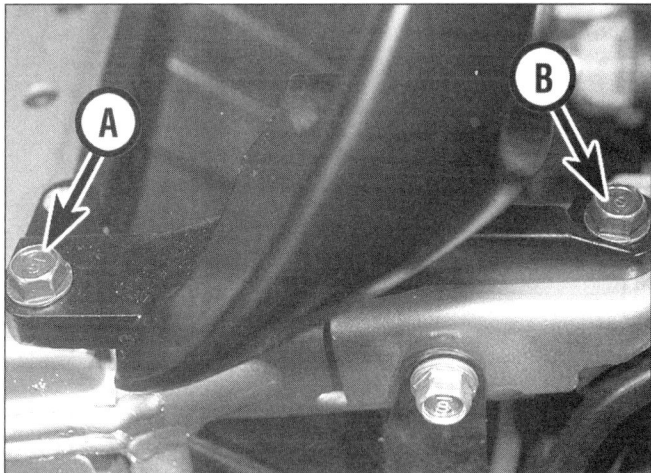

7.3 The grab-rail is secured by a bolt on each side at the front (A), and at the back (B)

8

Chapter 9
Electrical system

Contents

Degrees of difficulty

Easy, suitable for novice with little experience	✎	**Fairly easy,** suitable for beginner with some experience	✎	**Fairly difficult,** suitable for competent DIY mechanic	✎	**Difficult,** suitable for experienced DIY mechanic	✎	**Very difficult,** suitable for expert DIY or professional	✎

Specifications

Battery
Capacity . . . .   12 V, 8 Ah

Alternator
Output . . . .   345 W at 5000 rpm
Stator coil resistance . . . .   0.1 to 1.0 ohm at 20°C

Regulator/rectifier
Regulated voltage, current . . . .   13.5 to 15.5 V, 0.5 A

Starter motor
Brush length
    Standard . . . .   12.5 mm
    Service limit . . . .   6.5 mm

Fuel pump
Flow rate . . . .   600 cc/min at 10 V

9

Fusebox fuses

Main fuse 30A
Brake, turn signal, horn 15A
Fan, ignition, headlight, oil and neutral switches 10A

Bulbs

Headlight . . . . 60/55W H4 halogen
Sidelight . . . . 4.0 W
Brake/tail light . . . . 21/5 W
Turn signal lights . . . . 21 W

Torque settings

Oil pressure switch . . . . 12 Nm
Ignition (main) switch mounting bolts . . . . 25 Nm
Neutral switch . . . . 12 Nm
Alternator rotor bolt . . . . 130 Nm

1 General information

All models have a 12-volt electrical system. The components include a three-phase alternator unit and regulator/rectifier unit.

The regulator maintains the charging system output within the specified range to prevent overcharging, and the rectifier converts the ac (alternating current) output of the alternator to dc (direct current) to power the lights and other components and to charge the battery. The alternator is driven directly off the crankshaft.

The starter motor is mounted on the crankcase behind the cylinders. The starting system includes the motor, the battery, the relay and the various wires and switches. If the engine stop switch and the ignition (main) switch are both in the "Run" or "On" position, the starter relay allows the starter motor to operate only if the transmission is in neutral (neutral switch on) or, if the transmission is in gear, if the clutch lever is pulled into the handlebar (clutch switch on) and the side stand is up.

Note: *Keep in mind that electrical parts, once purchased, cannot be returned. To avoid unnecessary expense, make very sure the faulty component has been positively identified before buying a replacement part.*

2 Electrical troubleshooting

⚠ *Warning: To prevent the risk of short circuits, the ignition (main) switch must always be "OFF" and the battery negative (-ve) terminal should be disconnected before any of the bike's other electrical components are disturbed. Don't forget to reconnect the terminal securely once work is finished or if battery power is needed for circuit testing.*

1 A typical electrical circuit consists of an electrical component, the switches, relays, etc. related to that component and the wiring and connectors that hook the component to both the battery and the frame. To aid in locating a problem in any electrical circuit, refer to the wiring diagrams at the end of this Chapter.

2 Before tackling any troublesome electrical circuit, first study the wiring diagram (see end of Chapter) thoroughly to get a complete picture of what makes up that individual circuit. Trouble spots, for instance, can often be narrowed down by noting if other components related to that circuit are operating properly or not. If several components or circuits fail at one time, chances are the fault lies in the fuse or earth connection, as several circuits often are routed through the same fuse and earth connections.

3 Electrical problems often stem from simple causes, such as loose or corroded connections or a blown fuse. Prior to any electrical troubleshooting, always visually check the condition of the fuse, wires and connections in the problem circuit. Intermittent failures can be especially frustrating, since you can't always duplicate the failure when it's convenient to test. In such situations, a good practice is to clean all connections in the affected circuit, whether or not they appear to be good. All of the connections and wires should also be wiggled to check for looseness which can cause intermittent failure.

4 If testing instruments are going to be utilised, use the wiring diagram to plan where you will make the necessary connections in order to accurately pinpoint the trouble spot.

5 The basic tools needed for electrical fault finding include a battery and bulb test circuit, a continuity tester, test light and a jumper wire. For more extensive checks, a multimeter capable of measuring ohms, volts and amps will be required. Full details on the use of this test equipment are given in *Fault Finding Equipment* at the end of this manual.

3 Battery - removal, installation, inspection and maintenance

Caution: Be extremely careful when handling or working around the battery. The electrolyte is very caustic and an explosive gas (hydrogen) is given off when the battery is charging.

Removal and installation

1 Remove the seat (see Chapter 8) then unscrew the bolts securing the battery cover (four on J models, three on all other models) and remove the cover (see illustration). Disconnect the leads from the battery, disconnecting the negative (-ve) terminal first, and lift the battery out of its box (see illustrations).

2 On installation, clean the battery terminals and lead ends with a wire brush or knife and emery paper. Reconnect the leads, connecting the positive (+ve) terminal first, then fit the insulating cover over the positive (+ve) terminal. Fit the battery cover and install the seat (see Chapter 8).

HAYNES HiNT *Battery corrosion can be kept to a minimum by applying a layer of petroleum jelly to the terminals after the cables have been connected.*

3.1a Battery cover bolts (arrow)

3.1b Negative (-ve) terminal (A), positive (+ve) terminal (B), positive terminal cover (C)

Inspection and maintenance

3 The battery fitted to the models covered in this manual is of the maintenance-free (sealed) type and therefore requires no maintenance as such. However the following checks should still be regularly performed.

4 Check the battery terminals and leads for tightness and corrosion. If corrosion is evident, disconnect the leads from the battery, disconnecting the negative (-ve) terminal first, and clean the terminals and lead ends with a wire brush or knife and emery paper. Reconnect the leads, connecting the negative (-ve) terminal last, and apply a thin coat of petroleum jelly to the connections to slow further corrosion.

5 The battery case should be kept clean to prevent current leakage, which can discharge the battery over a period of time (especially when it sits unused). Wash the outside of the case with a solution of baking soda and water. Rinse the battery thoroughly, and then dry it.

6 Look for cracks in the case and replace the battery if any are found. If acid has been spilled, neutralise it with a baking soda and water solution, then dry it thoroughly. Make sure the battery vent tube is routed correctly and is not kinked or pinched.

7 If the motorcycle sits unused for long periods of time, disconnect the cables from the battery terminals, negative (-ve) terminal first. Refer to Section 4 and charge the battery once every month to six weeks. Refer to *Storage* in the Reference section of this Manual.

8 The condition of the battery can be assessed by measuring the voltage present at the battery terminals. Connect the voltmeter positive (+ve) probe to the battery positive (+ve) terminal and the negative (-ve) probe to the battery negative (-ve) terminal. When fully charged there should be approximately 13 volts present. If the voltage falls below 12.3 volts the battery must be removed, disconnecting the negative (-ve) terminal first, and recharged as described below in Section 4.

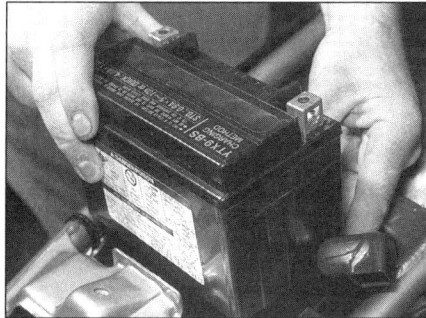

3.1c Lift the battery out of its case

4 Battery - charging

Caution: Be extremely careful when handling or working around the battery. The electrolyte is very caustic and an explosive gas (hydrogen) is given off when the battery is charging.

1 Remove the battery (see Section 3).

2 Honda recommend that the battery is charged at a maximum rate of 0.9 amps for 5 hours. Exceeding this figure can cause the battery to overheat, buckling the plates and rendering it useless. Few owners will have access to an expensive current controlled charger, so if a normal domestic charger is used check that after a possible initial peak, the charge rate falls to a safe level **(see illustration)**. **Note:** *In emergencies Honda state that the battery can be charged at a higher rate of 4.0 amps for a period of 1 hour. However, this is not recommended and the low amp charge is by far the safer method of charging the battery.*

Caution: If the battery becomes hot during charging stop - further charging will cause damage.

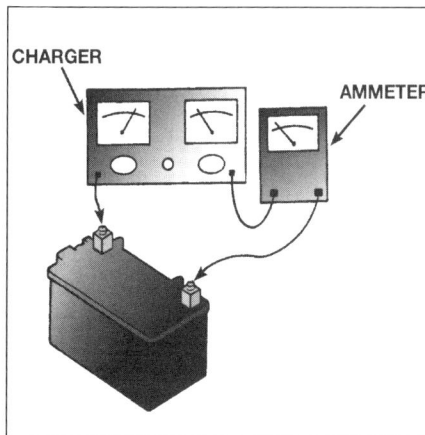

4.2 If the charger doesn't have ammeter built in, connect one in series as shown. DO NOT connect the ammeter between the battery terminals or it will be ruined

3 If the recharged battery discharges rapidly if left disconnected it is likely that an internal short caused by physical damage or sulphation has occurred. A new battery will be required. A sound item will tend to lose its charge at about 1% per day.

4 Install the battery (see Section 3).

5 If the motorcycle sits unused for long periods of time, charge the battery once every month to six weeks and leave it disconnected. Refer to *Storage* in the Reference section of this Manual.

5 Fuses - check and replacement

1 Most circuits are protected by fuses of different ratings. All fuses except the main fuse are located in the fusebox which is situated in between the handlebars on J, K and M models, and behind the right-hand side panel on P, S and T models **(see illustrations)**. On all models the main fuse is located behind the left side of the rear cowl and is incorporated in the starter relay.

2 To gain access to the fuses, on J, K and M models unscrew the two fusebox cover screws and remove the cover; on P, S and T models remove the right-hand side panel and unclip the fusebox lid **(see illustration)**. The fuses are labelled for easy identification. To access the main fuse, remove the rear cowl (see Chapter 8), then unclip the wiring connector on the top of the starter relay **(see illustration)**.

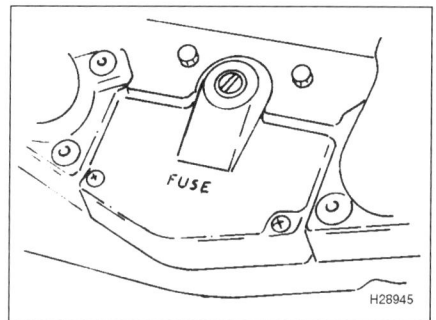

5.1a Fusebox - J, K and M models

5.1b Fusebox - P, S and T models

5.2a On P, S and T models, unclip the lid to access the fuses

5.2b The main fuse (arrow) is under the relay connector

3 The fuses can be removed and checked visually. If you can't pull the fuse out with your fingertips, use a pair of needle-nose pliers. A blown fuse is easily identified by a break in the element **(see illustration)**. Each fuse is clearly marked with its rating and must only be replaced by a fuse of the correct rating. *Caution: Never put in a fuse of a higher rating or bridge the terminals with any other substitute, however temporary it may be. Serious damage may be done to the circuit, or a fire may start. If the spare fuses are used, always replace them so that a spare fuse of each rating is carried on the bike at all times. A spare main fuse is located in the bottom of the starter relay.*

4 If a fuse blows, be sure to check the wiring circuit very carefully for evidence of a short-circuit. Look for bare wires and chafed, melted or burned insulation. If a fuse is replaced before the cause is located, the new fuse will blow immediately.

5 Occasionally a fuse will blow or cause an open-circuit for no obvious reason. Corrosion of the fuse ends and fusebox terminals may occur and cause poor fuse contact. If this happens, remove the corrosion with a wire brush or emery paper, then spray the fuse end and terminals with electrical contact cleaner.

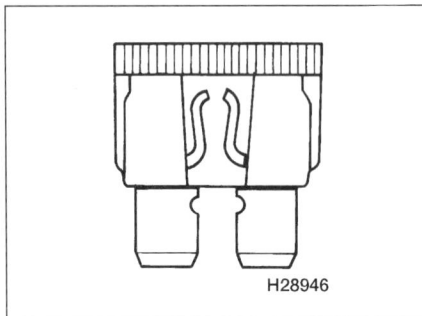

5.3 A blown fuse can be identified by a break in its element

6 Lighting system - check

1 The battery provides power for operation of the headlight, tail light, brake light and instrument cluster lights. If none of the lights operate, always check battery voltage before proceeding. Low battery voltage indicates either a faulty battery or a defective charging system. Refer to Section 3 for battery checks and Sections 31 and 32 for charging system tests. Also, check the condition of the fuses and replace any blown fuses with new ones.

Headlight

2 If the headlight fails to work, check the fuse first with the key "ON" (see Section 5) and the bulb, then unplug the electrical connector for the headlight (see Section 7) and use jumper wires to connect the bulb directly to the battery terminals. If the light comes on, the problem lies in the wiring or one of the switches in the circuit. Refer to Section 20 for the switch testing procedures, and also the wiring diagram at the end of this Chapter.

Tail light

3 If the taillight fails to work, check the bulbs and the bulb terminals first, then the fuses. Check for battery voltage at the tail light connector. If voltage is present, check the earth circuit for an open or poor connection.

4 If there is no voltage, check the wiring between the light and ignition switch, then check the switch. Also check the light switch.

Brake light

5 See Section 14 for the brake light switch checking procedure.

Neutral indicator light

6 If the neutral light fails to operate when the transmission is in neutral, check the fuses and the bulb (see Sections 5 and 17). If they are in good condition, check for battery voltage at the connector attached to the neutral switch under the left-hand side of the engine. If battery voltage is present, refer to Section 22 for the neutral switch check and replacement procedures.

7 If no voltage is indicated, check the wiring between the switch and the bulb for open-circuits and poor connections.

Oil pressure warning light

8 See Section 18 for the oil pressure switch check.

7 Headlight bulb and sidelight bulb - replacement

Note: *The headlight bulb is of the quartz-halogen type. Do not touch the bulb glass as skin acids will shorten the bulb's service life. If the bulb is accidentally touched, it should be wiped carefully when cold with a rag soaked in methylated spirit and dried before fitting.*

⚠️ *Warning: Allow the bulb time to cool before removing it if the headlight has just been on.*

Headlight

1 Unscrew the three screws securing the headlight rim to the headlight shell, and ease the rim out of the shell **(see illustration)**.

7.1 The headlight rim is secured to the shell by three screws

7.2 Disconnect the connector and remove the rubber cover

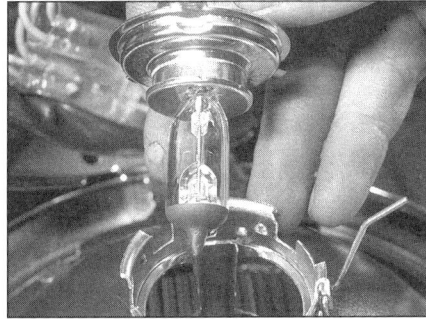

7.3 Release the clip and remove the headlight bulb

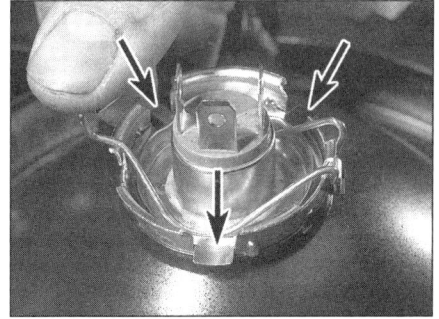

7.4 Make sure the three tabs fit correctly into the slots (arrows)

7.5 Fit the rubber cover with the TOP mark uppermost

7.6 Make sure the rim is correctly aligned with the shell

7.8a Remove the sidelight bulbholder from the headlight . . .

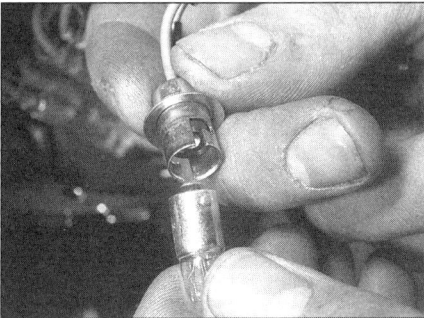

7.8b . . . and remove the bulb from the holder

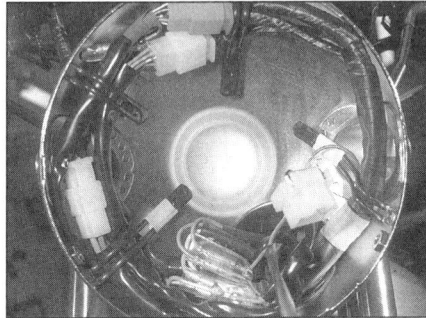

8.3a Free the wiring and pull it through the hole in the back of the shell

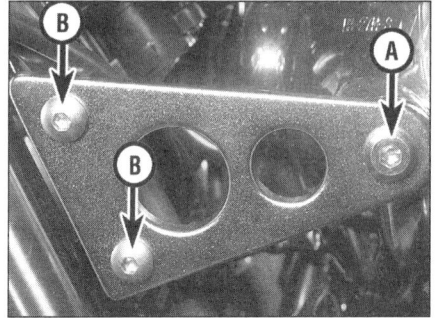

8.3b Headlight-to-bracket bolt (A), bracket-to-frame bolts (B)

2 Disconnect the wiring connector and remove the rubber dust cover, noting how it fits **(see illustration)**.

3 Release the bulb retaining clip, noting how it fits, then remove the bulb **(see illustration)**.

4 Fit the new bulb, bearing in mind the information in the **Note** above. Make sure the tabs on the bulb fit correctly in the slots in the bulb housing, and secure it in position with the retaining clip **(see illustration)**.

5 Install the dust cover, making sure it is correctly seated and with the "TOP" mark facing up, and connect the wiring connector **(see illustration)**.

6 Check the operation of the headlight, then install the rim into the shell and secure it with the screws **(see illustration)**.

Sidelight

7 Unscrew the three screws securing the headlight rim to the headlight shell, and ease the rim out of the shell **(see illustration 7.1)**.

8 Pull the bulbholder out from the headlight **(see illustration)**. Push the bulb inwards and twist it anti-clockwise to release it from the bulbholder **(see illustration)**. If the socket contacts are dirty or corroded, they should be scraped clean and sprayed with electrical contact cleaner before the new bulb is installed.

9 Install the new bulb in the bulbholder by pressing it in and twisting it clockwise. Press the bulbholder back into the headlight.

10 Check the operation of the sidelight, then install the headlight rim into the shell and secure with the screws **(see illustration 7.6)**.

8 Headlight assembly - removal and installation

Removal

1 Remove the three screws securing the headlight rim to the headlight shell, and ease the rim out of the shell **(see illustration 7.1)**.

2 Disconnect the wiring connector from the headlight bulb and pull the sidelight bulbholder out of the headlight **(see illustrations 7.2 and 7.8a)**.

3 To remove the headlight shell, free the wiring inside the shell from any clamps and ease it out the back of the shell, then unscrew the bolts securing the shell to the brackets and remove the shell **(see illustrations)**. If necessary,

9

9.2 Twist the bulbholder anti-clockwise to release it from the tail light

9.3 To release the bulb gently push it in and twist it anti-clockwise. Note that the pins on the bulb are offset

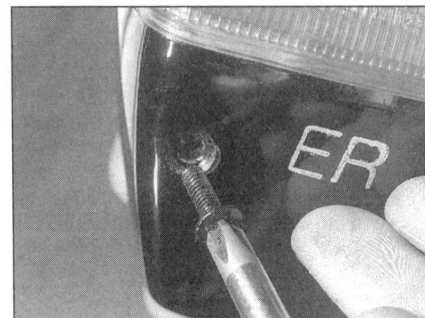

10.3 The tail light assembly is secured by two nuts (A). Note the wiring clamp (B)

unscrew the bolts securing the brackets to the frame and remove the brackets.

> **HAYNES HiNT** *When disconnecting wiring, label the connectors to avoid confusion on reconnection.*

Installation

4 Installation is the reverse of removal. Make sure all the wiring is correctly connected and secured. Check the operation of the headlight and sidelight. Check the headlight aim (see Chapter 1).

9 Tail light bulbs - replacement

1 Remove the seat (see Chapter 8).
2 Turn the bulbholder anti-clockwise and withdraw it from the tail light **(see illustration)**.
3 Push the bulb into the holder and twist it anti-clockwise to remove it **(see illustration)**. Check the socket terminals for corrosion and clean them if necessary. Line up the pins of the new bulb with the slots in the socket, then push the bulb in and turn it clockwise until it locks into place. **Note:** *The pins on the bulb are offset so it can only be installed one way. It is a good idea to use a paper towel or dry cloth when handling the new bulb to prevent injury if the bulb should break and to increase bulb life.*
4 Install the bulbholder into the tail light and turn it clockwise to secure it.
5 Install the seat (see Chapter 8).

10 Tail light assembly - removal and installation

Removal

1 Remove the seat (see Chapter 8).
2 Twist the bulbholders anti-clockwise and withdraw them from the taillight.
3 Unscrew the two nuts securing the tail light to the frame and carefully withdraw it from the back of the bike **(see illustration)**. Note the

wiring clip secured by the right-hand side nut, and the fitting of the washers and rubber grommets.

Installation

4 Installation is the reverse of removal. Check the operation of the tail and brake lights.

11 Turn signal bulbs - replacement

1 Unscrew the turn signal lens assembly retaining screw from the bottom of the turn signal cover and remove the lens assembly, noting which way round it fits **(see illustration)**.
2 Twist the bulbholder anti-clockwise to release it from the lens **(see illustration)**.
3 Push the bulb into the holder and twist it

11.1 The turn signal lens is secured to the cover by a single screw

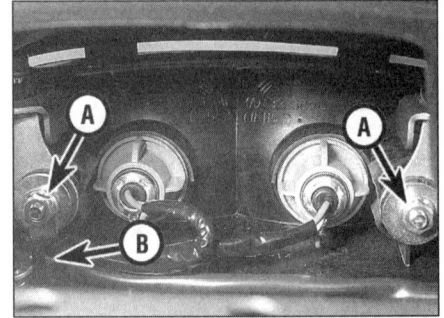

11.3 To release the bulb gently push it in and twist it anti-clockwise

anti-clockwise to remove it **(see illustration)**. Check the socket terminals for corrosion and clean them if necessary. Line up the pins of the new bulb with the slots in the socket, then push the bulb in and turn it clockwise until it locks into place. **Note:** *It is a good idea to use a paper towel or dry cloth when handling the new bulb to prevent injury if the bulb should break and to increase bulb life.*
4 Install the bulbholder back into the lens, and the lens assembly back into the cover, and tighten the retaining screw **(see illustration)**. Take care not to overtighten the screw as the assembly is easily cracked.

> **HAYNES HiNT** *If the socket contacts are dirty or corroded, scrape them clean and spray with electrical contact cleaner before a new bulb is installed.*

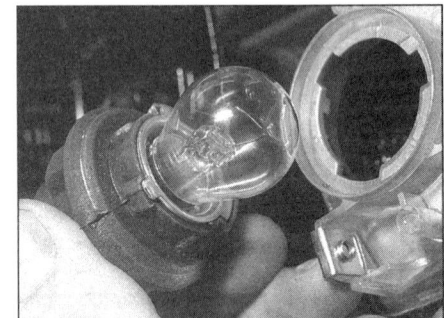

11.2 Twist the bulbholder anti-clockwise to release it from the lens

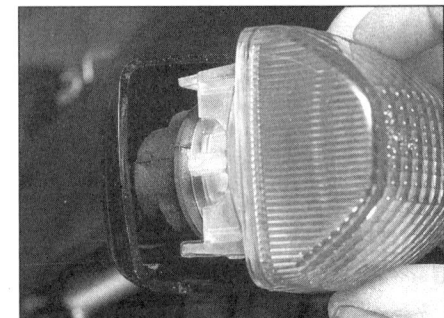

11.4 Install the lens back into the cover

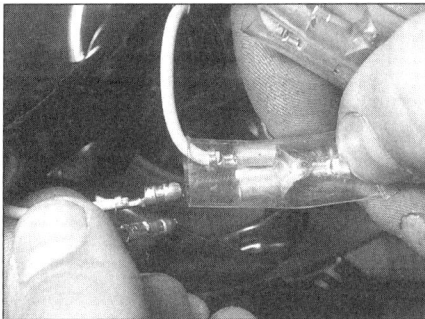

12.2 The front turn signal wiring connectors are inside the headlight shell

12.3 The lens and cover assembly is secured to the stalk by a single screw

12.4 The stalk fits around the fork and is bolted to the bottom yoke (arrow)

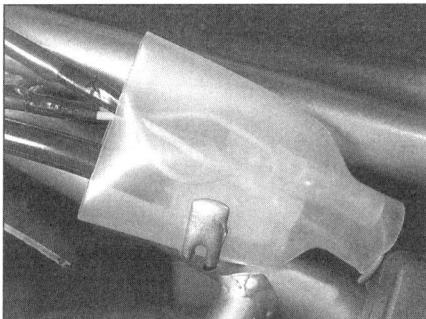

12.6 The rear turn signal wiring connectors are inside the rubber boot

12.8 The rear turn signal assembly is secured to the frame by a single nut

12 Turn signal assemblies - removal and installation

Front

Removal

1 Unscrew the three screws securing the headlight rim to the headlight shell, and ease the rim out of the shell **(see illustration 7.1)**.
2 Trace the turn signal wiring back from the turn signal and disconnect it at the connectors inside the headlight shell **(see illustration)**. Pull the wiring through to the turn signal mounting, noting its routing.
3 To remove the turn signal lens and cover assembly from its stalk, unscrew the screw on the bottom of the stalk and ease the turn signal off, taking care not to snag the wiring as you draw it through **(see illustration)**.
4 To remove the complete turn signal assembly, unscrew the bolt securing the stalk around the front fork and to its bracket on the bottom yoke, then remove the assembly as a unit **(see illustration)**. On P, S and T models, note that the bolt fits into a collar.

Installation

5 Installation is the reverse of removal. Make sure the wiring is correctly routed and securely connected. Check the operation of the turn signals.

Rear

Removal

6 Remove the seat (see Chapter 8). Trace the turn signal wiring back from the turn signal and disconnect it at the connectors inside the rubber boot behind the right-hand side of the rear cowl **(see illustration)**. Remove the rear cowl if access to the boot is too restricted (see Chapter 8) Pull the wiring through to the turn signal mounting, releasing it from any clips and noting its routing.
7 To remove the turn signal lens and cover assembly from its stalk, unscrew the screw on the bottom of the stalk and ease the turn signal off, taking care not to snag the wiring as you draw it through **(see illustration 12.3)**.
8 To remove the complete turn signal assembly, unscrew the nut under the rear mudguard securing the stalk to the frame, then remove the assembly, noting how the mounting plate and its rubber fit **(see illustration)**.

Installation

9 Installation is the reverse of removal. Make sure the wiring is correctly routed and securely connected. Check the operation of the turn signals.

13 Turn signal circuit - check

1 The battery provides power for operation of the turn signal lights, so if they do not operate,

always check the battery voltage first. Low battery voltage indicates either a faulty battery or a defective charging system. Refer to Section 3 for battery checks and Sections 31 and 32 for charging system tests. Also, check the fuses (see Section 5) and the switch (see Section 21).
2 Most turn signal problems are the result of a burned out bulb or corroded socket. This is especially true when the turn signals function properly in one direction, but fail to flash in the other direction. Check the bulbs and the sockets (see Section 11).
3 If the bulbs and sockets are good, check for power at the turn signal relay white/green wire (J and K models) or black/brown wire (all other models) with the ignition "ON". The relay is mounted behind the toolkit case behind the right-hand side panel **(see illustration)**. Turn the ignition OFF when the check is complete.

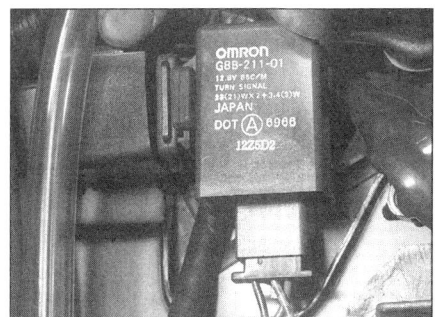

13.3 Turn signal relay location

14.5 Disconnect the front brake light switch wiring connectors

14.6 The brake light switch is secured by a single screw

10 Compress the switch adjuster nut retainer prongs and withdraw the complete switch from its bracket (see illustration).

11 Installation is the reverse of removal. Make sure the brake light is activated just before the rear brake pedal takes effect. If adjustment is necessary, hold the switch and turn the adjusting nut on the switch body until the brake light is activated when required.

15 Instrument cluster and speedometer cable - removal and installation

14.8 Disconnect the rear brake light switch wiring connector

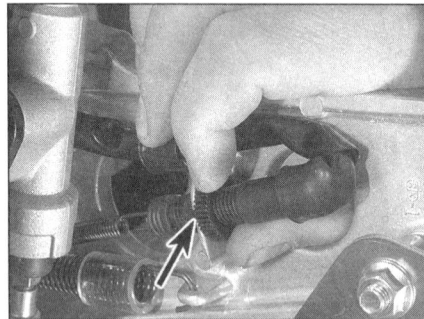

14.10 The retainer prongs are on the underside of the adjuster nut (arrow)

Instrument cluster

Removal

1 Unscrew the three screws securing the headlight rim to the headlight shell, and ease the rim out of the shell (see illustration 7.1).

2 Trace the wiring back from the instrument cluster, then disconnect it at the connectors inside the shell and release it from any ties.

3 Unscrew the speedometer cable retaining ring from the rear of the instrument cluster and detach the cable (see illustration 15.6).

4 Remove the two bolts securing the instrument cluster to the top yoke and carefully lift the assembly off the yoke, taking care not to snag the wiring and noting its routing (see illustration).

Installation

5 Installation is the reverse of removal. Make sure that the speedometer cable and wiring are correctly routed and secured.

Speedometer cable

Removal

6 Unscrew the speedometer cable retaining ring from the rear of the instrument cluster and detach the cable (see illustration).

7 Remove the screw securing the lower end of the cable to the drive housing on the left-hand side of the front wheel (see illustration).

8 Withdraw the cable from the guides on the brake caliper and front mudguard and remove it from the bike, noting its correct routing.

4 If no power was present at the relay, check the wiring from the relay to the ignition (main) switch for continuity.

5 If power was present at the relay, using the wiring diagram at the end of this Chapter, check the wiring between the relay, turn signal switch and turn signal lights for continuity. If the wiring and switch are sound, replace the relay with a new one.

14 Brake light switches - check and replacement

Circuit check

1 Before checking any electrical circuit, check the bulb (see Section 9) and fuses (see Section 5).

2 Using a test light connected to a good earth, check for voltage at the power wire of the brake light switch wiring connector (see illustration 14.5 or 14.8). The wiring connector should be connected to the switch for this test. If there's no voltage present, check the wire between the switch and the fusebox (see the *wiring diagram* at the end of this Chapter).

3 If voltage is available, touch the probe of the test light to the other terminal of the switch, then pull the brake lever in or depress the brake pedal. If the test light doesn't light up, replace the switch.

4 If the test light does light, check the wiring between the switch and the brake lights (see the *wiring diagrams* at the end of this Chapter).

Switch replacement

Front brake lever switch

5 Unplug the electrical connectors from the switch (see illustration).

6 Unscrew the single screw and detach the switch from the bottom of the front brake master cylinder (see illustration).

7 Installation is the reverse of removal. The switch isn't adjustable.

Rear brake pedal switch

8 The switch is mounted to the back of the right-hand footrest bracket. Trace the wiring and disconnect it at the connector which is mounted on top of the toolkit casing behind the right-hand side panel (see illustration).

9 Detach the lower end of the switch spring from the brake pedal.

15.4 The instrument cluster is secured to the top yoke by two bolts (arrows) - P, S and T models shown

15.6 Unscrew the knurled ring to release the speedometer cable

15.7 The speedometer cable is secured to the drive housing by a single screw (arrow)

15.9a Pass the cable through its guide on the mudguard . . .

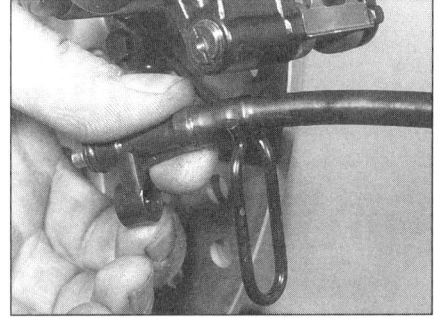

15.9b . . . and on the brake caliper

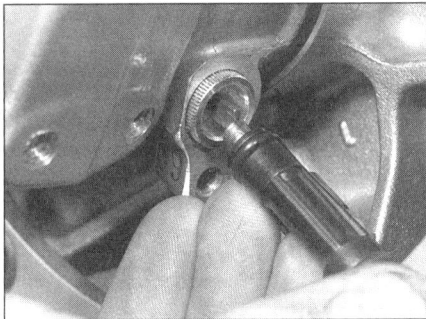

15.11a Align the slot in the cable with the drive tab . . .

15.11b . . . and secure the cable with its screw

Installation

9 Route the cable correctly and install it in its retaining guides on the front mudguard and the brake caliper **(see illustrations)**.

10 Connect the cable upper end to the instrument cluster and tighten the retaining ring securely **(see illustration 15.6)**.

11 Connect the cable lower end to the drive housing, aligning the slot in the cable end with the drive tab, and secure it with its screw **(see illustrations)**.

12 Check that the cable doesn't restrict steering movement or interfere with any other components.

16 Instruments - check and replacement

Tachometer

Check

1 No test procedure is provided for the tachometer. If it is believed to be faulty, take the motorcycle to a Honda dealer for assessment. Prior to condemning the tachometer, check the yellow/blue wire from the tachometer to its take-off point on the ignition HT coil for continuity.

Replacement

2 On J, K and M models, remove the three screws and the four nuts on the back of the cluster which secure the rear cover, noting the order of the washers and rubber grommets. Note the correct fitted position of the tachometer wires, then remove the wire retaining screws and detach the wires. Remove the bulbholders, then remove the rear cover and detach the tachometer from the front panel.

3 On P, S and T models, remove the screws securing the rear cover and remove the cover **(see illustration)**. Note the correct fitted position of the tachometer wires, then remove the wire retaining screws and detach the wires **(see illustration)**. Remove the bulbholders from their sockets. Unscrew the nuts securing the instrument bracket, the screws securing the tachometer, and the screws securing the front cover. Lift off the front cover and withdraw the tachometer from the cluster.

4 Install the tachometer by reversing the removal sequence. Make sure the wires are correctly and securely connected.

Speedometer

Check

5 Special instruments are required to properly check the operation of this meter. If it is believed to be faulty, take the motorcycle to a Honda dealer for assessment.

Replacement

6 On J, K and M models, unscrew the three screws and the four nuts on the back of the cluster which secure the rear cover, noting the order of the washers and rubber grommets. Unscrew the retaining screw from the centre of the odometer trip knob and remove the knob. Remove the bulbholders, then remove the rear cover and detach the speedometer from the front panel.

7 On P, S and T models, remove the screws securing the rear cover and remove the cover **(see illustration 16.3a)**. Remove the bulbholders

16.3a Remove the rear cover screws

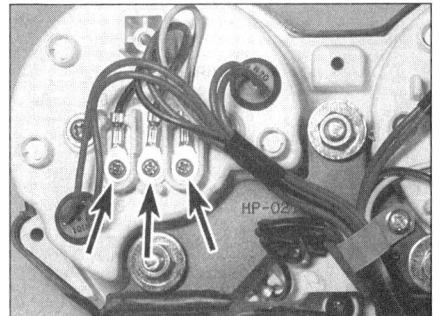

16.3b Note the position of the tachometer wires before removing them (arrows)

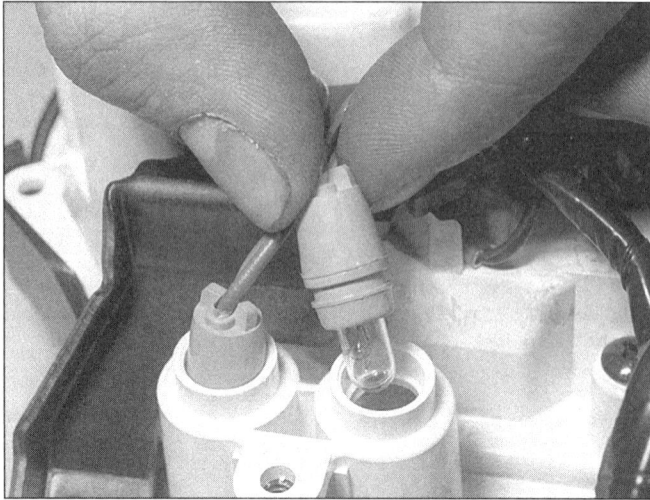

17.4a Pull the bulbholder out of the instrument cluster . . .

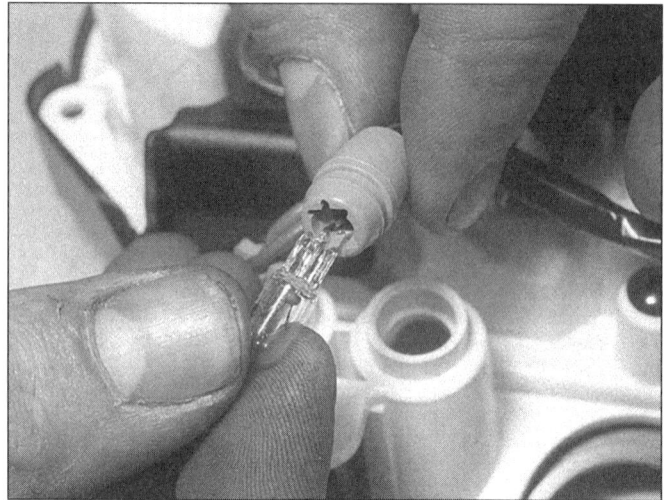

17.4b . . . and the bulb out of the holder

from their sockets. Unscrew the retaining screw from the centre of the odometer trip knob and remove the knob. Unscrew the nuts securing the instrument bracket, the screws securing the speedometer drive box and the speedometer, and the screws securing the front cover. Lift off the front cover and withdraw the tachometer from the cluster.

8 Install the speedometer by reversing the removal sequence.

Temperature gauge

Check

9 See Chapter 3.

Replacement

10 The temperature gauge is integral with the tachometer. See above for the tachometer replacement procedure.

17 Instrument and warning light bulbs - replacement

1 Remove the instrument cluster (Section 15).
2 On J, K and M models, remove the three screws and the four nuts on the back of the cluster which secure the rear cover, noting the order of the washers and rubber grommets.
3 On P, S and T models, remove the screws securing the rear cover and remove the cover (see illustration 16.3a).
4 Pull the relevant bulbholder out of the back of the cluster (see illustration). Gently pull the bulb out of the bulbholder (see illustration). If the socket contacts are dirty or corroded, scrape them clean and spray with electrical contact cleaner before a new bulb is installed.
5 Push the new bulb into position; push the bulbholder back into the rear of the cluster.
6 Install the rear cover and the instrument cluster (see Section 15).

18 Oil pressure switch - check, removal and installation

Check

1 The oil pressure warning light should come on when the ignition (main) switch is turned ON and extinguish a few seconds after the engine is started. If the oil pressure light comes on whilst the engine is running, stop the engine immediately and carry out an oil pressure check as described in Chapter 2.
2 If the oil pressure warning light does not come on when the ignition is turned on, check the bulb (see Section 17) and fuses (see Section 5).
3 The oil pressure switch is screwed into the left-hand side of the crankcase just ahead of the oil filter (see illustration). Pull back the rubber cover and detach the wiring connector from the switch. With the ignition ON, earth

18.3 The oil pressure switch is located just ahead of the oil filter

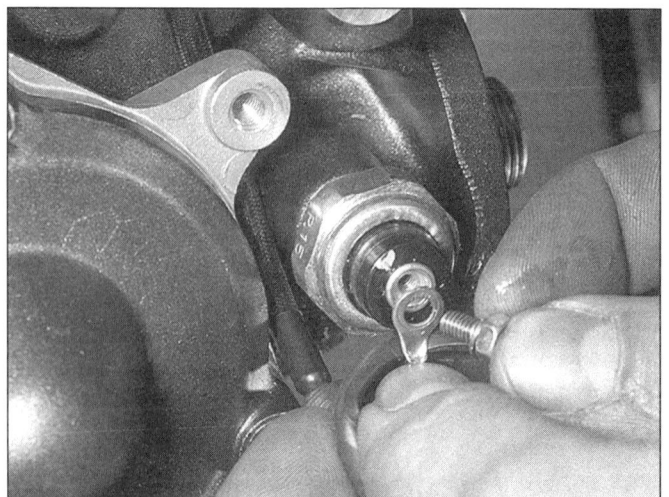

18.7 The connector is secured to the oil pressure switch by a bolt

19.4 The ignition (main) switch is secured to the top yoke by two Torx bolts (arrow)

21.2 The right-hand handlebar switch is secured by two screws

the wire on the crankcase and check that the warning light comes on. If the light comes on, the switch is defective and must be replaced.
4 If the light still does not come on, check for voltage at the wire terminal using a test light. If there is no voltage present, check the wire between the switch, the instrument cluster and fusebox for continuity (see the *wiring diagram* at the end of this Chapter).
5 If the warning light comes on whilst the engine is running, yet the oil pressure is satisfactory, remove the wire from the oil pressure switch. With the wire detached and the ignition switched ON the light should be out. If it is illuminated, the wire between the switch and instrument cluster must be earthed at some point. If the wiring is good, the switch must be assumed faulty and replaced.

Removal

6 Drain the engine oil (see Chapter 1).
7 Unscrew the bolt securing the wiring connector to the bolt **(see illustration)**. Unscrew the switch and withdraw it from the crankcase.

Installation

8 Apply a suitable sealant (3-Bond or equivalent) to the threads of the switch and install the switch; tighten it to the specified torque setting.
9 Refill the engine with oil (see Chapter 1).
10 Connect the wiring to the switch and check the operation of the switch (see Steps 1 to 5 above).

19 Ignition (main) switch - check, removal and installation

Note: *To prevent the risk of short-circuits, disconnect the battery negative (-ve) lead before making ignition (main) switch checks.*

Check

1 Remove the three screws securing the headlight rim to the headlight shell, and ease the rim out of the shell **(see illustration 7.1)**. Trace the ignition (main) switch wiring back from the base of the switch and disconnect it at the connector in the headlight shell.
2 Using an ohmmeter or a continuity tester, check the continuity of the terminal pairs (see the *wiring diagram* at the end of this Chapter). Continuity should exist between the terminals connected by a solid line on the diagram when the switch is in the indicated position.
3 If the switch fails any of the tests, replace it.

Removal and installation

4 Remove the instrument cluster (Section 15). Unscrew the two Torx bolts securing the switch to the underside of the top yoke and remove the switch **(see illustration)**. If access to the bolts is too restricted, also remove the top yoke (see Chapter 6, Section 8).
5 If the switch is being replaced, release the wiring from its clamp on the base of the switch, then unscrew the three screws and remove the contact plate from the base of the switch.
6 Installation is the reverse of removal. Tighten the switch mounting bolts to the specified torque setting.

20 Handlebar switches - check

1 Generally speaking, the switches are reliable and trouble-free. Most troubles, when they do occur, are caused by dirty or corroded contacts, but wear and breakage of internal parts is a possibility that should not be overlooked. If breakage does occur, the entire switch and related wiring harness will have to be replaced with a new one, since individual parts are not available.

2 The switches can be checked for continuity using an ohmmeter or a continuity test light. Always disconnect the battery negative (-ve) lead, which will prevent the possibility of a short-circuit, before making the checks.
3 Trace the wiring harness of the switch in question back to its connector(s) and disconnect it.
4 Using the ohmmeter or test light, check for continuity between the terminals of the switch harness with the switch in the various positions (ie switch off - no continuity, switch on - continuity) (see the *wiring diagram* at the end of this Chapter).
5 If the continuity check indicates a problem exists, refer to Section 21, remove the switch and spray the switch contacts with electrical contact cleaner. If they are accessible, the contacts can be scraped clean with a knife or polished with crocus cloth. If switch components are damaged or broken, it will be obvious when the switch is disassembled.

21 Handlebar switches - removal and installation

Right-hand handlebar switch

Removal

1 If the switch is to be removed from the bike, locate the switch wiring connector (either inside the headlight shell or under the fuel tank) and disconnect it. Work back along the harness, freeing it from all the relevant clips and ties, whilst noting its correct routing.
2 Disconnect the two wires from the brake light switch. Unscrew the switch retaining screw on its underside and remove the switch from the handlebar, noting how it fits **(see illustration)**. Remove the throttle cables and cable elbows from the switch (see Chapter 4 if necessary).

21.5 The left-hand handlebar switch is secured by two screws

21.6 The pin (arrow) locates in the hole in the handlebar

22.2 The neutral switch is located above the water pump

Installation

3 Installation is the reverse of removal. Make sure the locating pin in the lower half of the switch fits into hole in the underside of the handlebar **(see illustration 21.6)**. If necessary, refer to Chapter 4 for installation of the throttle cables.

Left-hand handlebar switch

Removal

4 If the switch is to be removed from the bike, locate the switch wiring connector (either inside the headlight shell or under the fuel tank) and disconnect it. Work back along the harness, freeing it from all the relevant clips and ties, whilst noting its correct routing.
5 Disconnect the two wires from the clutch switch. Unscrew the two switch retaining screws on the underside of the switch and remove the switch from the handlebar, noting how it fits **(see illustration)**. Remove the choke cable (see Chapter 4 if necessary).

Installation

6 Installation is the reverse of removal. Make sure the locating pin in the lower half of the switch fits into hole in the underside of the handlebar **(see illustration)**. If necessary, refer to Chapter 4 for installation of the choke cable.

22 Neutral switch - check and replacement

Check

1 Before checking the electrical circuit, check the bulb (see Section 17) and fuse (see Section 5).
2 The switch is located on the left-hand side of the crankcase above the water pump **(see illustration)**. Disconnect the wiring connector from the switch. Make sure the transmission is in neutral.
3 With the wire detached and the ignition switched ON, the neutral light should be out. If not, the wire between the switch and instrument cluster must be earthed at some point.

4 Earth the wire on the crankcase (using a jumper wire if necessary) and check that the neutral light comes on. If the light comes on, but doesn't when connected to the switch, the switch is confirmed defective.
5 If the light does not come on when the wire is earthed, check for voltage at the wire terminal using a test light. If there's no voltage present, check the wire between the switch, the instrument cluster and fusebox (see the *wiring diagram* at the end of this Chapter).

Replacement

6 Drain the engine oil (see Chapter 1).
7 Disconnect the wiring connector from the switch **(see illustration 22.2)**.
8 Unscrew the switch from the crankcase and remove it along with its sealing washer. Discard the washer as a new one must be used.
9 Clean the threads of the switch and fit a new sealing washer to it.
10 Install the switch and tighten it to the torque setting specified at the beginning of the Chapter, then reconnect the wiring connector.
11 Check the operation of the neutral light.
12 Fill the engine with oil (see Chapter 1).

23 Side stand switch - check and replacement

Check

1 The side stand switch is mounted on the frame just behind the side stand **(see illustration 23.6)**. The switch is part of the safety circuit which prevents or stops the engine running if the transmission is in gear whilst the side stand is down, and prevents the engine from starting if the transmission is in gear unless the side stand is up and the clutch is pulled in. A warning light on the instrument cluster indicates when the side stand is down. Before checking the electrical circuit, check the bulb (see Section 17) and fuse (see Section 5).
2 Trace the wiring back from the switch to its connector behind the left-hand side panel and disconnect it.

3 Check the operation of the switch using an ohmmeter or continuity test light. Connect the meter to the yellow/black and green wires on the switch side of the connector. With the side stand down there should be continuity (zero resistance) between the terminals, and with the stand up there should be no continuity (infinite resistance). Connect the meter to the green/white and green wires on the switch side of the connector. With the side stand up there should be continuity (zero resistance) between the terminals, and with the stand down there should be no continuity (infinite resistance).
4 If the switch does not perform as expected, it is defective and must be replaced. Check first that the fault is not caused by a sticking switch plunger due to the ingress of road dirt; spray the switch with a water dispersant aerosol.
5 If the switch is good, check the other components in the starter circuit as described in the relevant sections of this Chapter. If all components are good, check the wiring between the various components (see the *wiring diagram* at the end of this chapter).

Replacement

6 The side stand switch is mounted on the frame just behind the side stand **(see illustration)**. Trace the wiring back from the switch to its connector behind the left-hand side panel and disconnect it.
7 Work back along the switch wiring, freeing it from any relevant retaining clips and ties, noting its correct routing.

23.6 The side stand switch is secured by two bolts (arrows). Note the wiring clip on the right-hand bolt

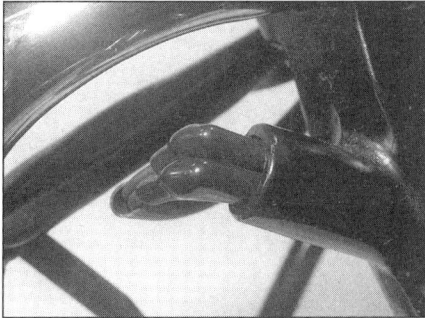

24.4 The clutch switch is a push fit into the lever bracket

26.2 Disconnect the horn wiring connectors

26.4 The horns are secured to the bracket by a single nut

8 Unscrew the two bolts securing the switch to the frame.

9 Fit the new switch to the frame and install the retaining bolts, tightening them securely.

10 Make sure the wiring is correctly routed up to the connector and retained by all the necessary clips and ties.

11 Reconnect the wiring connector and check the operation of the side stand switch.

24 Clutch switch -
check and replacement

Check

1 The clutch switch is situated on the base of the clutch lever bracket. The switch is part of the safety circuit which prevents or stops the engine running if the transmission is in gear whilst the side stand is down, and prevents the engine from starting if the transmission is in gear unless the side stand is up and the clutch is pulled in.

2 To check the switch, disconnect the wiring connectors from the switch **(see illustration 24.4)**. Connect the probes of an ohmmeter or a continuity test light to the two switch terminals. With the clutch lever pulled in, continuity should be indicated. With the clutch lever out, no continuity (infinite resistance) should be indicated.

3 If the switch is good, check the other components in the starter circuit as described in the relevant sections of this Chapter. If all components are good, check the wiring between the various components (see the *wiring diagram* at the end of this chapter).

Replacement

4 Disconnect the wiring connector from the clutch switch **(see illustration)**. Adjust the clutch lever freeplay adjuster to provide as much freeplay in the lever as possible (see Chapter 1), then unscrew the lever locknut and pivot bolt and displace the lever with the cable still attached. The clutch switch is a push fit into the bracket. Push the switch from its connector end and withdraw it from the bracket.

5 Install the new switch and the lever in a reverse of the removal procedure, then connect the wiring connector. Adjust the clutch lever freeplay (see Chapter 1).

25 Clutch diode -
check and replacement

Check

1 Remove the seat (see Chapter 8).

2 The diode is a small block that plugs into a connector in the main wiring harness. Disconnect the diode from the harness.

3 On J and K models, using an ohmmeter or continuity tester, connect its probes across the two terminals of the diode and note the reading. Reverse the meter probes and note the reading. The diode should only allow electricity to flow in one direction - if it indicates continuity in both directions or high resistance in both directions, the diode is faulty.

4 The diode block on M, P, S and T models contains two diodes. Using an ohmmeter or continuity tester, connect one of its probes to the single positive (+) terminal on the diode and the other probe to one of the two negative terminals on the diode. Note the reading and then reverse the probes. The diode should only allow electricity to flow in one direction - if it indicates continuity in both directions or high resistance in both directions, the diode is faulty. Now check the other diode, by making the same test across the single positive terminal and the other negative terminal.

5 If the diode is good, check the other components in the starter circuit as described in the relevant sections of this Chapter. If all components are good, check the wiring between the various components (see the *wiring diagrams* at the end of this chapter).

Replacement

6 Remove the seat (see Chapter 8).

7 The diode is a small block that plugs into a connector in the main wiring harness. Disconnect the diode and connect the new one.

26 Horns -
check and replacement

Check

1 The horns are mounted to a bracket on the bottom yoke **(see illustration 26.4)**.

2 Unplug the wiring connectors from the horn being tested **(see illustration)**. Using two jumper wires, apply battery voltage directly to the terminals on the horn. If the horn sounds, check the switch (see Section 20) and the wiring between the switch and the horn (see the *wiring diagrams* at the end of this Chapter).

3 If the horn doesn't sound, replace it.

Replacement

4 The horns are mounted to a bracket on the bottom yoke **(see illustration)**.

5 Unplug the wiring connectors from the horns **(see illustration 26.2)**, then unscrew the nut securing the horns to their mounting bracket and remove them from the bike.

6 Install the horns and securely tighten the nut. Connect the wiring connectors to the horns.

27 Fuel pump -
check, removal and installation

⚠️ *Warning: Petrol is extremely flammable, so be sure to take extra precautions when you work on any part of the fuel system. Don't smoke or allow open flames or bare light bulbs near the work area, and don't work in a garage where a natural gas-type appliance is present. If you spill any fuel on your skin, rinse it off immediately with soap and water. When you perform any kind of work on the fuel system, wear safety glasses and have a fire extinguisher suitable for a class B type fire (flammable liquids) on hand.*

Check

1 The fuel pump is located behind the left-hand side panel **(see illustration)**. The fuel

9

27.1 Fuel pump (arrow)

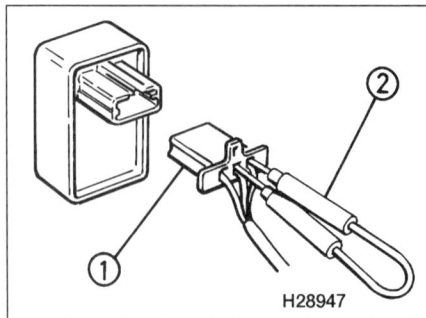

27.4 Disconnect the fuel pump relay wiring connector and connect across the terminals using a jumper wire

1 Relay wiring connector   2 Jumper wire

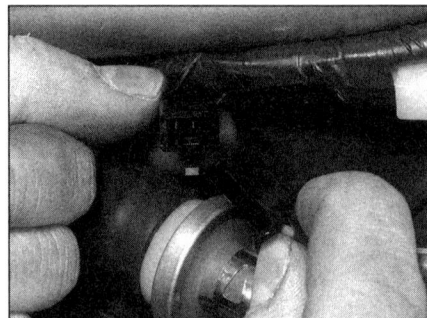

27.8 Disconnect the fuel pump wiring connector

pump relay is located behind the right-hand side panel. Remove the side panels for access (see Chapter 8).

2 The fuel pump is controlled through the fuel cut-off relay so that it runs whenever the ignition is switched "ON" and the ignition is operative (ie, only when the engine is turning over). As soon as the ignition is killed, the relay will cut off the fuel pump's electrical supply (so that there is no risk of fuel being sprayed out under pressure in the event of an accident).

3 It should be possible to hear or feel the fuel pump running whenever the engine is turning over - either place your ear close beside the pump or feel it with your fingertips. If you can't hear or feel anything, check the circuit fuse (see Section 5). If the fuse is good, check the pump and relay for loose or corroded connections or physical damage and rectify as necessary.

4 If the circuit is fine so far, switch the ignition "OFF", unplug the relay's wiring connector and connect across the black and black/blue terminals of the connector with a short length of insulated jumper wire **(see illustration)**. Switch the ignition "ON"; the pump should operate.

5 If the pump now works, either the relay or its wiring is at fault. Test the wiring as follows.

6 Check for full battery voltage at the relay's black terminal with the ignition switch "ON". If there is no battery voltage, there is a fault in the circuit between the relay and the fuse - trace and rectify the fault as outlined in Section 2; refer to the wiring diagram at the end of this Chapter Switch the ignition OFF. Next check for continuity on the blue/yellow wire between the relay and the ignition control unit, and on the black/blue wire between the relay and the pump. If there is no continuity on any of these wires, trace and rectify the fault as described in Section 2.

7 If these wiring checks reveal no faults, reconnect the relay and try the circuit again.

8 If the pump still does not work, trace the wiring from the pump and disconnect it at the black 2-pin wiring connector **(see illustration)**. Using a fully-charged 12 volt battery and two

insulated jumper wires, connect the positive (+ve) terminal of the battery to the pump's black/blue terminal, and the negative (-ve) terminal of the battery to the pump's green terminal. The pump should operate. If the pump does not operate it must be replaced.

9 If the pump works and all the relevant wiring and connectors are good, then the relay is at fault. The only definitive test of the relay is to substitute it with one that is known to be good. If substitution does not cure the problem, bear in mind that the ignition control unit could be faulty.

10 If the pump operates but is thought to be delivering an insufficient amount of fuel, first check the fuel tank breather and the condition and routing of the pipes between the tank, the pump and the filter (see Chapter 4). Check carefully for signs of kinked, trapped, pinched or blocked pipes.

11 The fuel pump's output can be checked as follows: make sure the ignition switch is "OFF", then remove the side panels (see Chapter 8).

12 Disconnect the fuel output hose (the inlet hose comes from the filter, the outlet hose goes to the carburettors) from the pump and connect a spare length of fuel hose from the

outlet and into a graduated beaker capable of holding about a litre **(see illustration)**.

13 Disconnect the fuel cut-off relay's wiring connector. Using a short length of insulated jumper wire, connect across the black and the black/blue wire terminals of the connector **(see illustration 27.4)**.

14 Turn the ignition switch "ON" and let fuel flow from the pump into the beaker for 5 seconds, then switch the ignition "OFF".

15 Record the amount of fuel that has flowed into the beaker, then multiply that amount by 12 to determine the fuel pump flow rate per minute. The minimum flow rate required is 600 cc per minute. If the flow rate recorded is below the minimum required, then the fuel pump must be replaced.

Removal

16 Make sure both the ignition and the fuel tap are switched "OFF". Remove the left-hand side panel (see Chapter 8).

17 Trace the wiring from the fuel pump and disconnect it at the black 2 pin connector **(see illustration 27.8)**.

18 Using a rag to mop up any spilled fuel, disconnect the two fuel hoses from the fuel pump, noting which hose fits on which

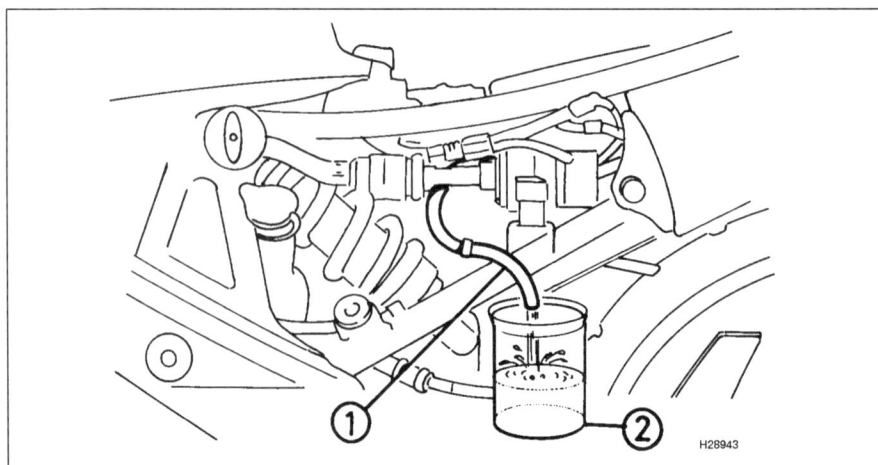

27.12 Connect a length of fuel hose (1) from the pump outlet and into a graduated beaker (2)

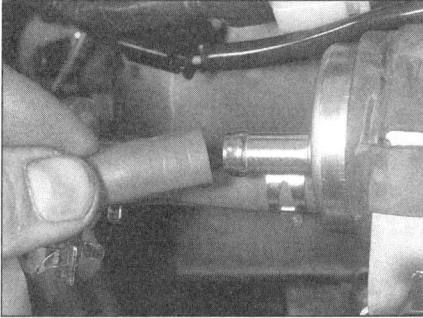

27.18a Disconnect the fuel hoses from the pump . . .

27.18b . . . and remove the pump rubber mounting from its tab

28.2 Starter relay is secured to the frame behind the left-hand side of the rear cowl

28.8 Starter relay terminals

nozzle. Remove the pump with its rubber mounting sleeve from the mounting bracket tab, taking care not to snag the wiring **(see illustrations)**.

19 To remove the fuel cut-off relay, disconnect its wiring connector and remove it from its mounting lug.

Installation

20 Installation is a reverse of the removal procedure. Make sure the fuel hoses are correctly and securely fitted to the pump. Start the engine and look carefully for any signs of leaks at the pipe connections.

28 Starter relay - check and replacement

Check

1 If the starter circuit is faulty, first check the fuses (see Section 5).

2 The starter relay is located behind the left-hand side of the rear cowl **(see illustration)**. Remove the cowl for access to the relay (see Chapter 8). With the ignition switch ON, the engine kill switch in RUN and the transmission in neutral, press the starter switch. The relay should be heard to click.

3 If the relay doesn't click, switch off the ignition. Remove the relay from the motorcycle as described below and test it as follows.

4 Set a multimeter to the ohms x 1 scale and connect it across the relay's starter motor and battery lead terminals. Using a fully-

charged 12 volt battery and two insulated jumper wires, connect the positive (+ve) terminal of the battery to the yellow/red wire terminal of the relay, and the negative (-ve) terminal to the green/red wire terminal of the relay. At this point the relay should be heard to click and the multimeter read 0 ohms (continuity). If this is the case the relay is proved good. If the relay does not click when battery voltage is applied and indicates no continuity (infinite resistance) across its terminals, it is faulty and must be replaced.

5 If the relay is good, check for battery voltage between the yellow/red wire and the green/red wire when the starter button is pressed. Check the other components in the starter circuit as described in the relevant sections of this Chapter. If all components are good, check the wiring between the various components (see the *wiring diagram* at the end of this chapter).

Replacement

6 Remove the rear cowl (see Chapter 8).

7 Disconnect the battery terminals, remembering to disconnect the negative (-ve) terminal first.

8 Disconnect the relay wiring connector, then unscrew the two bolts securing the starter motor and battery leads to the relay and detach the leads **(see illustration)**. Remove the relay with its rubber sleeve from its mounting lugs on the frame.

9 Installation is the reverse of removal ensuring that the terminal screws are securely tightened. Connect the negative (-ve) lead last when reconnecting the battery.

29 Starter motor - removal and installation

Removal

1 Remove the seat and the side panels (see Chapter 8). Disconnect the battery negative (-ve) lead.

2 Peel back the rubber cover and unscrew the nut securing the starter cable to the motor **(see illustration)**.

3 Unscrew the two bolts securing the starter motor to the crankcase **(see illustration)**. Note the earth cable secured by the front mounting bolt.

4 Slide the starter motor out from the crankcase and remove it from the left-hand side of the machine.

5 Remove the O-ring on the end of the starter motor and discard it as a new one must be used.

Installation

6 Install a new O-ring on the end of the starter motor and ensure it is seated in its groove **(see illustration)**. Apply a smear of engine oil to the O-ring to aid installation.

7 Manoeuvre the motor into position and slide it into the crankcase **(see illustration)**. Ensure that the starter motor teeth mesh correctly with those of the starter idler gear.

8 Install the retaining bolts and tighten them securely, not forgetting the earth cable on the front bolt **(see illustration 29.3)**.

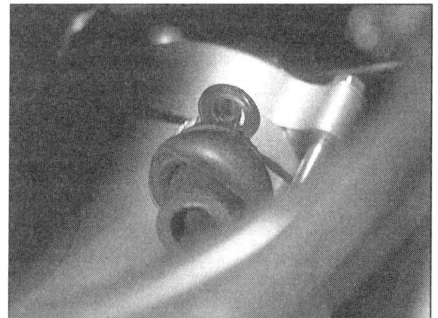

29.2 Pull back the rubber cover and unscrew the terminal nut

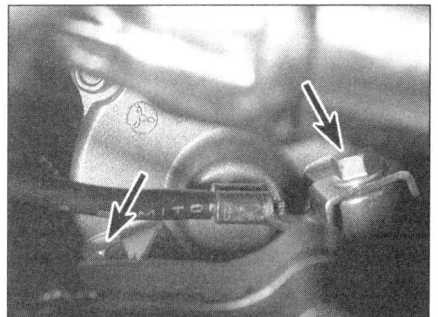

29.3 The starter motor is secured by two bolts (arrows). Note the earth cable secured by the front bolt

9

29.6 Fit a new O-ring to the starter motor

29.7 Manoeuvre the starter motor into position

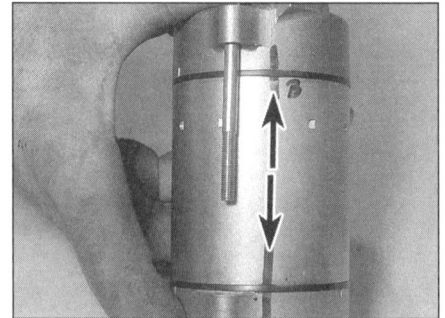
30.2 Make alignment marks between the main housing and the covers (arrows)

9 Connect the cable and spring washer, and secure them with the retaining nut **(see illustration 29.2)**. Make sure the rubber cover is correctly seated over the terminal.

10 Connect the battery negative (-ve) lead and install the seat.

30 Starter motor - disassembly, inspection and reassembly

Disassembly

1 Remove the starter motor (see Section 29).
2 Make alignment marks between the main housing and the two covers **(see illustration)**.

3 Unscrew the two long bolts then remove the rear cover from the motor along with its sealing ring **(see illustration)**. Discard the sealing ring as a new one must be used for reassembly. Remove the shim(s) from the rear end of the armature noting their correct fitted positions.
4 Remove the front cover from the motor along with its sealing ring. Discard the sealing ring as a new one must be used for reassembly. Recover the toothed washer from the cover and slide off the insulating washer and shim(s) from the front end of the armature, noting their correct fitted locations.
5 Withdraw the armature from the main housing.
6 Noting the correct fitted location of each washer, unscrew the nut from the terminal

bolt and remove the plain washer, the various insulating washers and the rubber O-ring. Withdraw the terminal bolt and brushplate assembly from the main housing and recover the insulator.
7 Lift each brush spring end onto the top of each brush holder and slide the brushes out from their holders **(see illustration)**.

> **HAYNES HiNT** *Lifting the end of the brush spring so that it is against the top of the brush holder and not pressing the brush inwards makes it much easier to install the armature on reassembly.*

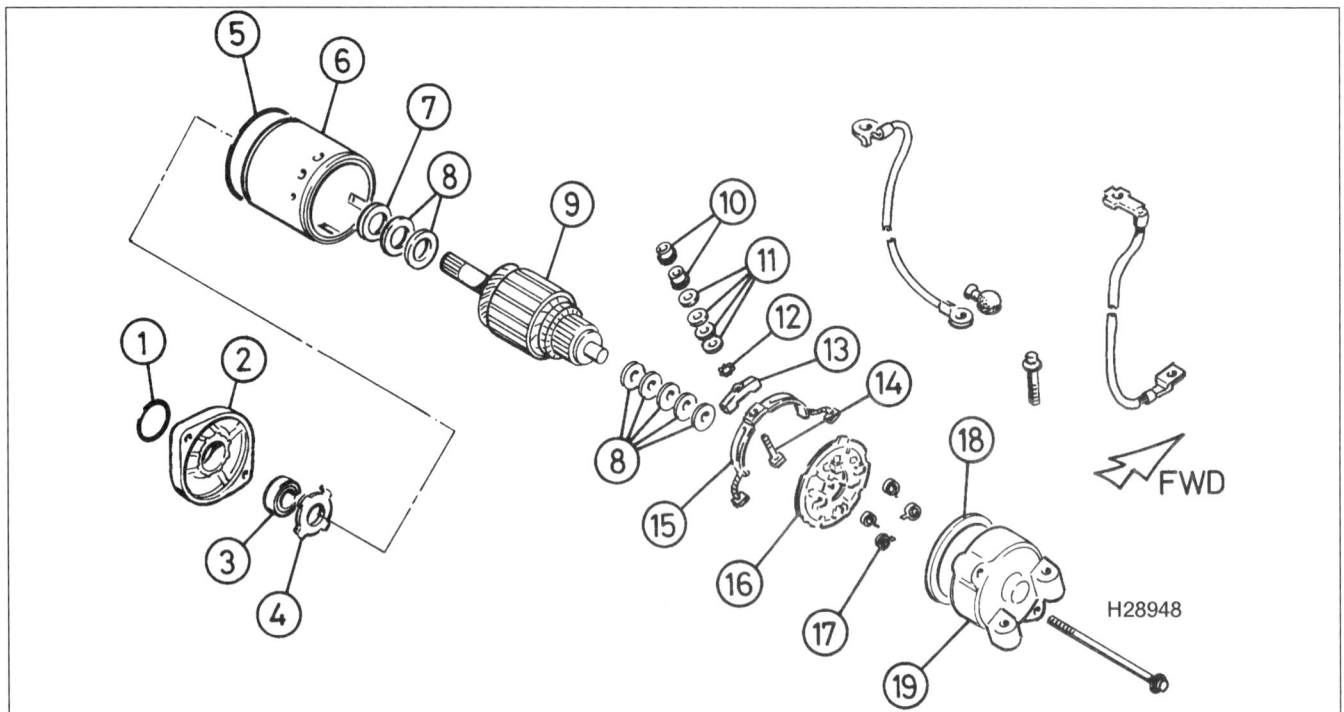
30.3 Starter motor components

1 O-ring	5 Sealing ring	9 Armature	13 Insulator	17 Brush springs
2 Front cover	6 Main housing	10 Nuts	14 Terminal bolt	18 Sealing ring
3 Oil seal	7 Insulating washer	11 Insulating washers	15 Brush assembly	19 Rear cover
4 Toothed washer	8 Shims	12 O-ring	16 Brush plate	

30.7 Lift the spring end off the brush and secure it against the top of the brush holder, then remove the brush

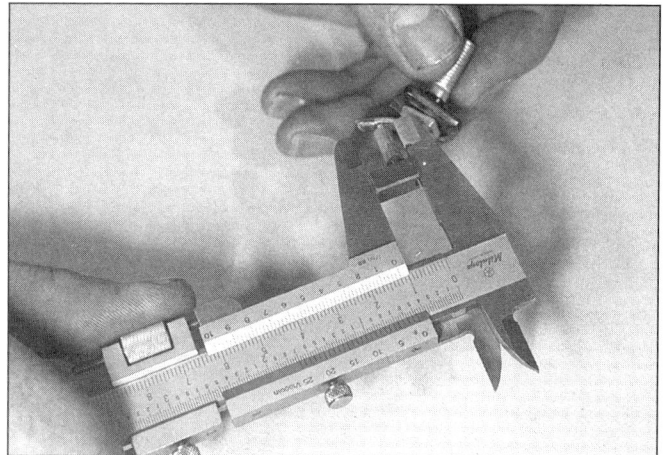

30.8 Measure the brush length

Inspection

8 The parts of the starter motor that are most likely to require attention are the brushes. Measure the length of the brushes and compare the results to the brush length listed in this Chapter's Specifications **(see illustration)**. If any of the brushes are worn beyond the service limit, replace the brush assembly with a new one. If the brushes are not worn excessively, nor cracked, chipped, or otherwise damaged, they may be re-used.

9 Inspect the commutator bars on the armature for scoring, scratches and discoloration. The commutator can be cleaned and polished with crocus cloth, but do not use sandpaper or emery paper. After cleaning, wipe away any residue with a cloth soaked in electrical system cleaner or denatured alcohol.

10 Using an ohmmeter or a continuity test light, check for continuity between the commutator bars **(see illustration)**. Continuity should exist between each bar and all of the others. Also, check for continuity between the commutator bars and the armature shaft **(see illustration)**. There should be no continuity (infinite resistance) between the commutator and the shaft. If the checks indicate otherwise, the armature is defective.

11 Check for continuity between each brush and the terminal bolt. There should be continuity (zero resistance). Check for continuity between the terminal bolt and the housing (when assembled). There should be no continuity (infinite resistance).

12 Check the starter pinion gear for worn, cracked, chipped and broken teeth. If the gear is damaged or worn, replace the starter motor.

13 Inspect the end cover for signs of cracks or wear. Inspect the magnets in the main housing and the housing itself for cracks.

14 Inspect the insulating washers, O-ring and front cover oil seal for signs of damage and replace if necessary.

Reassembly

15 Check that each brush spring is retained against the top of its brush holder so that it will not exert any pressure on the brush, then slide all the brushes back into position in their holders **(see illustration 30.7)**.

16 Fit the insulator to the main housing, then insert the terminal bolt through the brushplate and housing and install the brushplate assembly, making sure its tab is correctly located in the housing slot **(see illustrations)**.

17 Slide the rubber O-ring and small insulating washer(s) onto the terminal bolt, followed by the large insulating washer(s) and the plain washer. Fit the nut to the terminal bolt and tighten it securely **(see illustration)**.

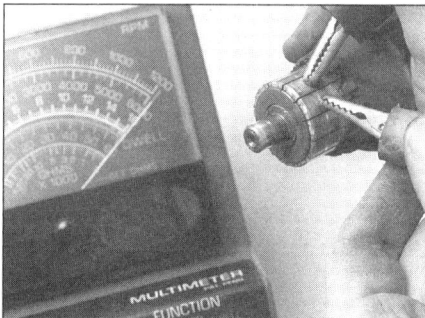

30.10a Continuity should exist between the commutator bars

30.10b There should be no continuity between the commutator bars and the armature shaft

30.16a Locate the insulator in the housing . . .

30.16b . . . and install the brushplate assembly and terminal bolt

30.17 Terminal assembly

9

30.18a Install the armature into the housing

30.18b Fit the brush spring ends onto the brushes

30.19 Fit the toothed washer to the front cover

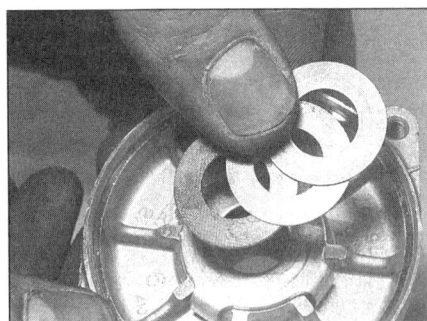
30.20a The insulating washer fits against the front cover, with the shims behind it

30.20b Fit a new sealing ring to the housing . . .

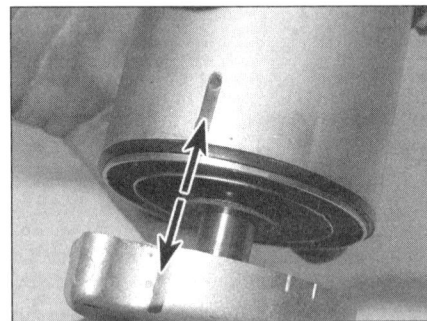
30.20c . . . then install the front cover, aligning the marks (arrows)

30.21 Fit the shims onto the end of the shaft

30.22a Fit a new sealing ring to the housing . . .

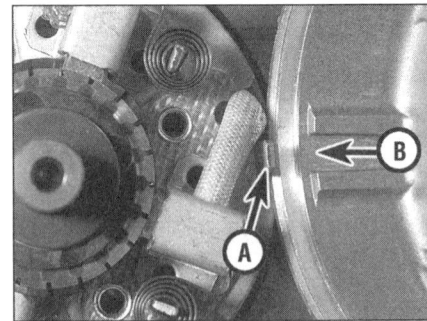
30.22b . . . then install the rear cover, aligning the tab on the brushplate (A) with the groove (B)

18 Insert the armature in the front of the housing and locate the brushes on the commutator bars. Slip each brush spring end on the top of the brush housing and onto the brush end **(see illustration)**. Check that each brush is securely pressed against the commutator by its spring and is free to move easily in its holder.
19 Fit the toothed washer to the front cover so that its teeth are correctly located with the cover ribs **(see illustration)**. Apply a smear of grease to the cover oil seal lip.
20 Slide the shim(s) onto the front end of the armature shaft, then fit the insulating washer **(see illustration)**. Fit a new sealing ring to the housing and carefully slide the front cover into position, aligning the marks made on removal **(see illustrations)**.

21 Fit the shims to the rear of the armature shaft **(see illustration)**.
22 Fit a new sealing ring to the housing **(see illustration)**. Align the rear cover groove with the brushplate outer tab and install the cover **(see illustration)**.
23 Check the marks made on removal are correctly aligned then fit the long bolts and tighten them securely **(see illustration 30.2)**.
24 Install the starter motor (see Section 29).

31 Charging system testing - general information and precautions

1 If the performance of the charging system is suspect, the system as a whole should be checked first, followed by testing of the individual components. **Note:** *Before beginning the checks, make sure the battery is fully charged and that all system connections are clean and tight.*
2 Checking the output of the charging system and the performance of the various components within the charging system requires the use of a multimeter (with voltage, current and resistance checking facilities).
3 When making the checks, follow the procedures carefully to prevent incorrect connections or short circuits, as irreparable damage to electrical system components may result if short circuits occur.
4 If a multimeter is not available, the job of checking the charging system should be left to a Honda dealer.

32 Charging system - leakage and output test

1 If the charging system of the machine is thought to be faulty, remove the seat (see Chapter 8) for access to the battery. Perform the following checks.

Leakage test

2 Make sure the ignition (main) switch is OFF and disconnect the lead from the battery negative (-ve) terminal.

3 Set the ammeter or multimeter to the mA (milli Amps) function, then connect its negative (-ve) probe to the battery negative (-ve) terminal, and its positive (+ve) probe to the disconnected negative (-ve) lead (see illustration). With the meter connected like this the reading should not exceed 0.1 mA.

4 If the reading exceeds the specified amount it is likely that there is a short-circuit in the wiring. Thoroughly check the wiring between the various components (see the wiring diagram at the end of this chapter).

5 If the reading is below the specified amount, the leakage rate is satisfactory. Disconnect the meter and connect the negative (-ve) lead to the battery, tightening it securely, Check the alternator output as described below.

Output test

6 Start the engine and warm it up to normal operating temperature.

7 Allow the engine to idle and connect a voltmeter or multimeter set to the 0-20 volts dc scale across the terminals of the battery (positive (+ve) lead to battery positive (+ve) terminal, negative (-ve) lead to battery negative (-ve) terminal). Slowly increase the engine speed to 3000 rpm and note the reading obtained. At this speed the voltage should be 13.5 to 15.5 volts. If the voltage is below this it will be necessary to check the alternator and regulator as described in the following Sections. **Note:** *Occasionally the condition may arise where the charging voltage is excessive. This condition is almost certainly due to a faulty regulator/rectifier which should be tested as described in Section 35.* Stop the engine and disconnect the meter.

> **HAYNES HINT** *Clues to a faulty regulator are constantly blowing bulbs, with brightness varying considerably with engine speed, and battery overheating.*

33 Alternator - removal and installation

Removal

1 Remove the right-hand side panel (see Chapter 8). Trace the wiring back from the alternator and disconnect it at the connector (see illustration). Release the wiring from any clips or ties.

2 Working in a criss-cross pattern, evenly slacken the left-hand side crankcase front cover retaining bolts. Lift the cover away from the engine, being prepared to catch any residual oil which may be released as the cover is removed. Remove the gasket and discard it. Note the positions of the two locating dowels fitted to the crankcase and remove them for safe-keeping if they are loose.

3 To remove the rotor bolt it is necessary to stop the rotor from turning. If the engine is in the frame, place the transmission in gear and have an assistant apply the rear brake, then unscrew the bolt - note that the bolt has a left-hand thread and so must be turned clockwise for removal (see illustration). If the engine is removed from the frame, a strap wrench can be used to hold the rotor or it can be locked with the Honda service tool (Pt. No. 07725-0040000).

4 Remove the idle/reduction gear along with its shaft (see illustration). To remove the rotor from the shaft it is necessary to use a rotor puller to release the rotor from the crankshaft taper. Use only the specified service tool (Pt. No. 07733-0020001) or a commericially available equivalent - the rotor might be damaged by other removal methods. Thread the rotor puller into the rotor threads and turn it clockwise until the rotor is displaced from the shaft (see illustration). Note how the Woodruff key in the crankshaft locates in the slot in the rotor.

5 To remove the stator from the crankcase cover, unscrew the four bolts securing the stator, and the bolt securing the wiring clip, then remove the assembly from the cover, noting how the rubber wiring grommet fits (see illustrations).

Installation

6 Make sure that no metal objects have attached themselves to the magnet on the inside of the rotor and that the Woodruff key is in its slot in the crankshaft, then align the slot

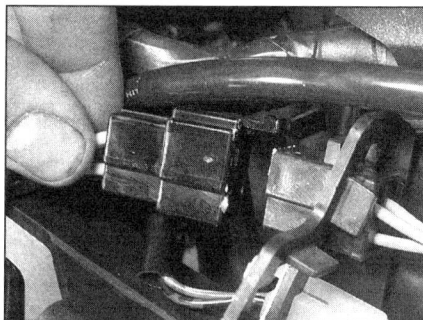

32.3 Checking the charging system leakage rate. Connect the meter as shown

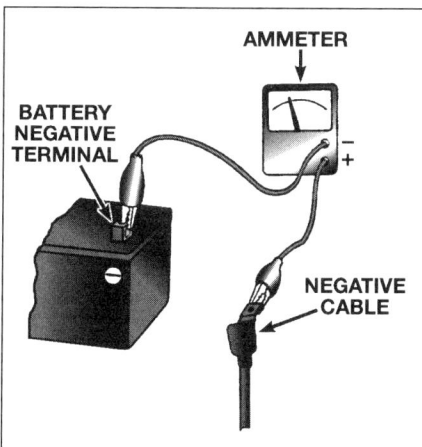

33.1 Disconnect the alternator wiring connector

33.3 Alternator rotor bolt (arrow)

33.4a Remove the idle/reduction gear and its shaft

33.4b Use only the specified tool to extract the alternator rotor

33.5a The stator is secured to the cover by four bolts (arrows)

33.5b Unscrew the bolt securing the wiring clamp (arrow)

33.6b Install the rotor bolt and its washer and tighten in an anti-clockwise direction

33.6a Check that the Woodruff key is in its slot (arrow)

in the rotor with the Woodruff key and install the rotor onto the shaft **(see illustration)**. Install the rotor bolt and tighten it to the torque setting specified at the beginning of the Chapter **(see illustration)**. To stop the rotor from rotating use a strap wrench, or place the transmission in gear and have an assistant apply the rear brake. Do not forget that the rotor has a left-hand thread and so must be tightened anti-clockwise. Install the idle/reduction gear, making sure the teeth of the smaller inner pinion face inwards and engage with the starter driven gear **(see illustration 33.4)**.

7 Install the stator into the cover, aligning the rubber wiring grommet with the groove in the cover. Apply a suitable non-permanent thread locking compound to the stator bolt threads, then install the bolts and tighten them securely. Apply a suitable sealant to the wiring grommet, then install it into the cut-out in the cover. Secure the wiring with its clamp **(see illustration 33.5b)**.

8 If removed, insert the dowels in the crankcase. Install the crankcase cover using a new gasket, making sure it locates correctly onto the dowels **(see illustration)**. Apply a suitable thread-locking compound to the top right-hand cover bolt, then tighten the cover bolts evenly in a criss-cross sequence.

33.8 Place a new gasket over the dowels (arrows) before installing the crankcase cover

9 Reconnect the wiring at the connector and secure it with any clips or ties.
10 Check the engine oil level and top up if necessary (see *Daily (pre-ride) checks*).

34 Alternator stator coils - check

1 Remove the right-hand side panel (see Chapter 8).
2 Trace the wiring back from the alternator and disconnect it at the 3-pin connector **(see illustration 33.1)**.
3 Using a multimeter set to the ohms x 1 scale, measure the resistance between each of the yellow wires on the alternator side of the connector, taking a total of three readings. These readings must be within the range shown in the Specifications at the beginning of this Chapter.
4 Next check for continuity between each yellow wire terminal and earth. If the stator

35.1 Disconnect the two regulator/rectifier unit wiring connectors (arrows)

UNIT: kΩ					
＋	RED/WHITE	YELLOW 1	YELLOW 2	YELLOW 3	GREEN
RED/WHITE		∞	∞	∞	∞
YELLOW 1	1-20		∞	∞	∞
YELLOW 2	1-20	∞		∞	∞
YELLOW 3	1-20	∞	∞		∞
GREEN	5-30	1-20	1-20	1-20	

2070-9-32,6 HAYNES

35.4 Regulator/rectifier unit resistance readings

35.8 The regulator/rectifier unit is mounted to a plate behind the toolkit and is secured by two bolts

coil windings are in good condition there should be no continuity (infinite resistance) between any of the terminals and earth.

5 If the stator coil tests do not produce the correct results and charging problems have been experienced, the alternator stator coil assembly is at fault and should be replaced. **Note:** *Before condemning the stator coils, check the fault is not due to damaged wiring between the connector and coils.*

35 Regulator/rectifier unit - check and replacement

Check

1 Remove the right-hand side panel (see Chapter 8) and disconnect the 4-pin white and 3-pin black regulator/rectifier unit wiring connectors **(see illustration)**.

2 Use a voltmeter or multimeter set to the 0-20 dc volts range to check the power supply to the regulator/rectifer. Connect the meter's positive (+ve) probe to either red/white terminal and its negative (-ve) probe to either green terminal on the wire harness side of the white wiring connector. Full battery voltage should be shown when the ignition is switched ON. Switch the ignition switch OFF and disconnect the meter.

3 Check the alternator stator coil resistance as described in Section 34.

4 Use an ohmmeter or multimeter set to the ohms scale to check the internal circuitry of the regulator/rectifer unit. Refer to the test table, noting that the checks are made on the regulator/rectifier side of the wire connectors, with the ignition OFF **(see illustration)**. **Note:** *The use of certain multimeters could lead to false readings being obtained. Therefore, if the above check shows the regulator/rectifier unit to be faulty take the unit to a Honda dealer for confirmation of its condition before replacing it.*

5 If the above checks do not provide the expected results check the wiring between the battery, regulator/rectifier and alternator (see the *wiring diagrams* at the end of this chapter).

6 If the wiring checks out, the regulator/ rectifier unit is probably faulty.

Replacement

7 Remove the right-hand side panel (see Chapter 8).

8 The regulator/rectifier unit is mounted to the back of the plate behind the toolkit **(see illustration)**. Trace the wiring back from the regulator/rectifier unit and disconnect it at the connectors **(see illustration 35.1)**.

9 Unscrew the two bolts securing the unit to its mounting plate and remove it.

10 Install the new unit and tighten its bolts securely. Connect the wiring at the connectors.

11 Install the right-hand side panel (see Chapter 8).

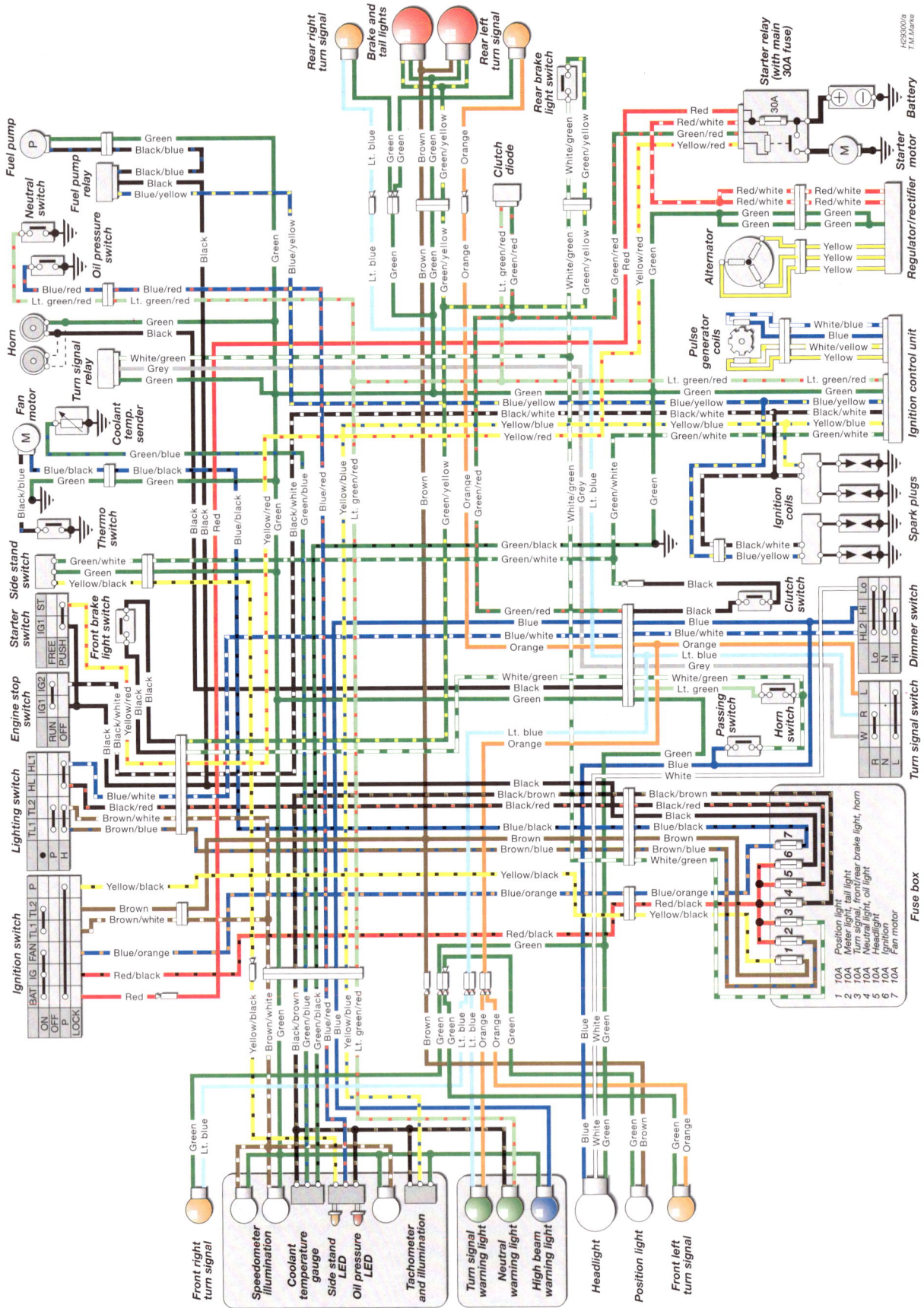

Wiring diagram - NTV600J and K models

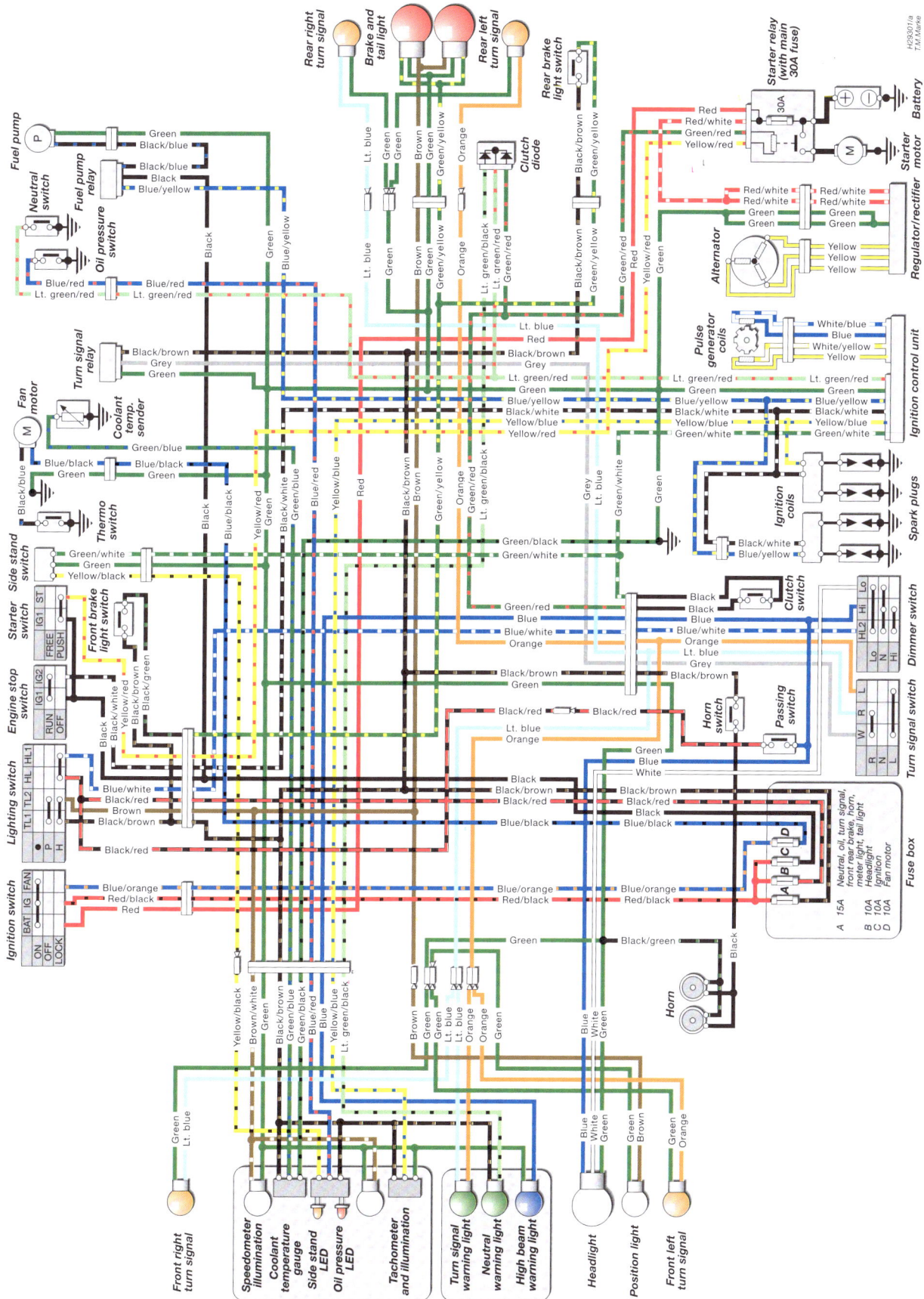

Wiring diagram - NTV600M, NTV650P, S and T models

Reference REF•1

Dimensions and Weights

NTV600

Wheelbase	1465 mm
Overall length	2150 mm
Overall width	710 mm
Overall height	1080 mm
Seat height	790 mm
Minimum ground clearance	165 mm
Weight (dry)	189 kg

NTV650

Wheelbase	1465 mm
Overall length	2190 mm
Overall width	765 mm
Overall height	1080 mm
Seat height	810 mm
Minimum ground clearance	165 mm
Weight (dry)	192 kg

Conversion Factors

Length (distance)

Inches (in)	x 25.4	= Millimetres (mm)	x 0.0394	= Inches (in)
Feet (ft)	x 0.305	= Metres (m)	x 3.281	= Feet (ft)
Miles	x 1.609	= Kilometres (km)	x 0.621	= Miles

Volume (capacity)

Cubic inches (cu in; in³)	x 16.387	= Cubic centimetres (cc; cm³)	x 0.061	= Cubic inches (cu in; in³)
Imperial pints (Imp pt)	x 0.568	= Litres (l)	x 1.76	= Imperial pints (Imp pt)
Imperial quarts (Imp qt)	x 1.137	= Litres (l)	x 0.88	= Imperial quarts (Imp qt)
Imperial quarts (Imp qt)	x 1.201	= US quarts (US qt)	x 0.833	= Imperial quarts (Imp qt)
US quarts (US qt)	x 0.946	= Litres (l)	x 1.057	= US quarts (US qt)
Imperial gallons (Imp gal)	x 4.546	= Litres (l)	x 0.22	= Imperial gallons (Imp gal)
Imperial gallons (Imp gal)	x 1.201	= US gallons (US gal)	x 0.833	= Imperial gallons (Imp gal)
US gallons (US gal)	x 3.785	= Litres (l)	x 0.264	= US gallons (US gal)

Mass (weight)

Ounces (oz)	x 28.35	= Grams (g)	x 0.035	= Ounces (oz)
Pounds (lb)	x 0.454	= Kilograms (kg)	x 2.205	= Pounds (lb)

Force

Ounces-force (ozf; oz)	x 0.278	= Newtons (N)	x 3.6	= Ounces-force (ozf; oz)
Pounds-force (lbf; lb)	x 4.448	= Newtons (N)	x 0.225	= Pounds-force (lbf; lb)
Newtons (N)	x 0.1	= Kilograms-force (kgf; kg)	x 9.81	= Newtons (N)

Pressure

Pounds-force per square inch (psi; lbf/in²; lb/in²)	x 0.070	= Kilograms-force per square centimetre (kgf/cm²; kg/cm²)	x 14.223	= Pounds-force per square inch (psi; lbf/in²; lb/in²)
Pounds-force per square inch (psi; lbf/in²; lb/in²)	x 0.068	= Atmospheres (atm)	x 14.696	= Pounds-force per square inch (psi; lbf/in²; lb/in²)
Pounds-force per square inch (psi; lbf/in²; lb/in²)	x 0.069	= Bars	x 14.5	= Pounds-force per square inch (psi; lbf/in²; lb/in²)
Pounds-force per square inch (psi; lbf/in²; lb/in²)	x 6.895	= Kilopascals (kPa)	x 0.145	= Pounds-force per square inch (psi; lbf/in²; lb/in²)
Kilopascals (kPa)	x 0.01	= Kilograms-force per square centimetre (kgf/cm²; kg/cm²)	x 98.1	= Kilopascals (kPa)
Millibar (mbar)	x 100	= Pascals (Pa)	x 0.01	= Millibar (mbar)
Millibar (mbar)	x 0.0145	= Pounds-force per square inch (psi; lbf/in²; lb/in²)	x 68.947	= Millibar (mbar)
Millibar (mbar)	x 0.75	= Millimetres of mercury (mmHg)	x 1.333	= Millibar (mbar)
Millibar (mbar)	x 0.401	= Inches of water (inH₂O)	x 2.491	= Millibar (mbar)
Millimetres of mercury (mmHg)	x 0.535	= Inches of water (inH₂O)	x 1.868	= Millimetres of mercury (mmHg)
Inches of water (inH₂O)	x 0.036	= Pounds-force per square inch (psi; lbf/in²; lb/in²)	x 27.68	= Inches of water (inH₂O)

Torque (moment of force)

Pounds-force inches (lbf in; lb in)	x 1.152	= Kilograms-force centimetre (kgf cm; kg cm)	x 0.868	= Pounds-force inches (lbf in; lb in)
Pounds-force inches (lbf in; lb in)	x 0.113	= Newton metres (Nm)	x 8.85	= Pounds-force inches (lbf in; lb in)
Pounds-force inches (lbf in; lb in)	x 0.083	= Pounds-force feet (lbf ft; lb ft)	x 12	= Pounds-force inches (lbf in; lb in)
Pounds-force feet (lbf ft; lb ft)	x 0.138	= Kilograms-force metres (kgf m; kg m)	x 7.233	= Pounds-force feet (lbf ft; lb ft)
Pounds-force feet (lbf ft; lb ft)	x 1.356	= Newton metres (Nm)	x 0.738	= Pounds-force feet (lbf ft; lb ft)
Newton metres (Nm)	x 0.102	= Kilograms-force metres (kgf m; kg m)	x 9.804	= Newton metres (Nm)

Power

Horsepower (hp)	x 745.7	= Watts (W)	x 0.0013	= Horsepower (hp)

Velocity (speed)

Miles per hour (miles/hr; mph)	x 1.609	= Kilometres per hour (km/hr; kph)	x 0.621	= Miles per hour (miles/hr; mph)

Fuel consumption*

Miles per gallon (mpg)	x 0.354	= Kilometres per litre (km/l)	x 2.825	= Miles per gallon (mpg)

Temperature

Degrees Fahrenheit = (°C x 1.8) + 32   Degrees Celsius (Degrees Centigrade; °C) = (°F - 32) x 0.56

It is common practice to convert from miles per gallon (mpg) to litres/100 kilometres (l/100km), where mpg x l/100 km = 282

Basic maintenance techniques

There are a number of techniques involved in maintenance and repair that will be referred to throughout this manual. Application of these techniques will enable the amateur mechanic to be more efficient, better organised and capable of performing the various tasks properly, which will ensure that the repair job is thorough and complete.

Fastening systems

Fasteners, basically, are nuts, bolts and screws used to hold two or more parts together. There are a few things to keep in mind when working with fasteners. Almost all of them use a locking device of some type (either a lock washer, locknut, locking tab or thread locking compound). All threaded fasteners should be clean, straight, have undamaged threads and undamaged corners on the hex head where the spanner fits. Develop the habit of replacing all damaged nuts and bolts with new ones.

Rusted nuts and bolts should be treated with a penetrating oil to ease removal and prevent breakage. After applying the rust penetrant, let it work for a few minutes before trying to loosen the nut or bolt. Badly rusted fasteners may have to be chiselled off or removed with a special nut breaker, available at tool shops.

If a bolt or stud breaks off in an assembly, it can be drilled out and removed with a special tool called an E-Z out (or screw extractor). Most dealer service departments and motorcycle repair shops can perform this task, as well as others (such as the repair of threaded holes that have been stripped out).

Washers should always be replaced exactly as removed. Replace any damaged washers with new ones. Always use a flat washer between a lock washer and any soft metal surface (such as aluminium), thin sheet metal or plastic. Special locknuts can only be used once or twice before they lose their locking ability and must be replaced.

Tightening sequences and procedures

When threaded fasteners are tightened, they are often tightened to a specific torque value (torque is basically a twisting force). Over-tightening the fastener can weaken it and cause it to break, while under-tightening can cause it to eventually come loose. Each bolt, depending on the material it's made of, the diameter of its shank and the material it is threaded into, has a specific torque value, which is noted in the Specifications. Be sure to follow the torque recommendations closely.

Fasteners laid out in a pattern (ie cylinder head bolts, engine case bolts, etc.) must be loosened or tightened in a sequence to avoid warping the component. Initially, the bolts/nuts should go on finger-tight only. Next, they should be tightened one full turn each, in a criss-cross or diagonal pattern. After each one has been tightened one full turn, return to the first one tightened and tighten them all one half turn, following the same pattern. Finally, tighten each of them one quarter turn at a time until each fastener has been tightened to the proper torque. To loosen and remove the fasteners the procedure would be reversed.

Disassembly sequence

Component disassembly should be done with care and purpose to help ensure that the parts go back together properly during reassembly. Always keep track of the sequence in which parts are removed. Take note of special characteristics or marks on parts that can be installed more than one way (such as convex washers and gear pinions). It's a good idea to lay the disassembled parts out on a clean surface in the order that they were removed. It may also be helpful to make sketches or take instant photos of components before removal.

When removing fasteners from a component, keep track of their locations. Sometimes threading a bolt back in a part, or putting the washers and nut back on a stud, can prevent mix-ups later. If nuts and bolts can't be returned to their original locations, they should be kept in a compartmented box or a series of small boxes or labelled plastic bags. A box of this type is especially helpful when working on assemblies with very small parts (such as the carburettors, tappets, shims etc).

Whenever wiring looms, harnesses or connectors are separated, it's a good idea to identify the two halves with numbered pieces of masking tape so they can be easily reconnected.

Gasket sealing surfaces

Gaskets are used to seal the mating surfaces between components and keep lubricants, fluids, vacuum or pressure contained in an assembly.

Many times these gaskets are coated with a liquid or paste type gasket sealing compound before assembly. Age, heat and pressure can sometimes cause the two parts to stick together so tightly that they are very difficult to separate. In most cases, the part can be loosened by striking it with a soft-faced hammer near the mating surfaces. A normal hammer can be used if a block of wood is placed between the hammer and the part. Do not hammer on cast parts or parts that could be easily damaged. With any particularly stubborn part, always recheck to make sure that every fastener has been removed.

Avoid using a screwdriver or bar to pry apart components, as they can easily mark the gasket sealing surfaces of the parts (which must remain smooth). If prying is absolutely necessary, use a piece of wood, but keep in mind that extra clean-up will be necessary if the wood splinters.

After the parts are separated, the old gasket must be carefully scraped off and the gasket surfaces cleaned. Stubborn gasket material can be soaked with a gasket remover (available in aerosol cans) to soften it so it can be easily scraped off. A scraper can be fashioned from a piece of copper tubing by flattening and sharpening one end. Copper is recommended because it is usually softer than the surfaces to be scraped, which reduces the chance of gouging the part. Some gaskets can be removed with a wire brush, but regardless of the method used, the mating surfaces must be left clean and smooth. If for some reason the gasket surface is gouged, then a gasket sealant thick enough to fill scratches will have to be used during reassembly of the components. For most applications, a non-drying (or semi-drying) gasket sealant is best.

Hose removal tips

Hose removal precautions closely parallel gasket removal precautions. Avoid scratching or gouging the surface that the hose mates against or the connection may leak. Because of various chemical reactions, the rubber in hoses can bond itself to the metal union that the hose fits over. To remove a hose, first loosen the hose clamps that secure it to the union. Then, with slip joint pliers, grab the hose at the clamp and rotate it around the union. Work it back and forth until it is completely free, then pull it off (silicone or other lubricants will ease removal if they can be applied between the hose and the outside of the union). Apply the same lubricant to the inside of the hose and the outside of the union to simplify installation.

If the hose is particularly stubborn, slit the hose with a sharp knife and peel it off the union. The hose will obviously be destroyed using this method.

If a hose clamp is broken or damaged, do not reuse it. Also, do not reuse hoses that are cracked, split or torn.

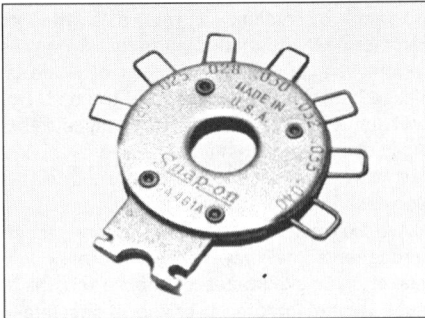

Spark plug gap adjusting tool

Feeler blade set

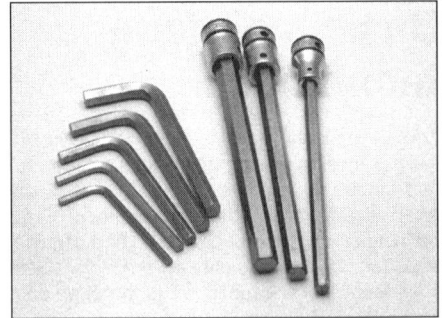

Allen keys (left), and Allen key sockets (right)

Tools

A selection of good tools is a basic requirement for anyone who plans to maintain and repair a motorcycle. For the owner who has few tools, if any, the initial investment might seem high, but when compared to the spiralling costs of routine maintenance and repair, it is a wise one.

To help the owner decide which tools are needed to perform the tasks detailed in this manual, the following tool lists are offered: Maintenance and minor repair, Repair and overhaul and Special. The newcomer to practical mechanics should start off with the Maintenance and minor repair tool kit, which is adequate for the simpler jobs. Then, as confidence and experience grow, the owner can tackle more difficult tasks, buying additional tools as they are needed. Eventually the basic kit will be built into the Repair and overhaul tool set. Over a period of time, the experienced do-it-yourselfer will assemble a tool set complete enough for most repair and overhaul procedures and will add tools from the Special category when it is felt that the expense is justified by the frequency of use.

Maintenance and minor repair tool kit

The tools in this list should be considered the minimum required for performance of routine maintenance, servicing and minor repair work. We recommend the purchase of combination spanners (ring end and open end combined in one spanner); while more expensive than open-ended ones, they offer the advantages of both types of wrench.

Combination spanner set (6 mm to 22 mm)
Adjustable wrench - 8 in
Spark plug socket (with rubber insert)
Spark plug gap adjusting tool
Feeler blade set
Standard flat-bladed screwdriver set
Phillips screwdriver set
Allen key set
Torx key set
Combination (slip-joint) pliers - 6 in
Hacksaw and assortment of blades
Tyre pressure gauge
Tyre tread depth gauge
Control cable pressure luber
Grease gun
Oil can
Fine emery cloth
Wire brush
Hand impact screwdriver and bits
Funnel (medium size)
Safety goggles
Drain tray

Repair and overhaul tool set

These tools are essential for anyone who plans to perform major repairs and are intended to supplement those in the Maintenance and minor repair tool kit. Included is a comprehensive set of sockets which, though expensive, are invaluable because of their versatility (especially when various extensions and drives are available). We recommend the 3/8 inch drive over the 1/2 inch drive for general motorcycle maintenance and repair (ideally, the mechanic would have a 3/8 inch drive set and a 1/2 inch drive set).

Socket set(s)
Reversible ratchet
Extension - 6 in
Universal joint
Torque wrench (same size drive as sockets)
Ball pein hammer - 8 oz
Soft-faced hammer (plastic/rubber)
Pliers - needle nose
Pliers - circlip (internal and external)
Cold chisel - 1/2 in
Scriber
Scraper
Centre punch
Pin punches (1/16, 1/8, 3/16 in)
Steel rule/straightedge - 12 in
A selection of files
Wire brush (large)
Clutch boss holder tool
Multimeter

Note: *Another tool which is often useful is an electric drill with a chuck capacity of 3/8 inch (and a set of good quality drill bits).*

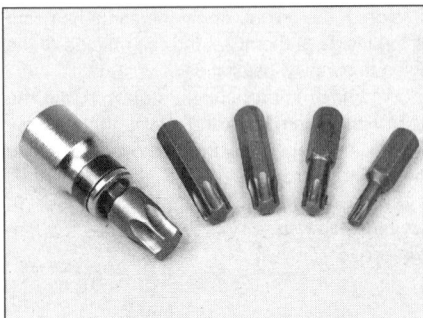

Torx bit set

Control cable pressure luber

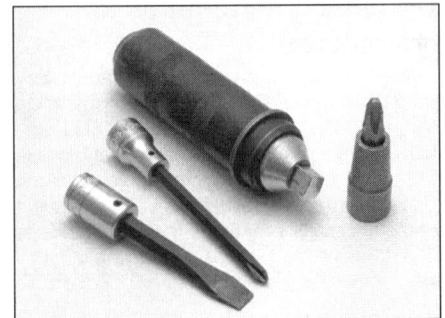

Hand impact screwdriver and bits

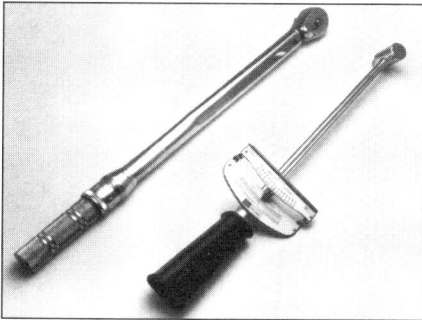

Torque wrenches
(left - click; right - beam type)

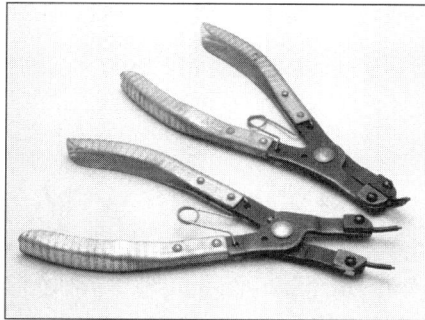

Circlip pliers
(top - external; bottom - internal)

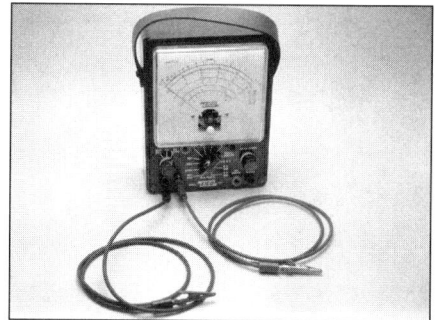

Multimeter (volt/ohm/ammeter)

Special tools

The tools in this list include those which are not used regularly, are expensive to buy, or which need to be used in accordance with their manufacturer's instructions. Unless these tools will be used frequently, it is not very economical to purchase many of them. A consideration would be to split the cost and use between yourself and a friend or friends (ie members of a motorcycle club).

This list primarily contains tools and instruments widely available to the public, as well as some special tools produced by the motorcycle manufacturer for distribution to dealers. As a result, references to the manufacturer's special tools are occasionally included in the text of this manual. Generally, an alternative method of doing the job without the special tool is offered. However, sometimes there is no alternative to their use. Where this is the case, and the tool can't be purchased or borrowed, the work should be entrusted to a dealer.

Valve spring compressor
Piston ring removal and installation tool
Piston pin puller
Oil pressure gauge
Telescoping gauges
Micrometer and Vernier calipers
Dial indicator set
Manometer or vacuum gauge set
Cylinder compression gauge
Cylinder surfacing hone
Small air compressor with blow gun and tyre chuck
Stud extractor set

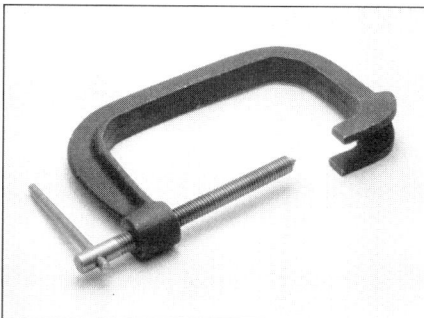

Buying tools

For the do-it-yourselfer who is just starting to get involved in motorcycle maintenance and repair, there are a number of options available when purchasing tools. If maintenance and minor repair is the extent of the work to be done, the purchase of individual tools is satisfactory. If, on the other hand, extensive work is planned, it would be a good idea to purchase a modest tool set from one of the large retail chain stores. A set can usually be bought at a substantial savings over the individual tool prices (and they often come with a tool box). As additional tools are needed, add-on sets, individual tools and a larger tool box can be purchased to expand the tool selection. Building a tool set gradually allows the cost of the tools to be spread over a longer period of time and gives the mechanic the freedom to choose only those tools that will actually be used.

Tool shops and motorcycle dealers will often be the only source of some of the special tools that are needed, but regardless of where tools are bought, try to avoid cheap ones (especially when buying screwdrivers and sockets) because they won't last very long. There are plenty of tools around at reasonable prices, but always aim to purchase items which meet the relevant national safety standards. The expense involved in replacing cheap tools will eventually be greater than the initial cost of quality tools.

It is obviously not possible to cover the subject of tools fully here. For those who wish to learn more about tools and their use, there is a book entitled *Motorcycle Workshop Practice Manual* (Book no. 1454) available from the publishers of this manual. It also provides an introduction to basic workshop practice which will be of interest to a home mechanic working on any type of motorcycle.

Care and maintenance of tools

Good tools are expensive, so it makes sense to treat them with respect. Keep them clean and in usable condition and store them properly when not in use. Always wipe off any dirt, grease or metal chips before putting them away. Never leave tools lying around in the work area.

Some tools, such as screwdrivers, pliers, spanners and sockets, can be hung on a panel mounted on the garage or workshop wall, while others should be kept in a tool box or tray. Measuring instruments, gauges, meters, etc. must be carefully stored where they can't be damaged by weather or impact from other tools.

When tools are used with care and stored properly, they will last a very long time. Even with the best of care, tools will wear out if used frequently. When a tool is damaged or worn out, replace it; subsequent jobs will be safer and more enjoyable if you do.

Valve spring compressor

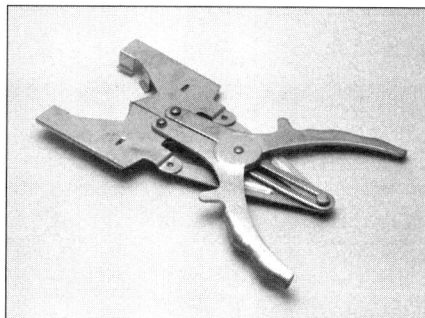

Piston ring removal/installation tool

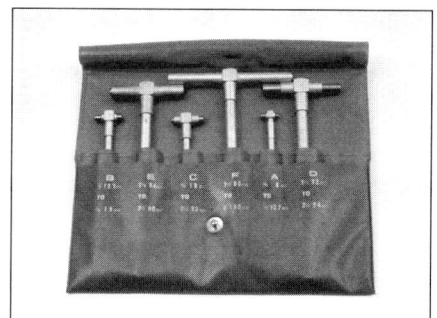

Telescoping gauges

Micrometer

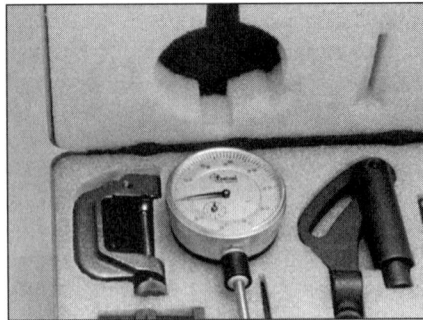

Dial indicator set

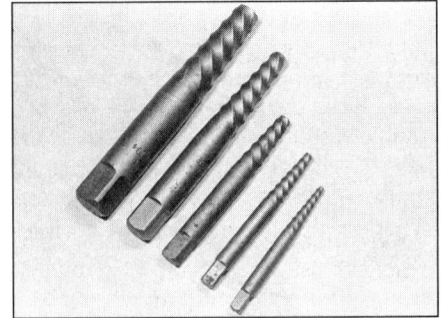

Stud extractor set

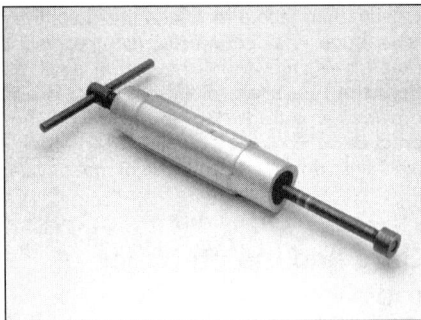

Piston pin puller

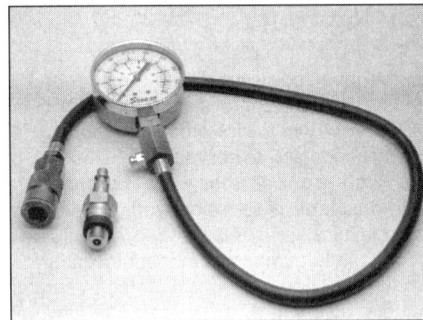

Cylinder comprerssion gauge

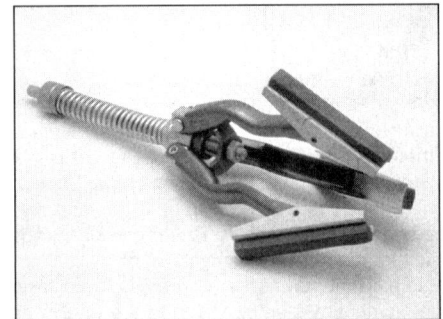

Cylinder surfacing hone

Working facilities

Not to be overlooked when discussing tools is the workshop. If anything more than routine maintenance is to be carried out, some sort of suitable work area is essential.

It is understood, and appreciated, that many home mechanics do not have a good workshop or garage available and end up removing an engine or doing major repairs outside (it is recommended, however, that the overhaul or repair be completed under the cover of a roof).

A clean, flat workbench or table of comfortable working height is an absolute necessity. The workbench should be equipped with a vice that has a jaw opening of at least four inches.

As mentioned previously, some clean, dry storage space is also required for tools, as well as the lubricants, fluids, cleaning solvents, etc. which soon become necessary.

Sometimes waste oil and fluids, drained from the engine or cooling system during normal maintenance or repairs, present a disposal problem. Do not pour them on the ground or into the drainage system, simply pour the used fluids into large containers, seal them with caps and take them to an authorised disposal site or garage.

Always keep a supply of old newspapers and clean rags available. Old towels are excellent for mopping up spills. Many mechanics use rolls of paper towels for most work because they are readily available and disposable. To help keep the area under the motorcycle clean, a large cardboard box can be cut open and flattened to protect the garage or workshop floor.

Whenever working over a painted surface (such as the fuel tank) cover it with an old blanket or bedspread to protect the finish.

A number of chemicals and lubricants are available for use in motorcycle maintenance and repair. They include a wide variety of products ranging from cleaning solvents and degreasers to lubricants and protective sprays for rubber, plastic and vinyl.

● **Contact point/spark plug cleaner** is a solvent used to clean oily film and dirt from points, grime from electrical connectors and oil deposits from spark plugs. It is oil free and leaves no residue. It can also be used to remove gum and varnish from carburettor jets and other orifices.

● **Carburettor cleaner** is similar to contact point/spark plug cleaner but it usually has a stronger solvent and may leave a slight oily reside. It is not recommended for cleaning electrical components or connections.

● **Brake system cleaner** is used to remove grease or brake fluid from brake system components (where clean surfaces are absolutely necessary and petroleum-based solvents cannot be used); it also leaves no residue.

● **Silicone-based lubricants** are used to protect rubber parts such as hoses and grommets, and are used as lubricants for hinges and locks.

● **Multi-purpose grease** is an all purpose lubricant used wherever grease is more practical than a liquid lubricant such as oil. Some multi-purpose grease is coloured white and specially formulated to be more resistant to water than ordinary grease.

● **Gear oil** (sometimes called gear lube) is a specially designed oil used in transmissions and final drive units, as well as other areas where high friction, high temperature lubrication is required. It is available in a number of viscosities (weights) for various applications.

● **Motor oil**, of course, is the lubricant specially formulated for use in the engine. It normally contains a wide variety of additives to prevent corrosion and reduce foaming and wear. Motor oil comes in various weights (viscosity ratings) of from 5 to 80. The recommended weight of the oil depends on the seasonal temperature and the demands on the engine. Light oil is used in cold climates and under light load conditions; heavy oil is used in hot climates and where high loads are encountered. Multi-viscosity oils are designed to have characteristics of both light and heavy oils and are available in a number of weights from 5W-20 to 20W-50.

● **Petrol additives** perform several functions, depending on their chemical makeup. They usually contain solvents that help dissolve gum and varnish that build up on carburettor and inlet parts. They also serve to break down carbon deposits that form on the inside surfaces of the combustion chambers. Some additives contain upper cylinder lubricants for valves and piston rings.

● **Brake and clutch fluid** is a specially formulated hydraulic fluid that can withstand the heat and pressure encountered in brake/clutch systems. Care must be taken that this fluid does not come in contact with painted surfaces or plastics. An opened container should always be resealed to prevent contamination by water or dirt.

● **Chain lubricants** are formulated especially for use on motorcycle final drive chains. A good chain lube should adhere well and have good penetrating qualities to be effective as a lubricant inside the chain and on the side plates, pins and rollers. Most chain lubes are either the foaming type or quick drying type and are usually marketed as sprays. Take care to use a lubricant marked as being suitable for O-ring chains.

● **Degreasers** are heavy duty solvents used to remove grease and grime that may accumulate on engine and frame components. They can be sprayed or brushed on and, depending on the type, are rinsed with either water or solvent.

● **Solvents** are used alone or in combination with degreasers to clean parts and assemblies during repair and overhaul. The home mechanic should use only solvents that are non-flammable and that do not produce irritating fumes.

● **Gasket sealing compounds** may be used in conjunction with gaskets, to improve their sealing capabilities, or alone, to seal metal-to-metal joints. Many gasket sealers can withstand extreme heat, some are impervious to petrol and lubricants, while others are capable of filling and sealing large cavities. Depending on the intended use, gasket sealers either dry hard or stay relatively soft and pliable. They are usually applied by hand, with a brush, or are sprayed on the gasket sealing surfaces.

● **Thread locking compound** is an adhesive locking compound that prevents threaded fasteners from loosening because of vibration. It is available in a variety of types for different applications.

● **Moisture dispersants** are usually sprays that can be used to dry out electrical components such as the fuse block and wiring connectors. Some types can also be used as treatment for rubber and as a lubricant for hinges, cables and locks.

● **Waxes and polishes** are used to help protect painted and plated surfaces from the weather. Different types of paint may require the use of different types of wax polish. Some polishes utilise a chemical or abrasive cleaner to help remove the top layer of oxidised (dull) paint on older vehicles. In recent years, many non-wax polishes (that contain a wide variety of chemicals such as polymers and silicones) have been introduced. These non-wax polishes are usually easier to apply and last longer than conventional waxes and polishes.

About the MOT Test

In the UK, all vehicles more than three years old are subject to an annual test to ensure that they meet minimum safety requirements. A current test certificate must be issued before a machine can be used on public roads, and is required before a road fund licence can be issued. Riding without a current test certificate will also invalidate your insurance.

For most owners, the MOT test is an annual cause for anxiety, and this is largely due to owners not being sure what needs to be checked prior to submitting the motorcycle for testing. The simple answer is that a fully roadworthy motorcycle will have no difficulty in passing the test.

This is a guide to getting your motorcycle through the MOT test. Obviously it will not be possible to examine the motorcycle to the same standard as the professional MOT tester, particularly in view of the equipment required for some of the checks. However, working through the following procedures will enable you to identify any problem areas before submitting the motorcycle for the test.

It has only been possible to summarise the test requirements here, based on the regulations in force at the time of printing. Test standards are becoming increasingly stringent, although there are some exemptions for older vehicles. More information about the MOT test can be obtained from the HMSO publications, *How Safe is your Motorcycle* and *The MOT Inspection Manual for Motorcycle Testing*.

Many of the checks require that one of the wheels is raised off the ground. If the motorcycle doesn't have a centre stand, note that an auxiliary stand will be required. Additionally, the help of an assistant may prove useful.

Certain exceptions apply to machines under 50 cc, machines without a lighting system, and Classic bikes - if in doubt about any of the requirements listed below seek confirmation from an MOT tester prior to submitting the motorcycle for the test.

Check that the frame number is clearly visible.

> **HAYNES HiNT** *If a component is in borderline condition, the tester has discretion in deciding whether to pass or fail it. If the motorcycle presented is clean and evidently well cared for, the tester may be more inclined to pass a borderline component than if the motorcycle is scruffy and apparently neglected.*

Electrical System

Lights, turn signals, horn and reflector

✔ With the ignition on, check the operation of the following electrical components. **Note:** *The electrical components on certain small-capacity machines are powered by the generator, requiring that the engine is run for this check.*

a) *Headlight and tail light. Check that both illuminate in the low and high beam switch positions.*

b) *Position lights. Check that the front position (or sidelight) and tail light illuminate in this switch position.*

c) *Turn signals. Check that all flash at the correct rate, and that the warning light(s) function correctly. Check that the turn signal switch works correctly.*

c) *Hazard warning system (where fitted). Check that all four turn signals flash in this switch position.*

d) *Brake stop light. Check that the light comes on when the front and rear brakes are independently applied. Models first used on or after 1st April 1986 must have a brake light switch on each brake.*

e) *Horn. Check that the sound is continuous and of reasonable volume.*

✔ Check that there is a red reflector on the rear of the machine, either mounted separately or as part of the tail light lens.

✔ Check the condition of the headlight, tail light and turn signal lenses.

Headlight beam height

✔ The MOT tester will perform a headlight beam height check using specialised beam setting equipment **(see illustration 1)**. This equipment will not be available to the home mechanic, but if you suspect that the headlight is incorrectly set or may have been maladjusted in the past, you can perform a rough test as follows.

✔ Position the bike in a straight line facing a brick wall. The bike must be off its stand, upright and with a rider seated. Measure the height from the ground to the centre of the headlight and mark a horizontal line on the wall at this height. Position the motorcycle 3.8 metres from the wall and draw a vertical

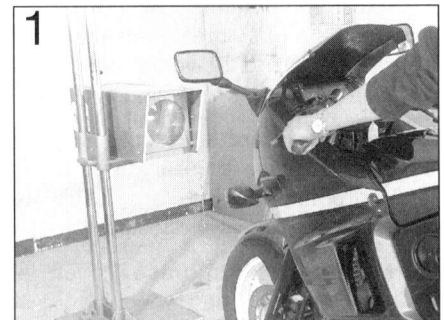

Headlight beam height checking equipment

line up the wall central to the centreline of the motorcycle. Switch to dipped beam and check that the beam pattern falls slightly lower than the horizontal line and to the left of the vertical line **(see illustration 2)**.

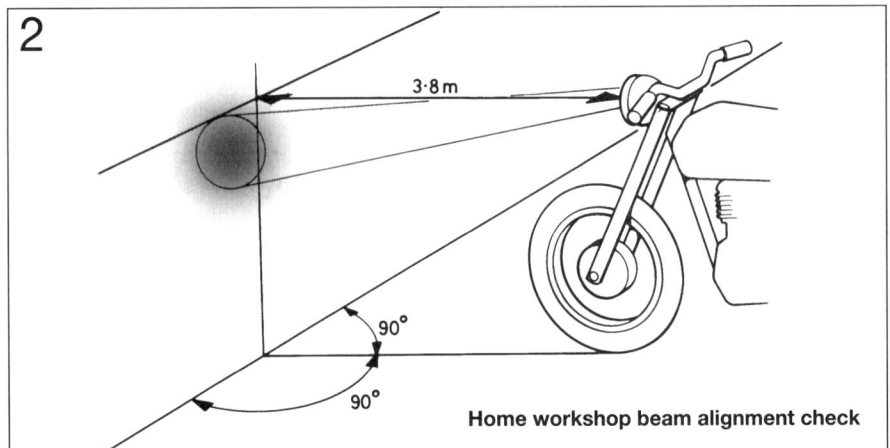

Home workshop beam alignment check

Exhaust System and Final Drive

Exhaust

✔ Check that the exhaust mountings are secure and that the system does not foul any of the rear suspension components.
✔ Start the motorcycle. When the revs are increased, check that the exhaust is neither holed nor leaking from any of its joints. On a linked system, check that the collector box is not leaking due to corrosion.

✔ Note that the exhaust decibel level ("loudness" of the exhaust) is assessed at the discretion of the tester. If the motorcycle was first used on or after 1st January 1985 the silencer must carry the BSAU 193 stamp, or a marking relating to its make and model, or be of OE (original equipment) manufacture. If the silencer is marked NOT FOR ROAD USE, RACING USE ONLY or similar, it will fail the MOT.

Final drive

✔ On chain or belt drive machines, check that the chain/belt is in good condition and does not have excessive slack. Also check that the sprocket is securely mounted on the rear wheel hub. Check that the chain/belt guard is in place.
✔ On shaft drive bikes, check for oil leaking from the drive unit and fouling the rear tyre.

Steering and Suspension

Steering

✔ With the front wheel raised off the ground, rotate the steering from lock to lock. The handlebar or switches must not contact the fuel tank or be close enough to trap the rider's hand. Problems can be caused by damaged lock stops on the lower yoke and frame, or by the fitting of non-standard handlebars.
✔ When performing the lock to lock check, also ensure that the steering moves freely without drag or notchiness. Steering movement can be impaired by poorly routed cables, or by overtight head bearings or worn bearings. The tester will perform a check of the steering head bearing lower race by mounting the front wheel on a surface plate, then performing a lock to lock check with the weight of the machine on the lower bearing (see illustration 3).
✔ Grasp the fork sliders (lower legs) and attempt to push and pull on the forks (see illustration 4). Any play in the steering head bearings will be felt. Note that in extreme cases, wear of the front fork bushes can be misinterpreted for head bearing play.
✔ Check that the handlebars are securely mounted.
✔ Check that the handlebar grip rubbers are secure. They should by bonded to the bar left end and to the throttle cable pulley on the right end.

Front suspension

✔ With the motorcycle off the stand, hold the front brake on and pump the front forks up and down (see illustration 5). Check that they are adequately damped.
✔ Inspect the area above and around the front fork oil seals (see illustration 6). There should be no sign of oil on the fork tube (stanchion) nor leaking down the slider (lower leg). On models so equipped, check that there is no oil leaking from the anti-dive units.
✔ On models with swingarm front suspension, check that there is no freeplay in the linkage when moved from side to side.

Rear suspension

✔ With the motorcycle off the stand and an assistant supporting the motorcycle by its handlebars, bounce the rear suspension (see illustration 7). Check that the suspension components do not foul on any of the cycle parts and check that the shock absorber(s) provide adequate damping.

Front wheel mounted on a surface plate for steering head bearing lower race check

Checking the steering head bearings for freeplay

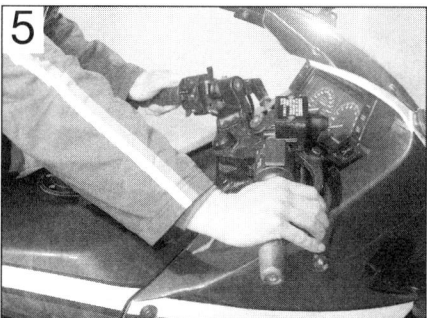

Hold the front brake on and pump the front forks up and down to check operation

Inspect the area around the fork dust seal for oil leakage (arrow)

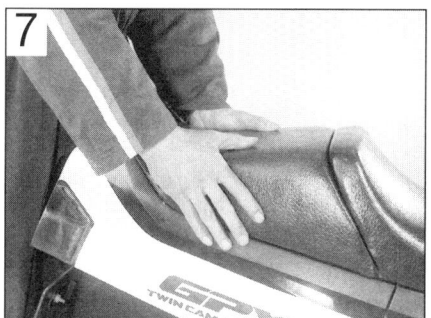

Bounce the rear of the motorcycle to check rear suspension operation

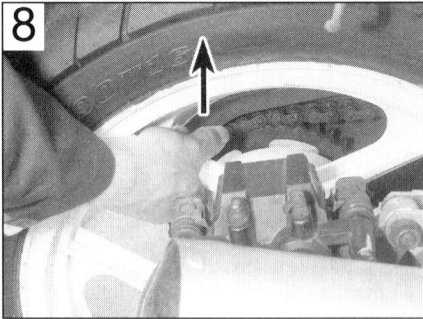

Checking for rear suspension linkage play

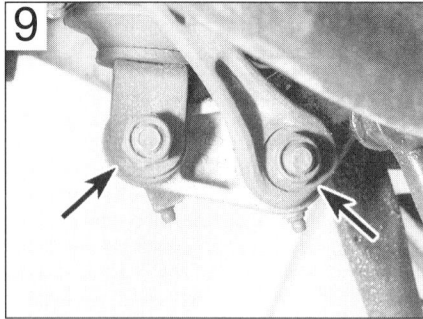

Worn suspension linkage pivots (arrows) are usually the cause of play in the rear suspension

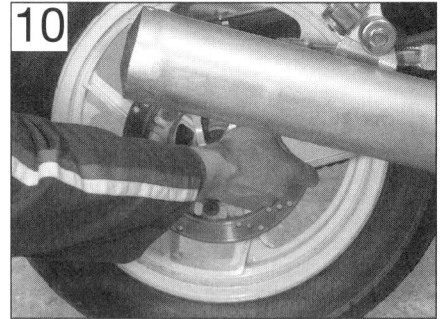

Grasp the swingarm at the ends to check for play in its pivot bearings

✔ Visually inspect the shock absorber(s) and check that there is no sign of oil leakage from its damper. This is somewhat restricted on certain single shock models due to the location of the shock absorber.

✔ With the rear wheel raised off the ground, grasp the wheel at the highest point and attempt to pull it up **(see illustration 8)**. Any play in the swingarm pivot or suspension linkage bearings will be felt as movement. **Note:** *Do not confuse play with actual suspension movement.* Failure to lubricate suspension linkage bearings can lead to bearing failure **(see illustration 9)**.

✔ With the rear wheel raised off the ground, grasp the swingarm ends and attempt to move the swingarm from side to side and forwards and backwards - any play indicates wear of the swingarm pivot bearings **(see illustration 10)**.

Brakes, Wheels and Tyres

Brakes

✔ With the wheel raised off the ground, apply the brake then free it off, and check that the wheel is about to revolve freely without brake drag.

✔ On disc brakes, examine the disc itself. Check that it is securely mounted and not cracked.

✔ On disc brakes, view the pad material through the caliper mouth and check that the pads are not worn down beyond the limit **(see illustration 11)**.

✔ On drum brakes, check that when the brake is applied the angle between the operating lever and cable or rod is **not** too great **(see illustration 12)**. Check also that the operating lever doesn't foul any other components.

✔ On disc brakes, examine the flexible hoses from top to bottom. Have an assistant hold the brake on so that the fluid in the hose is under pressure, and check that there is no sign of fluid leakage, bulges or cracking. If there are any metal brake pipes or unions, check that these are free from corrosion and damage. Where a brake-linked anti-dive system is fitted, check the hoses to the anti-dive in a similar manner.

✔ Check that the rear brake torque arm is secure and that its fasteners are secured by self-locking nuts or castellated nuts with split-pins or R-pins **(see illustration 13)**.

✔ On models with ABS, check that the self-check warning light in the instrument panel works.

✔ The MOT tester will perform a test of the motorcycle's braking efficiency based on a calculation of rider and motorcycle weight. Although this cannot be carried out at home, you can at least ensure that the braking systems are properly maintained. For hydraulic disc brakes, check the fluid level, lever/pedal feel (bleed of air if its spongy) and pad material. For drum brakes, check adjustment, cable or rod operation and shoe lining thickness.

Wheels and tyres

✔ Check the wheel condition. Cast wheels should be free from cracks and if of the built-up design, all fasteners should be secure. Spoked wheels should be checked for broken, corroded, loose or bent spokes.

✔ With the wheel raised off the ground, spin the wheel and visually check that the tyre and wheel run true. Check that the tyre does not foul the suspension or mudguards.

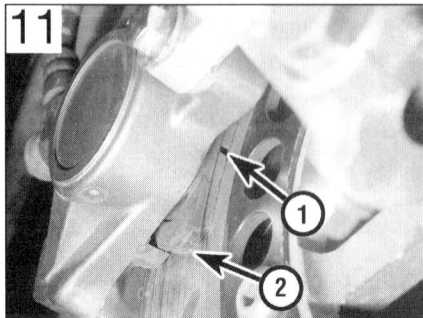

Brake pad wear can usually be viewed without removing the caliper. Most pads have wear indicator grooves (1) and some also have indicator tangs (2)

On drum brakes, check the angle of the operating lever with the brake fully applied. Most drum brakes have a wear indicator pointer and scale.

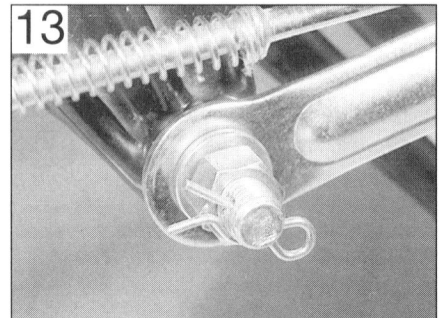

Brake torque arm must be properly secured at both ends

Check for wheel bearing play by trying to move the wheel about the axle (spindle)

Checking the tyre tread depth

Tyre direction of rotation arrow can be found on tyre sidewall

Castellated type wheel axle (spindle) nut must be secured by a split pin or R-pin

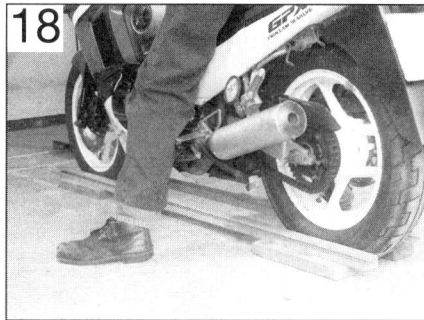

Two straightedges are used to check wheel alignment

✔ With the wheel raised off the ground, grasp the wheel and attempt to move it about the axle (spindle) **(see illustration 14)**. Any play felt here indicates wheel bearing failure.

✔ Check the tyre tread depth, tread condition and sidewall condition **(see illustration 15)**.

✔ Check the tyre type. Front and rear tyre types must be compatible and be suitable for road use. Tyres marked NOT FOR ROAD USE, COMPETITION USE ONLY or similar, will fail the MOT.

✔ If the tyre sidewall carries a direction of rotation arrow, this must be pointing in the direction of normal wheel rotation **(see illustration 16)**.

✔ Check that the wheel axle (spindle) nuts (where applicable) are properly secured. A self-locking nut or castellated nut with a split-pin or R-pin can be used **(see illustration 17)**.

✔ Wheel alignment is checked with the motorcycle off the stand and a rider seated. With the front wheel pointing straight ahead, two perfectly straight lengths of metal or wood and placed against the sidewalls of both tyres **(see illustration 18)**. The gap each side of the front tyre must be equidistant on both sides. Incorrect wheel alignment may be due to a cocked rear wheel (often as the result of poor chain adjustment) or in extreme cases, a bent frame.

General checks and condition

✔ Check the security of all major fasteners, bodypanels, seat, fairings (where fitted) and mudguards.

✔ Check that the rider and pillion footrests, handlebar levers and brake pedal are securely mounted.

✔ Check for corrosion on the frame or any load-bearing components. If severe, this may affect the structure, particularly under stress.

Sidecars

A motorcycle fitted with a sidecar requires additional checks relating to the stability of the machine and security of attachment and swivel joints, plus specific wheel alignment (toe-in) requirements. Additionally, tyre and lighting requirements differ from conventional motorcycle use. Owners are advised to check MOT test requirements with an official test centre.

Preparing for storage

Before you start

If repairs or an overhaul is needed, see that this is carried out now rather than left until you want to ride the bike again.

Give the bike a good wash and scrub all dirt from its underside. Make sure the bike dries completely before preparing for storage.

Engine

● Remove the spark plug(s) and lubricate the cylinder bores with approximately a teaspoon of motor oil using a spout-type oil can **(see illustration 1)**. Reinstall the spark plug(s). Crank the engine over a couple of times to coat the piston rings and bores with oil. If the bike has a kickstart, use this to turn the engine over. If not, flick the kill switch to the OFF position and crank the engine over on the starter **(see illustration 2)**. If the nature on the ignition system prevents the starter operating with the kill switch in the OFF position,

Squirt a drop of motor oil into each cylinder

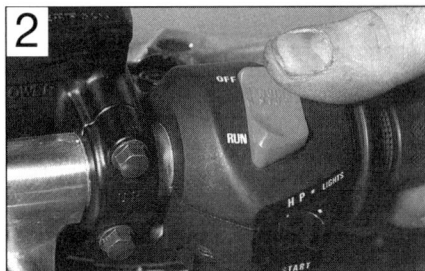

Flick the kill switch to OFF . . .

. . . and ensure that the metal bodies of the plugs (arrows) are earthed against the cylinder head

remove the spark plugs and fit them back in their caps; ensure that the plugs are earthed (grounded) against the cylinder head when the starter is operated **(see illustration 3)**.

⚠ *Warning: It is important that the plugs are earthed (grounded) away from the spark plug holes otherwise there is a risk of atomised fuel from the cylinders igniting.*

HAYNES HiNT *On a single cylinder four-stroke engine, you can seal the combustion chamber completely by positioning the piston at TDC on the compression stroke.*

Connect a hose to the carburettor float chamber drain stub (arrow) and unscrew the drain screw

● Drain the carburettor(s) otherwise there is a risk of jets becoming blocked by gum deposits from the fuel **(see illustration 4)**.

● If the bike is going into long-term storage, consider adding a fuel stabiliser to the fuel in the tank. If the tank is drained completely, corrosion of its internal surfaces may occur if left unprotected for a long period. The tank can be treated with a rust preventative especially for this purpose. Alternatively, remove the tank and pour half a litre of motor oil into it, install the filler cap and shake the tank to coat its internals with oil before draining off the excess. The same effect can also be achieved by spraying WD40 or a similar water-dispersant around the inside of the tank via its flexible nozzle.

● Make sure the cooling system contains the correct mix of antifreeze. Antifreeze also contains important corrosion inhibitors.

● The air intakes and exhaust can be sealed off by covering or plugging the openings. Ensure that you do not seal in any condensation; run the engine until it is hot, then switch off and allow to cool. Tape a piece of thick plastic over the silencer end(s) **(see illustration 5)**. Note that some advocate pouring a tablespoon of motor oil into the silencer(s) before sealing them off.

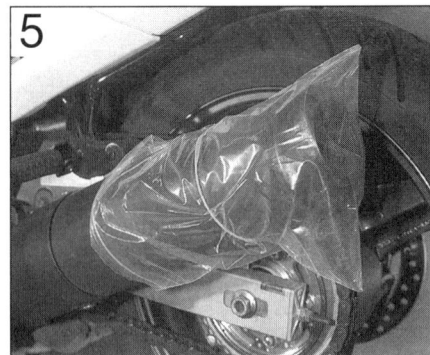

Exhausts can be sealed off with a plastic bag

Battery

● Remove it from the bike - in extreme cases of cold the battery may freeze and crack its case **(see illustration 6)**.

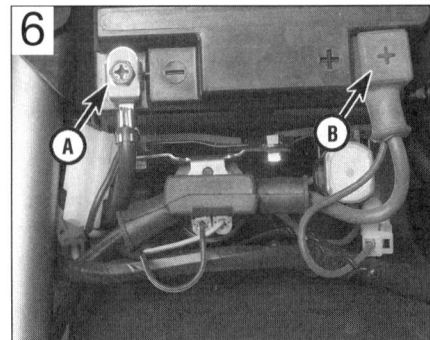

Disconnect the negative lead (A) first, followed by the positive lead (B)

● Check the electrolyte level and top up if necessary (conventional refillable batteries). Clean the terminals.

● Store the battery off the motorcycle and away from any sources of fire. Position a wooden block under the battery if it is to sit on the ground.

● Give the battery a trickle charge for a few hours every month **(see illustration 7)**.

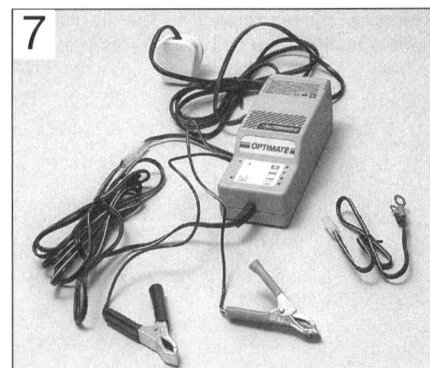

Use a suitable battery charger - this kit also assess battery condition

Tyres

● Place the bike on its centrestand or an auxiliary stand which will support the motorcycle in an upright position. Position wood blocks under the tyres to keep them off the ground and to provide insulation from damp. If the bike is being put into long-term storage, ideally both tyres should be off the ground; not only will this protect the tyres, but will also ensure that no load is placed on the steering head or wheel bearings.

● Deflate each tyre by 5 to 10 psi, no more or the beads may unseat from the rim, making subsequent inflation difficult on tubeless tyres.

Pivots and controls

● Lubricate all lever, pedal, stand and footrest pivot points. If grease nipples are fitted to the rear suspension components, apply lubricant to the pivots.

● Lubricate all control cables.

Cycle components

● Apply a wax protectant to all painted and plastic components. Wipe off any excess, but don't polish to a shine. Where fitted, clean the screen with soap and water.

● Coat metal parts with Vaseline (petroleum jelly). When applying this to the fork tubes, do not compress the forks otherwise the seals will rot from contact with the Vaseline.

● Apply a vinyl cleaner to the seat.

Storage conditions

● Aim to store the bike in a shed or garage which does not leak and is free from damp.

● Drape an old blanket or bedspread over the bike to protect it from dust and direct contact with sunlight (which will fade paint). This also hides the bike from prying eyes. Beware of tight-fitting plastic covers which may allow condensation to form and settle on the bike.

Getting back on the road

Engine and transmission

● Change the oil and replace the oil filter. If this was done prior to storage, check that the oil hasn't emulsified - a thick whitish substance which occurs through condensation.

● Remove the spark plugs. Using a spout-type oil can, squirt a few drops of oil into the cylinder(s). This will provide initial lubrication as the piston rings and bores comes back into contact. Service the spark plugs, or fit new ones, and install them in the engine.

● Check that the clutch isn't stuck on. The plates can stick together if left standing for some time, preventing clutch operation. Engage a gear and try rocking the bike back and forth with the clutch lever held against the handlebar. If this doesn't work on cable-operated clutches, hold the clutch lever back against the handlebar with a strong elastic band or cable tie for a couple of hours **(see illustration 8)**.

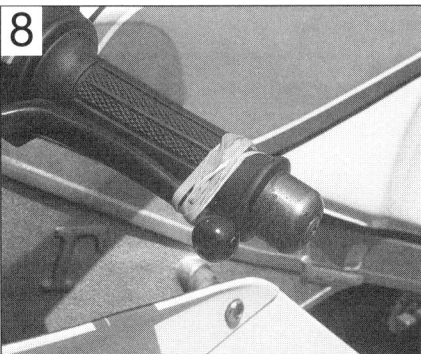

Hold clutch lever back against the handlebar with elastic bands or a cable tie

● If the air intakes or silencer end(s) were blocked off, remove the bung or cover used.

● If the fuel tank was coated with a rust preventative, oil or a stabiliser added to the fuel, drain and flush the tank and dispose of the fuel sensibly. If no action was taken with the fuel tank prior to storage, it is advised that the old fuel is disposed of since it will go off over a period of time. Refill the fuel tank with fresh fuel.

Frame and running gear

● Oil all pivot points and cables.

● Check the tyre pressures. They will definitely need inflating if pressures were reduced for storage.

● Lubricate the final drive chain (where applicable).

● Remove any protective coating applied to the fork tubes (stanchions) since this may well destroy the fork seals. If the fork tubes weren't protected and have picked up rust spots, remove them with very fine abrasive paper and refinish with metal polish.

● Check that both brakes operate correctly. Apply each brake hard and check that it's not possible to move the motorcycle forwards, then check that the brake frees off again once released. Brake caliper pistons can stick due to corrosion around the piston head, or on the sliding caliper types, due to corrosion of the slider pins. If the brake doesn't free after repeated operation, take the caliper off for examination. Similarly drum brakes can stick due to a seized operating cam, cable or rod linkage.

● If the motorcycle has been in long-term storage, renew the brake fluid and clutch fluid (where applicable).

● Depending on where the bike has been stored, the wiring, cables and hoses may have been nibbled by rodents. Make a visual check and investigate disturbed wiring loom tape.

Battery

● If the battery has been previously removal and given top up charges it can simply be reconnected. Remember to connect the positive cable first and the negative cable last.

● On conventional refillable batteries, if the battery has not received any attention, remove it from the motorcycle and check its electrolyte level. Top up if necessary then charge the battery. If the battery fails to hold a charge and a visual checks show heavy white sulphation of the plates, the battery is probably defective and must be renewed. This is particularly likely if the battery is old. Confirm battery condition with a specific gravity check.

● On sealed (MF) batteries, if the battery has not received any attention, remove it from the motorcycle and charge it according to the information on the battery case - if the battery fails to hold a charge it must be renewed.

Starting procedure

● If a kickstart is fitted, turn the engine over a couple of times with the ignition OFF to distribute oil around the engine. If no kickstart is fitted, flick the engine kill switch OFF and the ignition ON and crank the engine over a couple of times to work oil around the upper cylinder components. If the nature of the ignition system is such that the starter won't work with the kill switch OFF, remove the spark plugs, fit them back into their caps and earth (ground) their bodies on the cylinder head. Reinstall the spark plugs afterwards.

● Switch the kill switch to RUN, operate the choke and start the engine. If the engine won't start don't continue cranking the engine - not only will this flatten the battery, but the starter motor will overheat. Switch the ignition off and try again later. If the engine refuses to start, go through the fault finding procedures in this manual. **Note:** *If the bike has been in storage for a long time, old fuel or a carburettor blockage may be the problem. Gum deposits in carburettors can block jets - if a carburettor cleaner doesn't prove successful the carburettors must be dismantled for cleaning.*

● Once the engine has started, check that the lights, turn signals and horn work properly.

● Treat the bike gently for the first ride and check all fluid levels on completion. Settle the bike back into the maintenance schedule.

This Section provides an easy reference-guide to the more common faults that are likely to afflict your machine. Obviously, the opportunities are almost limitless for faults to occur as a result of obscure failures, and to try and cover all eventualities would require a book. Indeed, a number have been written on the subject.

Successful troubleshooting is not a mysterious 'black art' but the application of a bit of knowledge combined with a systematic and logical approach to the problem. Approach any troubleshooting by first accurately identifying the symptom and then checking through the list of possible causes, starting with the simplest or most obvious and progressing in stages to the most complex.

Take nothing for granted, but above all apply liberal quantities of common sense.

The main symptom of a fault is given in the text as a major heading below which are listed the various systems or areas which may contain the fault. Details of each possible cause for a fault and the remedial action to be taken are given, in brief, in the paragraphs below each heading. Further information should be sought in the relevant Chapter.

1 Engine doesn't start or is difficult to start

☐ Starter motor doesn't rotate
☐ Starter motor rotates but engine does not turn over
☐ Starter works but engine won't turn over (seized
☐ No fuel flow
☐ Engine flooded
☐ No spark or weak spark
☐ Compression low
☐ Stalls after starting
☐ Rough idle

2 Poor running at low speed

☐ Spark weak
☐ Fuel/air mixture incorrect
☐ Compression low
☐ Poor acceleration

3 Poor running or no power at high speed

☐ Firing incorrect
☐ Fuel/air mixture incorrect
☐ Compression low
☐ Knocking or pinging
☐ Miscellaneous causes

4 Overheating

☐ Engine overheats
☐ Firing incorrect
☐ Fuel/air mixture incorrect
☐ Compression too high
☐ Engine load excessive
☐ Lubrication inadequate
☐ Miscellaneous causes

5 Clutch problems

☐ Clutch slipping
☐ Clutch not disengaging completely (dragging)

6 Gear shifting problems

☐ Doesn't go into gear, or lever doesn't return
☐ Jumps out of gear
☐ Overshifts

7 Abnormal engine noise

☐ Knocking or pinging
☐ Piston slap or rattling
☐ Valve noise
☐ Other noise

8 Abnormal driveline noise

☐ Clutch noise
☐ Transmission noise
☐ Final drive noise

9 Abnormal frame and suspension noise

☐ Front end noise
☐ Shock absorber noise
☐ Brake noise

10 Oil pressure indicator light comes on

☐ Engine lubrication system
☐ Electrical system

11 Excessive exhaust smoke

☐ White smoke
☐ Black smoke
☐ Brown smoke

12 Poor handling or stability

☐ Handlebar hard to turn
☐ Handlebar shakes or vibrates excessively
☐ Handlebar pulls to one side
☐ Poor shock absorbing qualities

13 Braking problems

☐ Brakes are spongy, don't hold
☐ Brake lever or pedal pulsates
☐ Brakes drag

14 Electrical problems

☐ Battery dead or weak
☐ Battery overcharged

1 Engine doesn't start or is difficult to start

Starter motor doesn't rotate

☐ Engine kill switch OFF.
☐ Fuse blown. Check main fuse and starter circuit fuse (Chapter 9).
☐ Battery voltage low. Check and recharge battery (Chapter 9).
☐ Starter motor defective. Make sure the wiring to the starter is secure. Make sure the starter relay clicks when the start button is pushed. If the relay clicks, then the fault is in the wiring or motor.
☐ Starter relay faulty. Check it according to the procedure in Chapter 9.
☐ Starter switch not contacting. The contacts could be wet, corroded or dirty. Disassemble and clean the switch (Chapter 9).
☐ Wiring open or shorted. Check all wiring connections and harnesses to make sure that they are dry, tight and not corroded. Also check for broken or frayed wires that can cause a short to ground (earth) (see wiring diagram, Chapter 9).
☐ Ignition (main) switch defective. Check the switch according to the procedure in Chapter 9. Replace the switch with a new one if it is defective.
☐ Engine kill switch defective. Check for wet, dirty or corroded contacts. Clean or replace the switch as necessary (Chapter 9).
☐ Faulty neutral, side stand or clutch switch. Check the wiring to each switch and the switch itself according to the procedures in Chapter 9.

Starter motor rotates but engine does not turn over

☐ Starter motor clutch defective. Inspect and repair or replace (Chapter 2).
☐ Damaged idler or starter gears. Inspect and replace the damaged parts (Chapter 2).

Starter works but engine won't turn over (seized)

☐ Seized engine caused by one or more internally damaged components. Failure due to wear, abuse or lack of lubrication. Damage can include seized valves, followers, camshafts, pistons, crankshaft, connecting rod bearings, or transmission gears or bearings. Refer to Chapter 2 for engine disassembly.

No fuel flow

☐ No fuel in tank.
☐ Fuel pump failure or in-line filter blockage (see Chapters 1 and 9 respectively).
☐ Fuel tank breather hose obstructed (not California models).
☐ Fuel tap filter clogged. Remove the tap and clean it and the filter (Chapter 1).
☐ Fuel line clogged. Pull the fuel line loose and carefully blow through it.
☐ Float needle valve clogged. For all of the valves to be clogged, either a very bad batch of fuel with an unusual additive has been used, or some other foreign material has entered the tank. Many times after a machine has been stored for many months without running, the fuel turns to a varnish-like liquid and forms deposits on the inlet needle valves and jets. The carburetors should be removed and overhauled if draining the float chambers doesn't solve the problem.

Engine flooded

☐ Float height too high. Check as described in Chapter 4.
☐ Float needle valve worn or stuck open. A piece of dirt, rust or other debris can cause the valve to seat improperly, causing excess fuel to be admitted to the float chamber. In this case, the float chamber should be cleaned and the needle valve and seat inspected. If the needle and seat are worn, then the leaking will persist and the parts should be replaced with new ones (Chapter 4).
☐ Starting technique incorrect. Under normal circumstances (ie, if all the carburetor functions are sound) the machine should start with little or no throttle. When the engine is cold, the choke should be operated and the engine started without opening the throttle. When the engine is at operating temperature, only a very slight amount of throttle should be necessary. If the engine is flooded, turn the fuel tap OFF and hold the throttle open while cranking the engine. This will allow additional air to reach the cylinders. Remember to turn the fuel tap back ON after the engine starts.

No spark or weak spark

☐ Ignition switch OFF.
☐ Engine kill switch turned to the OFF position.
☐ Battery voltage low. Check and recharge the battery as necessary (Chapter 9).
☐ Spark plugs dirty, defective or worn out. Locate reason for fouled plugs using spark plug condition chart and follow the plug maintenance procedures (Chapter 1).
☐ Spark plug caps or secondary (HT) wiring faulty. Check condition. Replace either or both components if cracks or deterioration are evident (Chapter 5).
☐ Spark plug caps not making good contact. Make sure that the plug caps fit snugly over the plug ends.
☐ Ignition control module defective. Check the module, referring to Chapter 5 for details.
☐ Pulse generator defective. Check the unit, referring to Chapter 5 for details.
☐ Ignition HT coils defective. Check the coils, referring to Chapter 5.
☐ Ignition or kill switch shorted. This is usually caused by water, corrosion, damage or excessive wear. The switches can be disassembled and cleaned with electrical contact cleaner. If cleaning does not help, replace the switches (Chapter 9).
☐ Wiring shorted or broken between:

a) Ignition (main) switch and engine kill switch (or blown fuse)
b) Ignition control module and engine kill switch
c) Ignition control module and ignition HT coils
d) Ignition HT coils and spark plugs
e) Ignition control module and pulse generator

☐ Make sure that all wiring connections are clean, dry and tight. Look for chafed and broken wires (Chapters 5 and 9).

1 Engine doesn't start or is difficult to start (continued)

Compression low

☐ Spark plugs loose. Remove the plugs and inspect their threads. Reinstall and tighten to the specified torque (Chapter 1).

☐ Cylinder head not sufficiently tightened down. If the cylinder head is suspected of being loose, then there's a chance that the gasket or head is damaged if the problem has persisted for any length of time. The head bolts should be tightened to the proper torque in the correct sequence (Chapter 2).

☐ Improper valve clearance. This means that the valve is not closing completely and compression pressure is leaking past the valve. Check and adjust the valve clearances (Chapter 1).

☐ Cylinder and/or piston worn. Excessive wear will cause compression pressure to leak past the rings. This is usually accompanied by worn rings as well. A top-end overhaul is necessary (Chapter 2).

☐ Piston rings worn, weak, broken, or sticking. Broken or sticking piston rings usually indicate a lubrication or carburation problem that causes excess carbon deposits or seizures to form on the pistons and rings. Top-end overhaul is necessary (Chapter 2).

☐ Piston ring-to-groove clearance excessive. This is caused by excessive wear of the piston ring lands. Piston replacement is necessary (Chapter 2).

☐ Cylinder head gasket damaged. If the head is allowed to become loose, or if excessive carbon build-up on the piston crown and combustion chamber causes extremely high compression, the head gasket may leak. Retorquing the head is not always sufficient to restore the seal, so gasket replacement is necessary (Chapter 2).

☐ Cylinder head warped. This is caused by overheating or improperly tightened head bolts. Machine shop resurfacing or head replacement is necessary (Chapter 2).

☐ Valve spring broken or weak. Caused by component failure or wear; the springs must be replaced (Chapter 2).

☐ Valve not seating properly. This is caused by a bent valve (from over-revving or improper valve adjustment), burned valve or seat (improper carburation) or an accumulation of carbon deposits on the seat (from carburation or lubrication problems). The valves must be cleaned and/or replaced and the seats serviced if possible (Chapter 2).

Stalls after starting

☐ Improper choke action. Make sure the choke linkage shaft is getting a full stroke and staying in the out position (Chapter 4).

☐ Ignition malfunction. See Chapter 5.

☐ Carburetor malfunction. See Chapter 4.

☐ Fuel contaminated. The fuel can be contaminated with either dirt or water, or can change chemically if the machine is allowed to sit for several months or more. Drain the tank and float chambers (Chapter 4).

☐ Intake air leak. Check for loose carburetor-to-intake manifold connections, loose or missing vacuum gauge adapter screws or hoses, or loose carburetor tops (Chapter 4).

☐ Engine idle speed incorrect. Turn idle adjusting screw until the engine idles at the specified rpm (Chapter 1).

Rough idle

☐ Ignition malfunction. See Chapter 5.

☐ Idle speed incorrect. See Chapter 1.

☐ Carburetors not synchronized. Adjust carburetors with vacuum gauge or manometer set as described in Chapter 1.

☐ Carburetor malfunction. See Chapter 4.

☐ Fuel contaminated. The fuel can be contaminated with either dirt or water, or can change chemically if the machine is allowed to sit for several months or more. Drain the tank and float chambers (Chapter 4).

☐ Intake air leak. Check for loose carburetor-to-intake manifold connections, loose or missing vacuum gauge adapter screws or hoses, or loose carburetor tops (Chapter 4).

☐ Air filter clogged. Replace the air filter element (Chapter 1).

2 Poor running at low speeds

Spark weak

☐ Battery voltage low. Check and recharge battery (Chapter 9).

☐ Spark plugs fouled, defective or worn out. Refer to Chapter 1 for spark plug maintenance.

☐ Spark plug cap or HT wiring defective. Refer to Chapters 1 and 5 for details on the ignition system.

☐ Spark plug caps not making contact.

☐ Incorrect spark plugs. Wrong type, heat range or cap configuration. Check and install correct plugs listed in Chapter 1.

☐ Ignition control module defective. See Chapter 5.

☐ Pulse generator defective. See Chapter 5.

☐ Ignition HT coils defective. See Chapter 5.

Fuel/air mixture incorrect

☐ Pilot screws out of adjustment (Chapter 4).

☐ Pilot jet or air passage clogged. Remove and overhaul the carburetors (Chapter 4).

☐ Air bleed holes clogged. Remove carburetor and blow out all passages (Chapter 4).

☐ Air filter clogged, poorly sealed or missing (Chapter 1).

☐ Air filter housing poorly sealed. Look for cracks, holes or loose clamps and replace or repair defective parts.

☐ Fuel level too high or too low. Check the float height (Chapter 4).

☐ Fuel tank breather hose obstructed (not California models).

☐ Carburetor intake manifolds loose. Check for cracks, breaks, tears or loose clamps. Replace the rubber intake manifold joints if split or perished.

2 Poor running at low speeds (continued)

Compression low

- [ ] Spark plugs loose. Remove the plugs and inspect their threads. Reinstall and tighten to the specified torque (Chapter 1).
- [ ] Cylinder head not sufficiently tightened down. If the cylinder head is suspected of being loose, then there's a chance that the gasket and head are damaged if the problem has persisted for any length of time. The head bolts should be tightened to the proper torque in the correct sequence (Chapter 2).
- [ ] Improper valve clearance. This means that the valve is not closing completely and compression pressure is leaking past the valve. Check and adjust the valve clearances (Chapter 1).
- [ ] Cylinder and/or piston worn. Excessive wear will cause compression pressure to leak past the rings. This is usually accompanied by worn rings as well. A top end overhaul is necessary (Chapter 2).
- [ ] Piston rings worn, weak, broken, or sticking. Broken or sticking piston rings usually indicate a lubrication or carburation problem that causes excess carbon deposits or seizures to form on the pistons and rings. Top-end overhaul is necessary (Chapter 2).
- [ ] Piston ring-to-groove clearance excessive. This is caused by excessive wear of the piston ring lands. Piston replacement is necessary (Chapter 2).
- [ ] Cylinder head gasket damaged. If the head is allowed to become loose, or if excessive carbon build-up on the piston crown and combustion chamber causes extremely high compression, the head gasket may leak. Retorquing the head is not always sufficient to restore the seal, so gasket replacement is necessary (Chapter 2).

- [ ] Cylinder head warped. This is caused by overheating or improperly tightened head bolts. Machine shop resurfacing or head replacement is necessary (Chapter 2).
- [ ] Valve spring broken or weak. Caused by component failure or wear; the springs must be replaced (Chapter 2).
- [ ] Valve not seating properly. This is caused by a bent valve (from over-revving or improper valve adjustment), burned valve or seat (improper carburation) or an accumulation of carbon deposits on the seat (from carburation, lubrication problems). The valves must be cleaned and/or replaced and the seats serviced if possible (Chapter 2).

Poor acceleration

- [ ] Carburetors leaking or dirty. Overhaul the carburetors (Chapter 4).
- [ ] Timing not advancing. The pulse generator or the ignition control module may be defective. If so, they must be replaced with new ones, as they can't be repaired.
- [ ] Carburetors not synchronized. Adjust them with a vacuum gauge set or manometer (Chapter 1).
- [ ] Engine oil viscosity too high. Using a heavier oil than that recommended in Chapter 1 can damage the oil pump or lubrication system and cause drag on the engine.
- [ ] Brakes dragging. Usually caused by debris which has entered the brake piston seals, or from a warped disc or bent axle. Repair as necessary (Chapter 7).

3 Poor running or no power at high speed

Firing incorrect

- [ ] Air filter restricted. Clean or replace filter (Chapter 1).
- [ ] Spark plugs fouled, defective or worn out. See Chapter 1 for spark plug maintenance.
- [ ] Spark plug caps or HT wiring defective. See Chapters 1 and 5 for details of the ignition system.
- [ ] Spark plug caps not in good contact. See Chapter 5.
- [ ] Incorrect spark plugs. Wrong type, heat range or cap configuration. Check and install correct plugs listed in Chapter 1.
- [ ] Ignition control module defective. See Chapter 5.
- [ ] Ignition coils defective. See Chapter 5.

Fuel/air mixture incorrect

- [ ] Main jet clogged. Dirt, water or other contaminants can clog the main jets. Clean the fuel tap filter, the in-line filter, the float chamber area, and the jets and carburetor orifices (Chapter 4).
- [ ] Main jet wrong size. The standard jetting is for sea level atmospheric pressure and oxygen content.
- [ ] Throttle shaft-to-carburetor body clearance excessive. Refer to Chapter 4 for inspection and part replacement procedures.
- [ ] Air bleed holes clogged. Remove and overhaul carburetors (Chapter 4).
- [ ] Air filter clogged, poorly sealed, or missing (Chapter 1).
- [ ] Air filter housing poorly sealed. Look for cracks, holes or loose clamps, and replace or repair defective parts.
- [ ] Fuel level too high or too low. Check the float height (Chapter 4).
- [ ] Fuel tank breather hose obstructed (not California models).
- [ ] Carburetor intake manifolds loose. Check for cracks, breaks, tears or loose clamps. Replace the rubber intake manifolds if they are split or perished (Chapter 4).

Compression low

- [ ] Spark plugs loose. Remove the plugs and inspect their threads. Reinstall and tighten to the specified torque (Chapter 1).
- [ ] Cylinder head not sufficiently tightened down. If the cylinder head is suspected of being loose, then there's a chance that the gasket and head are damaged if the problem has persisted for any length of time. The head bolts should be tightened to the proper torque in the correct sequence (Chapter 2).
- [ ] Improper valve clearance. This means that the valve is not closing completely and compression pressure is leaking past the valve. Check and adjust the valve clearances (Chapter 1).
- [ ] Cylinder and/or piston worn. Excessive wear will cause compression pressure to leak past the rings. This is usually accompanied by worn rings as well. A top-end overhaul is necessary (Chapter 2).
- [ ] Piston rings worn, weak, broken, or sticking. Broken or sticking piston rings usually indicate a lubrication or carburation problem that causes excess carbon deposits or seizures to form on the pistons and rings. Top-end overhaul is necessary (Chapter 2).
- [ ] Piston ring-to-groove clearance excessive. This is caused by excessive wear of the piston ring lands. Piston replacement is necessary (Chapter 2).
- [ ] Cylinder head gasket damaged. If the head is allowed to become loose, or if excessive carbon build-up on the piston crown and combustion chamber causes extremely high compression, the head gasket may leak. Retorquing the head is not always sufficient to restore the seal, so gasket replacement is necessary (Chapter 2).
- [ ] Cylinder head warped. This is caused by overheating or improperly tightened head bolts. Machine shop resurfacing or head replacement is necessary (Chapter 2).

3 Poor running or no power at high speed (continued)

Compression low (continued)

☐ Valve spring broken or weak. Caused by component failure or wear; the springs must be replaced (Chapter 2).

☐ Valve not seating properly. This is caused by a bent valve (from over-revving or improper valve adjustment), burned valve or seat (improper carburation) or an accumulation of carbon deposits on the seat (from carburation or lubrication problems). The valves must be cleaned and/or replaced and the seats serviced if possible (Chapter 2).

Knocking or pinking

☐ Carbon build-up in combustion chamber. Use of a fuel additive that will dissolve the adhesive bonding the carbon particles to the crown and chamber is the easiest way to remove the build-up. Otherwise, the cylinder head will have to be removed and decarbonized (Chapter 2).

☐ Incorrect or poor quality fuel. Old or improper grades of fuel can cause detonation. This causes the piston to rattle, thus the knocking or pinking sound. Drain old fuel and always use the recommended fuel grade.

☐ Spark plug heat range incorrect. Uncontrolled detonation indicates the plug heat range is too hot. The plug in effect becomes a glow plug, raising cylinder temperatures. Install the proper heat range plug (Chapter 1).

☐ Improper air/fuel mixture. This will cause the cylinder to run hot, which leads to detonation. Clogged jets or an air leak can cause this imbalance. See Chapter 4.

Miscellaneous causes

☐ Throttle valve doesn't open fully. Adjust the throttle grip freeplay (Chapter 1).

☐ Clutch slipping. May be caused by loose or worn clutch components. Refer to Chapter 2 for clutch overhaul procedures.

☐ Timing not advancing.

☐ Engine oil viscosity too high. Using a heavier oil than the one recommended in Chapter 1 can damage the oil pump or lubrication system and cause drag on the engine.

☐ Brakes dragging. Usually caused by debris which has entered the brake piston seals, or from a warped disc or bent axle. Repair as necessary.

4 Overheating

Engine overheats

☐ Coolant level low. Check and add coolant (Chapter 1).

☐ Leak in cooling system. Check cooling system hoses and radiator for leaks and other damage. Repair or replace parts as necessary (Chapter 3).

☐ Thermostat sticking open or closed. Check and replace as described in Chapter 3.

☐ Faulty radiator cap. Remove the cap and have it pressure tested.

☐ Coolant passages clogged. Have the entire system drained and flushed, then refill with fresh coolant.

☐ Water pump defective. Remove the pump and check the components (Chapter 3).

☐ Clogged radiator fins. Clean them by blowing compressed air through the fins from the backside.

☐ Cooling fan or fan switch fault (Chapter 3).

Firing incorrect

☐ Spark plugs fouled, defective or worn out. See Chapter 1 for spark plug maintenance.

☐ Incorrect spark plugs.

☐ Faulty ignition HT coils (Chapter 5).

Fuel/air mixture incorrect

☐ Main jet clogged. Dirt, water and other contaminants can clog the main jets. Clean the fuel tap filter, the fuel pump in-line filter, the float chamber area and the jets and carburetor orifices (Chapter 4).

☐ Main jet wrong size. The standard jetting is for sea level atmospheric pressure and oxygen content.

☐ Air filter clogged, poorly sealed or missing (Chapter 1).

☐ Air filter housing poorly sealed. Look for cracks, holes or loose clamps and replace or repair.

☐ Fuel level too low. Check float height (Chapter 4).

☐ Fuel tank breather hose obstructed (not California models).

☐ Carburetor intake manifolds loose. Check for cracks, breaks, tears or loose clamps. Replace the rubber intake manifold joints if split or perished.

Compression too high

☐ Carbon build-up in combustion chamber. Use of a fuel additive that will dissolve the adhesive bonding the carbon particles to the piston crown and chamber is the easiest way to remove the build-up. Otherwise, the cylinder head will have to be removed and decarbonized (Chapter 2).

☐ Improperly machined head surface or installation of incorrect gasket during engine assembly.

Engine load excessive

☐ Clutch slipping. Can be caused by damaged, loose or worn clutch components. Refer to Chapter 2 for overhaul procedures.

☐ Engine oil level too high. The addition of too much oil will cause pressurization of the crankcase and inefficient engine operation. Check Specifications and drain to proper level (Chapter 1).

☐ Engine oil viscosity too high. Using a heavier oil than the one recommended in Chapter 1 can damage the oil pump or lubrication system as well as cause drag on the engine.

☐ Brakes dragging. Usually caused by debris which has entered the brake piston seals, or from a warped disc or bent axle. Repair as necessary.

Lubrication inadequate

☐ Engine oil level too low. Friction caused by intermittent lack of lubrication or from oil that is overworked can cause overheating. The oil provides a definite cooling function in the engine. Check the oil level (Chapter 1).

☐ Poor quality engine oil or incorrect viscosity or type. Oil is rated not only according to viscosity but also according to type. Some oils are not rated high enough for use in this engine. Check the Specifications section and change to the correct oil (Chapter 1).

Miscellaneous causes

☐ Modification to exhaust system. Most aftermarket exhaust systems cause the engine to run leaner, which make them run hotter. When installing an accessory exhaust system, always rejet the carburetors.

5 Clutch problems

Clutch slipping

- [ ] Cable freeplay insufficient. Check and adjust cable (Chapter 1).
- [ ] Friction plates worn or warped. Overhaul the clutch assembly (Chapter 2).
- [ ] Plain plates warped (Chapter 2).
- [ ] Clutch springs broken or weak. Old or heat-damaged (from slipping clutch) springs should be replaced with new ones (Chapter 2).
- [ ] Clutch release mechanism defective. Replace any defective parts (Chapter 2).
- [ ] Clutch center or outer drum unevenly worn. This causes improper engagement of the plates. Replace the damaged or worn parts (Chapter 2).

Clutch not disengaging completely (dragging)

- [ ] Cable freeplay excessive. Check and adjust cable (Chapter 1).
- [ ] Clutch plates warped or damaged. This will cause clutch drag, which in turn will cause the machine to creep. Overhaul the clutch assembly (Chapter 2).

- [ ] Clutch spring tension uneven. Usually caused by a sagged or broken spring. Check and replace the springs as a set (Chapter 2).
- [ ] Engine oil deteriorated. Old, thin, worn out oil will not provide proper lubrication for the plates, causing the clutch to drag. Replace the oil and filter (Chapter 1).
- [ ] Engine oil viscosity too high. Using a heavier oil than recommended in Chapter 1 can cause the plates to stick together, putting a drag on the engine. Change to the correct weight oil (Chapter 1).
- [ ] Clutch outer drum guide seized on mainshaft. Lack of lubrication, severe wear or damage can cause the guide to seize on the shaft. Overhaul of the clutch, and perhaps transmission, may be necessary to repair the damage (Chapter 2).
- [ ] Clutch release mechanism defective. Overhaul the clutch cover components (Chapter 2).
- [ ] Loose clutch center nut. Causes drum and center misalignment putting a drag on the engine. Engagement adjustment continually varies. Overhaul the clutch assembly (Chapter 2).

6 Gear shifting problems

Doesn't go into gear or lever doesn't return

- [ ] Clutch not disengaging. See Section 5.
- [ ] Shift fork(s) bent or seized. This is often caused by dropping the machine or from lack of lubrication. Overhaul the transmission (Chapter 2).
- [ ] Gear(s) stuck on shaft. Most often caused by a lack of lubrication or excessive wear in transmission bearings and bushings. Overhaul the transmission (Chapter 2).
- [ ] Gearshift drum binding. Caused by lubrication failure or excessive wear. Replace the drum and bearing (Chapter 2).
- [ ] Gearshift lever return spring weak or broken (Chapter 2).
- [ ] Gearshift lever broken. Splines stripped out of lever or shaft, caused by allowing the lever to get loose or from dropping the machine. Replace necessary parts (Chapter 2).

- [ ] Gearshift mechanism stopper arm broken or worn. Full engagement and rotary movement of shift drum results. Replace the arm (Chapter 2).
- [ ] Stopper arm spring broken. Allows arm to float, causing sporadic shift operation. Replace spring (Chapter 2).

Jumps out of gear

- [ ] Shift fork(s) worn. Overhaul the transmission (Chapter 2).
- [ ] Gear groove(s) worn. Overhaul the transmission (Chapter 2).
- [ ] Gear dogs or dog slots worn or damaged. The gears should be inspected and replaced. No attempt should be made to service the worn parts.

Overshifts

- [ ] Stopper arm spring weak or broken (Chapter 2).
- [ ] Gearshift shaft return spring post broken or distorted (Chapter 2).

7 Abnormal engine noise

Knocking or pinking

- [ ] Carbon build-up in combustion chamber. Use of a fuel additive that will dissolve the adhesive bonding the carbon particles to the piston crown and chamber is the easiest way to remove the build-up. Otherwise, the cylinder head will have to be removed and decarbonized (Chapter 2).
- [ ] Incorrect or poor quality fuel. Old or improper fuel can cause detonation. This causes the pistons to rattle, thus the knocking or pinking sound. Drain the old fuel and always use the recommended grade fuel (Chapter 4).
- [ ] Spark plug heat range incorrect. Uncontrolled detonation indicates that the plug heat range is too hot. The plug in effect becomes a glow plug, raising cylinder temperatures. Install the proper heat range plug (Chapter 1).
- [ ] Improper air/fuel mixture. This will cause the cylinders to run hot and lead to detonation. Clogged jets or an air leak can cause this imbalance. See Chapter 4.

Piston slap or rattling

- [ ] Cylinder-to-piston clearance excessive. Caused by improper assembly. Inspect and overhaul top-end parts (Chapter 2).
- [ ] Connecting rod bent. Usually caused by over-revving, trying to start a badly flooded engine or from ingesting a foreign object

into the combustion chamber. Replace the damaged parts (Chapter 2).
- [ ] Piston pin or piston pin bore worn or seized from wear or lack of lubrication. Replace damaged parts (Chapter 2).
- [ ] Piston ring(s) worn, broken or sticking. Overhaul the top-end (Chapter 2).
- [ ] Piston seizure damage. Usually from lack of lubrication or overheating. Replace the pistons and bore the cylinders, as necessary (Chapter 2).
- [ ] Connecting rod upper or lower end clearance excessive. Caused by excessive wear or lack of lubrication. Replace worn parts.

Valve noise

- [ ] Incorrect valve clearances. Adjust the clearances (see Chapter 1).
- [ ] Valve spring broken or weak. Check and replace weak valve springs (Chapter 2).
- [ ] Camshaft or cylinder head worn or damaged. Lack of lubrication at high rpm is usually the cause of damage. Insufficient oil or failure to change the oil at the recommended intervals are the chief causes. Since there are no replaceable bearings in the head, the head itself will have to be replaced if there is excessive wear or damage (Chapter 2).

7 Abnormal engine noise (continued)

Other noise

☐ Cylinder head gasket leaking.

☐ Exhaust pipe leaking at cylinder head connection. Caused by improper fit of pipe(s) or loose exhaust flange. All exhaust fasteners should be tightened evenly and carefully. Failure to do this will lead to a leak.

☐ Crankshaft runout excessive. Caused by a bent crankshaft (from over-revving) or damage from an upper cylinder component failure. Can also be attributed to dropping the machine on either of the crankshaft ends.

☐ Engine mounting bolts loose. Tighten all mountings (Chapter 2).

☐ Crankshaft bearings worn (Chapter 2).

☐ Cam chain tensioner defective. Replace according to the procedure in Chapter 2.

☐ Cam chain, sprockets or guides worn (Chapter 2).

8 Abnormal driveline noise

Clutch noise

☐ Clutch outer drum/friction plate clearance excessive (Chapter 2).

☐ Loose or damaged clutch pressure plate and/or bolts (Chapter 2).

Transmission noise

☐ Bearings worn. Also includes the possibility that the shafts are worn. Overhaul the transmission (Chapter 2).

☐ Gears worn or chipped (Chapter 2).

☐ Metal chips jammed in gear teeth. Probably pieces from a broken clutch, gear or shift mechanism that were picked up by the gears. This will cause early bearing failure (Chapter 2).

☐ Engine oil level too low. Causes a howl from transmission. Also affects engine power and clutch operation (Chapter 1).

Final drive noise

☐ Final drive oil level low (Chapter 1).

☐ Final drive gear lash incorrect. Refer to a Honda dealer for advice.

☐ Final drive gears worn or damaged (Chapter 6).

☐ Final drive bearings worn (Chapter 6).

☐ Driveshaft splines worn and slipping (Chapter 6).

9 Abnormal frame and suspension noise

Front end noise

☐ Low fluid level or improper viscosity oil in forks. This can sound like spurting and is usually accompanied by irregular fork action (Chapter 6).

☐ Spring weak or broken. Makes a clicking or scraping sound. Fork oil, when drained, will have a lot of metal particles in it (Chapter 6).

☐ Steering head bearings loose or damaged. Clicks when braking. Check and adjust or replace as necessary (Chapters 1 and 6).

☐ Fork triple clamps loose. Make sure all clamp pinch bolts are tight (Chapter 6).

☐ Fork tube bent. Good possibility if machine has been dropped. Replace tube with a new one (Chapter 6).

☐ Front axle or axle clamp bolt loose. Tighten them to the specified torque (Chapter 6).

Shock absorber noise

☐ Fluid level incorrect. Indicates a leak caused by defective seal. Shock will be covered with oil. Replace shock or seek advice on repair from a Honda dealer (Chapter 6).

☐ Defective shock absorber with internal damage. This is in the body of the shock and can't be remedied. The shock must be replaced with a new one (Chapter 6).

☐ Bent or damaged shock body. Replace the shock with a new one (Chapter 6).

Brake noise

☐ Squeal caused by pad shim not installed or positioned correctly - rear caliper (Chapter 7).

☐ Squeal caused by dust on brake pads. Usually found in combination with glazed pads. Clean using brake cleaning solvent (Chapter 7).

☐ Contamination of brake pads. Oil, brake fluid or dirt causing brake to chatter or squeal. Clean or replace pads (Chapter 7).

☐ Pads glazed. Caused by excessive heat from prolonged use or from contamination. Do not use sandpaper, emery cloth, carborundum cloth or any other abrasive to roughen the pad surfaces as abrasives will stay in the pad material and damage the disc. A very fine flat file can be used, but pad replacement is suggested as a cure (Chapter 7).

☐ Disc warped. Can cause a chattering, clicking or intermittent squeal. Usually accompanied by a pulsating lever and uneven braking. Replace the disc (Chapter 7).

☐ Loose or worn wheel bearings. Check and replace as needed (Chapter 7).

10 Oil pressure indicator light comes on

Engine lubrication system

☐ Engine oil pump defective, blocked oil strainer gauze or failed relief valve. Carry out oil pressure check (Chapter 2).

☐ Engine oil level low. Inspect for leak or other problem causing low oil level and add recommended oil (Chapter 1).

☐ Engine oil viscosity too low. Very old, thin oil or an improper weight of oil used in the engine. Change to correct oil (Chapter 1).

☐ Camshaft or journals worn. Excessive wear causing drop in oil pressure. Replace cam and/or cylinder head. Abnormal wear

could be caused by oil starvation at high rpm from low oil level or improper weight or type of oil (Chapter 1).

☐ Crankshaft and/or bearings worn. Same problems as paragraph 4. Check and replace crankshaft and/or bearings (Chapter 2).

Electrical system

☐ Oil pressure switch defective. Check the switch according to the procedure in Chapter 9. Replace it if it is defective.

☐ Oil pressure indicator light circuit defective. Check for pinched, shorted, disconnected or damaged wiring (Chapter 9).

11 Excessive exhaust smoke

White smoke

- [ ] Piston oil ring worn. The ring may be broken or damaged, causing oil from the crankcase to be pulled past the piston into the combustion chamber. Replace the rings with new ones (Chapter 2).
- [ ] Cylinders worn, cracked, or scored. Caused by overheating or oil starvation. The cylinders will have to be rebored and new pistons installed.
- [ ] Valve oil seal damaged or worn. Replace oil seals with new ones (Chapter 2).
- [ ] Valve guide worn. Perform a complete valve job (Chapter 2).
- [ ] Engine oil level too high, which causes the oil to be forced past the rings. Drain oil to the proper level (Chapter 1).
- [ ] Head gasket broken between oil return and cylinder. Causes oil to be pulled into the combustion chamber. Replace the head gasket and check the head for warpage (Chapter 2).
- [ ] Abnormal crankcase pressurization, which forces oil past the rings. Clogged breather hose is usually the cause.

Black smoke

- [ ] Air filter clogged. Clean or replace the element (Chapter 1).
- [ ] Main jet too large or loose. Compare the jet size to the Specifications (Chapter 4).
- [ ] Choke cable or linkage shaft stuck, causing fuel to be pulled through choke circuit (Chapter 4).
- [ ] Fuel level too high. Check and adjust the float height(s) as necessary (Chapter 4).
- [ ] Float needle valve held off needle seat. Clean the float chambers and fuel line and replace the needles and seats if necessary (Chapter 4).

Brown smoke

- [ ] Main jet too small or clogged. Lean condition caused by wrong size main jet or by a restricted orifice. Clean float chambers and jets and compare jet size to Specifications (Chapter 4).
- [ ] Fuel flow insufficient. Float needle valve stuck closed due to chemical reaction with old fuel. Float height incorrect. Restricted fuel line. Clean line and float chamber and adjust floats if necessary.
- [ ] Carburetor intake manifold clamps loose (Chapter 4).
- [ ] Air filter poorly sealed or not installed (Chapter 1).

12 Poor handling or stability

Handlebar hard to turn

- [ ] Steering head bearing adjuster nut too tight. Check adjustment as described in Chapter 1.
- [ ] Bearings damaged. Roughness can be felt as the bars are turned from side-to-side. Replace bearings and races (Chapter 6).
- [ ] Races dented or worn. Denting results from wear in only one position (eg, straightahead), from a collision or hitting a pothole or from dropping the machine. Replace races and bearings (Chapter 6).
- [ ] Steering stem lubrication inadequate. Causes are grease getting hard from age or being washed out by high pressure car washes. Disassemble steering head and repack bearings (Chapter 6).
- [ ] Steering stem bent. Caused by a collision, hitting a pothole or by dropping the machine. Replace damaged part. Don't try to straighten the steering stem (Chapter 6).
- [ ] Front tire air pressure too low (Chapter 1).

Handlebar shakes or vibrates excessively

- [ ] Tires worn or out of balance (Chapter 7).
- [ ] Swingarm bearings worn. Replace worn bearings by referring to Chapter 6.
- [ ] Rim(s) warped or damaged. Inspect wheels for runout (Chapter 7).
- [ ] Wheel bearings worn. Worn front or rear wheel bearings can cause poor tracking. Worn front bearings will cause wobble (Chapter 7).
- [ ] Handlebar clamp bolts loose (Chapter 6).
- [ ] Fork triple clamp bolts loose. Tighten them to the specified torque (Chapter 6).
- [ ] Engine mounting bolts loose. Will cause excessive vibration with increased engine rpm (Chapter 2).

Handlebar pulls to one side

- [ ] Frame bent. Definitely suspect this if the machine has been dropped. May or may not be accompanied by cracking near the bend. Replace the frame (Chapter 6).
- [ ] Wheels out of alignment. Caused by improper location of axle spacers or from bent steering stem or frame (Chapter 6).
- [ ] Swingarm bent or twisted. Caused by age (metal fatigue) or impact damage. Replace the arm (Chapter 6).
- [ ] Steering stem bent. Caused by impact damage or by dropping the motorcycle. Replace the steering stem (Chapter 6).
- [ ] Fork tube bent. Disassemble the forks and replace the damaged parts (Chapter 6).
- [ ] Fork oil level uneven. Check and add or drain as necessary (Chapter 6).

Poor shock absorbing qualities

- [ ] Too hard:

  a) *Fork oil level excessive (Chapter 6).*
  b) *Fork oil viscosity too high. Use a lighter oil (see the Specifications in Chapter 6).*
  c) *Fork tube bent. Causes a harsh, sticking feeling (Chapter 6).*
  d) *Shock shaft or body bent or damaged (Chapter 6).*
  e) *Fork internal damage (Chapter 6).*
  f) *Shock internal damage.*
  g) *Tire pressure too high (Chapter 1).*

- [ ] Too soft:

  a) *Fork or shock oil insufficient and/or leaking (Chapter 6).*
  b) *Fork oil level too low (Chapter 6).*
  c) *Fork oil viscosity too light (Chapter 6).*
  d) *Fork springs weak or broken (Chapter 6).*
  e) *Shock internal damage or leakage (Chapter 6).*

13 Braking problems

Brakes are spongy, don't hold

- [ ] Air in brake line. Caused by inattention to master cylinder fluid level or by leakage. Locate problem and bleed brakes (Chapter 7).
- [ ] Pad or disc worn (Chapters 1 and 7).
- [ ] Brake fluid leak. See paragraph 1.
- [ ] Contaminated pads. Caused by contamination with oil, grease, brake fluid, etc. Clean or replace pads. Clean disc thoroughly with brake cleaner (Chapter 7).
- [ ] Brake fluid deteriorated. Fluid is old or contaminated. Drain system, replenish with new fluid and bleed the system (Chapter 7).
- [ ] Master cylinder internal parts worn or damaged causing fluid to bypass (Chapter 7).
- [ ] Master cylinder bore scratched by foreign material or broken spring. Repair or replace master cylinder (Chapter 7).
- [ ] Disc warped. Replace disc (Chapter 7).

Brake lever or pedal pulsates

- [ ] Disc warped. Replace disc (Chapter 7).
- [ ] Axle bent. Replace axle (Chapter 7).
- [ ] Brake caliper bolts loose (Chapter 7).
- [ ] Brake caliper sliders damaged or sticking (rear caliper), causing caliper to bind. Lube the sliders or replace them if they are corroded or bent (Chapter 7).
- [ ] Wheel warped or otherwise damaged (Chapter 7).
- [ ] Wheel bearings damaged or worn (Chapter 7).

Brakes drag

- [ ] Master cylinder piston seized. Caused by wear or damage to piston or cylinder bore (Chapter 7).
- [ ] Lever balky or stuck. Check pivot and lubricate (Chapter 7).
- [ ] Brake caliper binds. Caused by inadequate lubrication or damage to caliper sliders (Chapter 7).
- [ ] Brake caliper piston seized in bore. Caused by wear or ingestion of dirt past deteriorated seal (Chapter 7).
- [ ] Brake pad damaged. Pad material separated from backing plate. Usually caused by faulty manufacturing process or from contact with chemicals. Replace pads (Chapter 7).
- [ ] Pads improperly installed (Chapter 7).

14 Electrical problems

Battery dead or weak

- [ ] Battery faulty. Caused by sulfated plates which are shorted through sedimentation. Also, broken battery terminal making only occasional contact (Chapter 9). Refer to *Fault Finding Equipment* for battery voltage and specific gravity checks.
- [ ] Battery cables making poor contact (Chapter 9).
- [ ] Load excessive. Caused by addition of high wattage lights or other electrical accessories.
- [ ] Ignition (main) switch defective. Switch either grounds (earths) internally or fails to shut off system. Replace the switch (Chapter 9).
- [ ] Regulator/rectifier defective (Chapter 9).
- [ ] Alternator stator coil open or shorted (Chapter 9).
- [ ] Wiring faulty. Wiring grounded (earthed) or connections loose in ignition, charging or lighting circuits (Chapter 9).

Battery overcharged

- [ ] Regulator/rectifier defective. Overcharging is noticed when battery gets excessively warm (Chapter 9).
- [ ] Battery defective. Replace battery with a new one (Chapter 9).
- [ ] Battery amperage too low, wrong type or size. Install manufacturer's specified amp-hour battery to handle charging load (Chapter 9).

Fault Finding Equipment

Checking engine compression

● Low compression will result in exhaust smoke, heavy oil consumption, poor starting and poor performance. A compression test will provide useful information about an engine's condition and if performed regularly, can give warning of trouble before any other symptoms become apparent.

● A compression gauge will be required, along with an adapter to suit the spark plug hole thread size. Note that the screw-in type gauge/adapter set up is preferable to the rubber cone type.

● Before carrying out the test, first check the valve clearances as described in Chapter 1.

1 Run the engine until it reaches normal operating temperature, then stop it and remove the spark plug(s), taking care not to scald your hands on the hot components.

2 Install the gauge adapter and compression gauge in No. 1 cylinder spark plug hole (see illustration 1).

3 On kickstart-equipped motorcycles, make sure the ignition switch is OFF, then open the throttle fully and kick the engine over a couple of times until the gauge reading stabilises.

4 On motorcycles with electric start only, the procedure will differ depending on the nature of the ignition system. Flick the engine kill switch (engine stop switch) to OFF and turn

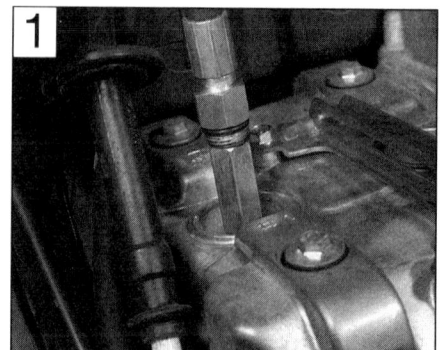

Screw the compression gauge adapter into the spark plug hole, then screw the gauge into the adapter

the ignition switch ON; open the throttle fully and crank the engine over on the starter motor for a couple of revolutions until the gauge reading stabilises. If the starter will not operate with the kill switch OFF, turn the ignition switch OFF and refer to the next paragraph.

5 Install the spark plugs back into their suppressor caps and arrange the plug electrodes so that their metal bodies are earthed (grounded) against the cylinder head; this is essential to prevent damage to the ignition system as the engine is spun over **(see illustration 2)**. Position the plugs well away from the plug holes otherwise there is a risk of atomised fuel escaping from the combustion chambers and igniting. As a safety precaution, cover the top of the valve cover with rag. Now turn the ignition switch ON and kill switch ON, open the throttle fully and crank the engine over on the starter motor for a couple of revolutions until the gauge reading stabilises.

All spark plugs must be earthed (grounded) against the cylinder head

6 After one or two revolutions the pressure should build up to a maximum figure and then stabilise. Take a note of this reading and on multi-cylinder engines repeat the test on the remaining cylinders.

7 The correct pressures are given in Chapter 2 Specifications. If the results fall within the specified range and on multi-cylinder engines all are relatively equal, the engine is in good condition. If there is a marked difference between the readings, or if the readings are lower than specified, inspection of the top-end components will be required.

8 Low compression pressure may be due to worn cylinder bores, pistons or rings, failure of the cylinder head gasket, worn valve seals, or poor valve seating.

9 To distinguish between cylinder/piston wear and valve leakage, pour a small quantity of oil into the bore to temporarily seal the piston rings, then repeat the compression tests **(see illustration 3)**. If the readings show a noticeable increase in pressure this confirms that the cylinder bore, piston, or rings are worn. If, however, no change is indicated, the cylinder head gasket or valves should be examined.

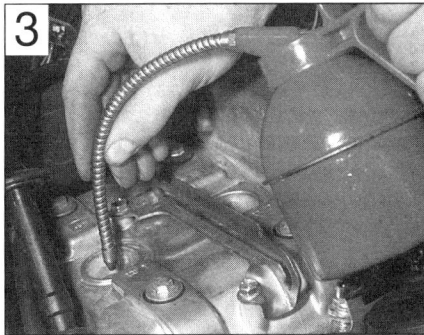

Bores can be temporarily sealed with a squirt of motor oil

10 High compression pressure indicates excessive carbon build-up in the combustion chamber and on the piston crown. If this is the case the cylinder head should be removed and the deposits removed. Note that excessive carbon build-up is less likely with the used on modern fuels.

Checking battery open-circuit voltage

⚠ *Warning: The gases produced by the battery are explosive - never smoke or create any sparks in the vicinity of the battery. Never allow the electrolyte to contact your skin or clothing - if it does, wash it off and seek immediate medical attention.*

● Before any electrical fault is investigated the battery should be checked.

● You'll need a dc voltmeter or multimeter to check battery voltage. Check that the leads are inserted in the correct terminals on the meter, red lead to positive (+ve), black lead to negative (-ve). Incorrect connections can damage the meter.

● A sound fully-charged 12 volt battery should produce between 12.3 and 12.6 volts across its terminals (12.8 volts for a maintenance-free battery). On machines with a 6 volt battery, voltage should be between 6.1 and 6.3 volts.

1 Set a multimeter to the 0 to 20 volts dc range and connect its probes across the

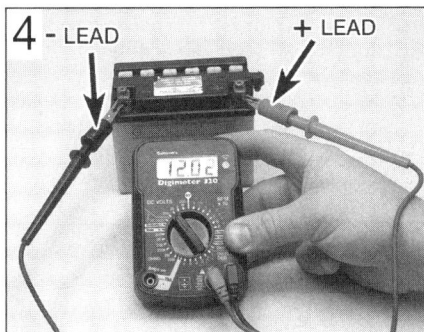

Measuring open-circuit battery voltage

battery terminals. Connect the meter's positive (+ve) probe, usually red, to the battery positive (+ve) terminal, followed by the meter's negative (-ve) probe, usually black, to the battery negative terminal (-ve) **(see illustration 4)**.

2 If battery voltage is low (below 10 volts on a 12 volt battery or below 4 volts on a six volt battery), charge the battery and test the voltage again. If the battery repeatedly goes flat, investigate the motorcycle's charging system.

Checking battery specific gravity (SG)

⚠ *Warning: The gases produced by the battery are explosive - never smoke or create any sparks in the vicinity of the battery. Never allow the electrolyte to contact your skin or clothing - if it does, wash it off and seek immediate medical attention.*

● The specific gravity check gives an indication of a battery's state of charge.

● A hydrometer is used for measuring specific gravity. Make sure you purchase one which has a small enough hose to insert in the aperture of a motorcycle battery.

● Specific gravity is simply a measure of the electrolyte's density compared with that of water. Water has an SG of 1.000 and fully-charged battery electrolyte is about 26% heavier, at 1.260.

● Specific gravity checks are not possible on maintenance-free batteries. Testing the open-circuit voltage is the only means of determining their state of charge.

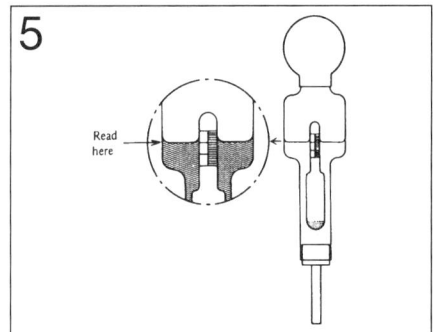

Float-type hydrometer for measuring battery specific gravity

1 To measure SG, remove the battery from the motorcycle and remove the first cell cap. Draw some electrolyte into the hydrometer and note the reading **(see illustration 5)**. Return the electrolyte to the cell and install the cap.

2 The reading should be in the region of 1.260 to 1.280. If SG is below 1.200 the battery needs charging. Note that SG will vary with temperature; it should be measured at 20°C (68°F). Add 0.007 to the reading for every 10°C above 20°C, and subtract 0.007 from the reading for every 10°C below 20°C. Add 0.004 to the reading for every 10°F above 68°F, and subtract 0.004 from the reading for every 10°F below 68°F.

3 When the check is complete, rinse the hydrometer thoroughly with clean water.

Checking for continuity

● The term continuity describes the uninterrupted flow of electricity through an electrical circuit. A continuity check will determine whether an **open-circuit** situation exists.

● Continuity can be checked with an ohmmeter, multimeter, continuity tester or battery and bulb test circuit **(see illustrations 6, 7 and 8)**.

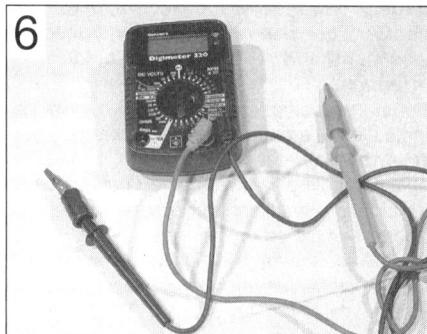

Digital multimeter can be used for all electrical tests

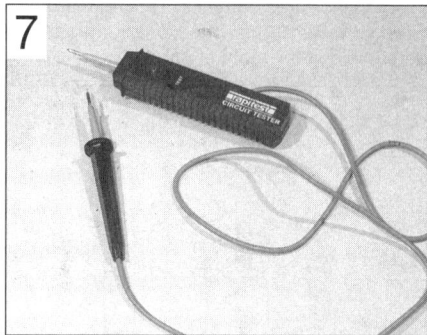

Battery-powered continuity tester

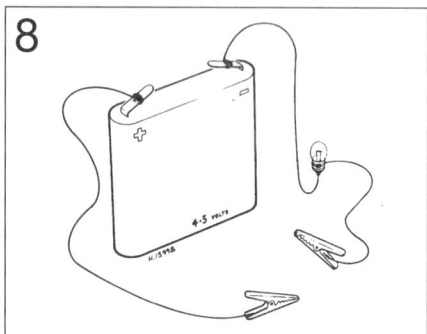

Battery and bulb test circuit

● All of these instruments are self-powered by a battery, therefore the checks are made with the ignition OFF.

● As a safety precaution, always disconnect the battery negative (-ve) lead before making checks, particularly if ignition switch checks are being made.

● If using a meter, select the appropriate ohms scale and check that the meter reads infinity (∞). Touch the meter probes together and check that meter reads zero; where necessary adjust the meter so that it reads zero.

● After using a meter, always switch it OFF to conserve its battery.

Switch checks

1 If a switch is at fault, trace its wiring up to the wiring connectors. Separate the wire connectors and inspect them for security and condition. A build-up of dirt or corrosion here will most likely be the cause of the problem - clean up and apply a water dispersant such as WD40.

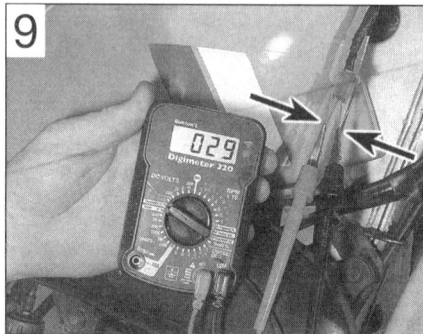

Continuity check of front brake light switch using a meter - note split pins used to access connector terminals

2 If using a test meter, set the meter to the ohms x 10 scale and connect its probes across the wires from the switch **(see illustration 9)**. Simple ON/OFF type switches, such as brake light switches, only have two wires whereas combination switches, like the ignition switch, have many internal links. Study the wiring diagram to ensure that you are connecting across the correct pair of wires. Continuity (low or no measurable resistance - 0 ohms) should be indicated with the switch ON and no continuity (high resistance) with it OFF.

3 Note that the polarity of the test probes doesn't matter for continuity checks, although care should be taken to follow specific test procedures if a diode or solid-state component is being checked.

4 A continuity tester or battery and bulb circuit can be used in the same way. Connect its probes as described above **(see illustration 10)**. The light should come on to indicate continuity in the ON switch position, but should extinguish in the OFF position.

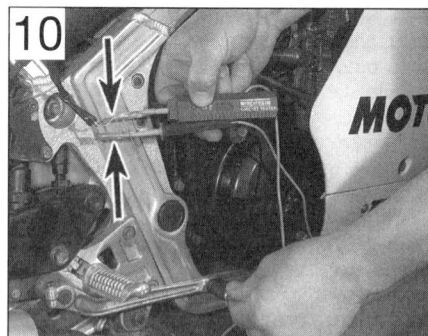

Continuity check of rear brake light switch using a continuity tester

Wiring checks

● Many electrical faults are caused by damaged wiring, often due to incorrect routing or chaffing on frame components.

● Loose, wet or corroded wire connectors can also be the cause of electrical problems, especially in exposed locations.

1 A continuity check can be made on a single length of wire by disconnecting it at each end and connecting a meter or continuity tester across both ends of the wire **(see illustration 11)**.

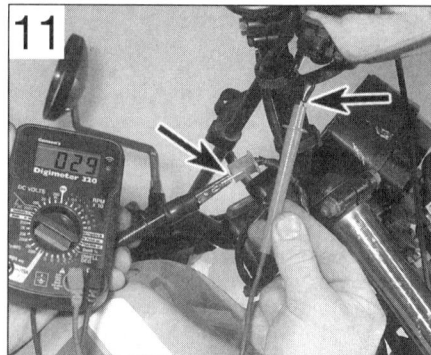

Continuity check of front brake light switch sub-harness

2 Continuity (low or no resistance - 0 ohms) should be indicated if the wire is good. If no continuity (high resistance) is shown, suspect a broken wire.

Checking for voltage

● A voltage check can determine whether current is reaching a component.

● Voltage can be checked with a dc voltmeter, multimeter set on the dc volts scale, test light or buzzer **(see illustrations 12 and 13)**. A meter has the advantage of being able to measure actual voltage.

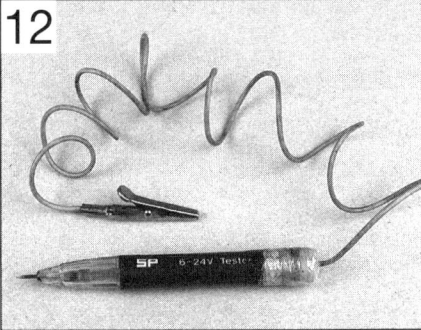

A simple test light can be used for voltage checks

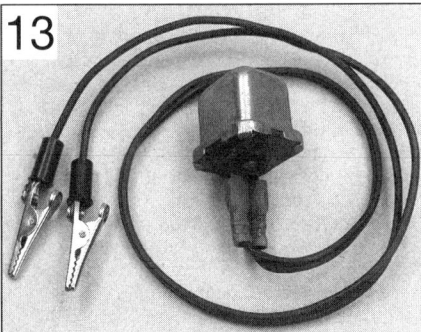

A buzzer is useful for voltage checks

● When using a meter, check that its leads are inserted in the correct terminals on the meter, red to positive (+ve), black to negative (-ve). Incorrect connections can damage the meter.

● A voltmeter (or multimeter set to the dc volts scale) should always be connected in parallel (across the load). Connecting it in series will destroy the meter.

● Voltage checks are made with the ignition ON.

1 First identify the relevant wiring circuit by referring to the wiring diagram at the end of this manual. If other electrical components share the same power supply (ie are fed from the same fuse), take note whether they are working correctly - this is useful information in deciding where to start checking the circuit.

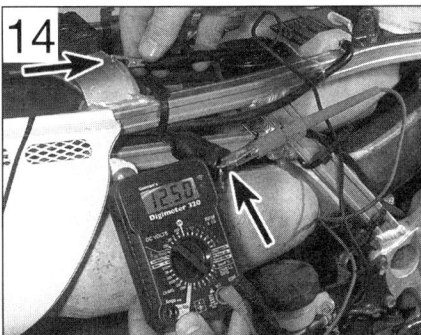

Checking for voltage at the rear brake light power supply wire using a meter . . .

2 If using a meter, check first that the meter leads are plugged into the correct terminals on the meter (see above). Set the meter to the dc volts function, at a range suitable for the battery voltage. Connect the meter red probe (+ve) to the power supply wire and the black probe to a good metal earth (ground) on the motorcycle's frame or directly to the battery negative (-ve) terminal **(see illustration 14)**. Battery voltage should be shown on the meter with the ignition switched ON.

3 If using a test light or buzzer, connect its positive (+ve) probe to the power supply terminal and its negative (-ve) probe to a good earth (ground) on the motorcycle's frame or directly to the battery negative (-ve) terminal **(see illustration 15)**. With the ignition ON, the test light should illuminate or the buzzer sound.

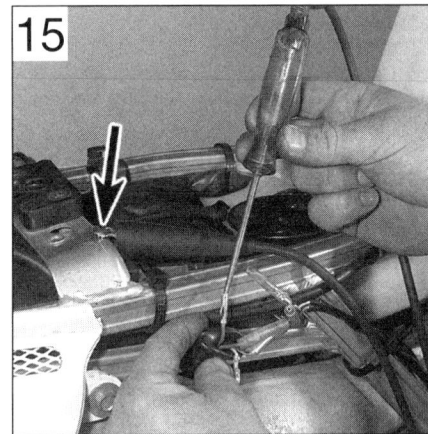

. . . or a test light - note the earth connection to the frame (arrow)

4 If no voltage is indicated, work back towards the fuse continuing to check for voltage. When you reach a point where there is voltage, you know the problem lies between that point and your last check point.

Checking the earth (ground)

● Earth connections are made either directly to the engine or frame (such as sensors, neutral switch etc. which only have a positive feed) or by a separate wire into the earth circuit of the wiring harness. Alternatively a short earth wire is sometimes run directly from the component to the motorcycle's frame.

● Corrosion is often the cause of a poor earth connection.

● If total failure is experienced, check the security of the main earth lead from the negative (-ve) terminal of the battery and also the main earth (ground) point on the wiring harness. If corroded, dismantle the connection and clean all surfaces back to bare metal.

1 To check the earth on a component, use an insulated jumper wire to temporarily bypass its earth connection **(see illustration 16)**. Connect one end of the jumper wire between the earth terminal or metal body of the component and the other end to the motorcycle's frame.

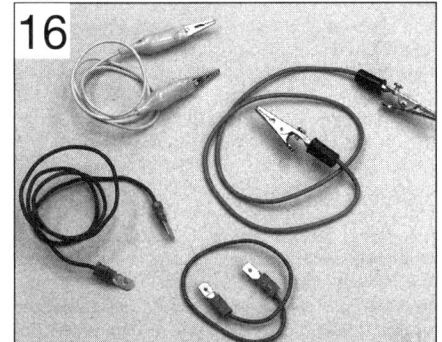

A selection of jumper wires for making earth (ground) checks

2 If the circuit works with the jumper wire installed, the original earth circuit is faulty. Check the wiring for open-circuits or poor connections. Clean up direct earth connections, removing all traces of corrosion and remake the joint. Apply petroleum jelly to the joint to prevent future corrosion.

Tracing a short-circuit

● A short-circuit occurs where current shorts to earth (ground) bypassing the circuit components. This usually results in a blown fuse.

● A short-circuit is most likely to occur where the insulation has worn through due to wiring chafing on a component, allowing a direct path to earth (ground) on the frame.

1 Remove any bodypanels necessary to access the circuit wiring.

2 Check that all electrical switches in the circuit are OFF, then remove the circuit fuse and connect a test light, buzzer or voltmeter (set to the dc scale) across the fuse terminals. No voltage should be shown.

3 Move the wiring from side to side whilst observing the test light or meter. When the test light comes on, buzzer sounds or meter shows voltage, you have found the cause of the short. It will usually shown up as damaged or burned insulation.

4 Note that the same test can be performed on each component in the circuit, even the switch.

A

ABS (Anti-lock braking system) A system, usually electronically controlled, that senses incipient wheel lockup during braking and relieves hydraulic pressure at wheel which is about to skid.

Aftermarket Components suitable for the motorcycle, but not produced by the motorcycle manufacturer.

Allen key A hexagonal wrench which fits into a recessed hexagonal hole.

Alternating current (ac) Current produced by an alternator. Requires converting to direct current by a rectifier for charging purposes.

Alternator Converts mechanical energy from the engine into electrical energy to charge the battery and power the electrical system.

Ampere (amp) A unit of measurement for the flow of electrical current. Current = Volts ˆ Ohms.

Ampere-hour (Ah) Measure of battery capacity.

Angle-tightening A torque expressed in degrees. Often follows a conventional tightening torque for cylinder head or main bearing fasteners **(see illustration)**.

Angle-tightening cylinder head bolts

Antifreeze A substance (usually ethylene glycol) mixed with water, and added to the cooling system, to prevent freezing of the coolant in winter. Antifreeze also contains chemicals to inhibit corrosion and the formation of rust and other deposits that would tend to clog the radiator and coolant passages and reduce cooling efficiency.

Anti-dive System attached to the fork lower leg (slider) to prevent fork dive when braking hard.

Anti-seize compound A coating that reduces the risk of seizing on fasteners that are subjected to high temperatures, such as exhaust clamp bolts and nuts.

API American Petroleum Institute. A quality standard for 4-stroke motor oils.

Asbestos A natural fibrous mineral with great heat resistance, commonly used in the composition of brake friction materials. Asbestos is a health hazard and the dust created by brake systems should never be inhaled or ingested.

ATF Automatic Transmission Fluid. Often used in front forks.

ATU Automatic Timing Unit. Mechanical device for advancing the ignition timing on early engines.

ATV All Terrain Vehicle. Often called a Quad.

Axial play Side-to-side movement.

Axle A shaft on which a wheel revolves. Also known as a spindle.

B

Backlash The amount of movement between meshed components when one component is held still. Usually applies to gear teeth.

Ball bearing A bearing consisting of a hardened inner and outer race with hardened steel balls between the two races.

Bearings Used between two working surfaces to prevent wear of the components and a build-up of heat. Four types of bearing are commonly used on motorcycles: plain shell bearings, ball bearings, tapered roller bearings and needle roller bearings.

Bevel gears Used to turn the drive through 90°. Typical applications are shaft final drive and camshaft drive **(see illustration)**.

Bevel gears are used to turn the drive through 90°

BHP Brake Horsepower. The British measurement for engine power output. Power output is now usually expressed in kilowatts (kW).

Bias-belted tyre Similar construction to radial tyre, but with outer belt running at an angle to the wheel rim.

Big-end bearing The bearing in the end of the connecting rod that's attached to the crankshaft.

Bleeding The process of removing air from an hydraulic system via a bleed nipple or bleed screw.

Bottom-end A description of an engine's crankcase components and all components contained there-in.

BTDC Before Top Dead Centre in terms of piston position. Ignition timing is often expressed in terms of degrees or millimetres BTDC.

Bush A cylindrical metal or rubber component used between two moving parts.

Burr Rough edge left on a component after machining or as a result of excessive wear.

C

Cam chain The chain which takes drive from the crankshaft to the camshaft(s).

Canister The main component in an evaporative emission control system (California market only); contains activated charcoal granules to trap vapours from the fuel system rather than allowing them to vent to the atmosphere.

Castellated Resembling the parapets along the top of a castle wall. For example, a castellated wheel axle or spindle nut.

Catalytic converter A device in the exhaust system of some machines which converts certain pollutants in the exhaust gases into less harmful substances.

Charging system Description of the components which charge the battery, ie the alternator, rectifer and regulator.

Circlip A ring-shaped clip used to prevent endwise movement of cylindrical parts and shafts. An internal circlip is installed in a groove in a housing; an external circlip fits into a groove on the outside of a cylindrical piece such as a shaft. Also known as a snap-ring.

Clearance The amount of space between two parts. For example, between a piston and a cylinder, between a bearing and a journal, etc.

Coil spring A spiral of elastic steel found in various sizes throughout a vehicle, for example as a springing medium in the suspension and in the valve train.

Compression Reduction in volume, and increase in pressure and temperature, of a gas, caused by squeezing it into a smaller space.

Compression damping Controls the speed the suspension compresses when hitting a bump.

Compression ratio The relationship between cylinder volume when the piston is at top dead centre and cylinder volume when the piston is at bottom dead centre.

Continuity The uninterrupted path in the flow of electricity. Little or no measurable resistance.

Continuity tester Self-powered bleeper or test light which indicates continuity.

Cp Candlepower. Bulb rating common found on US motorcycles.

Crossply tyre Tyre plies arranged in a criss-cross pattern. Usually four or six plies used, hence 4PR or 6PR in tyre size codes.

Cush drive Rubber damper segments fitted between the rear wheel and final drive sprocket to absorb transmission shocks **(see illustration)**.

Cush drive rubbers dampen out transmission shocks

D

Degree disc Calibrated disc for measuring piston position. Expressed in degrees.

Dial gauge Clock-type gauge with adapters for measuring runout and piston position. Expressed in mm or inches.

Diaphragm The rubber membrane in a master cylinder or carburettor which seals the upper chamber.

Diaphragm spring A single sprung plate often used in clutches.

Direct current (dc) Current produced by a dc generator.

Decarbonisation The process of removing carbon deposits - typically from the combustion chamber, valves and exhaust port/system.

Detonation Destructive and damaging explosion of fuel/air mixture in combustion chamber instead of controlled burning.

Diode An electrical valve which only allows current to flow in one direction. Commonly used in rectifiers and starter interlock systems.

Disc valve (or rotary valve) A induction system used on some two-stroke engines.

Double-overhead camshaft (DOHC) An engine that uses two overhead camshafts, one for the intake valves and one for the exhaust valves.

Drivebelt A toothed belt used to transmit drive to the rear wheel on some motorcycles. A drivebelt has also been used to drive the camshafts. Drivebelts are usually made of Kevlar.

Driveshaft Any shaft used to transmit motion. Commonly used when referring to the final driveshaft on shaft drive motorcycles.

E

Earth return The return path of an electrical circuit, utilising the motorcycle's frame.

ECU (Electronic Control Unit) A computer which controls (for instance) an ignition system, or an anti-lock braking system.

EGO Exhaust Gas Oxygen sensor. Sometimes called a Lambda sensor.

Electrolyte The fluid in a lead-acid battery.

EMS (Engine Management System) A computer controlled system which manages the fuel injection and the ignition systems in an integrated fashion.

Endfloat The amount of lengthways movement between two parts. As applied to a crankshaft, the distance that the crankshaft can move side-to-side in the crankcase.

Endless chain A chain having no joining link. Common use for cam chains and final drive chains.

EP (Extreme Pressure) Oil type used in locations where high loads are applied, such as between gear teeth.

Evaporative emission control system Describes a charcoal filled canister which stores fuel vapours from the tank rather than allowing them to vent to the atmosphere. Usually only fitted to California models and referred to as an EVAP system.

Expansion chamber Section of two-stroke engine exhaust system so designed to improve engine efficiency and boost power.

F

Feeler blade or gauge A thin strip or blade of hardened steel, ground to an exact thickness, used to check or measure clearances between parts.

Final drive Description of the drive from the transmission to the rear wheel. Usually by chain or shaft, but sometimes by belt.

Firing order The order in which the engine cylinders fire, or deliver their power strokes, beginning with the number one cylinder.

Flooding Term used to describe a high fuel level in the carburettor float chambers, leading to fuel overflow. Also refers to excess fuel in the combustion chamber due to incorrect starting technique.

Free length The no-load state of a component when measured. Clutch, valve and fork spring lengths are measured at rest, without any preload.

Freeplay The amount of travel before any action takes place. The looseness in a linkage, or an assembly of parts, between the initial application of force and actual movement. For example, the distance the rear brake pedal moves before the rear brake is actuated.

Fuel injection The fuel/air mixture is metered electronically and directed into the engine intake ports (indirect injection) or into the cylinders (direct injection). Sensors supply information on engine speed and conditions.

Fuel/air mixture The charge of fuel and air going into the engine. See **Stoichiometric ratio.**

Fuse An electrical device which protects a circuit against accidental overload. The typical fuse contains a soft piece of metal which is calibrated to melt at a predetermined current flow (expressed as amps) and break the circuit.

G

Gap The distance the spark must travel in jumping from the centre electrode to the side electrode in a spark plug. Also refers to the distance between the ignition rotor and the pickup coil in an electronic ignition system.

Gasket Any thin, soft material - usually cork, cardboard, asbestos or soft metal - installed between two metal surfaces to ensure a good seal. For instance, the cylinder head gasket seals the joint between the block and the cylinder head.

Gauge An instrument panel display used to monitor engine conditions. A gauge with a movable pointer on a dial or a fixed scale is an analogue gauge. A gauge with a numerical readout is called a digital gauge.

Gear ratios The drive ratio of a pair of gears in a gearbox, calculated on their number of teeth.

Glaze-busting see **Honing**

Grinding Process for renovating the valve face and valve seat contact area in the cylinder head.

Gudgeon pin The shaft which connects the connecting rod small-end with the piston. Often called a piston pin or wrist pin.

H

Helical gears Gear teeth are slightly curved and produce less gear noise that straight-cut gears. Often used for primary drives.

Installing a Helicoil thread insert in a cylinder head

Helicoil A thread insert repair system. Commonly used as a repair for stripped spark plug threads **(see illustration).**

Honing A process used to break down the glaze on a cylinder bore (also called glaze-busting). Can also be carried out to roughen a rebored cylinder to aid ring bedding-in.

HT High Tension Description of the electrical circuit from the secondary winding of the ignition coil to the spark plug.

Hydraulic A liquid filled system used to transmit pressure from one component to another. Common uses on motorcycles are brakes and clutches.

Hydrometer An instrument for measuring the specific gravity of a lead-acid battery.

Hygroscopic Water absorbing. In motorcycle applications, braking efficiency will be reduced if DOT 3 or 4 hydraulic fluid absorbs water from the air - care must be taken to keep new brake fluid in tightly sealed containers.

I

lbf ft Pounds-force feet. An imperial unit of torque. Sometimes written as ft-lbs.

lbf in Pound-force inch. An imperial unit of torque, applied to components where a very low torque is required. Sometimes written as in-lbs.

IC Abbreviation for Integrated Circuit.

Ignition advance Means of increasing the timing of the spark at higher engine speeds. Done by mechanical means (ATU) on early engines or electronically by the ignition control unit on later engines.

Ignition timing The moment at which the spark plug fires, expressed in the number of crankshaft degrees before the piston reaches the top of its stroke, or in the number of millimetres before the piston reaches the top of its stroke.

Infinity (∞) Description of an open-circuit electrical state, where no continuity exists.

Inverted forks (upside down forks) The sliders or lower legs are held in the yokes and the fork tubes or stanchions are connected to the wheel axle (spindle). Less unsprung weight and stiffer construction than conventional forks.

J

JASO Quality standard for 2-stroke oils.

Joule The unit of electrical energy.

Journal The bearing surface of a shaft.

K

Kickstart Mechanical means of turning the engine over for starting purposes. Only usually fitted to mopeds, small capacity motorcycles and off-road motorcycles.

Kill switch Handebar-mounted switch for emergency ignition cut-out. Cuts the ignition circuit on all models, and additionally prevent starter motor operation on others.

km Symbol for kilometre.

kph Abbreviation for kilometres per hour.

L

Lambda (λ) sensor A sensor fitted in the exhaust system to measure the exhaust gas oxygen content (excess air factor).

Lapping see **Grinding**.
LCD Abbreviation for Liquid Crystal Display.
LED Abbreviation for Light Emitting Diode.
Liner A steel cylinder liner inserted in a aluminium alloy cylinder block.
Locknut A nut used to lock an adjustment nut, or other threaded component, in place.
Lockstops The lugs on the lower triple clamp (yoke) which abut those on the frame, preventing handlebar-to-fuel tank contact.
Lockwasher A form of washer designed to prevent an attaching nut from working loose.
LT Low Tension Description of the electrical circuit from the power supply to the primary winding of the ignition coil.

M

Main bearings The bearings between the crankshaft and crankcase.
Maintenance-free (MF) battery A sealed battery which cannot be topped up.
Manometer Mercury-filled calibrated tubes used to measure intake tract vacuum. Used to synchronise carburettors on multi-cylinder engines.
Micrometer A precision measuring instrument that measures component outside diameters **(see illustration)**.

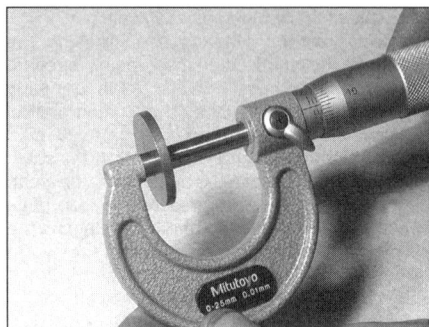

Tappet shims are measured with a micrometer

MON (Motor Octane Number) A measure of a fuel's resistance to knock.
Monograde oil An oil with a single viscosity, eg SAE80W.
Monoshock A single suspension unit linking the swingarm or suspension linkage to the frame.
mph Abbreviation for miles per hour.
Multigrade oil Having a wide viscosity range (eg 10W40). The W stands for Winter, thus the viscosity ranges from SAE10 when cold to SAE40 when hot.
Multimeter An electrical test instrument with the capability to measure voltage, current and resistance. Some meters also incorporate a continuity tester and buzzer.

N

Needle roller bearing Inner race of caged needle rollers and hardened outer race. Examples of uncaged needle rollers can be found on some engines. Commonly used in rear suspension applications and in two-stroke engines.
Nm Newton metres.
NOx Oxides of Nitrogen. A common toxic pollutant emitted by petrol engines at higher temperatures.

O

Octane The measure of a fuel's resistance to knock.
OE (Original Equipment) Relates to components fitted to a motorcycle as standard or replacement parts supplied by the motorcycle manufacturer.
Ohm The unit of electrical resistance. Ohms = Volts ÷ Current.
Ohmmeter An instrument for measuring electrical resistance.
Oil cooler System for diverting engine oil outside of the engine to a radiator for cooling purposes.
Oil injection A system of two-stroke engine lubrication where oil is pump-fed to the engine in accordance with throttle position.
Open-circuit An electrical condition where there is a break in the flow of electricity - no continuity (high resistance).
O-ring A type of sealing ring made of a special rubber-like material; in use, the O-ring is compressed into a groove to provide the seal.
Oversize (OS) Term used for piston and ring size options fitted to a rebored cylinder.
Overhead cam (sohc) engine An engine with single camshaft located on top of the cylinder head.
Overhead valve (ohv) engine An engine with the valves located in the cylinder head, but with the camshaft located in the engine block or crankcase.
Oxygen sensor A device installed in the exhaust system which senses the oxygen content in the exhaust and converts this information into an electric current. Also called a Lambda sensor.

P

Plastigauge A thin strip of plastic thread, available in different sizes, used for measuring clearances. For example, a strip of Plastigauge is laid across a bearing journal. The parts are assembled and dismantled; the width of the crushed strip indicates the clearance between journal and bearing.
Polarity Either negative or positive earth (ground), determined by which battery lead is connected to the frame (earth return). Modern motorcycles are usually negative earth.
Pre-ignition A situation where the fuel/air mixture ignites before the spark plug fires. Often due to a hot spot in the combustion chamber caused by carbon build-up. Engine has a tendency to 'run-on'.
Pre-load (suspension) The amount a spring is compressed when in the unloaded state. Preload can be applied by gas, spacer or mechanical adjuster.
Premix The method of engine lubrication on older two-stroke engines. Engine oil is mixed with the petrol in the fuel tank in a specific ratio. The fuel/oil mix is sometimes referred to as "petroil".
Primary drive Description of the drive from the crankshaft to the clutch. Usually by gear or chain.
PS Pfedestärke - a German interpretation of BHP.
PSI Pounds-force per square inch. Imperial measurement of tyre pressure and cylinder pressure measurement.
PTFE Polytetrafluroethylene. A low friction substance.

Pulse secondary air injection system A process of promoting the burning of excess fuel present in the exhaust gases by routing fresh air into the exhaust ports.

Q

Quartz halogen bulb Tungsten filament surrounded by a halogen gas. Typically used for the headlight **(see illustration)**.

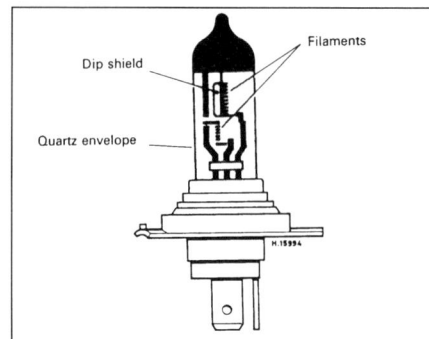

Quartz halogen headlight bulb construction

R

Rack-and-pinion A pinion gear on the end of a shaft that mates with a rack (think of a geared wheel opened up and laid flat). Sometimes used in clutch operating systems.
Radial play Up and down movement about a shaft.
Radial ply tyres Tyre plies run across the tyre (from bead to bead) and around the circumference of the tyre. Less resistant to tread distortion than other tyre types.
Radiator A liquid-to-air heat transfer device designed to reduce the temperature of the coolant in a liquid cooled engine.
Rake A feature of steering geometry - the angle of the steering head in relation to the vertical **(see illustration)**.

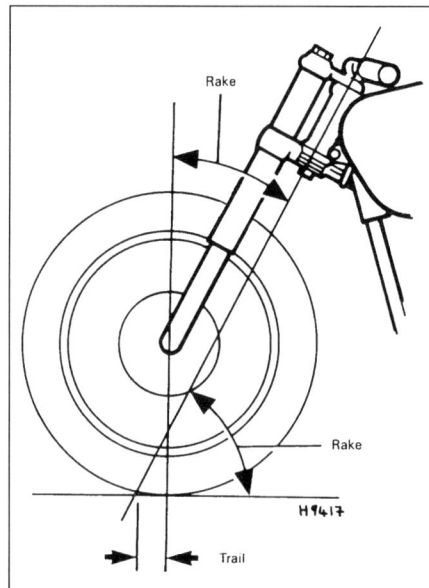

Steering geometry

Rebore Providing a new working surface to the cylinder bore by boring out the old surface. Necessitates the use of oversize piston and rings.

Rebound damping A means of controlling the oscillation of a suspension unit spring after it has been compressed. Resists the spring's natural tendency to bounce back after being compressed.

Rectifier Device for converting the ac output of an alternator into dc for battery charging.

Reed valve An induction system commonly used on two-stroke engines.

Regulator Device for maintaining the charging voltage from the generator or alternator within a specified range.

Relay A electrical device used to switch heavy current on and off by using a low current auxiliary circuit.

Resistance Measured in ohms. An electrical component's ability to pass electrical current.

RON (Research Octane Number) A measure of a fuel's resistance to knock.

rpm revolutions per minute.

Runout The amount of wobble (in-and-out movement) of a wheel or shaft as it's rotated. The amount a shaft rotates `out-of-true'. The out-of-round condition of a rotating part.

S

SAE (Society of Automotive Engineers) A standard for the viscosity of a fluid.

Sealant A liquid or paste used to prevent leakage at a joint. Sometimes used in conjunction with a gasket.

Service limit Term for the point where a component is no longer useable and must be renewed.

Shaft drive A method of transmitting drive from the transmission to the rear wheel.

Shell bearings Plain bearings consisting of two shell halves. Most often used as big-end and main bearings in a four-stroke engine. Often called bearing inserts.

Shim Thin spacer, commonly used to adjust the clearance or relative positions between two parts. For example, shims inserted into or under tappets or followers to control valve clearances. Clearance is adjusted by changing the thickness of the shim.

Short-circuit An electrical condition where current shorts to earth (ground) bypassing the circuit components.

Skimming Process to correct warpage or repair a damaged surface, eg on brake discs or drums.

Slide-hammer A special puller that screws into or hooks onto a component such as a shaft or bearing; a heavy sliding handle on the shaft bottoms against the end of the shaft to knock the component free.

Small-end bearing The bearing in the upper end of the connecting rod at its joint with the gudgeon pin.

Spalling Damage to camshaft lobes or bearing journals shown as pitting of the working surface.

Specific gravity (SG) The state of charge of the electrolyte in a lead-acid battery. A measure of the electrolyte's density compared with water.

Straight-cut gears Common type gear used on gearbox shafts and for oil pump and water pump drives.

Stanchion The inner sliding part of the front forks, held by the yokes. Often called a fork tube.

Stoichiometric ratio The optimum chemical air/fuel ratio for a petrol engine, said to be 14.7 parts of air to 1 part of fuel.

Sulphuric acid The liquid (electrolyte) used in a lead-acid battery. Poisonous and extremely corrosive.

Surface grinding (lapping) Process to correct a warped gasket face, commonly used on cylinder heads.

T

Tapered-roller bearing Tapered inner race of caged needle rollers and separate tapered outer race. Examples of taper roller bearings can be found on steering heads.

Tappet A cylindrical component which transmits motion from the cam to the valve stem, either directly or via a pushrod and rocker arm. Also called a cam follower.

TCS Traction Control System. An electronically-controlled system which senses wheel spin and reduces engine speed accordingly.

TDC Top Dead Centre denotes that the piston is at its highest point in the cylinder.

Thread-locking compound Solution applied to fastener threads to prevent slackening. Select type to suit application.

Thrust washer A washer positioned between two moving components on a shaft. For example, between gear pinions on gearshaft.

Timing chain See **Cam Chain.**

Timing light Stroboscopic lamp for carrying out ignition timing checks with the engine running.

Top-end A description of an engine's cylinder block, head and valve gear components.

Torque Turning or twisting force about a shaft.

Torque setting A prescribed tightness specified by the motorcycle manufacturer to ensure that the bolt or nut is secured correctly. Undertightening can result in the bolt or nut coming loose or a surface not being sealed. Overtightening can result in stripped threads, distortion or damage to the component being retained.

Torx key A six-point wrench.

Tracer A stripe of a second colour applied to a wire insulator to distinguish that wire from another one with the same colour insulator. For example, Br/W is often used to denote a brown insulator with a white tracer.

Trail A feature of steering geometry. Distance from the steering head axis to the tyre's central contact point.

Triple clamps The cast components which extend from the steering head and support the fork stanchions or tubes. Often called fork yokes.

Turbocharger A centrifugal device, driven by exhaust gases, that pressurises the intake air. Normally used to increase the power output from a given engine displacement.

TWI Abbreviation for Tyre Wear Indicator. Indicates the location of the tread depth indicator bars on tyres.

U

Universal joint or U-joint (UJ) A double-pivoted connection for transmitting power from a driving to a driven shaft through an angle. Typically found in shaft drive assemblies.

Unsprung weight Anything not supported by the bike's suspension (ie the wheel, tyres, brakes, final drive and bottom (moving) part of the suspension).

V

Vacuum gauges Clock-type gauges for measuring intake tract vacuum. Used for carburettor synchronisation on multi-cylinder engines.

Valve A device through which the flow of liquid, gas or vacuum may be stopped, started or regulated by a moveable part that opens, shuts or partially obstructs one or more ports or passageways. The intake and exhaust valves in the cylinder head are of the poppet type.

Valve clearance The clearance between the valve tip (the end of the valve stem) and the rocker arm or tappet/follower. The valve clearance is measured when the valve is closed. The correct clearance is important - if too small the valve won't close fully and will burn out, whereas if too large noisy operation will result.

Valve lift The amount a valve is lifted off its seat by the camshaft lobe.

Valve timing The exact setting for the opening and closing of the valves in relation to piston position.

Vernier caliper A precision measuring instrument that measures inside and outside dimensions. Not quite as accurate as a micrometer, but more convenient.

VIN Vehicle Identification Number. Term for the bike's engine and frame numbers.

Viscosity The thickness of a liquid or its resistance to flow.

Volt A unit for expressing electrical "pressure" in a circuit. Volts = current x ohms.

W

Water pump A mechanically-driven device for moving coolant around the engine.

Watt A unit for expressing electrical power. Watts = volts x current.

Wear limit see **Service limit**

Wet liner A liquid-cooled engine design where the pistons run in liners which are directly surrounded by coolant **(see illustration).**

Wet liner arrangement

Wheelbase Distance from the centre of the front wheel to the centre of the rear wheel.

Wiring harness or loom Describes the electrical wires running the length of the motorcycle and enclosed in tape or plastic sheathing. Wiring coming off the main harness is usually referred to as a sub harness.

Woodruff key A key of semi-circular or square section used to locate a gear to a shaft. Often used to locate the alternator rotor on the crankshaft.

Wrist pin Another name for gudgeon or piston pin.

Note: *References throughout this index are in the form – "Chapter number" • "page number"*

Haynes Motorcycle Manuals – The Complete List

Title	Book No.
BMW	
BMW 2-valve Twins (70 - 93)	0249
BMW K100 & 75 2-valve Models (83 - 93)	1373
BSA	
BSA Bantam (48 - 71)	0117
BSA Unit Singles (58 - 72)	0127
BSA Pre-unit Singles (54 - 61)	0326
BSA A7 & A10 Twins (47 - 62)	0121
BSA A50 & A65 Twins (62 - 73)	0155
BULTACO	
Bultaco Competition Bikes (72 - 75)	0219
CZ	
CZ 125 & 175 Singles (69 - 90)	◊ 0185
DUCATI	
Ducati 600, 750 & 900 2-valve V-Twins (91 - 96)	3290
HARLEY-DAVIDSON	
Harley-Davidson Sportsters (70 - 93)	0702
Harley-Davidson Big Twins (70 - 93)	0703
HONDA	
Honda PA50 Camino (76 - 91)	0644
Honda SH50 City Express (84 - 89)	◊ 1597
Honda NB, ND, NP & NS50 Melody (81 - 85)	◊ 0622
Honda NE/NB50 Vision & SA50 Vision Met-in (85 - 93)	◊ 1278
Honda MB, MBX, MT & MTX50 (80 - 93)	0731
Honda C50, C70 & C90 (67 - 95)	0324
Honda ATC70, 90, 110, 185 & 200 (71 - 85)	0565
Honda XR80R & XR100R (85 - 96)	2218
Honda XL/XR 80, 100, 125, 185 & 200 2-valve Models (78 - 87)	0566
Honda CB/CL100 & 125 Singles (70 - 76)	0188
Honda CB100N & CB125N (78 - 86)	◊ 0569
Honda H100 & H100S Singles (80 - 92)	◊ 0734
Honda CB/CD125T & CM125C Twins (77 - 88)	◊ 0571
Honda CG125 (76 - 94)	◊ 0433
Honda NS125 (86 - 93)	◊ 3056
Honda CB125, 160, 175, 200 & CD175 Twins (64 - 78)	0067
Honda MBX/MTX125 & MTX200 (83 - 93)	◊ 1132
Honda CD/CM185 200T & CM250C 2-valve Twins (77 - 85)	0572
Honda XL/XR 250 & 500 (78 - 84)	0567
Honda CB250RS Singles (80 - 84)	◊ 0732
Honda CB250 & CB400N Super Dreams (78 - 84)	◊ 0540
Honda Elsinore 250 (73 - 75)	0217
Honda TRX300 Shaft Drive ATVs (88 - 95)	2125
Honda CB400 & CB550 Fours (73 - 77)	0262
Honda CX/GL500 & 650 V-Twins (78 - 86)	0442
Honda CBX550 Four (82 - 86)	◊ 0940
Honda XL600R & XR600R (83 - 96)	2183
Honda CBR600F1 & 1000F Fours (87 - 96)	1730
Honda CBR600F2 Fours (91 - 94)	2070
Honda CB650 sohc Fours (78 - 84)	0665
Honda NTV600 & 650 V-Twins (88 - 96)	3243
Honda CB750 sohc Four (69 - 79)	0131
Honda V45/65 Sabre & Magna (82 - 88)	0820
Honda VFR750 & 700 V-Fours (86 - 94)	2101
Honda CB750 & CB900 dohc Fours (78 - 84)	0535
Honda CBR900RR FireBlade (92 - 95)	2161
Honda GL1000 Gold Wing (75 - 79)	0309
Honda GL1100 Gold Wing (79 - 81)	0669

Title	Book No.
KAWASAKI	
Kawasaki AE/AR 50 & 80 (81 - 95)	1007
Kawasaki KC, KE & KH100 (75 - 93)	1371
Kawasaki AR125 (82 - 94)	◊ 1006
Kawasaki KMX125 & 200 (86 - 96)	◊ 3046
Kawasaki 250, 350 & 400 Triples (72 - 79)	0134
Kawasaki 400 & 440 Twins (74 - 81)	0281
Kawasaki 400, 500 & 550 Fours (79 - 91)	0910
Kawasaki EN450 & 500 Twins (Ltd/Vulcan) (85 - 93)	2053
Kawasaki EX500 (GPZ500S) Twins (87 - 93)	2052
Kawasaki ZX600 (Ninja ZX-6, ZZ-R600) Fours (90 - 95)	2146

Title	Book No.
Kawasaki ZX600 & 750 Liquid-cooled Fours (85 - 97)	1780
Kawasaki 650 Four (76 - 78)	0373
Kawasaki 750 Air-cooled Fours (80 - 91)	0574
Kawasaki ZX750 (Ninja ZX-7 & ZXR750) Fours (89 - 95)	2054
Kawasaki 900 & 1000 Fours (73 - 77)	0222
Kawasaki ZX900, 1000 & 1100 Liquid-cooled Fours (83 - 97)	1681
MOTO GUZZI	
Moto Guzzi 750, 850 & 1000 V-Twins (74 - 78)	0339
MZ	
MZ TS125 (76 - 86)	◊ 1270
MZ ES, ETS, TS150 & 250 (69 - 86)	◊ 0253
MZ ETZ Models (81 - 95)	◊ 1680
NORTON	
Norton 500, 600, 650 & 750 Twins (57 - 70)	0187
Norton Commando (68 - 77)	0125
SUZUKI	
Suzuki FR50, 70 & 80 (74 - 87)	◊ 0801
Suzuki GT, ZR & TS50 (77 - 90)	◊ 0799
Suzuki TS50X (84 - 95)	◊ 1599
Suzuki 100, 125, 185 & 250 Air-cooled Trail bikes (79 - 89)	0797
Suzuki GP100 & 125 Singles (78 - 93)	◊ 0576
Suzuki GS & DR125 Singles (82 - 94)	◊ 0888
Suzuki 250 & 350 Twins (68 - 78)	0120
Suzuki GT250X7, GT200X5 & SB200 Twins (78 - 83)	◊ 0469
Suzuki GS/GSX250, 400 & 450 Twins (79 - 85)	0736
Suzuki GS500E Twin (89 - 97)	3238
Suzuki GS550 (77 - 82) & GS750 Fours (76 - 79)	0363
Suzuki GS/GSX550 4-valve Fours (83 - 88)	1133
Suzuki GSF600 & 1200 Bandit Fours (95 - 97)	3367
Suzuki GS850 Fours (78 - 88)	0536
Suzuki GS1000 Four (77 - 79)	0484
Suzuki GSX-R750, GSX-R1100, GSX600F, GSX750F, GSX1100F (Katana) Fours (85 - 96)	2055
Suzuki GS/GSX1000, 1100 & 1150 4-valve Fours (79 - 88)	0737

Title	Book No.
TOMOS	
Tomos A3K, A3M, A3MS & A3ML Mopeds (82 - 91)	◊ 1062
TRIUMPH	
Triumph Tiger Cub & Terrier (52 - 68)	0414
Triumph 350 & 500 Unit Twins (58 - 73)	0137
Triumph Pre-Unit Twins (47 - 62)	0251
Triumph 650 & 750 2-valve Unit Twins (63 - 83)	0122
Triumph Trident & BSA Rocket 3 (69 - 75)	0136
Triumph Triples & Fours (91 - 95)	2162
VESPA	
Vespa P/PX125, 150 & 200 Scooters (78 - 95)	0707
Vespa Scooters (59 - 78)	0126
YAMAHA	
Yamaha FS1E, FS1 & FS1M (72 - 90)	◊ 0166
Yamaha RD50 & 80 (78 - 89)	◊ 1255
Yamaha DT50 & 80 Trail Bikes (78 - 95)	◊ 0800
Yamaha T50 & 80 Townmate (83 - 95)	◊ 1247
Yamaha YT, YFM, YTM & YTZ ATVs (80 - 85)	1154
Yamaha YB100 Singles (73 - 91)	◊ 0474
Yamaha 100, 125 & 175 Trail bikes (71 - 85)	0210
Yamaha RS/RXS100 & 125 Singles (74 - 95)	0331
Yamaha RD & DT125LC (82 - 87)	◊ 0887
Yamaha TZR125 (87 - 93) & DT125R (88 - 95)	◊ 1655
Yamaha TY50, 80, 125 & 175 (74 - 84)	◊ 0464
Yamaha XT & SR125 (82 - 96)	1021
Yamaha 250 & 350 Twins (70 - 79)	0040
Yamaha XS250, 360 & 400 sohc Twins (75 - 84)	0378
Yamaha YBF250 Timberwolf ATV (92 - 96)	2217
Yamaha YFM350 Big Bear and ER ATVs (87 - 95)	2126
Yamaha RD250 & 350LC Twins (80 - 82)	0803
Yamaha RD350 YPVS Twins (83 - 95)	1158
Yamaha RD400 Twin (75 - 79)	0333
Yamaha XT, TT & SR500 Singles (75 - 83)	0342
Yamaha XZ550 Vision V-Twins (82 - 85)	0821
Yamaha FJ, FZ, XJ & YX600 Radian (84 - 92)	2100
Yamaha XJ600S (Seca II, Diversion) & XJ600N Fours (92 - 95 UK) (92 - 96 USA)	2145
Yamaha 650 Twins (70 - 83)	0341
Yamaha XJ650 & 750 Fours (80 - 84)	0738
Yamaha XS750 & 850 Triples (76 - 85)	0340
Yamaha FZR600, 750 & 1000 Fours (87 - 93)	2056
Yamaha XV V-Twins (81 - 96)	0802
Yamaha XJ900F Fours (83 - 94)	3239
Yamaha FJ1100 & 1200 Fours (84 - 96)	2057
PRACTICAL MANUALS	
ATV Basics	10450
Motorcycle Basics Manual	1083
Motorcycle Carburettor Manual	0603
Motorcycle Electrical Manual (2nd Edition)	0446
Motorcycle Workshop Practice Manual	1454

◊ denotes manual not available in the USA.

The manuals featured on this page are available through good motorcycle dealers and accessory shops. In case of difficulty, contact:
Haynes Publishing (UK) on 01963 440635
Haynes Publications (USA) on 805 4986703
Haynes Publishing Nordiska AB (Sweden) on +46 18 124016
Editions Haynes S.A. (France) on +33 1 47 03 61 80

C6685.CL04.04/97

Notes

Preserving Our Motoring Heritage

< *The Model J Duesenberg Derham Tourster. Only eight of these magnificent cars were ever built – this is the only example to be found outside the United States of America*

Almost every car you've ever loved, loathed or desired is gathered under one roof at the Haynes Motor Museum. Over 300 immaculately presented cars and motorbikes represent every aspect of our motoring heritage, from elegant reminders of bygone days, such as the superb Model J Duesenberg to curiosities like the bug-eyed BMW Isetta. There are also many old friends and flames. Perhaps you remember the 1959 Ford Popular that you did your courting in? The magnificent 'Red Collection' is a spectacle of classic sports cars including AC, Alfa Romeo, Austin Healey, Ferrari, Lamborghini, Maserati, MG, Riley, Porsche and Triumph.

A Perfect Day Out

Each and every vehicle at the Haynes Motor Museum has played its part in the history and culture of Motoring. Today, they make a wonderful spectacle and a great day out for all the family. Bring the kids, bring Mum and Dad, but above all bring your camera to capture those golden memories for ever. You will also find an impressive array of motoring memorabilia, a comfortable 70 seat video cinema and one of the most extensive transport book shops in Britain. The Pit Stop Cafe serves everything from a cup of tea to wholesome, home-made meals or, if you prefer, you can enjoy the large picnic area nestled in the beautiful rural surroundings of Somerset.

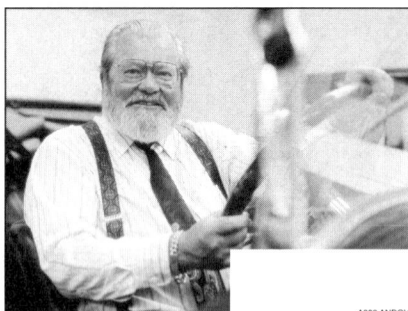

> *John Haynes O.B.E., Founder and Chairman of the museum at the wheel of a Haynes Light 12.*

< *The 1936 490cc sohc-engined International Norton – well known for its racing success*

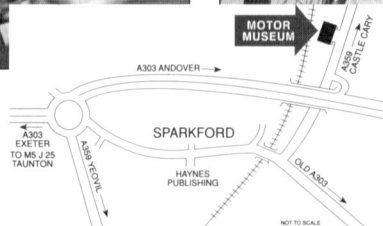

The Museum is situated on the A359 Yeovil to Frome road at Sparkford, just off the A303 in Somerset. It is about 40 miles south of Bristol, and 25 minutes drive from the M5 intersection at Taunton.
Open 9.30am - 5.30pm (10.00am - 4.00pm Winter) 7 days a week, *except Christmas Day, Boxing Day and New Years Day*
Special rates available for schools, coach parties and outings Charitable Trust No. 292048